The Essex Institute
Historical Collections
(Volume XLIII) 1907

Unknown

Alpha Editions

This edition published in 2020

ISBN: 9789354187896 (Hardback)
ISBN: 9789354188152 (Paperback)

Design and Setting By
Alpha Editions
www.alphaedis.com
email - alphaedis@gmail.com

CONTENTS.

iv   CONTENTS.

GW. SHINGTON

HISTORICAL COLLECTIONS

OF THE

ESSEX INSTITUTE

VOL. XLIII.   JANUARY, 1907   No. 1

AN ETCHED PROFILE PORTRAIT OF WASHINGTON BY JOSEPH HILLER, JR., 1794.

BY CHARLES HENRY HART.

To the Historical Collections of the Essex Institute, Vol. XVI, p. 161, I had the honor to contribute a brief "Notice of a Portrait of Washington." The portrait there noticed was the etched profile made by Joseph Wright, in 1790, and at the period I wrote, 1879, we were in our infancy in the study of Washington iconography; indeed that "Notice" was my first important contribution, in print, to the subject. Since then I have published enough to have earned the illustrious name of "Washington," as a sobriquet, and while engaged in the preparation of my *Catalogue of the Engraved Portraits of Washington*, issued by the Grolier Club, New York, January, 1904, in a sumptuous quarto of 406 pages, I discovered in the cabinet of the Massachusetts Historical Society, an etched profile of Washington, which was new to me and evidently copied from the one by Wright, signed "J HILLER Ju^r Sculp^t, 1794." In seeking the history of this print, I found, in the Proceedings of the Society, for February 12, 1874, (Vol. 13, p. 243) the following note ;—

(1)

Mr. Brooks presented, in the name of Mr. A. H. Safford, of Cambridge, a pen and ink sketch of Washington, executed by J. Hiller Jr., in 1794. Mr. Safford's belief was that the miniature was presented by General Washington to Captain Thomas Hartshorn, of Reading, who died in 1819. It had been in Mr. Safford's possession for over fifty years, he having been a foster son of Captain Hartshorn. The drawing is sketched on the back of a playing card,—the ten of diamonds. The name of " George Washington " is inscribed on a scroll beneath the picture and beneath the oval, in which the picture is enclosed, is, " J. Hiller, Jr. scrip (or sculp.) 1794."

This note is a curiosity for its stupid errors. The profile was, of course, neither " a pen and ink sketch," a "miniature " or a " drawing," and there is not the least likelihood that Washington presented it to Captain Hartshorn.* It is what is technically known as *a dry point etching* and is *printed* on the back of a ten of diamonds playing card. I am saved from a minute description of the print by the impressions from the original copper plate which accompany this monograph.

As has often been said nothing can be claimed as unique that has emanated from the press, so, close upon the heels of this *find*, in the cabinet of the the Massachusetts Historical Society, in Boston, I was sent by C. W. Darling, of Utica, New York, a reproduction of a similar etching, which he had given to the Oneida Historical Society, with this inscription ;

" Gen. Washington, 1794. The original of this portraiture, presented by Gen. Darling, Corresponding Secretary of the Oneida Historical Society, was given by an artist named J. Hiller, Jr., in 1794 to Harriet Paine,† then a young lady of sixteen. At a reception the artist took from his pocket a package of playing cards and on the back of the King of Clubs, began this sketch of Washington."

The errors of this inscription are as amusing as those already noticed, both of which are only fair examples of the romances that hang around so many portraits of the

*Capt. Hartshorn married Abigail Cleveland, aunt of young Joseph Hiller, and no doubt received the print from his nephew.
†The Cleveland and Paine families intermarried.

Father of his Country, which it has been my province and
duty to correct and expose. From the two impressions of
the Hiller etching of Washington I gleaned the imforma-
tion contained in my catalogue where the following description will be found on page 66.

" 140 J. Hiller, Jr.
    Bust, profile to right, in uniform. Title, on rib-
    bon, below bust. Oval, of a single line, without
    background.   *Dry-point etching.*
G. WASHINGTON / J HILLER JU^R SCULP^T, 1794/.
Oval height, 2. 9.   Oval width, 1. 14.

This is an extremely close copy of the Wright etching,
No. 138, but without a worked background. All the impressions that I know are printed on the backs of playing
cards."

A few months after the publication of my Grolier Club
volume I received a communication from the Secretary of
the Essex Institute, who wrote as follows :—

" A friend of mine and a member of the Essex Institute,
has in her possession two interesting profiles of Washington,
etched in 1794, by Joseph Hiller, only son of Major Joseph
Hiller of Salem. The etching may familiarly be called card
photograph in size and very generally resembles the rare etching by Joseph Wright. The Essex Institute owns a very
beautiful seal, cut in London for Major Hiller and showing in
profile the head of Washington. The etching by his son, I am
inclined to think, may have been made for the purpose of
sending to London a representation for the use of the seal
cutter, for the portrait cut upon the seal and the etching are
nearly identical. The etching, of which two copies are known
to exist, is now in the possession of a descendant of Major
Hiller and I am writing to you at this time, not only to bring
to your attention this, to me, interesting portrait of Washington, but also to inquire in behalf of its present owner, if the
two copies in her possession may not have a commercial value
that may warrant the sale of the same."

Here then were two more original prints of the Hiller
etching of Washington and what is yet more remarkable

these two impressions were clearly what would be described, chalcographically, as two different states, the first and second. The lettering of the first state corresponded with that given in Hart 140, and of the second state, with the plate as it now exists. The differences are very slight, the only important change being the addition of "N 1", in the lower right corner of the margin. There are also dots or periods, ".", added after "Washington," "J", "Ju^r", and "1794"; and "Sculp^t", is "Sculp". I had the pleasure of disposing of these prints and now am able to communicate additional information relative to the Joseph Hillers, father and son, furnishing some interesting data concerning this early Massachusetts engraver.

Joseph Hiller, Jr., was born in Salem, Mass., June 21, 1777, and was drowned August 22, 1795, being washed overboard from a vessel off the Cape of Good Hope, so that he was only in his seventeenth year when he essayed the copy of Wright's etching of Washington. He was the fourth child, and only son, of six children born to Major Joseph Hiller (1748-1814) and his wife Margaret Cleveland (1748-1804). His father was a revolutionary officer who led " a uniformed company from Salem, on the day of the Lexington fight. The uniform of this company was quite elaborate and fully vindicates the truthfulness of Col. Trumbull's painting. It consisted of a green coat, white waist-coat and breeches, black gaiters, cocked hat with three black feathers and ruffles."* He saw active service in August, 1778, in Rhode Island, where he commanded a company of volunteers from Salem.† In 1784, he was appointed by the General Court of Massachusetts and commissioned by Governor Hancock, to collect the custom revenues at the port of Salem, which appointment was confirmed by commission from President Washington, August 5, 1789, as first Collector of the Port of Salem under the government of the United States. This office Major Hiller held until August 12, 1802, when he was superceded by President Jefferson and there hangs in the

*Rantoul's Port of Salem. Essex Institute Historical Collections, Vol. x, pt. 1, p. 65.

†Letter from Joseph Hiller to Major Sprague, dated "Camp before Newport, August 21, 1778." Essex Institute Historical Collections, Vol. xxix, p. 167.

Custom House at Salem, a portrait of him, painted from life, which was presented by his descendants. He is said to have been " the first American by birth who espoused the doctrines of Swedenborg." He was a Mason and admitted to Essex Lodge, January 25, 1780, elected Master, March 30, and re-elected under the new charter when the Lodge was re-established, July 5, 1791.* In early life Major Hiller was a silversmith† and jeweller‡ and was possessed of "great mechanical ingenuity."§ It was undoubtedly this last quality, with the taste that was naturally acquired from following the artistic trades of silversmith and jeweller, transmitted from father to son, that led the youth of seventeen to attempt the engraving of the Washington profile and doubtless the father, from his trade experience, was able to instruct his son in the mechanical part of his work, for in the early days every practical silversmith and jeweller understood something of chasing and engraving which were very important branches of their business. This plate, too, it will be remembered, is " dry-point etching "—engraved with the point and not bitten in with acid, and as far as is known is the only attempt of Joseph Hiller, Jr., at engraving. The supposition that this etching was primarily made, to be sent to England, for the use of the gem engraver, employed by Major Hiller, to cut in stone, at a cost of £20,¶ the seal, with the profile head of Washington, now in the cabinet of the Essex Institute, seems very reasonable. The profiles are as much alike as an intaglio cut in hard stone could be to a flat one engraved on soft copper, in addition to which they both face in the same direction, which would indicate copying without reversing, the easiest method for an ordinary copyist, and which reverses the head when impressed in wax. Nor is it too much a stretch of the imagination to conceive that the Wright etching copied by young Hiller, was the identical impression that belonged to

*Leavitt's History of Essex Lodge. Essex Institute Historical Collections. Vol. III, p. 123.

†Essex Institute Historical Collections. Vol. IV. p. 11.

‡Id. Vol. X, pt. 1, p. 65.

§Cleveland's Genealogy of the Cleveland and Cleaveland Families. Hartford, 1899. Vol. I, p. 234.

¶Essex Institute Historical Collections, Vol. X. pt. 1, p. 66, states that the sum of £40, but living descendants name £20, as the correct amount.

Benjamin Goodhue and which was the subject of my former communication to the Essex Institute. Stranger coincidences than this have happened and this is not at all an unreasonable supposition while it may be a hopeless one to follow to a satisfactory determination.

This story would be interesting enough if it ended here, but it does not and its sequel is quite remarkable. In May, 1906, I learned that the original copper plate of the Hiller etching of Washington was in existence. That it had been found lying upon a beam in the attic of an old house located on Turner street, in Salem, and although somewhat corroded, yet yielded a fair impression. Thus the past is brought up to the present and through the courtesy of its owner, Mr. Albert I. Whipple, the plate has been secured to illustrate this monograph, so that one hundred and thirteen years after its execution, restrike impressions from the original plate are published in the birthplace of the youthful engraver as a fitting memorial of him. Of original prints the four mentioned in the text are the only ones so far known.

REVOLUTIONARY LETTERS
WRITTEN TO COLONEL TIMOTHY PICKERING.

BY GEORGE WILLIAMS OF SALEM.

(*Continued from Vol. XLII, page 830.*)

At Boston, March 22, 1778.

D^r. Sir.

I received yours of 22 Feby ye 6th Instant. I thank you for them. Have let the Counciel of this State see y^n of 6th. Some Friends to our cause we are contending for, are surprised to hear of the wants of the Army for Bread & Meat in a plentyfull cuntry. Am Sorry the good Genl did not order the Commissory's, or a force, to have Bread & Meat taken and Brought into the Army so thay should not complain for the want of the above, and every Farmer that did not send or deliver it, it should be Taken away from him. It would be the case if the Army was in this State, with out Money, if the Treasure was out. You mentioned a Return from our friend Carlton in Brewer's reg^t is distressing. Some Thousands Sutes of Cloathes compleat, has bin sent to Peeks Kill. There many Lay am informed, a Rotten when so many brave men are Fresing. Ware is the Fault. We Judge it must be to the Southard. Lt. Col. Colman of Wiggelsworth reg^t told me Two days past, the 300 Sutes compleat he sent of got to Peeks Kill in 17 days, from this, and there stoped, for what reason I cant conceive, but suppose partly the defect is the want of money, to give the Waggener, as I am very Sensible is the want hear, but hope the [Mint?] will not stop Till all Departments is well Supply'd and every Soilder pay'd monthly.

The high prise of provisions in the Southern States, I hope will Influance Congres to have an embargo Layed on, that no provisions shall be shiped to any part of the West Indies. If it had bin Layed on Sep^t 1775 to this day, we should have bin in much happerer Surçumstances, tho some marchants has got money, Like the North Carelinio man by exchanging to make his barrell of pork net £90. The March's hear has on the whole suffred greatly, and will in a year or Two, Fail. Privertering Turns out much the Same this year as Trade.

The Council has ordered Gen¹ Hancock to have a return of the Militia & of there Armes &c. This State has emported about 7,000 Armes &c. About 5,000 Armes, 30 ton of Lead, 1000 Gunlocks with a proporsion of Flints & powder, has bin delivered out to each Town in proporsion to the Tax thay pay to the State. Am in hopes the Militia is in better Order for the Above Articales then ever thay ware. In Store about 50 Tons Lead & Ball, 2,000 Armes, 1000 Gunlocks, emported powder 260 barrills. The Forts round the coast Supplyd. At Mʳ Sam¹ Phillips mill, ready to prove 5,000ᵗᵇ. Colᵒ Burbank a few days past proved 15ᵗᵇ of ˢᵈ Phillips [and] sayes it is better then any emported. Is gon up to Andover to prove yᵉ above. Hope it will Turn out as good. Mʳ. Phillips has Taken a great deal of paines [and] has got to such perfection that he judges he can produce as good as any in the world. At the State Mill Majʳ. Crane told me he was on the Same plan with Mʳ Phillips. He Told me he had 6 tons ready to prove. When Colᵒ Burbank comes from Andover he is to go & prove it. The mill at Springfield makes also good. The quanity there I dont no. Meterels we have plenty, making dayly.

What this State Expects is a Brig from France, with Cloathing &c, every day, and a Brig in about 2 months. Two Large Ships that went with Masts is to Bring Salt & Blankets. A Brig gon to Bilboa for Cordage & Cloathing. A Brig, a Ship, to South Carolinio & France.

Schedule of what is ordered in Most of yᵉ above Vessels, viz :—3 point Blanketts, of a good quality. Blue Cloath, White Cloath, Red Cloath, propootioned 7/8 Blue, 1/16 White, 1/16 Red, for Soilders Cloath. Linnen for shirts for dᵒ frᵒ 30 to 50 fols. Hose of White yarn. Shose Large & Strong. Felt hats Large. White Flannell (Thin) for Linings. Do Swanskin. Russia Sheeting 30

Ells a p⁵ cost in London 42 to 45. Brown or some other kind of your own fabrick in Stead to make Rifle Shirts or Frocks principally. Boxes of Sheet Tin a third X. Sewing thread of all Collors, & for Linnen. Russia Duck. Raven's do. Ticklingburg. Sail Twine. Lead. Armes. Powder.

Three State arm'd Brigs out, Ordered on ye Coast of Spain [and] portugal. Hope thay will send in some prizes with goods. The above Schedule is what is ordered for the State and am in hopes we shall have success in the Armed Brigs & the other adventures.

Provissions, Beef, & pork provided for only the State Troopes &c. (Bread only from day to day. It must come from the State of York, Connecticut & the upper part of this State.)

You mentioned the difficulty of giting Seaman to man the Vessels to Bring provissions up the Bay for the Army. States Privertering marchant Vessels, what few is employed, wages is up to 15 to 20 £ p⁺ m°. Insurance 70 to 75 p⁺ Ct. You may see we are distressed for men to Serve the publick, as well as other States. Congress sent a resolve with a Warrent on the Loan Office, to the Board of War to emport Flouer from Virginia, to hire or purchas Vessels. Not one can be hired as yet. Two only Bought. Got men, and then thay Left, and now [am] after men. Am fearful shall not be Able to git them, for the risk is so great to Virginia, men dont incline to go at any Wages. The order came to Late. All the Small Vessells was gone. This adventure should have bin gone into early in the fall past, when the risk was not half as much. The Ship that had a number of our men from Halifax bound to York, was Brot into Marblehead some Time past has given the Small pox to a number of the Inhabitants of each Town thay went Throu. This Town had so many Taken down that the Gen¹ Court was Obliag'd to Brake up, and are to Meet the first day of April next. This Town has gon into anoculation. In my Last I mention'd the Towns are call'd on for there quota of men. The Committes from each Town has reported, that each Town is endevering to git there quota of men and are determed to git them. The Town

of Salem has Taxed a number of the Inhabitants, the Am⁰
is £3,000, to git yᵉ men wanted for said Town, and hope
each Town will git them Soon. This State sends Two
regᵗ to the State of Road Island. I suppose Millet Broᵗ
some orders for men for the State of New York. I believe
this State will due every thing that Layes in there power,
to see the Army filled, & to assist the other States. I wish
Congres had order'd that this State Should send men to
the State of Road Island for what Conneticut was to send
to sᵈ Road Island, & Conneticut, to send to the State of
New York the Same number thay was to send to the
State of Road Island, which would save Time & expence.
Suppose each in the Like danger. Majʳ. Wadesworth,
formerly Genˡ Wards A. D. C. proposed a plan for the
Town or Towns to Turn out Volinters to make up a Company to March to the Army with out pay, to be found
provission & a Waggon to cary there Baggage, and stay in
Camp Till Janʸ. next, and due duty as good Soilderes.
You may see by one of the Late Boston papers a supposed
plan of the Same. The resolve you enclosed me, in ye
Last of 2ᵈ March of much the same plan for Horsman. I
have sent it to Salem this Morning. Council received one
by Millet yesterday. I have acquainted a number of
Gentᵐ hear of it. Thay begin to Talk away that it is a
good plan. I wish thay will due as well as Talk. I hope
something will be dun as the Members of Court when
thay adjourn'd sayed thay would due all that Layed in
there power to have there Towns git there men and all
members was desired to atend at the First Meeting.
Nothing to be dun Till the Army is settled.

A Fleet for Burgoine & men is at Cape Cod. A flag of
Truse has bin up and gone back, to know if thay will Land
the provissions thay have in the Fleet for the Army. I
hope thay will so the Farmers may have Beef &c Left on
there hands, for our Farmers are as cruel as Death in there
Demands on the Inhabitants, for wood is at 6 to 9£ pʳ
Cord, Beef is 6 to 2-3 pʳ ˡᵇ Indian Corn 24. Hope we
shall at Last weather the Storm, and we to have a free
Cours by warter, which will soon Loar these high prises.
You will see by this our State. I wish it was better.

April 4, 1778.

Since y[e] above, Burgoine Fleet is return'd toward's Newport or York, and the Gen[l] Court is got together again, and are now on filling up the Continental rig[t] & men for y[e] State of York. A prise arrived at Salem with Shoes & Stockings & other goods fit[d] for y[e] Army, and am in hopes the Army in Time will be benifet[d] by them. All m[r] Phillips powder is proved and is all Good. The Bad weather has prevent'd proving Crane's. By my next hope shall be able to Acquaint you of its proving good.

Pickering MSS. Vol. 17, p. 119.

At Boston, May 4, 1778

• D[r] Sir

This morning I Left home. Have not had any of your Favors Since 25 March Last. Our honered Farther, is in a very weak State and I Judge he will not continue Long with us, as he is confind to his house. All other of our Friends is well and am in hopes this will meet you well. A Ship at portsmouth from France with Cloathing. One at Cape Ann. One arrived hear with do. and a Ship, Snow & Brig in sight. Cap[t] Harreden arrived with a prise Snow from Bristol with Flour Salt &c. for New York. The Brig Lyon, Warren, arrived at Salem. Taken a Brig from Bristol. Left her 5 days ago. The Ship Cumberland arrived hear, with a ship from England with Coales &c for the Army. A prise at portsmouth with Beef &c belong to a priverter of Newbury port. On the whole privertering Turns out but poorly and our Marchant men mostly Taken, and Trade is all most over with us as we have nothing to send in our Vessels but Lumber. I wish it was interly over. Orders is gon out for men for Gen[l] Washington's Army & for the North river and am very Sorry—our Cuntry men is so Backward, but hope the good News you have by M[r] Dean Some dayes past from hear is with you, and old England I beleve is got into Bad Bread for M[r] French man at Last is put a Trick on them in declaring our independant. Now for Continental Ships.

In this Harbour, the Ship Warren, Rawla,* [and] Two Brigs. The brave Hindman of the Alfred is Taken by the nelect of Capt Thomson. All the men that is got home from the Alfred, sayes if Capt Thompson had come down they would have Taken ye Two English Ships in one hours engagement. I wish Some care might be Taken when officers is appointed so the navy of the United States may not be in disgrace. Some Spur is wanted hear to git the ships to Sea. Now is the Time for them to be at Sea. I hope soon to have the pleasure of Seeing you as your wife Told me you expected to be at home Soon.

Pickering MSS. Vol. 17, p. 147.

Salem June 7, 1778.

Dr Freind

This is to Informe you this day at noon, our Honour'd Farther departed this Life, and I have no doubt for a Better, and it is no Small comfort to Serviving Freinds that we have so good a hope of him, that he is gone to rest, and when it should please god to call us home we may be so prepared to Leave this, as he has don. He has offen expressed he was willing to depart, & allso sayed he hoped he should not Long be a burthen to any one, and no Freind has thought it any Trouble to atend on so worthy a Freind.

Yesterday received yours of 24 may, which I thank you for. Mother is much Troubled with her old complaint. Brother Jn° is much the Same State of health as usal, and also all other Freinds, and desires to be remembered to you. Brother Jn° has ingag'd Powars & willes paper† to be sent to you. Dont direct any more Letters to me, as member of the Board of war as I am determind to resine. The Town at the New Chose of representitives, would not excus Br Jn° & me. I cant Serve Two Masters by resining my seat at the Board of war, I may have one hour's Leasure to Serve myself & my Friends, for I have not had since

*Ship Raleigh.
†The Independant Chronicle.

you Left us, one hour Time for myself.   Nothing remark-
bal since my Last.   Hope in a few days to be able to informe you all the men ord'ed, has gone Forrow'd.

To Timothy Pickering Esqr member of the Board of
War, York Town.

Pickering MSS. Vol. 17, p. 161.

Boston, July 10, 1778.

Dr Sir

Yours of 23 & 24th June, also one from Wm Duer Esqr
p^r order of the Board of war, came to my hand 9th Instant
at Salem.   Am very Sorry of my appointment, which I
can not Accept.   The honnour due me in it I asteam the
greatest Faver.   It gives me pain to make excuse for not
accepting.   I have Served ever since the war my Town &
the public, I may say for nothing and also I would have
served the United States one year, if I had not promised
the Following—Sister Gooll's* Estate to settel, Capt Har-
radens Last Cruse, Brig Lyons two d^o, Brig Montgomerys
d^o, Ship Black Prince & Some others.   As for my own
privet Affairs, allthough I have not Taken any care only
in the evens at my being from Court & Boston,—should
not have hindred me of Accepting.   By the Above you
will see my ingagements before I received yours &c.   As you
know I allways indever'd to fulfill my engagements before
I engaged in any other and for fear the public should Suffer by my Accepting I have deliver'd the Letter & papers
to the Council.   Hope thay will appoint a good man.   I
am much obliaged to you for this recommendation, and
with great pain I Reffused it, only on your Acco^t, as it is
not in my power to accept and due my duty.   You mention'd allso the Board are directed to purchas Linnen,
Stockings & Shoes, untill the Cloathing department is ar-
arranged.   Who is the Best Man to Appoint to purchase
in our State; can you undertake—I say no, for the same
reasons as before.   It is hard for any man in these dayes
to say who is the Best man to Appoint.   You must know

*Lois, widow of John Gooll who died at St. Christopher's, Mar. 23, 1776.

who is at the head of business, who has Served faithfull, and the faithfull ought to be incurraged. I wish if it was for your honour you was hear to Accept, of that emportant place of purchasing & the whole matter of Cloathing, and I make no doubt you would find some faithfull men to Serve with you. This I have found by experance. Two many employed in any one business has bin the means of enhancing the price of Goods. You have inclosed a Letter from y^r wife & Brother John. I suppose he will give you Account how your dece'd Farther has disposed of his Estate. I hope it will be agreeable to you. By y^{rs} of 6 June you mentiond you have not received any Letters from your Freinds only one from me 4th May. Have wright you Several. I hope you will Still wright, and if you have Time give me Acco^t of our Army, and your Opinion consarning a place or not, as it will Serve me much in Trade, if we should enter into it, as the enemy has Left Pheledelphia. If you should go down there, please to make inquire of our Freind Newman, if the Schooner & Stores that belongs to Mason & me is Left by the enemy. Let me know by the First Oppertunity. Some Time past a resolve of Congress desiring each State to appoint a Committe to the old money of ye Southering States. The State has not appointed any, and as I have some by me, should be Glad to know how I may pas it. If ye Schooner is Safe & I can Spare time in 6 weeks hence, I would come and fit her out. If the United States should want a Vessel I will sell her to them. Please to inquire & Let me know.

Pickering MSS. Vol. 17, p. 179.

Salem, July 12 1778.

Dr Sir

At my return from Boston received yours 26th. You will see my reasons by the within of my not Accepting. I hope it will satisfy you, & all others, and as for the Bills of Lading &c, shall be emeaditly sent to Boston or go myself as soon as I know who is appointed. Shall call on M^r

Hopkins to know this night. I am very sorry our Kinsman Gardner should meat with any disappointment. I hope it wont put a check on his Spirits, as he had a good Spur in the other Voyage, if he had made good emprovement. You mention'd a Villainous Scheme to raise the price of provisions wanted for the Army. It an't only with you. Other parts is all most as bad. A scheme of some packers of Beef [was] this way; in the fall of the year thay barrill'd it, and before they was to deliver it, drawed of ye pickel & put in fresh warter so it might soak into it, and by that meanes make it whol out its wieght, and as soon as the hot weather Seats in it is Stinking. Our State was cheat'd in this way Last year, which we could not Account for till we was informed of this Villainous practis and while I was at the war office, it offen Occurred. To my mind the saying, our cuntry men are cheates, this war has fullfilled. You have inclosed your wifes Letter. Nothing remarable hear. We are wating to know the faite of the British Army. Am verry Sorry the Great State of Philedelphia Should be so Backward in Turning out, so thay might have part of ye honnour of Taking Mr Clinton, but am in fear he will Slip away.

Pickering MSS. Vol. 17, p. 181.

On Road Island, Augt 20, 1778.

Dr Sir,

You will wonder at my being on Road Island. I am a Volinteer in Company of about 80 men, & 25 Boat Men for Landing ye men. Wee Landed hear last Sunday Morning about 9 a Clock which the enemy Left ye North end. Had no body to oppose us, and now we are advanced within a mile & a 1-2. Have got three redoubts oppen on them. The Last 48 hours past thay Sent us about 600 Shot, & yesterday we return'd them about 60 18lb shot in exchange. We have had a very hard storm of Rain & wind & very Fogge weather, ever since we Landed. The French Fleet went out after the English fleet that came of this harbour Last Munday week. At this

Instant a Number of Ships is in Sight. Hope it is the French Fleet, if not we shall be in Bad Bread, but we must see it out with them. We are on in the Left of ye Front Line. If call'd to Battel hope we shall behave well as any old Seeman as we have Jon^a Gardner J^r, Jon^a Peele, Jno Felt, Jno Fish, Jon^a Harredin, Saml Webb, Barth^o Putnam, B. Moses, Orsborn,* Tucker,† & Tucker,‡ Geo. Smith, B. Goodhue, Jacob Ashton, Nathl Ropes, Saml Ward, Jno Andrew, 4 Persies, B. Ropes, Saml Flag, Miles Greenough, Fra^s Cabbot, Capt Foster. The other names cant remember. Our Turing out has Turned out 100 Boat men fr^o Marblehead, 60 from Newburyport, about 80 fr^o Boston, in 3 smale Companys, and a number of Voluntiers from other Towns from our State, also New Hampshire a number. It is say'd we have 14,000 men. I judge not so many. I wish you was hear. Rece^d yours of 1 Instant 2 days past. Miller this Instant has come hear. Shall give you Acco^t of priverturing by my next as I have not Time, for you know a Soldur has nothing but [   ] and his knapsack for his writing table. Miller can Let you know how all Freinds is as I am bin from Home all most 3 weeks past.

N. B. Jon^a Peele is unwell & says cant wright you, as he sayes. The ships are the French Fleet, and the report is the Admerel has Lost her main Mast & rudder & a 80 Gun Ship Missing. They Tuk a Frigate & a Bum Ship & if the Gale of wind had not come on so soon thay would ingaged each other.

To Timothy Pickering Esqr member of the Board of the Board of War, Philedelphia.

Pickering MSS. Vol. 17, p. 210.

*William Osborne.
†Jonathan Tucker.
‡Samuel Tucker.

(*To be continued.*)

THE BURYING GROUND AT SAWYER'S HILL, NEWBURYPORT.

This plate is from Currier's "Ould Newbury."

INSCRIPTIONS FROM THE OLD BURYING GROUND AT SAWYER'S HILL, NEWBURYPORT, MASS.

COPIED AND ANNOTATED BY MRS. ANNA BARTLETT
BOYNTON OF WEST NEWBURY.

The Sawyer's Hill burying ground was set aside for burial purposes by a grant from the town of Newbury, dated Dec. 18, 1695. It was then one acre in extent. On Mar. 25, 1707-8, the parish voted to enclose the burying place with a stone wall, but the next year it was voted that the committee should "fence in the burying place either with board fence or stone wall," at their discretion. The ground is now within the limits of Newburyport, and is nearly three miles from the city, on the road leading to Curson's mill. The oldest stone marks the grave of Mrs. Hannah Bartlett, who died May 1, 1705. She was the grandmother of Josiah Bartlett, the signer of the Declaration of Independence.

Miss Elizabeth Atkins daughter of William Atkins Esq. of Newburyport, died July 30, 1838, aged 88 yrs.

Daughter of William and Abigail (Beck) Atkins.

John Barnard son of yᵉ Revᵈ Mʳ Thomas and Mʳˢ Mary Barnard died Novʳ 3ᵈ 1743 aged 12 days.

Rev. Thomas Barnard was the third minister of the Second Parish, 1739-1751. Rev. Thomas Barnard m. Mrs. Mary Woodbridge, Apr. 9, 1741.

Here lies buried the body of Samuel Bartlet who departed this life Ma——

Here lyes buried the body of Richard Bartlett who died Aprail the 17, 1724 in ye 76 year of his age

Son of Richard, immigrant from England, 1635, and Abigail, his wife. Born in Newbury, Feb. 21, 1649; married Hannah, daughter of John Emery. They had nine sons and three daughters.

Here lyes buried the body of Hannah Bartlett ye wife of Richard Bartlett who died May ye furst in 1705 aged 50 years

First interment in this yard. Daughter of John Emery, 2nd, and Mary (Webster) his wife. Born April 26, 1654; married Nov. 18, 1673.

Here lyes buried the body of Mrs Margrat Bartlet the wife of Sargent Richerd Bartlet* who died April 6, 1718 in ye 42 year of her age

Margaret (Woodman) Bartlett, daughter of Edward Woodman, jr., and Mary (Goodridge) his wife. Born Aug. 31, 1676. Married, Apr. 12, 1699. (Richard Bartlett's first wife.)

Here l—— buried the b—— of Mr Richard Bartlet who died Novr 3rd 1753 in ye 74 year of his age

Son of Samuel and Elizabeth (Titcomb) Bartlett; m. (1),; Abigail Ropes of Salem, 1706; (2), Sarah (Titcomb) Bayley, 1727.

Abigail Bartlett the wife of Richard Bartlet junr who died May the 16, 1727 in 47th year of her age

Here lies buried the body — Mr Samuel Bartlet who —— rted this —— May 16th [1753] —— ye 78thy —— his age.

Son of Samuel and Elizabeth (Titcomb) Bartlett. Born March 28, 1876.

Here lyes buried the body of Mrs Durkes Bartlet the wife of Mr John Bartlet who died Jenewary ye 18, 1719 in the 53 year of her

Mary (Rust), first wife of John (Richard?) Bartlett; m. Sept. 29, 1680; d. after 1693. Daughter of Nathaniel and Dorothy of Ipswich.

In memory of Mr Tristram Bartlet who decest Janr^y ye 3rd 1760 in ye 30th year of his age

Son of Samuel and Judith (Coffin) Bartlett; born Sept. 13, 1730.

*Son of Richard and Hannah (Emery) Bartlett.

Eunice Bartlet in ye —1—0—

Daughter of Joseph and Sarah (Adams) Bartlet); born Mar. 22, 1737; died about 1747.

In memory of Mr. John Bartlett, son of Mr. Jonathan Bartlett; who died Oct. 12, 1819, aged 65. He left no children.

Son of Jonathan and Mary (Jones) Bartlett.

In memory of Hannah Bartlet dau^r of Mr Moses & Mrs Judith Bartlet died Sept 16th 1770 in ye 18th year of her age.

In memory of Moses Bartlett who died Dec. 19, 1800 aged 89.

Son of John and Mary (Ordway) Bartlett, b. Jan. 2, 1714.

In memory of Judith Bartlett wife of Moses Bartlett, who died March 1800 aged 81.

Judith (Rogers), m. Moses Bartlett May 17, 1744; bapt. Mar. 27, 1720; dau. of Thomas jun. and Hannah Rogers.

In memory of Mary Delpratt, widow of James Delpratt, & daughter of Moses & Judith Bartlett who died Dec. 22, 1816, aged 63.

Thomas K. son of Jonathan & Sarah Bartlett born May 22, 1816, died March 7, 1895.

Susan T. wife of Thomas K. Bartlett and daughter of Amos & Charlotte Chamberlain born April 22, 1823, died Sept. 14, 1890.

Susan, daughter of Thomas K. & Susan T. Bartlett born Nov. 9, 1859, died May 1, 1880.

Helen R. daughter of Thomas K. & Susan T. Bartlett died Sept. 20, 1851, aged 5 yrs. 2 mos. 10 ds.

Here lyes buried the body of Isaac Bayley who died May the 26th 1726 in the 43 year of his age

Son of Isaac and Sarah (Emery) Bayley, b. 1654; m. Sarah Titcomb May 18, 1708.

Here lyes buried the body of Mr Isaac Bayley who ——
13, —r— 174– & — — 35 —— of his ——

Son of Isaac and Sarah (Titcomb) Bayley; b. Mar. 21, 1709; d.
Oct. 13, 1743; m. Abigail (Hills), 1731.

Isaac Bayley son of Mr Isaac and Abigail Bayley died
August 10, 1736 in ye 5th year of his age

Here lyes ye body of Mr David Bayley dec^d Decr ye 26,
1721 in ye 34 year of his age

Son of Isaac and Sarah Emery; m. Experience Putnam Nov. 11,
1713.

Here lys ye body of Mary wife of John Baily who died
March ye 19, 1707–8 aged 24 years

Daughter of John and Mary (Rust) Bartlett; b. Apr. 27, 1684; m.
July, 1700.

This stone is erected to the memory of Dea^n Edmund
Bayley who departed this life Novr 24, 1801 Æt 91.

Edmund, son of Isaac and Sarah (Titcomb), m. Mary Parkhurst;
(2), Abigail Bartlett.

(Death's head).   Here lies buried the body of Mrs Abigail the wife of Deacon Edmund Bayley who departed this
life Jan^{ry} 21st 1757 in the 47th year of her age

Daughter of Richard and Abigail (Ropes) Bartlett; m. May 22, 1739.
(Footstone in fragments.)

Sarah, daughter of Dea^n Edmund and Prudence Bayley
died June 24, 1759 aged 3 mons 3 days

Deacon Edmund Bayley, m. (third wife) Prudence (Ordway),
widow of Joshua Morse, Jan. 4, 1758.

David Bayley son of Deacon Edmund and Abigail Bay-
ley, who died Janr^y 8th 1757 in ye 5th year of his age

Here lyes buried the body of Mrs Mary Bayley the wife
of Mr Edmund Bayley, who died September the 24th 1736
& in the 27 year of her age.

Mary (Parkhurst) first wife of Deacon Edmund Bayley.

Here lyes the body of Lydea Bayley who died June the
27th 1736 & in the 22nd year of her age

Daughter of Isaac and Sarah (Titcomb) Bayley.

Here lyes buried the body of Samuel Bayley who died Febrvary the 10th 1731 & in the 19th year of his age.

Son of Isaac and Sarah (Titcomb) Bayley, b. Aug. 18, 1712.

Here lyes the body of Judith Bayley who died July ye 7th 1736 & in the 17th year of her age.

Daughter of Isaac and Sarah (Titcomb) Bayley.

Here lies buried the body of Mrs Mary Bayley who died March 24, 1760 ye 24th year of her age

Perhaps daughter of Deacon Edmund and Mary (Parkhurst) Bayley; b. Aug., 1736. (The distinction between *Mrs.* and *Miss* is more modern.)

Here lyes the body of Joseph Bayley who died July the 12, 1736 & in the 14th year of his age

Son of Isaac and Sarah (Titcomb) Bayley.

In memory of Mrs Abigail Bayley wife of Mr Abner Bailey, died Novr 28th 1783 in ye 48th year of her age

Abigail (Cheney) Bayley, m. Dea. Abner (first wife), May 24, 1758.

In memory of Dea. Abner Bayley born March 20, 1739 died Jan. 29, 1821, aged 82. Judith his wife born Oct. 1, 1744 died Aug 17, 1837, aged 93.

Daughter of Dea. Edmund and Abigail (Bartlett) Bayley; m. (1), James Kindrick, Dec. 17, 1763; (2), Dea. Abner Bailey, April 7, 1785.

In memory of Judith Bayley, who died Nov. 12, 1845, aged 48.

Judith, probably daughter of Abner and Mary (Kendrick) Bayley, born March 5, 1799.

Mary R., widow of William H. Bishop, of Portsmouth, N. H. Died March 18, 1876, aged 78 yrs.

In memory of Mrs Martha Bowley wife of Mr James Bowley who died Octr ye 11 1773 in ye 28 year of her age.

Here lyes buried the body of Dockter Daniel Brodstreet who died April ye 24, 1723 & in the 23rd year of his age

Son of Dr. Humphrey and Sarah (Pierce) Bradstreet, b. Feb. 13, 1701.

Here lyes buried the body of Deacon Joshua Brown who died March the 20, 1720 in the 78 year of his age

Joshua, son of Richard and Edith, the immigrants, born April 10, 1642; m. Sara Sawyer Jan. 15, 1669.

Here lieth Mrs Sarah the wife of Decon Joshua Brown who died August the 2nd 1732 aged 80 one years.

Born Nov. 20, 1651; daughter of William and Ruth (Bidfield) Sawyer.

In memory of Joseph Brown, who died July 4, 1742, aged 42 years.

Joseph, son of Joseph and Lydia (Emery), b. Nov. 1, 1699; m. Abigail Hills.

In memory of Mrs. Abigail Brown, relict of Mr. Joseph Brown, who died March 1774, aged 69 years

Abigail Hills m. Joseph Brown, Dec. 26, 1723.

Frances ye son of Mr Joseph & Abigail Brown died June 14 1736 aged in ye 29 years

Abigail & Samuel children of Mr Joseph & Abigal Brown died Decr 6, 1736. Abigail in ye 12 year & Samuel 26 days old

Lydiah Brown daughter of Joseph & Abigail Brown who died February ye 11, 1730 aged 3 years & 2 days

Samuel son of Mr Joseph & Abigail Brown died June 8th [1736] aged 4 year of his age

Here lyes buried the body of Samuel Brown who died February the 19, 1735 in the 22 year of his age

Mrs. Dolly Brown daughter of Caleb & Dorothy Moody d. Sept. 17, 1863, æt. 94 & 5 mos.

Eliphelet, son of Mr Joseph and Abigail Brown —— June 8th 1736 —— 6 years

In memory of Joseph Brown who died Jany 15th 1810, Æt. 80.

Joseph Brown m. Susanna Bailey Nov. 23, 1752. His five children were baptized in Newbury between Sept., 1767, and 1776, the entries calling him successively Lieut., Corp., and Capt.

John Campbell died July 21, 1821; aged 31. Judith Ann his widow died Dec. 24, 1833; aged 39.

Mrs Mary Carlton consort of Mr John Carlton died Sept. 8th 1801, Ætat. 26.

Here lyes buried y° body of Ann Chase y° wife of Ensign Moses Chase aged 40 years died April y° 18 1708 being y° Lords day

Ensign Moses Chase m. Ann Follansby Nov. 10, 1680; m. (2), Sarah Jacobs, Dec. 13, 1713.

In memory of Ruth Chase relict of Nathan Chase, who died July 28th 1795, Æt. 85.

Ruth (Davis), third wife of Nathan, son of Thomas and Rebecca (Follansby) Chase; m. 1763.

1789   Aquila Chase —— 75 —— age

Son of James and Martha (Rolfe) Chase; bapt. June, 1715.

In memory of John Chase who died Jan. 11, 1804; aged 73 yrs.   Hannah Chase wife of John Chase, died Oct. 25, 1807; aged 82 yrs.

John Chase m. Hannah Hoyt, July 30, 1728.

In memory of Nathan Chase son of John & Hannah Chase who died April 15, 1777 aged 16 years.

Anna Chase wife of Aquila Chase died July 14th 1826; aged 70.

The Rev. Plummer Chase late Pastor of the Congregational Church in Carver, Mass.   Born March 13, 1794, died Sept 17, 1835.

Amos Chase died May 27, 1872, aged 81 yrs. 2 mos.

Patience H. wife of Amos Chase, died Aug. 18, 1854, aged 47.

Lydia wife of Amos Chase died July 13, 1850, aged 63.

In memory of Leonard Gardner son of Amos & Lydia Chase, who died Dec. 13, 1827, Æt. 7 yrs. 8 mo.

Amos Chase died Oct. 5, 1844 aged 79.

Samuel Chase died Feb. 22, 1834 aged 80.

Samuel, son of John Chase, bapt. Sept. 22, 1754.

Priscilla his wife died Sep. 17, 1814, aged 60.

Priscilla, dau. of Henry and Priscilla (Lowell) Merrill, bapt. Jan. 27, 1754.

Nathaniel C. son of Josiah & Susanna Chase died Sep^t 22nd 1810, Æt 25.

Eunice wife of Amos Chase, died March 22, 1842 aged 79.

Amos Chase m. Eunice Merrill, Aug. 2, 1787.

Esther S. Chase died Sept. 24, 1855, aged 57 y'rs, 6 mo's, 16 days.

Josiah Chase died Aug. 4, 1835, aged 51 y'rs, 6 mo's, 23 days.

Anna M. L. dau. of Josiah & Esther S. Chase, died Aug. 26, 1823 : aged 3 yrs. 5 mo's. 3 days.

Lydia Esther dau. of Josiah & Esther S. Chase, born Dec. 20, 1827, died Aug. 14, 1839, aged 11 y^{rs} 7 mo^s & 25 days.

In memory of Sarah Cheney dau^r of Mr Daniel & Mrs Elizth Cheney died April 6th 1772, aged 18 months

Daniel Cheney m. Elizabeth Davis, Feb. 17, 1757.

Daniel son of John and Joanna Cheney who died April ye 2nd 1736 aged 9 year.

Hannah Chisemore daughter of Daniel & Abigail Chisemore died Nov. 21st 1801, Æt. 31.

Mrs. Abigail Chisemore wife of Mr. Danl Chisemore died March 31st 1804 Ætat. 71.

Daniel Chisemore m. Abigail Morse, March 7, 1759.

In memory of Anna Chisemore daughter of Daniel and Abigail Chisemore who died Nov. 27th 1792, Æt. 20.

Thomas Coker died May 5th 1804 : Æt. 46.

Son of Samuel and Miriam (Collins) Coker, who were pub. Sept. 30, 1752.

Sarah wife of Thomas Coker died Feb. 8, 1832 : aged 72.

Greenleaf Coker died July 9, 1817 ; aged 17.

Daughter of Edmund and Sarah (Woodman) Greenleaf.

In memory of Mr. Thomas Colby who died Augst 27th 1789 : in the 31st year of his age.

Mr^s Mary Cooper wife of Mr Moses Cooper who died Feb^{ry} 13, 1763 in the 27 year of her age.

In memory of Mr. Simeon Cooper who died August 6, 1814 : aged 66.
Son of Moses and Mary Cooper; baptized July 28, 1750.

Hannah consort of Dea. Moses Cooper died June 10, 1800, Æt. 72.

Rebekah Cooper died Apr. 16, 1807, Æt. 47.
Rebecca, daughter of Moses and Hannah —— Cooper, bapt. Sept. 14, 1760.

Elisabeth daughter of Simeon & Elisabeth Cooper died May 21, 1798, aged 8 years.

Dea. Moses Cooper, died Novr 10, 1803: in his 86 year.
Simeon Cooper m. Elizabeth Brown in South Hampton, N. H., May 30, 1776.

Abigail consort of Dea. Moses Cooper, died April 27, 1758, Æt. 43.

Lydia Cooper died Aug. 15, 1801, Æt. 38.

Charles Edward son of Hon. Robert and Mary Cabot Cross, born Sept. 24, 1837, died June 5, 1863, aged 25 yrs. 9 mos. Graduated at West Point Military Academy, the second in the class of April, 1861. He was appointed First Lieut. of Engineers in May, 1861, and for service at Yorktown and Fredericksburg was made a captain in the same corps. He was killed instantly while crossing the Rappahannock near Falmouth.

Robert Cross died at Lawrence Nov. 19, 1859, aged 60 yrs.

Mary Ruth, daughter of Robert and Mary C. Cross, died at Lawrence August 31, 1854, aged 24.

In memory of Samuel Curson who died Jan. 12, 1847; aged 65.
Samuel Curson, son of Samuel and Elizabeth (Burling) Curson.

Margaret wife of Samuel Curson died June 18, 1877, aged 90.

Daughter of George and Mary Rapell (Atkins) Searl.

Enoch son of John & Priscilla Davis died Oct 17th 1806 Æt. 16.

John Davis m. Priscilla, daughter of David and Priscilla (Huldgate) Bartlett, April 18, 1784.

Deacon Benjamin Davis died March 5, 1871, aged 64 yrs.

Martha Eveline wife of Benjamin Davis died January 11, 1892, aged 84 yrs.

Martha Eveline daughter of Benjamin & Martha E. Davis, died Sept. 12, 1854, aged 20 years.

William Henry, son of Benjamin & Martha E. Davis, died July 5, 1865, aged 23 yrs.

Mary Annie, daughter of Benjamin & Martha E. Davis, died Aug. 10, 1889, aged 40 yrs.

Charles M. Davis, died at Cheviot, Ohio, Oct. 24, 1858, aged 28.

Anna Josephine, daughter of Charles M. & Anna C. Davis died at Worcester, Mass. Jan. 1, 1860, aged 7 1-2 yrs.

Abigail relict of Jeremiah Dole, died Jan. 15, 1837, aged 81.

Paul P. Downer died Oct. 16, 1852, aged 58.

Joseph S. son of Paul & Hannah Downer died at San Francisco, Cal. Jan. 5, 1851, aged 30.

Hannah Moody wife of Paul P. Downer, died Sept. 5, 1872, aged 79 yrs. 10 mos.

Daughter of Samuel and Hannah (Emery) Moody; m. March 28, 1811.

In memory of Mr Hanameel Emeroson died Decer ye 7th 1776

Here lyes buried the body of Mr Josiah Emery who died March the 16, 1718 & in the 39 year of his age.

Son of John and Mary (Webster) Emery.

Here lies buried the body of Mr John Emery who died July the 14, 1730 in the 74——

John Emery, b. Sept. 12, 1656; son of John and Mary (Webster).

Here lies buried the body of En^s Stephen Emery who died February 1st 1746-7 in the 81st year of his age

Born Sept. 6, 1666; son of John and Mary (Webster).

Here lies buried the body of Mr^s Ruth Emery wido and relick of Mr Stephen Emery who departed this this life Jany 9, 1764 in the 92nd year of her age

Daughter of Henry and Anna (Knight) Jaques; born April 14, 1672; m. Nov. 29, 1692.

Here lyes buried the body of Hittey Emery daughter of Mr John and Mehetabal Emery who died June ye 29, 1739 in the 16 year of her age.

Here lies buried Lef^t John Emery who died June 30, 1750 in the 64th year of his age

Son of John and Mary (Sawyer) Emery; m. Mehetabel, daughter of Henry and Ann (Longfellow) Short, Dec. 30, 1714.

Here is intered Mehetabel Emery the wife of Lieut. John Emery who des—— June ye 11th 1773 in the 78th year of her age

Here lyes buried the body of John the son of Mr John and Mehetebel Emery who died August ye 16, 1736 in ye 15 year of his age

Janne Emery the daughter of Leutn. John & Mehetabel Emery died June the 19, 1736 in ye 7th year of her age

Here lyes buried the body of Mr Daniel Emery who died January the 28, 1729 in the 36th year of his age

Daniel, son of John and Mary (Sawyer) Emery, born June 15, 1693. Daniel Emery m. Hannah Tappan Nov. 26, 1718.

Here lyes buried the body of Mrs Hannah Emery wife of Mr Daniel Emery who died Oct. ye 15th 1719 & in the 41 year of her age

Daughter of Jacob Tappan and Hannah (Sewall) born Mar. 4, 1679.

Stephen Emery, Esq. departed this life Sept. 16th 1795 Ætat. 85.

Son of Stephen and Ruth (Jaques) Emery; colonel of the 7th
Regt., 1767, and of the 2nd Division of the 2nd Regt., 1771.

In memory of Mrs Hannah Emery late consort of Col°
Stephen Emery who died Jany 10th 1779 in ye 71 year of
her age

Daughter of Henry and Hannah (Tappan) Rolfe; m. May 5, 1732.

Baniamin the son of Mr. Stephen & Hannah Emery ye
3rd who died 13th May 1736 aged one year

Here lyes buried the body of Josiah Emrey the son of
Mr John & Mehitebel Emrey who died December ye 8th
1729 in ye 12^h year of his age

Here lies buried the body of Mr Daniel Emery who departed this life Jany 24th 1760 in the 26 year of his age.

Samuel Emery died Aug 31st 1805, Æt. 68.

Son of John and Mehetabel (Short) Emery; b. July 26, 1737; m.
Ruth (Annis), Nov. 25, 1760.

In memory of Ruth wife of Samuel Emery who died
March 20, 1800, in the 62 year of her age.

Daughter of Christopher and Ruth (Merrill) Annis.

Sarah Emery daughter of Saml & Ruth Emery, died
Oct. 4, 1838, aged 76.

In memory of Anna daughter of Samuel & Ruth Emery, who died Sep. 16, 1778, Æt. 10.

Miss Polly Emery died Sept 8, 1854, aged 77.

Daughter of Samuel and Ruth (Annis) Emery.

Daniel Emery, Esq. died Jan. 18, 1841, aged 74 y^{rs}.
Hannah Emery died August 26, 1857, aged 86 yrs.

Children of Samuel and Ruth (Annis) Emery.

Sacred to the memory of Mr. Nathaniel Emery, who
died July 14, A. D. 1822 : aged 81 years.

Son of Stephen and Hannah (Rolfe) Emery; Revolutionary soldier.

In memory of Mrs Sarah Emery late consort of M^r
Natha^{ll} Emery & only Daugh^r of Mr Nicholas Short who
died Dece^r ye 22^d 1783 in ye 30th year of her age

In memory of Mr. Stephen Emery who died April 16, 1799 : in the 67 year of his age.

Son of Stephen and Hannah (Rolfe) Emery; m. Sarah Moody, Nov. 6, 1760; m. (2), Sarah Bartlett.

In memory of Mrs Sarah Emery wife of Mr Stephen Emery who died Novr 4th 1777 in ye 36th year of her age.

Here lies interrd Mr^s Hannah Emery who departed this life August ye 7th 1772 in the 61st year of her age.

Here lies intered Doc^t Eliphalet Emery who departed this life Oct. ye 15th 1773 in the 26th year of his age

Son of Stephen and Ruth (Jaques) Emery; surgeon of a privateer.

Miss Mary Emery departed this life May 21st 1803, Ætat. 57.

Daughter of Stephen and Ruth (Jaques) Emery.

In memory of Mrs. Abigail relict of Nathaniel Emery, who died Dec. 9, 1843; aged XCVII.

Abigail (Longfellow), second wife of Lieut. Nathaniel Emery.

In memory of Hannah relict of Benjamin Greeley, who died Novr 30th 1802, in her 89th year.

Benj. Greeley m. (1), Ruth Whittier, Jan. 1, 1723; m. (2), Hannah Poore; bapt. Dec., 1716; child of Samuel and Hannah (Morse) Poore.

Here lies burid ye body of Capt Tristram Greenleaf June^r who departed this life Nouember ye 12th 1754 aged 51 year & 7 days

Son of Tristram and Margaret (Piper) Greenleaf; m. Nov. 5, 1728, Dorothy Rolfe.

In memory of Mrs. Dorothy Greenleaf relict of Mr. Tristram Greenleaf who died Dec. 21st 1782: Ætat. 77.

Marthy daughter of — Mr Trustram & Dorathy Greenlef died Nouem^r 16, 1735 aged 5 year^s

Here lies buried the body of Capt Tristram Greenleaf who died Sepr 15, 1742 in the 73rd year of his age

Son of Stephen and Elizabeth (Coffin) Greenleaf; born Feb. 11, 1668; m., Nov. 12, 1689, Margaret Piper of Ipswich.

Here lies buried the body of Enoch Greenleaf who departed life April ye 3rd —— in ye 29 year of his age

Here lies buried the body of In[s] Edmund Greenleaf who departed this life Oct[r] 14, 1759 in ye 65 year of his age
Son of Tristram and Margaret (Piper) Greenleaf.

Here lies buried the body of Mr[s] Sarah the wife of Mr Edmund Greenleaf who departed this life April 23, 1761 in ye 28 year of her age
Sarah (Woodman) m. Edmund Greenleaf, jun., April 18, 1754.

Francis Greenleaf died Febr[y] 25, 1797, Æt. 77.
Eldest son of Edmund and Lydia (Brown) Greenleaf; m. Anne Wycomb, 1748.

Enoch, son of Francis Greenleaf, died at Newfoundland Jany 1779, Æt. 20.
Son of Francis and Anna (Wycomb).

*Charles How son of Abner & Sarah Greenleaf, died Aug. 29, 1806, aged 4 years 9 m[o]

In memory of *Mehetable, daughter of Abner & Sarah Greenleaf, who died Dec. 31, 1811, aged 21 years.

Here lies interrd Shimuel Griffin, who departed this life April ye 15, 1762, in ye 89 year of his age.
Shimuel Griffin m. (1), Rebecca Annis, Nov., 1715; m. (2), widow Susanna Worth, Jan. 18, 1749.

Here lyes buried the body of Thomas Hale Esqr who departed this life Jany 6th 1746-7 Æ[t] 64. He was long a captain in the militia & for several years one of His Majestie's Justice of the Peace of the County of Essex.
Son of Capt. Thomas and Sara (Northend); pub. to Anna (Short), Nov. 25, 1704.

Here lies buried the body of Mrs Anna Hale the relict of Thomas Hale Esqr who departed this life Nouember the 15th 1770, and in the 89[h] year of her age

Here lie the remains of the Rev. Moses Hale, M. A. Pastor of the Second Church in Newbury who died Jan[y] 18, 1779 in the 64th year of his age and the 28th of his ministry. In him were united the sincere and exemplary Chriftian, the judicious and sound divine, the prudent,

*Children of Abner and Sarah (Hale) of Salem.

vigilant and faithfull Pastor, the tender husband and parent, the warm and active friend of his country and mankind.

Fourth minister of the Second Church in Newbury (first in West Newbury); son of Joseph and Sarah (Symonds), and nephew of Rev. Moses Hale of Byfield; graduated from Harvard, 1734; m. Mehitabel, daughter of Nathaniel and Sarah (Moody) Dummer, 1744 ; ordained at Newbury, Feb. 20, 1751; died there Jan. 15, 1779.

Here lies buried the body of Mr Matthew Hale who departed this life July ye 2, 1773 aged 56 years 3 mo & 6 days

Son of Thomas and Anna (Short) Hale; b. March 15, 1717; m. Mehitabel (Short).

Mehetable, relict of Matthew Hale, died March 6th 1824; aged 93.

Matthew Hale m. Mehitabel Short of West Amesbury, Feb. 21, 1760.

In memory of Thomas Hale son of Mr Matthew and Mrs Mehitabl Hale who died Nou^r the 1, 1776 aged 4 year 2 months 27 ds

Here lies buried ye body of Matthe Hale the son of Mr Mathew & Mrs Mehetabel Hale who departed this life March ye 14th 1767 aged 5 years 10 mo and 5 days

In memory of Mrs Judith Hale wife of Capt. Oliver Hale who died Dec. 26th 1790 in the 53^d year of her age.

Judith, daughter of Daniel and Judith (Emery) Hale; m. May 4, 1758.

In memory of Mary Hale dau^r of Capt. Oliver & Mrs Judith Hale died March 18th 1778 aged 7 mos.

Mary, daughter of Oliver Hale; bapt. Aug. 14, 1777.

In memory of Mr. Silas Hale son of Capt Oliver & Judith Hale, who died Feby 12, 1797 aged 26 years 26 days.

In memory of Miss Elizabeth Hale daughter of Capt. Oliver Hale & Mrs. Judith Hale who died May 24th 1791 Ætat. 23

In memory of Miss Sarah Hale dau^r of Capt Oliver & Mrs Judith Hale who died Nov. 5th 1785 in ye 26th year of her age.

In memory of a son of Cap. Oliver & Mrs Judith Hale born & died Octr 5th 1781

In memory of Lydia wife of Lieut Oliver Hale J^r who died Octr 4^t 1801, in the 38 year of her age

Daughter of Eliphalet and Lydia (Emery) Coffin; first wife of Oliver Hale, jr.

This stone marks the grave of William Hersey, a native of Ireland; who died Dec. 27, 1804.

Thomas Quincy, son of William and Mary Ann Hill, died Oct. 31, 1897, aged 62.

Here lies buried the body of Mr Abel Huse who died March ye 11th 1757 in the 94th year of his age

Son of Abel and Mary (Sears) Huse.

Here lies buried the body of M^s Judith the wife of Mr Abel Huse who died April 24, 1753 in the 82nd year of her age

Daughter of John and Mary (Webster) Emery.

Here lyes buried the bod3 of Mr Thomas Huse — who died Nouember ye 7^h 1734 aged 69 year

Son of Abel and Mary (Sears) Huse.

Here lyes buried the body of Hannah Huse wife of Thomas Huse who died Apr ye 12, 1737 aged 65 years

Here lies buried ye body of Mr William — Huse who departed this life March ye 7th 1756 in ye 55th year of his age

Son of William and Annie (Russell) Huse; b. Oct. 30, 1701.

Here lies buried ye body of Mrs Annie Huse wife to Mr William Huse She departed this life June the 2nd 1733 & in ye 61st year of her age

Annie (Russell) Huse, m. 1699.

Here lies buried the body of Mr William Huse who departed this — life May ye 6th 1754 & in ye 87th year of his age

Son of Abel and Mary (Sears) Huse; b. Oct., 1667.

(To be Continued.)

SALEM TOWN RECORDS.

TOWN MEETINGS, VOLUME II.

1659—1680.*

(*Continued from Vol. XLII. page 272.*)

Th acc° Aboue is Credito[r]

It. pd Nathaniel ffelton	04 : 17 : 06
It. pd Lef[t] Tho Putnam	07 : 04 : 08
It. pd Anthony Buxton	01 : 14 : 08
It. pd William fflint	01 : 14 : 00
It. pd to m[r] Higginſon	32 : 00 : 00
It. pd Josiah Southwicke	00 : 05 : 00
It. by Thomas Goofys rate he being gone	00 : 05 : 00
It. pd the Country Treaſurer	05 : 13 : 01
It pd to Edmond Batter	03 : 10 : 04
It pd to M[r] Jn° Gedney ſen	05 : 03 : 00
It pd to M[r] Daniell Epps Jun	10 : 00 : 00

	72 : 7 : 03
and for his pay is	01 : 0 : 0
	06 : 00 : 00

Acc[td] with Nath Ing[r]ſoll Rest to ballanc
To wh paymt of fixe pounds he do Ingage to pay or Caufe to be pd vnto the felect men in beinge at or before the last of the fift moneth next enfuinge the Date hereof as witnes his hand this 30 : 11 : 73

Nathanaill Ingerſoll

Nath[l] Ingerson : Cred[r]
payd W[m] Dounton p noate 18 : 9[mo] 1674   6 : 00 : 00

[174]   Att A meeting of the Select men the 28[th] January 1672 Being p[r]sent as in the m[r]gent

Maj[r] Hathorne
m[r] W[m] Browne   Bills Granted to pay The Townes Debts

*Copied from the original by Martha O. Howes and verified by Sidney Perley, Esq.

Capt Corwine   To Corporall Putnam for ^{li}   ^{sh}   ^d
m^r Edm^o Batter   Expenses about the high-
Capt Price
Corporall Putnam   ways   01 : 15 : 00
Wm Browne Junr   To m^r Norice for Keeping
                      skoole   10 : 00 : 00
To ffrancis Skery for Keeping Sarah Lam-
bert this year & one months time nurſing her
and her childe & one load brush for ye high
ways   06 : 08 : 00
   To W^m fflint about high ways   02 : 04 : 00
To m^r Henery Bartholmew for his deputy
shipp   07 : 00 : 00
To Daniel Epps for Keeping Skoole wch is
all that was due to him till he went out of
Towne   06 : 05 : 08
To Jno Willms Conſtable for Charges in
Carying the french woman wch m^r Pipon
brought into the Towne abord his Shipp agen 00 : 08 : 00
To Jno Smith for Worke at Strong water
brooke   00 : 03 : 00
To Josiah Southwick & Joshua Buffum w^{ch}
is for worke done on the high ways   02 : 06 : 06
   To m^r Wm Browne Senr   07 : 08 : 07
To Capt Corwine : for his deputy shipp : 7^{li}
& 27^s for other Difburſmts for the Towne   08 : 07 : 00
   To Capt Price a bill for   00 : 13 : 02
To m^r Gedny Senr for Expences in takeing
downe the old meeting houſe & the Select mens
Expences   05 : 03 : 00
To m^r Gedny Senr for m^r Bartholmews
Expences when he was deputy in the year : 66
or 67: at boston he being pd short that year
by the towne   03 : 00 : 00
To m^r Batter for what was due him form^rly
wch should haue bine pd by m^r Phipeny&Keaſer 03 : 10 : 04
To Nath Pickman Senr for worke to ye old
meeting houſe   00 : 04 : 00

                                                  64 : 16 : 03

[175]   Att A meeting of the Selectmen together with

m^r Higginfon Paftor of the Church: January: 13th 1672 Being p^{r}sent as in the m^{r}gent :

Maj^r Hathorne
m^r Wm Browne
Capt Geo: Corwine
m^r Edm^o Batter
Capt Walter Price
Wm Browne Junr

It is Agreed that m^r Wm Browne Senr Capt Geo : Corwin Wm Browne Junr & Docter Weld shall each of them haue liberty to Build a pew for each of ther familys Between the Eaft Door & the South Corner of the meeting houfe. And That Majer Hathorne m^r Edm^o Batter Capt Walter Price and m^r Jno Corwine shall haue liberty to Build each of them a pew for ther familys on the South Syde of the Weft Door, and it is alfoe Agreed that m^r Vearen Senr shall haue liberty to Build a pew for his wife to Sett in at ye south weft Corner of the Meeting houfe and m^{rs} Emery and m^{rs} Norice hath liberty to Sett in the Said pew if they are willing

Att A meeting of the Select men together wth m^r Higginfon the 27th January: 1672: being p^{r}sent as in the m^{r}gent

Maj^r Hathorne
m^r Wm Browne
Capt Geo: Corwine
m^r Edm^o Batter
Capt Walter Price
Corporal Putnam
Wm Browne Junr

It is Agreed that m^r Endecott shall haue liberty to build a pew in the firft place on the North Syde of the East Door for himfelfe & his family : And m^r James Browne hath liberty Granted him to Build apew for himfelfe & family next to m^r Endecotts on ye north Syde Andm^r Jno Turner hath liberty Granted him to Build A pew for himfelfe & family next to m^r James Browns on the North Syde of ye East Window And ther is liberty Granted to m^r Jos Grafton Jun^{rs} Widow & Mr Jno Graftons wife & Nathaniel Graftons Widow to Build A pew from the North Eaft Corner to the midle of the Next Window on the North Syde of ye meeting houfe And m^r Sam^{ll} Gardner hath liberty Granted him to Build a pew from the midle of the North Window to ye Stayers on the Eaft Syde of the North Door.

And m^r Higginfon hath liberty to Build a pew for his family & Relations the firft place on the Weft Syde of the North Door next to the Stayers.

And ffarmer Porter hath liberty Granted him to Build A pew the firft place on the North Syde of the Weft Door. And

[176] *And* m^r John Ruck hath liberty Granted him to Build a pew next to ffarmer Porters, on the North Syde of it.

And m^r Gedny Senr for himfelfe & wife & Jn° Gednys wife and his Sone Barth° Gedny & Wife next to m^r Rucks pew. 8th 7mo 1673. wheras m^r Gedny Senr & his wife are plac'd otherwise the Seat is Granted to m^r Barth° Gedny for his family together wth his Sifter Sufanah

m^r Eleaz^r Gednys Wife hath liberty to Set in one of the pews in the weft Galery.

Sergt Jn° Pickerings Wife hath liberty Granted her to Sett in one of the pews in the Weft Gallery. and m^r Richard Hollingworths wife hath liberty to Set in one of the pews in the Weft Gallery.

[177] Att A meeting of the Select men the 18th : 12mo : 1672 being p^{r}sent as in the m^{r}gent

Major Hathorne
Mr Wm Browne
Capt Corwine
Capt Price
Corporall Putnam
Wm Browne Junr

The Select men made Choice of Lef^t Tho: Putnam: and Jacob Barny Senr of Jn° Raiment : of Beuerly to Eftimate the high way that was layd out by ffarmer Porter & Serg^t Richard Leach through Jacob Barnys land Nigh froft fifh Riuer, and it is alfoe left to them to Judge wch is best to haue barrs through his fence or a Gate, and they are to make a returne to the Select men that soe the S^d Barny may haue Satiffaction for his land.

Joseph Herick & Edward Bithopp Junr made a Complaint to the Select men that they were oppof'd by W^m ffilke and James ffreind and Seu^{r}all others of wenham from falling trees in the Grt Swampe nigh wenham and from bringing away Some wch they had fallen:

Nathaniel Ingerfon is allowed to Sell beer & Syder by the quart for the tyme whyle the farmers are a building of ther meeting houfe and on Lords Days afterwards.

Jn° Smith, Taylor, is abated his towne Rate this year wch is 3^s for Seruice done to the bridge at strong water brooke

Samuel Williams vpon the paym^t of three pownds ten shillings to Jn° Clifford is difcharg'd from the Rates Com-

mitted to him the year that he was Conftable in: And
this Sume of three pownds ten shill was pd Clifford as p
his receipt doth appear:

[178]   Att A Meeting of the Select men the 28th ffeb
1672 being p'sent as in the m'gent

Majr Hathorne
Mr Wm Browne
Capt Corwine
Capt Price
Mr Batter
Corporal Putnam
Wm Browne Junr

Accounted wth mr Higginfon this p'sent
day || & || he Gaue an accquittance, as
appear at the latter End of this booke
for the full of his maintenance from the
Towne to the laft of Decembr 1671:
Philip Cromwell was abated ten shillings of his rate this year:

Granted to the ꝓprieters of the Southfeild through
whofe land the Country high way is layd out the hill of
land by John Holmses, and they are to Run a fence from
the Corner of the fence of the Southfeild by the high way
to the Corner of mr Eleazer Hathorns fence, and this is in
Confideration of the Country high way laid through the
South-feild aforefaid:

Its Ord'd that the ffreemen of this towne be Warn'd to
meet on thirfday the 13th of m'ch next for the nomination
of Majestrates and Choice of a County Treafurer and for
the Choice of Deputies for the Generall Court:

Its Ord'd that A Generall Towne Meeting be Warn'd
for the Inhabitants of the Towne to meet on fryday the
14th of m'ch at Eight of the Clock in the morning for the
Choice of Select men, and Conftables, and to Confidr of a
motion made by mr Higginfon to the Select men & whether the Towne Intend to Gett mr Nichollatt to stay wth
them another year: and to ᵱfect the lyne between this
Towne & Beuerly, and to Confider of the petition of
Some of the ffarmers Deliuered in to the Towne the Laft
Towne meeting in January laft, and what Elce may fall in
wherin the Towne is Confern'd

[179]   Att A meeting of the ffreemen: m'ch the 13th
1672: 73 Capt Geo: Corwine is Chofsen Comifsionr to
Carry in the voats for the Nomination of Majestrates at
the Meeting of the Comifsion'rs of other Towns vppon the
day apointed by law.

Its Voated that ther shall be two Deputyes chofen to
Serue at the Generall Court and that they shall Serue for
the whole year:

m^r Wm Browne Senr & m^r Henery Bartholmew are
Chofsen Deputies for the year Enfueing:

Att a meetinge of the Town in Gen^{r}all vppon the 14th
of 1: 72/3

Choffen for Constabls   Xtpher Babbidge
                        Jno Marston Jun

Capt Corwine m^r Jno Corwine Leith Joseph Gardn^r are
defired & Impowred to apeare at the next gen^{r}all Court in
the behalfe of the Towne & to Anfwer to the pettion of
Sergeant Jno Porter fen & Compay & they are to Receiue
there Instrucons from the felect men

Mr Charls Nicolate is defired to stay at Salem for another yeare when the form^r yeare is expered vpon the
fame Tearms

Capt Corwine haue pmifed to pay m^r Higginfons 100^l
in money & 40 Cords of wood for the next yeare now enfuing & he to haue the 160^{ll} Towne pay as the yeare past:
if any pd to him in money to abate the fourth pt.

Mr Sam^{ll} ‖Gardn^r m^r Bart Gidney ‖ & franc Nurce are
Impowred to Inquire out w^t Comon Land about ye farmes
in or bounds & to bringe Report to ye next Gen^{r}all
Towne meeting that it may be Improued to pay m^r Higginfons debts

In Anfwer to Cornelius Baker m^r Samll Gardner &
franc Nurce ar apoynted to view it & to bringe the Report
to next Towne meetinge

[180] Corp^{ll} Jno Putname Nath Putnam & Sam^{ll}
Gardn^r are Impowred to fetle the line & bounds from a
Marked Tree neare Ipswich River fo called & foe to Crom-
well Rocke

Nathanell Putname is apoynted & Impowred to Exchange about four Acres of Land of the Towns with
Samll Cutler for his better accomeda

Choffen for Select men

Mr Will Browne   Mr Bart Gidney
Mr Hen Bartholmew   Jno Pickeringe
Mr Jno Corwine   Edm Batter

Jnº Becket	Helliard Veren Jun	
Tho Gould	James Powlin	tooke the
Dan Andrews	Ed Woolen fen	oath of fidelity
Manaffes Marston	Elez Gidney	

Jno Cliford haue liberty to cutt the graffe that wilbe on Chery Iland for one yeare

Graunted to Jeremiah Butman & foe to his childr after him : a pcell of land to Build a houfe on neare Bucklys accordinge the cpporton of the other lotts If it be ther to be hade or any wher ther abouts as yᵘ goe to the feaward

[181] Att a Generall Towne meeting: held this 29ᵗʰ : mʳch 73 Chosen for felect men : to make the full nomber of feauen

Maijor William Hawthorne :

Liftenant Joseph Gardner :

Corporall John Puttnam :

Jno Peafe Chosen Constable : Tho fflinte Refufing not beinge Capable by law.

Agreed with ffranc Skery that for keeping Sarah Lamberts Child for the tyme past to this ||day|| he is alowed fiue pounds pfently to haue a bill for it. Agred with him for the enfueing yeare to keep Sarah Lambert fiue pound, for the further difpofe of her Child to ye felect men the Towne to pay the Chardge

Left to ye felect men to cpuide a belringer

The felect men are Impowred to cpuide ordrs for the keepinge out of Cattell & sheep that they doe not anoy oʳ Comons by any of oʳ towne or elfe to feed on them

Left to the felect men to fell the fencinge ftuffe about the buryinge place

Select men ar defired to take of the Town heurd : or to gett a keepʳ & Bulls & to agree about them with the keep or elfe

James Symons his pettion for that lote layd for him amongst the Lots in the Comon below Daniell Rumbals lote the towne faw good to giue it him

Will Traske : his Request about Change of Land Refered to the felect men : to do it for him accordg to his Request

Ben ffel[t]on is Choffen to Ring the bell & to take care of ye meeting houfe only the own^{rs} of the pews to looke them themfelus & to haue feauen pounds p Anum & if the Towne foe good to add 20^d more

[182] At A Meetinge of the Select men the third day of Aprill 1673 beinge p^{r}fent The fame Ord^r about fwine

Mr Jno Corwine
Mr Bart : Gidney
L Jos: Gardn^r
Ed: Batter

that was the yeare past to be for the yeare enfuing & Jno Cooke & will Reeues apoynted to excekate the ordr

||Nath Beadle|| is Choffen fealer of meafurs & waights
Anthony Needham & will Traske ar apoynted to take care about Stone horfes as for the yeare past, for the yeare enfuinge

Mr Jno Corwine & m^r Barth Gidney are apoynted to lay out the widow Reade fpote of land neare Sam^{ll} Ebourns: as alfo to anfwere Jno Burtons Graunt about a peec of fwampe land for his Tan fates: as alfo to anfwr the request of Will Traske: about exchange of foure or fiue pole of land

wee apoynte for furuey^{rs} for the fouthfield fencs for the yeare enfuing: Jno Maffy & Jermah Neale

Wee apoynte for furueyr^s for the North field fencs for the yeare enfuing Georg Keifour & Nich Mani[n]ge

Wee apoynte for furvei^{rs} for the glaffe houfe fencs & all other therabouts without the Northfield : Jofiah Southwicke & Samll Gaskell

Wee apoynte for furvier^s for all the fencs from the Caufeway to the end of the towne vnto mordechai Creuets ffranc Skery & Steven Hasket

Wee ord^r that all the fencs be made vp & inclofed at or before the eight of this Instant month

Wee apoynte & Impower to goe in pambilacon between Lyne and Salem m^r Barth Gidney Jno: Pickering m^r Jn^{thn} Corwine Hilliard ,Veren Jno Price Saml Gardn^r Jun & Thomas Gardn^r & will Hathorn ||jun|| the third *third* day of this Instant moneth

[183] Laid out to Jeremiah Butname about eighteene Roods of Land next adoyninge vnto Buckleys land

James Symons vpon his Request to the Towne for to

Remite the fiue pounds due for a fpote of ground layd out to him amongst the fmall pcons of land in the Comon below Rumbals Anfwered in the Afirmatiue

At a meeting of the select men the fifteenth day of aprill 1673

present

major hawthorne
mr Edmund batter
mr Jno Corwine
Left Joseph Gardner
Jno pickring
Bartlemew Gedney

Bartlemew Gedney Is chosen to keep the towne Bookes this year Ensuing mr Jnᵒ Corwin & Bartlemew Gedney & Sarjant Jnᵒ pickering are desired to finish the high way by the widow Cookes & to bring It thorough to the Comon acording as It now Ranges

Left Joseph Gardner Is allso Joined with them for the setling thatt & all other ways In the north feild & they or any three of yᵐ are Empowred to setle & lay out all ways needfull In the north feilld

Samuell Getchell Is admited an Inhabitant of this towne agreed thatt mr Joseph Gardner hath Roome for a pew alowed him next to mr Jno higinson

And thear Is Libertie granted to Capt Georg Corwin to take In thatt pew In the Corner next to his & thatt mr Eleazer hawthorne & his wife hath Libertie to Sit thear & docter welds hath Libertie to build a pew between thatt & the pulpit stairs If he Coesent to It

Agreed with Tho greenslets wife to keep Sarah Lamberts child Soe Long as to make up the time two months from 29 of march Last upon the same terms She hath kept It hitherto

[184] Its ordered that A generall towne meeting Be warned for thee Inhabitants of the towne to meet together on munday next being the 21ᵗʰ of Aprill at twelve of the Clock to Consider what Instructions shall be given to the select men : & Concerning building a schoole houfe & watch houfe of the timber of the old meeting-house or otherways to dispose of It

& alsoe to make Choice of sum persons to seat the people In the metinghouse

And that wee may Confer with oʳ neighboʳs the farmers About the matter In question between them & us Con-

cerning their ministers maintenance & w^t els may fall in
wherin the towne Is Concerned

ordered that ffrancis Scery Shall haue a bill for four
pound granted him to Niclis maning for keeping Sarah
Lamberts Child

ordered that all persons Inhabitants of this thatt shall
take In from other townes any Cattle : horses or Sheep &
feed them on the towne Comons shall pay thwelve pence
pr head for Evry weeke

An agreement made with Joseph miles & Jn° milke for
the keeping of the towne heard of Cowes

Inp^r they the said miles & milke are to begin to keep the
towne heard vpon the eighteenth day of this Instant month
& to Continue keeping of them untill the fourteenth of
octob^r next & to keep them evry second Lordsday &
those Lords days that they doe not keep them they or one
of them are : to : goe & help to Bring the Cows home before Night & this they are to Attend Seasonably from time
to time & that till their time of keeping be Expired & If
any Cattle be Lost : to Looke them out with all Speed and
to provide two Sufitient Buls

2   And for their payment to have four shilings thre
pence p^r head for all Cattle put before them & keept By
them & to have twelv pence p^r Cow for those that goe on
the Neck without a keeper : & four pence p^r Cow for those
att the upward part of the towne that goe without a keeper
toward the payment of ye buls & for those Catle that goe
with the keeper half the time are to pay for them but half
pay

but If they goe fourteen dayes more than half : to pay
for the whole sum^r & the Select men doe promise to afist
them In Cafe any Refuse to pay

the County treasurer having sent his war-
rent for our County Rate being 7^{li} 16^s 8^d 7   16   08
Is thus paid by 4^{li} 12^s 8^d alowed us by the
County Court toward the Repairing the bridg
or Caufway In o^r towne   4   12   08
tt by Left Gardner 57^s mor by m^r Batter 7^s 3   04   0
                                                _____
                                                 7   16   08

[185]   The Returne of those that were Apointed to
Lay out Sum Land of the townes In Exchange with william Traske & likewise to Satisfie the widow Read for the
high way that Coms thorough her ground by Samuell
Aberns

we have Laid out to W^m traske 5 pole of Land 2 pole
depe from his fence & 2 pole & 1-2 front this between :
their now dweling houſe & their Barne we have taken In
Exchang for the towne about the Same quantitie of Land
Begining at his Barne & soe on vpon a stra‖i‖t Line about
12 Rod In Length Leaving out 2 of the Aple trees of his
orchard Into the towne Comon & Is about a pole Broad In
the midle and Sharpe of to nothing att Each End

& vnto ye widdow Read we have Laid out about the
Same quantitie of Land as Is taken from her for ye hiegh
way : on the west Side of her Land It Lies in anguler
13 poles upon that Side next the North feild fence : & 9
pole on the other Side next her Land soe a strait line
makes the other side we have alowed both high wais 4 Rod
wide

13 Aprill 1673   p^r Jn° Corwin
                                        Bartlemew Gedney

At a generall towne meeting held this 21th : of aprill
1673

Voted that the Instructians Given to the Select men In
the year 1668 are giuen to the select men for this year

Voated that m^r Wm Browne Senr Capt Price & m^r Samuell Gardner are apointed & Empowred to Agree with a
Carpenter or Carpenters to build a houſe for the towne
which may Serve for a Schoole houſe & watch house &
towne houſe of the timber of the old meetinghouſe acording as the timber will bear

Voated that the Select men : and the undertakers for
the meetinghouse with m^r higginson ar appointed and
Empoured to Seat the people In the meetinghouse

Voated thatt the Select men ar Empoured to take Care
for the finding out & setling all such land as belongs to the
towne In any part therof & In Spetiall they are appointed and Empowred to act In behalfe of the towne what Is
Convenient Concening Wenham Swamp

[186]   the Returne of those that were Appointed to
Enquire what *what* Comon Land the town hath amongst
or about the farmes

Wee whose names ar under writen being chosen And
appointed by the towne to Enquire what Comon land belonging to the towne Lieth amongst or about the farmes
doe find as foloweth

Inp^rmis we find a tract of Land Lieing partly on Bev-
erly bounds b||e||gining at goodman howards Soe Runs up
Beetweene Rich^rd Leeches & Jacob barnie Senr their Land
on the on : Side & Cornelious Baker Edward bishop & hosea
traske their Land on the other side soe quite up to the
high way by Jeremy wats his houfe Aboute an hundred
Acres of which ther Is about eight acres of low land very
good almost cleared & well Spread with English gras : We
found ther a bound tree newly Cut downe & hewed on the
Sids   It was marked to deface the markes we Conceave
thear Is Reason for the towne further to Enquire Concerning thatt matter : It is said to be the antient bounds between Ed Bishop & the towns Comon. The land which
Cornelious Baker petitioned for lies within this Aboue mentioned tract & Is about fifteen acres not of the Best of the
Land

2   we find ther Is neer to Jn° harwoods land beetween
goodman Nurs his land & Zacery marsh his land about
fifteen acres of land which is towns Comon

3   neer to Samuell Cutlers land about the like quantety

4   neer to wiliam Shaws land about sixteen acres of *of*
Comon

5   we are Enformed that betweene Nathaniell putman
Nath felton & Antony neehams lands Is land belonging to
the towne to a Conciderable value

6   that ther is within the land wch Jacob barnie Senr
Claims a parcell of land which belongs to the towne

7   that ther Is neer wenham Caufeway above Joseph
porters land Sum land that belongs to the towne

8   between farmer porters meadow & topsfeald bounds
about fourteen acres of Comon

9   ther Is Sum Comon land whear the timber was Cut
for the meetinghoufe

10   neer the landing place by m^r Reads farme a peec of *of* Sault marsh with Sum up land

11   alsoe at Ipswitch River neer Capt Corwins farm ther is Comon land

Dated 21 Aprill 1673   p^r Bartlemew Gedny
                                          Samuell Gardner
                                          francis nurce

[187]   At A meeting of the select men 26 Arill 1673 being present as In the margent

m^r Batter
Mr Jno Corwin
Left Joseph Gardner
Bartlemew Gedney

Agreed with wiliam lord to Ring the bell boath on Saboath dayes and all other publicke ocations except on Coart daies and alsoe to Ring the nine a clocke bell and to Sweep all the Seats and pewes both aboue and below in ye metinghouse And likewise to Call m^r Higinson At his house both morning and afternoone Evry Saboath day and alsoe to dig the graves for all Such as he is desired and to be paid by those that Imploy him In It

& thees things to doe Constantly as the ocation Requires the Space of one whole year from this present day

And In Concideration of the p^rmises he Is to have the full Sum of Seven pounds paid him out of the towne Rate the one halfe of said Sum to be paid him att or before michalmas next

on the 24th da of this Instant month ther was a p^rambulation upon the bounds which are setled between Lin & Salem from midle of m^r Blano his house to the noated Spring & soe to ‖ye‖ tre at the further end of the long pond toward Lin In all wch space we have Renewed the bounds Evry twenty Rod by ading to the heaps of Stons formerly made & this Run by

for Salem   for Lin
m^r Jonathan Corwin   Andrew mausfeeld
Mr Jno Price   Serjant Basett
m^r Hilyard Verin Junr   Wm Basett Junr
    Tho Gardner   Benja. Colins
    Sargt Pickring
    Bart Gedney

The Returne of the Setling the bounds betwene Reading and o^r towne.

23: 2 ᵐᵒ : 1673. Know all by thees pʳsents that wee whose names are under written being Chosen by the townes of Salem and Reading to Run a devitionall line and to state Bounds Betweene the two towns above mentiond wee hav agreed on a small white oake tree on yᵉ south side of the River neer to Jno Phelps his house And to Run from that tree on a straight liue to Cromwels Rock this to be for the towne of Reading for their line till they meet with the farme yt Is now In the hand or posetian of Goodman fuler

for Salem	for Reading
Samuell Gardner	Jonathan Poole
Nathaniell Putnam	Mathew Edwards
John Putnam	John Browne

[188]   At a meeting of the Select men: 3 may 1673 being pʳsent wee Appoint & Empower
mʳ Batter
mʳ Jnᵒ Corwin   Jnᵒ Dodg Junʳ to Execute the orders
Levt Joseph Gardner thatt are made for the pʳservation of
Jnᵒ Pickring   timbʳ and young trees on the townes
Bartlemew Gedney   Comon on Riall Side and to Seaz on
such wood as Is now or that he shall find Cut on yᵉ said Comon Contrary to orders made by the towne   Aggreed that Richʳd Roberts shall have a spot of ground to Build vpon abovt 2 pole wide In the front at the lower End of the Rang of lots sould by the towne next to george hodge his house lott

At a meeting of the select men this 26 may 1673 Being present   agreed that Nathaniell Putman Is Dismist from Being a laier out of Land &
mʳ Batter
mʳ Jnᵒ Corwin   that he shall make Returne unto the
Levt Joseph Gardner select men of all that he hath already
Jnᵒ Pickring   done as a laier out of land for the towne
Bartlemew Gedney   toany person wᵗsoeuer And that Care
be taken the next towne meeting that new laiers out be chosen &

Agreed that ther shall Be a generall towne meeting warned for the Inhabitants of the towne to meet together on the 9ᵗʰ day of June being the second day of yᵉ week that the towne may finish the mater about mʳ higginsons debts and to shuse new laiers out of land and to Considʳ of m^r Jno Browne Senr his Request for the laieng out of land formerly granted to him by the towne and alsoe of fletcher his demand of Land granted to true

Samuell williams doth acknowledg Rebeca outen to be his servant for one wholl year begining the 15th day of aprill Last & the select men doe setle her with him as a servant for that time & hee to furnish her with things needful for such a servant

John Pickring Is chosen and Appointed to Rebuild or Repaire forest River Bridg If Marblehead apoint one to act with them for their part And notis Is to be given to ye select men of marblehead that they apoint sum man or men to Joine with o^{r}s about It

Caried over leaf

[189] Wee Appoint and Impoure Antonie needham and wiliam tra‖s‖ke to take pay out of ye horses y^t they take Runing on the Comons Contrarie ‖to law‖ we say that they take the penaltie appointed by the Law unles ye ouners Compound with them to satisfaction

the o^{r}der made By the Select men ye 8th may 1672 about those twelv persons Is Renewed and Confermed and the Select men doe now ad to y^t number thees folowing viz Giles: Lee Jno mason and w^m holis humphrie Coombes & mordecay Crafort ‖who:‖ are alsoe prohibited from frequenting the ordinaries only we Dismis francke Colins from y^t prohibition

At A meeting of the select men 3 day of June 1673 being present as In the margent

m^r Batter
m^r Jno Corwin
Levt Joseph Gardner
Jno Putnam
Jno Pickring
Bartlemew Gedney

Sould to henry Scery Senr the fence on the buriall place he to pay to the Select men for the townes use twentie and five Shilings

Benjamin Garish and Company have libertie to build a Seat over the Staires : In the meetinghouse

wee Apoint and Impoure Antonie needham and wiliam trask to Execute the Law about horses made Last Court of Election

wee Appoint and Impo^r Bartlemew Gedney to prosecute an action against Joseph Phipen Senr In behalfe of the Select men for his detaining p^t of the Rates Comited to

him when he was Constable and this to be done the next
County Court

*agreed with Isack Cooke that for 35ˢ to be paid
to yᵉ Select men for the towns vse In good and Curant
pay he shall have the high way that goes thorough his
grownd and the Land of the pound thatt Stands neer his
Land alsoe pʳvided that he purchase vpon his owne Charge
for the townes use two pole and half of the north angle of
of that ground Lately Laid out to widow Read the towne
Ading soe much as will make a Convenient pound

Joseph gray hath paid unto mʳ Batter five pound for
that Land which was granted Nicho maning for him

[190]   At A Generall towne meeting held the 9ᵗʰ June
1673

voated that mʳ Samuell Gardner Bartlemew Gedney
and franc Nurce Are Chosen Appointed and Impoʳed to
make Sale of Soe much of the townes Land mentioned In
the Keturne made By them to the towne of Land found
amongst the farmes : as will Amount to the Sum of
Eighty pounds and mʳ Higginson to have itt to pay his
debts this to be done by the Land yᵗ Lies nerest to Beverly

voated thatt mʳ Jnº Browne Senʳ Shall have twentie
Acres of Land added to his former grant of thirtie Acres
to be Laid out In sum Convenient place not to pʳjudice
the bodie of the Comon nor that wᶜʰ Is to be Sould to pay
mʳ Higginsons Debts the wholl Sum to be Laid out Is 50
acres

voated thatt Leivt Joseph Gardner Sargt Richʳd Leach
are Chosen & Appointed to Lay out Lands granted by yᵉ
towne to any and to make Returnes In writing of what
they Soe Lay out at any time and alsoe ffrancis nurce
Is also Joined with them any two of them together have
powʳ to Lay out Land granted

voated that mʳ Batter and mʳ Joseph Gardner are
Chosen appointed and Impoʳed to Answer In behalfe of the
towne att the Next Court the Complaint of Joseph ffletch-
er In behalfe of the Children of ‖henry‖ true for Land
formerly Granted

* " which he has paid to Jnᵒ Higginson wᶜʰ Sd Higⁿ has alowed in his Accᵗ 78."
written in the margin.

(To be continued)

(Continued from Vol. XLII, page 354.)

Agreement. Samuel Sewall, merchant in Boston, on behalf of John Ashley, merchant in Barbados, and Madam Margaret Matson, widow, in Barbados, on the one part, and Peter Henderson, mariner, master of the sloop Salley, of which John Ashley and Margaret Matson are owners, on the other part. Said Henderson with his mate and two men more shall navigate the sloop with all speed and shall receive as wages for himself and crew so much per month as is shown by the "portlidge" bill hereunto annexed, viz. for himself mate and two men from the time they entered into pay until the sloop was unloaded in Barbados or at discharge of the owners and also one month's pay after such discharge " towards Defraying their Charge & Expence they may be at in returning home to New England." Witnesses: John Higginson, Jun', John Everton, Stephen Sewall. Jan. 14, 1714/15.

Deed. Ebenezer Glover, shipwright in Salem, to Samuel Sewall, in behalf of John Ashley and Margaret Matson equal owners, for the new sloop Salley, 34 tons, and her appurtenances for £101, 5 s. Witnesses: Jane Sewall, Stephen Sewall, John Everton. Jan. 26, 1714/15.

[104] " Portlidge Bill for y⁰ Sloop Salley Peter Henderson master

When Shipt 1714/15	Mens Names	at what p. month	Wages advanced
Dec 20	Peter Henderson, master	4 10 -	
Jan'' 6	Stephen Dyke	3 5 -	– 11 –
Dec' 20	John Hilliard	2 10 -	2 2 11
Jan 10	John Everton	2 10 -	2 1 10
		£12. 15 -	£4 15 9

" Mem⁰ A copy attested sent to y⁰ Owners & Deliv⁴
Henderson Another

Sam¹ Sewall

Peter Henderson

"ye particulars of ye advance wages to ye Two Seamen
Ditto Jno Everton 1 yd 3/4 Serge 4/   0 - 7 - 0
            2 yds 1/2 ozenbriggs 18/   3 - 4½
            1 Do 1/2 buttons 6^d p   1 - 0
            Mohair 6^d thred 4^d - 10
            a handke 2/6 1 rundlet 18   4 -
            a box 8, 3 gallo rum 4/6   14 - 8
            4 sugar 3/, a blanket 8/   8 -

                              ———————
                              2 - 1 - 10½

                                  s   d
viz: Jno Hilliard 3 yds flannel 2/4 ⎫
                 thread   3^d ⎬   7   3
         "   pr Shoes & Hose   8   6
         "   rundlet 18^d 3 gall^o rum   15 - 6
         "   4 Sugar 3,   box 8 ^{d} 3 - 8
         "   1/2 blanket   8 -

                              ———————
                              2 - 2 - 11"

     Protest.   Capt Habakuk Gardner made declaration that
on Feb. 23, 1714/15, being at anchor in Salem harbour in
the ship Hopewell of which he was master, that " there
arose a violent Storme of wind and raine from the North
East to ye East and forc't in a very high tide and blew so
Extream hard as somewhat before high water it caused y^e
Ship to drive and all her anchors came home not with-
standing a Large Scope of Cable out and so drove upon y^e
rocks in ye Southfeild in Salem aforesaid on ye top of high
water being Loaden with merchantable fish for Bilboa and
being an Exceeding high tide they were forc't to unload a
considerable part of her Lading and Digg away ye Sand
and Stones to get her off and and that there is part of y^e
Keele beaten off and ye planke some of it brusid and
Rubbed and what further Damage cannot yet be fully
Knowne."

     Signed. Hab^k Gardner, William Stacey, John Swasey."

     [105]   Power of attorney given by Phillip Papillion,
Thomas Lovering, John Capell, Johnathan Capell, John

Thompson, John Parsons, James Wagstafe "y⁰ Elder,"
William Wagstafe of London, merchants, owners of the
ship called the Hanover " lately built att New England William Oulder Master " to James Wagstafe jr, of London to
sell the said ship and appurtenances, to pay for the building, the master's wages, any other claims against her and
reasonable commission.

Witnesses : Joseph Knapton, Joseph Parsons, Nathaniel
Long, Daniel White, James Pitson, Elisha Barlow, Wm
Tilladores.   April 12, 1714

[106]   " Goods left by Mr. John Cabbott
Invoice of goods receiv⁰ of Mr Joshua Madox of New
Yorke and left in his hand till further order from me.

		£	s	d
one ps and 26 yards Searge		£ 8	18	10
26 yards Drugget black	5/6	7	3	
2 ps Stuff at 60/ each		6		
1 ps Anterine 40 yds at 2/		4		
26 yds Silk	8/6	11	1	
27 yds ditto		11	9	6
26 1/4 yds Tabby	5/8	7	5	
6 Bleath white Thread at 4/6		1	7	
5 1/2 ditto		1	4	9
24 yards Stuff	3/	3	10	
20 yards blue Silk	3/6	3	10	
8 yards Tammy	3/	1	4	
26 yards Graggᵗ	4/3ᵈ	5	10	6
21 yards Caleminco	4/	4	4	
1/2ᵘ of N: of N: 26,	3/4	1	12	
1/2ᵘ of N: of N: 13. 10.	2/10ᵈ		15	
1/4ᵘ of N: of N: 16. 10. 10ᵈ N: 18, 1/4 at 12/6		1	02	6
5 Silke Belts	4/	1		
11 pr Garters	3/6	1	18	6
2 ps Silke Cord		1	4	
10 3/4 green Poppling	5/2	2	15	5
10 yards ditto		2	11	8
40 yards Stuff	2/6	5		
30 yards white Durant	2/10ᵈ	4	5	
one box of Ivory knives		1	7	
one box of Maple			18	
2 ps Mogling 40 yards at 3/6		7		

2 diamond cut Bottles	24/	2	8
2 ditto	18	1	16
7 Bosome ditto	7/	2	9
1 doz & 8 at 2/6		2	10
4 Carses of Studs at 10^d		2	
1 bathmettle Stone Necklace		2	10
1 pr. Silver Buckles			9
30 yards Broad Cloth at 24/		36	
32 yards White Flannell 2/8^d		4	5	4
13 1/4 yards Silke	at 13/	8	12	4
2 ps Gauge	3/8	3	18
40 yards Stuff	2/6	5	
26 yards ditto	1/6	2	14
27 1/2 yards ditto	2/9	3	15	4
40 yards ditto	1/8	3	6	8
80 yards dyaper	1/6	6	
2 ps Silk crape valued	at 2/6	13	10
30 pr hose	4/6	4	
20 yards Brocade Ribon	4	4	
50 yards ditto plaine & figured	3/8	6	13	4
5 pr mens hose	at 8/6	2	2	6
2 ps Linces 61 yards	3/	9	3
1 doz^n Silk handkerch^s		2	10
1 doz^n ditto		3	
1 doz^n ffanns		1	
2 doz^n Ribon	at 16/	1	12
10 yards Ribbon flower'd wth Silver			
and Gold	at 6/	3	
3^{ll} Nuttmegs	21/	3	3

£248 4 2

"November the 10th 1714   I acknowledge to have rec^d
the goods above mentioned (lately the Goods of Mr John
Brand of Boston) of Mr John Cabbot, amonting to as p.
Invoice to Two hundred forty eight pounds 4 2^d & prom-
ise to follow his order in ye dispose or Sending them to
Boston as Witness my hand   Joshua Maddox."

Protest. Capt. Patrick Aikman, commander of the ship
Hanniball Galley, made declaration that by a charterparty

dated Feb. 6, 1715, between Messrs Chetham, Winder & Co. merchants in Livonia in behalf of Thomas Pillans of London, merchant on the one part, and said Aikman on the other part, whereby the said Aikman should sail from Livonia to Sicily and after loading with salt, sail to Marblehead where he should stay three months or until Aug. 1, and load with dry codfish or poor Jack, demurrage to be paid at the rate of 40s per day. Aikman fulfilled his part of the contract but Francis Borland and Gilbert Simpson, factors of Thomas Pillans, up to Aug 2, had supplied him with only 200 odd quintalls of fish whereas he could carry 2 or 3000 quintalls. Witnesses: Ga⁵ Gambell, first mate, Geo Adams, second mate. Aug. 2, 1715.

Order from James Wagstaffe jr., with power of attorney from James Wagstaffe & Co. to William Gedney, sheriff of Essex County, to deliver the ship Hannover, 400 Tons, lately built by Andrew and Jonathan Belcher for James Wagstaffe, to Andrew and Jonathan Belcher to whom he had given the bill of sale. Boston, Mar. 5, 1714/15.

[108] Protest. Capt. Jonas Motts of London, commander of the ship Mary, made declaration that in London he shipped as sailors, John Salter, boatswain, John Hock, Richard Mackbread, James Gould and William Smith, for a voyage to New England and then to the "Streights or Mediterranean" and return to Great Britian. They arrived at Marblehead June 18, 1715, and the sailors oftentimes neglected and deserted the service of the ship and greatly hindered the loading with fish. Salem, Aug. 28, 1715.

Protest. Capt. James Comerford, commander of the ship Swallow, made declaration that he sailed from Belfast, Ireland, June 21, 1715, to New England, "but by reason of Contrary winds he put into Loughswilly on yᵉ Norwest part of Ireland & on yᵉ 29ᵗʰ Day of y Same month of June he Set Sayle for New England that on his passage to New England on yᵉ 25 Day of July 1715 met with very stormy weather yᵉ wind being Southerly veering out to Southsoeast which storme continued Severall Dayes so that y^t Sea brocke vpon them very Dangerously & made them very Leaky carried away their maintopmast pumpt out much wheat & haue Just cause to fear much more Damage in ye Hold." Aug. 30, 1715.

[110] Protest. Archeball Hamleton and Capt. James Comerford, commander of the bark Swallow of Belfast, Ireland, made declaration that June 2 they shipped two apprentices or servants of William Bell, viz. Hector Macknab and John Mackallester, as sailors for a voyage to New England, to Bilboa and back to Ireland, and " both of them on the Eleventh Day of August last past being Sabath Day privately and secretly deserted the said service and run clear away and tho he was at great cost charge and trouble to search for them many miles through severall towns but could by no means find them, all which is to the great detriment of the said Comerford and owners of the ship " Whereby they protest against William Bell the master of said servants, the said servants themselves, " And who shipt them." Witnesses; Benjamin Marston, John Higginson. Sworn to by William Fisher, mate, and John Carr, sailor. Oct. 2, 1715.

[111] Protest. John Guy, commander of the ship Grundey, made declaration that by a charterparty dated June 7, 1715, between the said Guy on the one part and Richard Merrey of London, merchant, on the other part, whereby it was agreed that said ship should remain thirty days after arrival in Boston or Marblehead and should load on board such fish and other merchandise as the agents of said Merrey might supply and that at each place the ship might be kept 20 days after said 30 days, at 40 s. per day demurrage. He arrived at Marblehead, Sept. 2, 1715, and reported to Mr Oulton and Cornelius Waldo, merchants, factors of said Merrey, waited until Oct. 30th "allowing for Sabbath Dayes & both ye running Days & ye Twenty Dayes of Demurrage ye said John Guy attended with his boat & hands according to ye Customs & usages of ye Countrey to load," etc. but could obtain no loading. Salem, Nov. 1, 1715.

[112]   Protest.   Capt. Thomas Wright, commander of the ship Mary Galley of London, Redness Smith, one of the mates, George Cox, carpenter, and Walter Mantell, Steward, made declaration, viz. " bound for ye West Indies & New Foundland : / First ye 20 Day of March 1715 at eight in ye Morning weighed from Graues End bound for Barbados where arrived ye Eighth of May where disposed of my Cargoe & tooke in rum Sugar & Molasses for Newfoundland afores^d & departed from Barbados ye Eleventh of —— Designed to touch in Anteguo but ye wind inclining to ye Northward bore to Leward of Gwardeloop & ye 18 of June came to an anchor in ye Island Gwardo. where tooke in Salt for Newfoundland the 30th tooke my departure from Virgin Guardo ye 10 of July had an obseruation & found our Selues in ye Lat 37. 17^m & by ye best of our Judgment by our reckoning were 50 or 60 Leagues to ye Eastward of Burmudos & Steared our Course N. E. or N. E. & by N. & on Sunday in ye Morning being ye Seuenteenth of July houe ye lead had no Soundings with Six lines at fiue or Six in ye afternoon Sounded againe & had about 115 fathom Water or thereabouts to ye best of our Judgment, at Six handed our Small Sayles & Halled vp our Mainsail with Much fogg, at Two on Munday Morning our Ship Struck aground, ye wind at S. S. E. wearing ye Ship ye wind came to ye S. S. W. ye Ship Stuck fast.   Imediatly Hoised out Boat & carried out our best Bow Anchor & Houe ye Ships head to wind & Sea, ye Anchor coming home carried out our sheet anchor heauing a great Strain, our Windless Gaue way & one of ye bolts drew out of ye Cleeke of ye windless upon y^t brought our runners and Tackles on both our Cables with what purchase we could make but finding ye water falling ye Ship laid fast between two rocks and finding could not doe no good Lowered both our yards and Topmasts to Save ye Ship in an hours time after ye Ship Stuck fast ye Rudder broke Close to ye upper Gudgeon and in halfe an hour after had near five foot water in ye hold and in less then halfe an hour after ye hold was full of water finding ye made ye best of our time to get Some provisions on Shore for to Subsist with which did get some on Shore when

Come on Shore found it to be a very Small Island neither tree nor brush nor fresh water thereon, about four in ye afternoon Cutt our foremast by ye board to save ye Ship whole from parting Containing little wind, Saved our Sails and gott Some Casks of Rum on Shore and Severall of our Stores and other goods to a Considerable value : Saturday ye 30th of July at ten in ye morning were Surrounded by twenty two Indians with arms which Seazed on us and made us Cry for quarter and Said war were Declaired in Cape Britton. Wee Said no but were a good peace between us : upon their Coming on ye Island one of ye Indians seeing my Doctor setting on ye beach fired at him and Shot him Stone dead and Imediatly forced my men to goe into our boat to goe over to another Island about a Gun Shott from itt and Said would send us provisions for a month but as soon as Came to y^t Island ordered two of my men to goe on Shore to fill a Small two Gallon Kag with water wch did as soon as wee had Got it Row'd of but one of ye Indians seeing of us goe off Came downe and weaved his hatt for us to goe on Shore. I answered him again with waving to ye Shore, as soon as I goott out of gun Shott Sat our mast and Sail and made ye best of our way to ye Sea Standing off Sea a Sail, made for him, Came So near him wave our hatts to him he finding we Come near him made Sail from us we, haveing no bread nor Compass Could not follow him but Stood into ye Shoar again and found ye Indians there wch Came Down and fired Severall arms to make us Come to them. I seeing y^t Stood to Sea again till ye Evening and then went for ye Shoare and got a harbour about 6 Leagues Distance from ye Island where ye Indians had forced us from where ye Ship were Stranded and Continued till Monday morning then went to ye Island againe wch found ye Indians still there ye Indians See us by off ye Island in our boat, they mann^d three or four Canoos and gave me Chase three or four Leagues to Sea finding ye fogg Coming on gave over their Chace, it proving foggy wee Could not See ye Shore but were forced to Continue in our boat with fourteen Souls with neither bread nor water till Wednesday morning ten of ye Clock Came on board ye John and

Sarah, Henry Elkins master, belonging to Salem in New England wch told him my misfortunes. he and one neighbor of his more in another Sloop went down to ye Island to See whether ye Indians were gon finding them gon went on Shore wch found a Small matter part of my goods there of Rum and Rigging left but ye wind blowing hard Could not Stay there y^t night but were forced to goe into Island harbour about two Leagues Distance from y^t place. when arrived in this Island harbour found one Scooner and one Sloop belonging to ye french one Pettepaws master of ye Scooner and one Moyzene Labaver master of ye Sloop. whereupon Inquiry found ye undermentioned goods on board ye Scooner and Sloop wch is attested to as vizt: Two Bar^{ll} of Rum, two brass Blunderbuses, three Coyles, three Iron pump Speare, two hides of Leather, a quantity of Iron, one Cask of Tallow, a large Quantity of new and old Canvis, Cut to peices by ye french out of ye Bolt ropes, one large Copper pump, three Caine Chaires, and Seventy peices of Beef and about 100 w^t of fine Sugar found on board ye Said vesell ye fifth day of August 1715. ye next day went to ye Island where my goods were and took them off and y^e —— of September arrived at Salem."
Salem, Sept. 10, 1715.

[113] Protest. Capt. Thomas Landell of Portsmouth, N. H., master of the Sloop Paradox, made declaration that, being laden with wood and fish on a voyage from Pascataqua to Boston on Nov. 27, 1715, "the wind being out and ye weather Dark & cloudy, for Safety he put into Marblehead harbour & came to an Anchor there & veered out as good a Scope as they could but a Storm Came on in ye night ye wind at E. N. East and blew very hard So that ye Cable parted & ye Sloop drove ashore on ye rocks at Waldrons head & Staved & filled with Water, Lost their wood & Damnifyed ye fish." Salem, Nov. 30, 1715.

Brandford, March 30, 1714/15. Receipt by Joseph ffoot to Wm English on account of Phillip English of Salem for 50 gallons of molasses to be disposed for said English & Co.

Guilford, April 6, 1714.   Receipt by Samuel Hill to
Wm. English of 3 hogshead of molasses and a Caske of
sugar belonging to Phillip English.

[114] Protest. Ebenezer Glouer of Salem, shipwright,
made declaration that by an agreement dated Feb. 25,
1715/16, between the said Glouer on the one part and
John Wyet of Boston, lighterman, on the other part,
whereby the said Glouer was to rebuild and lengthen a
sloop belonging to said Wyet, provided the said Wyet
should furnish the "Iron Worke Nayles Ocum & Tarr"
which he failed to do to such a degree that said Glouer
could not proceed on the work for want of material and
two of his hands, viz. Theodor Atkinson and Edward Cox
have gone away on a fishing voyage and said Wyet himself
has sailed. Witnesses : Daniel Bacon jr., Joseph Allen jr.
    Salem, April 18, 1716.

Protest.   Samuel Northey, master of the Sloop Newe
Tryall, and Richard Newcomb, mate, made declaration that
on March 17, 1715/16, while on a voyage from North
Carolina to Saint Christophers " they met with a Violent
Easterly Storm insomuch that ye Sea run so high ye wind
so fierce & ye Sloop so Walt that they were in great Danger of being all lost so that they were constrained to
heave thier boat ouerboard for ye preseruacon of ye whole
& it continued such hard blowing Stormy Southeasterly
weather for 14 dayes together that they droue farr to y^e
Norward & on 6th Aprill it blew so hard a Storm at S. S.
E. ye Sloop lay all along & would not hold up her side &
ye Sea run ouer & there was 3 foot water in ye hold
whereby for ye Saving of thier liues they were forct to
Stave thier Water that was on Deck & other Caske so that
they were left in a Miserable Condition for ye Saving of
y^r lives Endeavored to get to ye first Suitable English
place they could possible for recruit & not being able to
get to ye Southward to ye Intended port but forc'd by
long continued Storming & hard Southerly Gales & y^e
Waltness & Insufficiency of y^t Sloop were droue wthin
about 40 L. of Long Island & then concluded ye likelyest
place would be N. England where wee arrived ye first day
of May at Marblehead."

Sworn to by Samuel Northy, R^d Newcombe, and Jeremiah Symons, passenger. "Swore to by all three, Two of them after ye Manner of Quakers." Salem, May 2, 1716.

[115]   Servant's indenture of James Stoy of Salem, to Benjamin Marston of Salem, merchant, for the term of 3 1/2 years, from Nov. 1, 1712, and he "shall faithfully Serve his Lawful Comands obey & in all things behaue himselfe towards his said Master & all his as a faithfull Servant ought to doe during all ye said Term and ye said Master shall find & provide meat, drink, Washing & lodging as well in Sickness as in health." Witnesses: Samuel Upton, Elizabeth Upton.   Recorded June 11, 1716.

Depositions of Daniel Webb of Salem, mariner, aged 64 years, and Daniel Caton, "Taylor," formerly of Bandonbridge in Ireland, now of Salem, aged 61 years, that they were well acquainted with John Dyn of Kingsate, Ireland, merchant or Shopkeeper, deceased, "who dwelt nigh ye Water gate" and that Elizabeth Comer, wife of Richard Comer, "Taylor," of Providence, Rhode Island, was the daughter of said John Dyn who had been dead 30 years. Daniel Webb further testified that he was master of the ketch Tryall of Salem and brought over the aforesaid Elizabeth Comer whose maiden name was then Elizabeth Dynn about 1679 and that the year before he took the son of said John Dynn, William Dunn, as an apprentice and brought him to New England and further that "Elizabeth Comer alias Dynn is ye very person alive & well at ye taking these affidavits being present at ye Caption." They also add that the aforesaid William Dynn died several years before and that the only two children he had viz John Dynn and William Dynn, also were dead. Salem, June 18, 1716.

Power of attorney. Dated June 11, 1716, given by Thomas Lyndall of Portsmouth, N. H., mariner, to Samuel Swan, also of Portsmouth. Witnesses: Benjamin Gambling, Eleazer Russell.

[116]   Deposition of John Ward, minister of Haverhill, that he had "lived in New England upward of fforty

years at my ffirst Coming into ye Country I had knowledge of one known & called by ye name of M^r ——— ffawne
who fformerly as I heard lived at Ipswich in New England
and after that at Haverhill in New England where I knew
him, who had there two daughters living with him whereof one of them by name Elizabeth is yet Alive & now y^e
wife of Robert Clement of s^d Haverhill which s^d Elizabeth
was always Accounted & called by ye name of Elizabeth
ffawne before her Marriage so ffar as ever I knew & was
all along in s^d M^r ffawnes time in this Country owned by
him to be his own Naturall Daughter She being ye Eldest
of ye Two & hath lived ffull or neare fforty years in Haverhill where now she is living." Haverhill, Aug. 19, 1681.

Deposition of Lieut. Daniel Lad Senr that at his first
coming to New England he knew John ffawne and his wife
and their daughter, later the wife of Robert Clement of
Haverhill and further that John ffawne never had but one
wife.

Ann Ladd, wife of Daniel Ladd Senr deposed that for
thirty years she knew John ffawne, his wife, and Elizabeth,
wife of Robert Clement, who lived with them and was owned
by them to be their daughter. Haverhill, Aug. 27, 1681.

Robert Clement Senr of Haverhill and Elizabeth Clement his wife daughter of John ffawne, formerly of Haverhill,
deed to ffawne Clement, of Newbury, their son, all money
given to either of them by will as a legacy, and especially
referring to a legacy given by Mr Luke ffawne formerly
of London, stationer. Witnesses: James Saunders,
Joseph Kingsberry. Haverhill, March 5, 1707/8.

[117] Depositions of Joseph Peasely, Yeoman, aged
69 years, and Thomas Whitcher, husbandman, aged 62
years, both of Haverhill, that they were neighbors and well
acquainted with Robert Clements of Haverhill, deceased,
about four years before, Elizabeth Clements, his wife and
ffawne Clement their eldest surviving son, and they "have
often heard ye s^d Elizabeth Clements Say that they named
their Sons Christian Name (ffawne) to Bear up ye Name
of his Mothers Relations." Salem, June 27, 1716.

Affidavit by Tobias Colman, and Lydia Colman, his wife, both of Newbury, that Thomas Colman his son "was named Thomas Colman by the Desire of his Grandfather Thomas Coleman, late of Nantucket, deceased, and that it was his Desier that he Should Enjoye all that Estate in Nantucket mentioned in a deed beareing Date the Third Day of november one thousand Six hundred Seventy & three and we do further Testify that our now Son Thomas Colman was named Thomas Colman to beare up his grandfathers name and by his Desier Should Enjoy all his Estate." July 1, 1713.
Witnesses : Thomas Noyes, Joseph Woodbridge.

John Wicomb and Abigail Wicomb testify that Tobias Colman bound his son Thomas as an apprentice to them, a short time after he came from Nantucket, and he served them for upwards of ten years. They also testify that said Thomas was the son of said Tobias. July 6, 1713.

[118] Protest. Thomas Steel and George Bethune of Boston, merchant's agents and factors for Messrs Thomas Kirkpatrick and John Porter of Dublin, Ireland, merchants, made declaration that by a charterparty dated May 7, 1716, made between the aforementioned party on the one part and Jeffrey Farmer, commander of the Briganteen the Good Fellow, wherein it was agreed that said Farmer should sail from Marblehead six days after the said factors had finished shipping the quantity of fish they were obliged by the charterparty to ship, the said factors protest that although they agreed with the terms and the ship was loaded by July 5, and wind and weather were favorable the said Farmer had up to the date of protest neglected to sail. Salem, July 17, 1716.

Protest. William Diamond of Marblehead, innholder, owner of the shallop Rebecah, made protest against John Harris of Boston, now resident in Marblehead, in that the said Harris " did sometime this last Sumer take charge of y° said Shallop as a Skipper or Master for y° remainder of y° Summer Voiage whereupon y° s⁴ Wm Diamond had been at considerable charge in disbursements for y° Generall and perticulars on said voiage yet Notwithstanding contrary to all reason, custom & vsage in Such cases ye said John Harris & William Pitts, a Sojourner in Marblehead, one of ye Crew belonging to ye said Shallop, did on or about ye 25th Day of August Instant at Marblehead afore-sd Illegaly & Injuriously desert ye sd Shallop upwards or about a month sooner y^n is vsual & left her unmoar'd in a careless furlorn condition." Salem, Aug. 29, 1716.

[119]   Protest.   Samuel Swasey of Salem, shipwright, made declaration that by a charterparty, dated May 21, 1716, between said Swasey and Samuel Reed it was agreed that said Swasey should build a shallop for said Reed and the latter should " find all Iron Works mast yards ocum Tarr &c " and pay five payments, " as ye vessel went forward in her being built reserving one paymen^t till she should be finish't & Delieured."   And said Swasey testified that the building of the ship had gone on " till she is almost finished " but said Reed had failed on his part " in not paying of one or more of ye payments " and not providing him with nails to his great hindrance.
Salem, Aug. 30, 1716.

" Severall writings belonging to ffawn Clements recorded Sepr 15th 1716.

"Memorial of ffawn Clements Son of Mrs Eliz^a Clements who was daughter of Mr John & Elizabeth Fawn wch Eliz^a Clements was Niece to one Mr Luke alias Look Fawn a Stationer in Pauls Church yard at ye Sign of ye parrot who died a little before ye fire and gave ye s^d Mrs Elizabeth Clements £800 and left it in ye hands of Mr John Cressit in Charter house yard in London Mr Edward Clements at ye Sign of ye Lamb in Abchurch lane Mr Edward Henning Merch^t in London & Mr Jerrat Marshal in London.   Exam^d "

[120]   Salem, Oct. 16, 1715.   Receipt given by John Brett to Abraham Purchass for £7 with a promise to lay out said sum for him in Barbados and to make returns for the same.   Recorded Sept. 16, 1716.

Protest. Patrick French of Galloway, Ireland, now resident in Salem, merchant, made protest "that Capt. Dauid Gentleman, Master or Comander of ye Pinke Elizabeth, burthen ab^o 110 Tunn, which Pinke is Consigned to ye s^d Patrick French & at his disposall & altho' ye s^d Patrick French hath dispatcht ye said David Gentleman & furnished him with loading provision & Everything necessary for his voyage in so much that on or about ye 15th Instant he ye s^d David Gentleman aplyed to ye s^d Patrick French for Sayling orders aleadging he was ready to Sayl & accordingly ye s^d french gaue him his orders to set Sayl ye first oportunity of wind & weather & direct his course for ye Island of Madera there to aply to Mr Fra^s Brown yet notwithstanding he ye s^d David Gentleman Master afores^d not regarding to Comply wth his orders hath Neglected Sayling to this Day tho a fair wind has blown Ever Since & Neglects his Duty on board his Ship hauing been gone to Boston for about nine days where he yet remains & did at Boston before ye s^d pinke came about to Salem hinder Much of ye Merchts time & business by taking out a Mast or Masts." Salem, Sept. 18, 1716.
Witnesses: James Lindall, Richard Newcombe.

Protest. Capt. John Harrison, Commander of the ship Mercury of Teneriffe, one of the Canary Islands, made declaration that by a charterparty between the said Harrison on the one part and Peter D^e Keyser and Barnard Welch of the port of Oratawa in Teneriffe, merchants, it was agreed that the said ship should proceed from Teneriffe to New England and there remain 30 days and then might be kept 10 days longer for which demurrage should be paid at the rate of fifty shillings per day, and protests that although he arrived Aug. 3, 1716 and had always been ready to take freight on board up to Sept. 29, 1716, he still needed several tons to complete his loading. Salem, Sept. 25, 1716. Witnesses: Richard Rowland, Richard Newcombe.

[121] Protest. Capt. William Scott of London, commander of the ship Princess Galley, made declaration that

by a charterparty made in London, June 15, 1716, between himself and Disney Stanyforth of London, merchant, it was agreed that he should proceed to New England and there remain 25 days and take on board all such merchantable fish that the factors of said freightor shall supply to her full loading, and said Scott may be detained thirty days in all at the rate of 25s. per day. And the said Scott affirms that he arrived in Boston, August 26, 1716, and that by direction of the factor of said Stanyforth he went to Marblehead and that as late as Oct. 12, 1716, the date of the protest there were still needed   quintals to complete the loading. Salem, Oct. 11, 1716.

Protest. Capt. John Robinson, master of the pink or snow called the Richard and Elizabeth, and Richard Main, mate, made declaration that on Oct. 14, 1716, while on a voyage from Barbados to New England, in lat. 38° north " they mett with a violent Storm of wind at S. E. and so shifted to W. S. W. which raised ye Sea to such a height that it broke upon them & shiffted thier goods & ballast in ye Hold so that they were in great Hazard of Loosing ship & liues & all by all which they cannot but conclude they have Suffered Great Damage & y^t on Sabath Day ye 21 Instant they made Piscataqua riuer & were in hopes of getting in but it proving a dark Day & ye wind Spring up Northerly & blowing hard they were forc't to bare away & ariued at Marblehead ye 21 Day of October." Salem, Oct. 22, 1716.

(To be continued.)

EDMUND LEWIS OF LYNN, AND SOME OF HIS DESCENDANTS.

BY GEORGE HARLAN LEWIS OF LOS ANGELES, CAL.

Edmund Lewis, who came to this country and first settled in Watertown, is said to have come from Lynn Regis (King's Lynn), England, but there is no record of him or any of his family on the church registers there. Alonzo Lewis, in his history of Lynn (second edition), states that he was a brother of William Lewis, who was at Roxbury in 1630, and was a founder of Lancaster, Mass., in 1653, who descended from a good Welsh family, with a pedigree running back centuries. (Some Welsh pedigrees run back to Noah.) Where Lewis obtained his information is not at my command. I have searched the records of this colony and visited England and Wales, used the library of the British Museum, and consulted the records of Somerset House and Fetter Lane, London, without success. Alonzo Lewis has his pedigree upon his monument in the Western Burying Ground, Lynn, running from William, through Isaac, his son, who died childless. In point of fact, Alonzo Lewis was descended from Isaac, son of John, of Charlestown and Malden. If Alonzo Lewis had stated his Welsh pedigree, giving the name of the Welsh ancestor, or the place from which he emigrated, it might have been traced.

There is no authoritative connection of any of the Lewis immigrants to New England, during the 17th century, with any Welsh or English family. Without knowing his English home, it is impossible to trace a Welshman. It was not until the middle of the 16th century that the prominent families of Wales begun to adopt the surname as used by the English. They then took the name of the father, and William ap Lewis became William Lewis;

(65)

Lewis ap Edward became Lewis Edwards; Thomas ap Richard became Thomas Prichard or Richards; John ap Robert became John Probert or Roberts; John ab Owen became John Bowen; John ap Evan became Bevan or Evans; John ap Harry became Parry,—and so on through the whole list.

The name of Lewis was as popular in Wales as Washington and Franklin in this country. It was adopted as the English form for Llewellyn, who was the last ruling prince in Wales, and was killed in 1282, and whose head hung over the entrance to the Tower of London, after having been paraded through the streets as a warning to others who might rebel. Nearly every Welsh family had a son Lewis, and when the surname was adopted there were many Lewises.

But this did not take place universally at any given time, for at the beginning of the 19th century not half the people had surnames, and to-day in some of the northern parts of Wales the old ap or ab is used between father and child. Edmund might have been the first to adopt the surname, and his father may have been Lewis ap John, or some other name, therefore it is impossible to trace the ancestry in Wales without knowing the place of nativity and parents names, and even then it cannot be done with certainty.

All coats of arms are without authority for the same reasons. Ion Lewis, son of Alonzo, states in his biographical sketch of his father, that they descended from the family in Glamorgan. I have been to Cardiff and Greenmeadow, and inspected the family chart of Henry Lewis, M. P., who is the head of the family at this time, and find no connection. I have also consulted the printed records of the family and find none. The parish registers do not run back earlier than 1725, therefore all recorded connection is impossible. When a member of the family emigrated from England his record was discontinued, and no entry was made even if the family knew where the individual had gone.

That the Lewises came from a good family cannot be doubted. Thomas Lewis, who was the first, came to Saco in 1628, and was an educated man of means, or he could not have obtained the grant which he did. Philip Lewis of Greenland (Portsmouth), 1650, was a relative of —— Tucker, of Cleaves and Tucker. William Lewis of Roxbury was probably one of the young sons of a numerous family, where the eldest son inherited the estates, and the other sons had to look elsewhere. He was of an adventurous spirit, and came out when a mere youth, and returned to England where he may have interested his brothers in the colony, and possibly Edmund and John were brothers of his, as the similarity of names in the families will be noticed. After William's children were driven out of Lancaster (1675-6) by the Indians, Isaac is found fighting the Indians with John, the son of Edmund, and he received £3. 2. 0. from Lynn. (Bodge's Indian Wars, p. 371.) Later he is found in Malden, Chelsea, and Charlestown, where John's descendants are living.

There is no doubt but that Edmund was brought up by the sea. He had a good estate at Watertown, but it was away from the water, and he went to Lynn, where he found an ideal place, and bought forty acres directly upon the seashore. He may have been a sailor, as in his inventory appears a " cutlas," a weapon used in battle, at close quarters, on vessels. He may have bought his land of John Wood, as his lands are called " Wood end fields," and that end of the town was called " Wood end." In his will he mentions John and Thomas as having some property, and is solicitous for the welfare of the five youngest children, of whom only James and Nathaniel are recorded at Watertown, so the others were born in Lynn, and no record made. Whether he had five children younger than John, as Savage thinks, or five younger than Thomas, is uncertain. Of James I find no certain trace. Nathaniel, with his brother Joseph, sailed away to New London, Conn., in 1666.

It has been said that Benjamin Lewis of Stratford, Conn., who went from New Haven, Conn., in 1670, as one of the founders of Wallingford, and later sold out to Dr. John Hall and returned to Stratford, was a son of Edmund. Did he, like Nathaniel and Joseph, sail away, and not finding a place at New London, continue until he reached New Haven and Stratford? Did he later, like Edmund, leave the inland town for the seashore? The habits of youth are hard to eradicate. Another connection may be found in the fact that the names of his children are almost identical with those of Edmund, and some of John's, viz.: John, Mary, James, Edmund, Joseph, Hannah, Martha, Benjamin and Eunice. John had John, Hannah, and Benjamin. This is not positive proof, but is strong circumstantial evidence in support of the claim that Benjamin was the youngest child of Edmund. I do not include him, for want of absolute proof.

But with Joseph it is quite different, for I consider the written proof made over two hundred years ago identifying Nathaniel with Lynn, and Joseph with Nathaniel at Swansea, together with the presence there of their brother Thomas, as superior to the uninvestigated theory of Mr. Deane, who, in his History of Scituate, assumes that they were children of George Lewis of Barnstable. Other writers have repeated his statement, save Savage, who rejects it, and Amos Otis, who, in his Barnstable Families, throws it out entirely, and states that neither town, colony, or church records confirm the statement.

On April 10, 1634, Edmund Lewis, aged 33 years, his wife Mary, aged 32, son John, aged 3, and son Thomas, aged ¾ years, embarked in the Elizabeth, William Andrews, master, at Ipswich, England. He settled at Watertown, Mass., and shared in the first great division of lands. His homestead was on what is now the east side of Lexington street. He was granted land July 25, 1636, lot 26, 30 acres in the 1st division; Feb. 28, 1636-7, lot 82, 5 acres ; June 16, 1637, lot 61, 5 acres ; April 9, 1638, 6 acres. In the book of possessions he held in lands : (1) A Homestall of 6 acres. (2) One acre of meddow in Rockmeddow. (3) Thirty acres of upland being a great Divident in the 1st Division, the 25th Lott. (4) Five acres of Plowland in the further Plaine and the 91 lott. (5) Five acres of meddow in the remote meddows & the 61 lott. (6) A farme of hundred acres of upland. (7) One acre of remote meddow by estimation. He was admitted a freeman May 24, 1636, and was elected a selectman for the year 1638. Oct. 14, 1638, he was one of a committee chosen " To lay out the farmes as they were ordered, near the Dedham line." (Barker's Watertown, p. 4.) Alonzo Lewis' History of Lynn says he removed to Lynn in 1639. Bond's Genealogies of Watertown says he removed after 1642. He buried a child there Nov. 6, 1642; Savage says 1643. He had lived near the sea, and when he removed to Lynn he settled in the eastern part of the town, on what is now Lewis street. He died in January, 1650. His wife died Sept. 7, 1658.

In his will, made the 13, 11th month, 1650, he mentions five young children. The date of birth of two of them is not recorded, and the name of one of them is not known. His will, on file in Essex County Probate Records, Vol. 1, f. 119, is as follows :

" Line the 13th of the 11th mo. 1650. Memorandum that I Edmund Lewis beinge Sick & Weake, but of perfect remembrance, doe make & conferm this my last Will and testyment as followeth,

First. My Will is that my land att Watertown shall be soaled, & that my eldest son John Lewis shall have a double portyon & the rest of my children namely, the five youngest to have every one of them a licke portyon of my Estate.

Secondly. My deare & lovinge wife to have the third of all my whole Estate.

Thirdly. I desire that my wife may have a cow over & above towards bringinge upe of my youngest children.

Fourthly :—my desire is my wife to be my whole executor to dispose of my body & goods accordinge to my Will.

Fifthly :—my request to my son John is, to give his mother a Cow to helpe her towards the bringinge up of my youngest children.

Sixthly :—my request to my son Thomas Lewis is to give to his mother half of his Sheepe to help her as aforesaid.

Seventhly :—My desire and meaninge is that the Cow I

ask of John & the Sheepe I ask of Thomas is of them
that they now have in their possession. Also my request
is to Thomas Hastings to be my supervisor to assist my
lovinge wife.

Witnesses   Edmund X Lewis
                                        mark
John Deakin
Edward Burcham.

This will, with an inventory, was brought into court
by Mary, widow of Edmund Lewis, on the 25th 12 mo
1650-1, and Edward Burcham swore to the truth of it, and
the Court ordered "that the children shall have their several portyons paid them at the age of twentie & one years."
"The Inventory of the goods of Edmund Lewis of
Line laite deceased, tacken by us whose names are heare
under subscribed this 12th day of the 12th mo 1650-1

Imprimis: One payer of Oxen,	13	00	0
one payer of Oxen,	14	00	0
foure working steares,	24	00	0
one two year oulde heffer,	3	00	0
six shots at	3	00	0
one heffer at	2	00	0
too milch kine & a calfe,	9	00	0
three yearlings,	5	00	0
fouer wether sheepe,	2	16	0
fouer ewe sheepe,	6	00	0
three lames of this yeare,	1	06	0
hay £2 10s, too little harrowes 10s,	3	00	0
one plow with coulter & share,		06	0
one cheane,		2	6
one payer of old wheles,		10	0
A cart & draughts,	1	00	0
The Waine,	1	10	0
An old plow,		2	6
too yockes,		6	0
one bede with the furniter,	3	3	0
one bede with the furnituer,	1	1	0
Purse & aparell	2	0	0
Five pilar coverings & five napkins,		13	6
A table cloth,	0	2	0

A bedsteade,		5	0
A chiste,		3	4
Three wheeles & too littell chayers,		10	0
In yaren, flaxe & wooll,	1	17	0
In wheate 10 bushells,	2	10	0
In oats £5 7s a fan 3s 4d,	1	10	4
too sithes & fouer hooks,		9	0
three score bushells of Indyan Coren,	9	0	0
A sword belte & bandeleres,		12	0
too muskets & too rests,	1	16	0
A foulinge pece,	1	6	0
too small gunes,		16	0
A Cettell & too iern pots,		14	8
A gird ieren & a iern Kettell & a ould posnett,		6	0
Peuter 10s A frying pan & a hooke, 7s,		17	0
too trayes & a meale sive & other lumber,		11	0
three axes, too wedges & a drawing knife,			
three augers and a handsaw,		11	8
too drink barrels,		3	0
A bibell 8s A pece of lether, 6s,		14	0
a churn, a bottell, & a little tube,		5	0
too tubes, a brake & a crackell,		7	0
		122	7 6

John Deakin
James Arry
Edward Burcham
William X Tilton
     mark
       Appraisers."

Children :

2. JOHN, b. 1631, in England.
3. THOMAS, b. 1633, in England.
4. JAMES, b. 15, 11 mo, 1635-6, in Watertown.
5. NATHANIEL, born 25, 6mo, 1639, in Watertown.
5a. A CHILD, aged 20 days, was buried Nov. 6, 1642, in Watertown.
6. JOSEPH.

There is no record of the 6th and 7th children, who were alive at the time he made his will, and who must have been born after 1642, in Lynn.

2 John Lewis, yeoman, innholder, lieutenant, captain, and deacon, was born in England in 1631. He came into possession of his father's lands in Wood end fields, 40 acres fronting on the sea and through which Lewis street now passes. At that time the eastern end of Lynn was called "Wood end," and the western end, "Breed's end," and the locality back of where Samuel Graves settled was called "Graves end." For years these names appeared in the description of lands given in deeds.

On the 19, 5mo., 1669, John Lewis of Lynn, yeoman, and wife Hannah, sold to Ralph King for £23, four acres of upland in Lynn bounded on William King, said Lewis, and south by the sea. (Essex Deeds, Vol. 3, f. 95.) In 1699 he married for his second wife the widow of this Ralph King. Nov. 9, 1699, he deeded his lands to his two sons, John and Thomas, as follows:—John Lewis, sen. of Lynn, yeoman, for £160, to his two sons, John and Thomas, yeomen, in equal halves "all my housing and lands in Lynn, viz: a dwelling house where I formerly lived, a barn, with 40 acres tillage at Wood End fields, Also a parcel of Salt marsh in Rumney Marsh 12 acres." (Essex Deeds, Vol. 3. f. 191.) A division of the above was made, June 5, 1708, "the dividing line to begin at a flat rock about a pole & a half from the back side of John Lewis Jr. house and so running easterly on a straight line to a flat rock in the field where it has been formerly broke up, so from thence South East straight to a stake with a heap of stones, thence East to a stake with a heap of stones by the ditch that parts said lands formerly of Ezekiel Needham's, and all lands South of said line to be John's, and all lands North, with the house and barn, till it comes to the brook that runs from Collins' fresh meadow, to be Thomas, John to have all lands North of said brook, it to be the bound betwixt them in that place. As to the Marsh land, John to have the Easterly half, and Thomas to have Westerly half." (Essex Deeds, Vol. 21, f. 50.)

John Lewis was a lieutenant under Capt. Henchman in King Philip's War, and received £1. 14. 3. Aug. 20, 1675. He was granted land at Souhegan West, now Amherst, N. H., for his services, which his grandson, Edmund, secured in 1728. (Bodge's King Philip's War, p. 422.)   He was paid £1. 16. 0. June 24, 1676, for services in Capt. Nick Manning's Co. (N. E. Hist. Gen. Register, Vol. 42, p. 95.)   He was made a freeman, April 18, 1691, and was then called "lieutenant." (N. E. Hist. Gen. Register, Vol. 5, p. 352.)   He was elected a deacon in the church at a town meeting held January 8, 1692:— "That Lieut. Lewis & Lieut. Fuller should sit at table." He kept a tavern in the eastern part of Saugus, known as the "Blue Anchor," probably being the successor of his father in law, Capt. Thomas Marshall, who died in 1683. This inn was later kept by his son Thomas (9) and grandson John (41), and is mentioned by travellers of that day.*

Madam Knight in her Diary also mentions this tavern.

He died in 1710, at the age of 79 years.   His will† is as follows :—

I John Lewis Sr. of Lynn being of sound understanding & memory thro the goodness of God, considering the frailty of human nature in general and my own age in particular, not knowing how soon it may please God to take me out of this transitory life and, being desirous of making allotment of my outward estate and prevent any differences which might otherwise arise after my death between my wife and my children, do make this my last Will and Testament as followeth [commits his soul to God, and his body to the earth].   And as for that outward estate which God in his goodness hath lent unto me, I do dispose of it as hereafter is expressed.   For as much as I have formerly done for my children what I judge meet, and sufficient and am now desirous according to my duty and ability to provide for yᵉ comfortable livelyhood and subsistance of my now wife after my decease, if it be the pleasure of God that she outlive me, I do therefore give unto my said wife, Sarah Lewis, and my Will is that she shall receive, have and enjoy to her own absolute use and disposal, my whole Estate not formerly by me other-

*Samuel Sewall writing in his Diary regarding the funeral of his mother on Jany. 14, 1700-1, says, "Hired horses at Charlestown, set out about 10 o'clock in a great Fogg. Dined at Lewis' with Mr. Cushing of Salisbury.   Sam and I kept on in Ipswich Rode."

†Essex Co. Probate, Vol. 310, f. 242.

wise disposed of, both reall and personal, whether in money
or household stuff, or stock or cloathing, and also all debts
& dues owing unto me from any and every person, whither
by bill, bond or otherwayes, and I do constitute, ordain &
appoint my sd loving wife Sarah Lewis to be my sole Executrix of this my last Will. Desiring and appointing my
loving ffriends Mr. John Floyd of Rumney Marsh, &
William Meriam of Lynn, to be my overseers, whom I pray
to be assisting unto my loving wife, in y⁰ execution of
this my Will which I do hereby declare to be my last Will
and Testament, nulling and making void all former or
other Wills by me made or pretended to be made, so that
this only shall be taken for my last Will & Testament. In
confirmation whereof I doe Signe, Seal and publish the
same this twenty fifth day of ffebruary, one thousand
seven hundred six-seven.

Signed, sealed and published   John Lewis ⎡SEAL⎤
    in presence of   ⎣ L ⎦
    John ffloyd,
    Samuel ffloyd,
    Edmund Chamberlaine.

John Lewis married (Lynn records:—Jonathan), first,
June 17th, 1659, Hannah, daughter of Capt. Thomas
Marshall of Lynn. She died May 15, 1699. He married,
second, Sept. 2, 1699, widow Elizabeth King, relict of
Ralph King of Swampscott, and daughter of Capt. Richard
and Jane (Talmage) Walker. (Essex Inst. Hist. Colls.,
Vol. 16, p. 77.) He married, third, Feb. 10, 1706-7, Mrs.
Sarah Jenks, born Sept. 14, 1665, and died Jan. 4, 1740,
widow of John Jenks, the son of Joseph and Elizabeth
Jenks. She was the daughter of William and Elizabeth
(Breed) Merriam of Lynn. At this time John Lewis was
75 years of age, and his wife was 41. He made his will
fifteen days after this marriage. His land had been deeded
to his two sons two months after his second marriage.

Children of John and Hannah:

7. JOHN, b. Mar. 30, 1660.
8. HANNAH, b. Feb. 25, 1661; m., May 12, 1686, Capt. Edward
    Fuller.

9. THOMAS, b. June 2, 1663.
10. MARY, b. Feb. 24, 1665; m., July 10, 1689, Thomas Baker.
11. BENJAMIN, b. Apr. 27, 1667; d. young.
12. NATHANIEL, b. Apr. 16, 1672; d. Nov. 25, 1692.
13. SAMUEL, b. July 25, 1675; d. Aug. 12, 1675.
14. ABIGAIL, b. May 16, 1679; d. May 30, 1706.
15. EBENEZER, b. July 16, 1681; not provided for by his father, or mentioned in his will.
16. REBECCA, d. Nov. 22, 1692.

Child of John and Sarah:

17. BENJAMIN, b. April 23, 1708.

3. **Thomas Lewis,** born in England in 1633, removed from Lynn to Northampton in 1661-1662, where he had a home lot of four acres, which he sold to Matthew Clesson in 1667. He was chosen to assist in building a mill, 27, 6 mo., 1666. He removed from there to Swansea, where, at a town meeting held Dec. 1, 1669, " Thomas Lewis was admitted inhabitant and member of this township, and to have a twelve acre lot where any two of the Com'te for admission of inhabitants shall approve of his settlement." At a town meeting held Feb. 9, 1670, it was ordered that all lots and divisions of land thereafter be granted according to the three-fold rank, by the selectmen. First rank, three acres; second rank, two acres; and third rank, one. Thomas Lewis was in the second rank. He was elected a selectman, May 21, 1672. He is mentioned at Bristol, R. I., as early as 1681, and was taxed at Mendon, Mass., in 1691, 1692 and 1693. He was elected a selectman, May 1, 1693, for the year, but declined to serve. The following is taken from the Annals of Mendon, p. 129, where it is used as a model for the peaceful settlement of a land dispute.

" Know all men by these Presents that I Thomas Lewis of Bristol, Doe Constitute and Appoint my well beloved Capt. Josiah Chapin of Mendon, In my Roome and Stead for to Joyne with sergent Abraham Staples of Mendon aforesaid to Devid A percell of medow that belonged to John Parris's Lot in Mendon, Now Eaqually belonging to me the said Lewis and ye Above sd Staples, and doe by these presents bind myself my heyers, Executors, administrators and Assigns, to stand to their Agreement about ye devision of sd medow, and after the decision is made to cause the same to be recorded, as Witness my hand this 9th of January, 1695-6. Thomas Lewis [Seal]."

In 1696, he was called of Mendon, with wife Hannah. In 1692, Thomas Lewis of Bristol, R. I., sold land to Capt. John Andrews. He also sold land there in 1701. In the Book of Possessions of Swansea his lands are recorded on page 9, and in the various proceedings of the town his name appears in regard to lands. On Dec. 23, 1704, he, with his wife Hannah, executed a deed of gift for good will and affection, of the " north part of my dwelling house in Bristol," to his daughter, Hepzebah Lewis. (Bristol Co. Deeds, Vol. 4, p. 319.)

The will of Thomas Lewis of Bristol, recorded in Bristol Co. Probate Records, Vol. 2, f. 257: " In the name of God, Amen, I Thomas Lewis of Bristol in ye County of Bristol in New England, being aged and very Infirm, and not knowing when or how soon I may be Removed out of a Chaingable world, to prevent Jarrs & Contentions after my Decease do make constitute and ordaine this to be my last Will & Testament in manner and form following ; that is to say, I commend my Soul into ye hands of God and body to ye earth to be decently buried at the Discrefion of my friends, and as to my temporal estate which it hath pleased God of his mercy to lend me, I give bequeath and bestow in the following manner, Viz: After my ffuneral Charges and Just Debts are payed and sattisfyed by my Executrix hereafter mentioned, I give and bequeath unto my aged and beloved wife all my whole estate both Reall and personal after my decease During her natural Life with full power and Authority by Virtue of these presents to make sale of ye whole my Two acre lott in Bristol with the Dwelling house thereon except what I have before given by deed of Gift to my Daughter Hepzebath or any part or parsell of my said lott to such person or persons who shall appear to purchass the same hereby Impowering of my said wife Hannah Lewis to make, sign, seal and fully to Execute a good and sufficient Deed and Legall Convayance of the said two acre lott or any part or parcell thereof so sold as aforesaid for her necessary & Comfortable livelyhood During her natural life and after her Decease what shall be Remaining of my estate to be Devided to and among my Children in as Just and equal proportion as may be according to the direction of the law in such case made and provided, having a regard allwayes to what any of my Sons or Daughters have had formerly of my estate before my decease. And of this my Last Will & Testament I constitute and ordain my Beloved wife Hannah Lewis my sole Executrix Hereby making null & voydd all other and former Wills Legacies or Executors by me in any wise before this time named willed or bequeathed and in Testimony hereof I Thomas Lewis have hereunto sett my hand and fixed my seal the Eleventh day of August, A. D. 1708. Thomas Lewis [Seal]"

Proved July 6, 1709. Presented and sworn to by Hannah Lewis.

The widow Hannah Lewis sold, April 22, 1710, to Nath¹ Byfield, "one half of the two acre lot of land where ye dwelling house now stands being the eastern most half of those two acre lot with ye barn and house thereon" bounded East on High St, South on Queen St. West by land of said Thomas Lewis, being the other half, and northerly by land of Nath'l Byfield. (Bristol Co. Deeds, Vol. 6, f. 174.)

Thomas Lewis married, Nov. 11, 1659, Hannah, daughter of Edward and Joan Baker. They both died at Bristol, R. I., he dying April 26, 1709, aged about 76 years, and his widow following him in January, 1717.

Children of Thomas and Hannah:

18. EDWARD, b. July 28, 1660, at Lynn; d. July 15, 1662, at Northampton, Mass.

19. HANNAH, m. Jan. 22, 1683, George Morey. Their children, born in Bristol, R. I., were: (1) John, b. Oct. 3, 1684, who m., about 1700, Margaret Linsford, b. in Braintree, Feb. 6, 1682-3, dau. of Edward and Hannah (Plumley) Linsford; (2) Mary, b. Mar. 24, 1687-8; (3) Sarah, b. Mar. 4, 1690-1; (4) Hannah, b. Mar. 18, 1693-4; d. Dec., 1717; (5) George, b. Aug. 31, 1696; (6) Martha, b. Mar. 12, 1698-9; (7) Abigail, b. Feb. 27, 1701-2; (8) Benjamin, b. Apr. 18, 1705; (9) Thomas, b. Jan. 1, 1708-9.

20. MARY, b. 1663; d. Mar. 26, 1666.

21. ESTHER, b. 1665; m., Jan. 7, 1684, Jeremiah Finney, at Bristol,
    R. I., where they had children born : (1) Mary, b. Mar. 26,
    1686; (2) Hannah, b. Jan. 14, 1687-8; (3) Mehitable, b. May
    8, 1689; (4) John, b. Aug. 3, and d. Oct. 23, 1690; (5) Rebec-
    ca, b. Feb. 24, 1691; (6) Esther, b. May 5, 1693; (7) John, b.
    April 13, 1696; (8) Abigail, b. April 17, 1697.
22. THOMAS, b. Sept. 28, 1666, at Northampton, Mass.; d. Jan. 11,
    1666-7, at Northampton.
23. THOMAS, b. Apr. 29, 1668, at Lynn.
24. ELIZABETH, b. Dec. 7, 1669, at Swansea.
25. PERSITHE, b. June 15, 1671, at Swansea.
26. SAMUEL, b. Apr. 23, 1673, at Swansea.
27. HEPSEBAH, b. Nov. 15, 1674, at Swansea; m., Dec. 25, 1706,
    James Thurber, at Bristol, R. I. He died June 10, 1747.
    She died Nov. 11, 1753, at Bristol, R. I.
28. JOSEPH, b. May 13, 1677, at Swansea.
29. DEBORAH, b. Mar. 19, 1679, at Swansea.

5. Nathaniel Lewis was born at Watertown, 25th,
6 m., 1639. Caulkins' History of New London, p. 296,
says, " Nathaniel and Joseph Lewis are names that appear
on the rate list of 1667, as partners in estate. They were
transient residents." They removed to Swansea and became inhabitants.

At a town meeting, Dec. 1, 1669, " Nathaniel Lewis is
admitted townsman, and is to have a 12 acre lot where it
may be Judged Convenient." He was of the 3d rank Feb.
7, 1670. In the Book of Possessions his lands are recorded on page 107, except his lot No. 85 in the sheep pasture,
alias Towoset Neck, which is recorded by a mistake with
his brother Joseph's lands on page 53. He married Mary
——, and died Oct. 13, 1683.

Children of Nathaniel and Mary :

30. NATHANIEL, b. July 17, 1673; d. Aug. 20, 1676.
31. MARY, b. Dec. 4, 1677, at Lynn; m., June 10, 1693, John Cole, jr.,
    in Swansea, and had born there: (1) Lewis, b. Oct. 23, 1694;
    (2) Joanna, b. Feby. 20, 1696-7 ; (3) Nathan, b. Mar. 20, 1703.

6. Joseph Lewis. There is no record of his birth.
His father died in 1650, and in 1658 his mother was taken
away, and John, his eldest brother, did not marry until the
next year (17 June, 1759), so that his childhood was not
very propitious and early in life he had to start to build
his own fortune. Being used to the water, with his brother

Nathaniel, he sailed along the coast, and was at New London, Conn., on Dec. 2, 1667, where they were transient residents and taxed £2. 3s. 9d. for the minister's rate. (New London, Ct., Records.) He removed to Swansea with his brothers, Thomas and Nathaniel, and became an inhabitant, and was granted land in the third rank, Feb. 7, 1670. At town meeting 9th, 12 mo., 1671, he was elected to assist the committee to " lay out the lands recently purchased at Metapoisett." His lands are recorded in the Book of Possessions on pages 53 and 54, and with them are recorded part of the lands of his brother Nathaniel (5) on page 53 by a mistake made at that time. The following certificate is self-explanatory.

Office of Town Clerk and Treasurer.

Swansea, Mass., Aug. 3, 1906.

" Nathaniel Lewis his land in the Sheep pasture alis Towoset Neck by a mistake were Recorded in page 53 with his Brother Joseph's Lands."

I hereby certify that the above is a true copy of the record as it appears on page 107 of the original " Proprietors Records " in the town of Swansea.

Henry O. Wood, Town Clerk.

[Seal of the Town of Swansea.]

There has been considerable discussion as to who were the parents of this Joseph Lewis. Mr. Deane's Scituate and Mr. Shepherd in the N. E. Hist. Gen. Register state that he was a son of George of Barnstable. There appears to be no foundation for such statement, as George had no son by that name, as is shown by Otis' Barnstable Families. There is ample evidence that Nathaniel was from Lynn, and the above is evidence that his brother Joseph was with him.

There is a tradition that Joseph Lewis was the first white man slain in King Philip's War. He was killed at Swansea, June 24, 1675. (Bodge's King Philip's War, p. 463.) A list of the slain reported by the clerk of the town at the time is : Joseph Lewis, Robert Jones, John Jones,* Nehemiah Allen, William Cohun, John Salisbury,

*The Joneses were relatives of Mrs. Joseph Lewis. The deaths probably occurred in the order named.

William Salisbury, John Hall. (Plymouth Colonial Records.)

" As the inhabitants of Swansea were returning from public worship, a number of Indians who lay in ambuscade, fired upon them, killed one of their company and wounded another. They next intercepted and killed two men, who were sent for a surgeon. The same night they entered the town of Swansea and murdered six men." (Hannah Adams' N. E. History, p. 120.)

" In the afternoon of June 24, 1675, being a fast day at Swansea, people were coming from Public Worship the Indians attacked them, killed one and wounded others, and killed two men who were going for a Surgeon, beset a house in another part of the town and murdered 6 more." (Hutchinson's History of Mass., Vol. 1, page 261.)

Joseph Lewis married Mary Jones, June 13, 1671. (Swansea Records.) She was the daughter of Robert and Anne (Bibble) Jones of Hull. Anne was the daughter of John and Sibyll Bibble of Malden. After the massacre Mary returned to Malden to live with her grandmother.* Mary, the widow of Joseph, married, Jan. 11, 1677, at Malden, Obadiah Jenkins. He died in 1720, and his sons Joel and Obadiah gave bond April 1, 1720, and were appointed administrators of his estate. His wife Mary must have died before that time, as she had no share in his estate. Their children were: (1) Joel, (2) Mary, (3) Annabel, (4) Lydia, (5) Sarah, m. —— Taylor; (6) Anna, m. Benj. Teal; (7) Obadiah, m. Mary Grover.

*The Will of John Bibble (N. E. Hist. Gen. Register, Vol. 9, p. 306-7) mentions son in law Robert Jones of Hull, daughter Annie and wife Sibyll, and calls himself " of Maldon being now of Hull," July 23, 1653. Ann Bibble was a petitioner for a minister to be settled at Malden, Oct. 28, 1651, so she must have married Robert Jones between that day and July 1, 1653, when her father made his will. Sybil Bibble, widow, married Miles Nutt, and on Oct. 30, 1674, became the wife of John Doolittle of Malden, where she lived and died Sept. 23, 1690, aged about 82 years. Her will, made at Malden, Dec. 25, 1683, proved in 1690, gives "to Obadiah Jenkins and Mary Jenkins his wife and their children, all my housing and lands in Malden, with all movables, he paying out of it to my grandchildren, Robert, Zachery, Benjamin and Rebeccah Jones £5, a piece when they become of age. * * * I make my grandson Obadiah Jenkins my Executor of this my last Will."

Sybil Doolittle [Seal.

Children of Joseph and Mary, born in Swansea:

32. JOSEPH, b. Aug. 6, 1672.
33. SYBIL, b. Mar. 18, 1674; m. in 1700, at Malden, Samuel Howard of Malden, and had: (1) Samuel, b. Apr. 25, 1701; m. July 12, 1727, Elizabeth Wayte; lived in Malden. (2) Joseph, b. Nov., 1702; d. May 18, 1725. (3) Mary, b. about 1708; m. Sept. 6, 1733, Thomas Mighills of Pomfret, Conn. (4) Sybill, b. about 1712; m. Dec. 27, 1738, Reuben Darbe of Pomfret, Conn. (5) Benjamin, b. in 1714; d. 1763; m. June 19, 1740, Abigail Walton of Reading. Settled at Malden, and removed to Holden, Mass., in 1749.

The following memorandum, filed in Middlesex County Probate, file 8876, is interesting proof of the relationship of all the parties thereto.

"Deacon Samuel Howard's mother was sister to the deceased* by his mother's side, i. e.: Obadiah's mother before she married his Father—married a Lewis & had 2 children. Viz:—Joseph and Sibilla, which Sibilla was mother to the said Samuel Howard, who claims Joseph was father to Benj^m Lewis, who also claims Sibilla's children are Samuel and Sibella. Joseph's children are Benjamin, Joseph and Abigail."

The claims were allowed and settlement made as above.

7 John Lewis, born in Lynn, Mar. 30, 1660, was a lieutenant, and was made a freeman Apr. 18, 1691. In the division of his father's lands he had the south half next the sea. He died intestate about a year after his father, and his widow Elizabeth was appointed administratrix, June 27, 1711. The inventory of his estate, taken July 11, 1711, is as follows:

To an house, barn, & land adjoining to about twenty acres or more,	160	00	00
To 15 acre upland & meadow in same field,	60	00	00
To 7 acres Salt Marsh,	42	00	00
To Common Lotte,	42	00	00
To Forty sheep & two swine,	10	00	00
To Cow & Tools for husbandry,	4	07	00
To Wareing Cloth & Gun,	11	11	00

*Obadiah Jenkins.

To Fodder, beds & bedding, £8, & house-
hold stuff, £4 05,   12   05   00
To Cash,   4   10   00
Real Estate £304, Personal, £67 13 0
Debt due the estate,   12 0
                                       _____
                                       £68   5 0
Dr to sundry creditors,   83   9 8
Allowance for youngest son
until 6 years of age,   24   0 0
                                       _____
        Total,   £118 16   2

John Lewis married Elizabeth Brewer, April 18, 1683,
in Lynn.
Children of John and Elizabeth, born in Lynn :

34. ELIZABETH, b. April 7, 1684; m. Feb. 8, 1708-9, Samuel
    Graves, Jr., b. Aug. 2, 1684, in Lynn, son of Samuel and
    Sarah (Brewer) Graves, and had the following children
    born in Lynn : (1) Samuel, b. Jan. 19, 1710; (2) Sarah, b.
    Feb. 1, 1713; m. (int. Nov. 16, 1735), Job Collins.
35. HANNAH, b. Jan. 22, 1685-6; m. Nov. 13, 1711, Lieut. Samuel
    Stocker,* b. Nov. 29, 1684, son of Ebenezer and Sarah (Mar-
    shall) Stocker of Lynn. She died Dec. 16, 1760. Children,
    born in Lynn : (1) John, b. Feb. 15, 1711-12; m. 1st, Hannah
    Richards, m., 2nd, Ruth Breed; (2) Samuel, b. July 28, 1717,
    (twin); m., 1st, Elizabeth——, pub. Oct. 21, 1743; m., 2d, May
    25, 1757, Priscilla Rhodes; (3) Joseph, b. July 28, 1717, (twin).
36. SARAH, b. April 5, 1688; d. young
37. JOHN, b. Sept. 23, 1690; d. young.
38. NATHANIEL, b. Jan. 18, 1692-3; d. young.
39. EDMUND, b. Dec. 8, 1695.
40. REBECCA, b. June 18, 1699; m. Feb. 17, 1725-6, Grover Pratt,
    son of Richard and Rebecca Pratt of Malden. He died Jan.
    14, 1790. Had : (1) Richard, b. Nov. 27, 1728, in Lynn; d.
    Apr. 25, 1816; m. his cousin, Rebecca, dau. of Nathaniel, Jr.
    and Tabitha (Lewis) Ingalls, born Dec. 20, 1732. His
    " Common Place Book " has been published.
41. TABATHA, b. July 22, 1702; m. Jan. 1, 1722, at Lynn, Nathan-
    iel Ingalls, Jr., b. Dec. 25, 1692, son of Nathaniel and Anne
    Ingalls. He d. Sept. 23, 1772.
42. THOMAS, b. May 10, 1708.

*Samuel Stocker's mother and his wife Hannah Lewis' grandmother, were
sisters, both being daughters of Capt. Thomas Marshall.

9 Thomas Lewis, born June 2, 1663, in Lynn, married Mary Breed born in Lynn, Aug. 24, 1664, daughter of Allen jr. and Elizabeth (Ballard) Breed.

He was a yeoman and innholder, succeeding his father. He died Jan. 28, 1713-14, aged 50 years.   She died Jan. 19, 1736-7, aged 74 years. His will made Jan. 27, 1713-14, the day before his death, follows: " I Thomas Lewis of Lynn in ye County of Essex in ye Province of ye Massachusetts Bay in New England being weak of Body yet God affording to me my Reason & perfect understanding...I will and bequeath as followeth.   Imp—That all my honest & Just debts be truly & honestly payd.   I give to my beloved wife Mary one third part of all my movable estate of what kind soever to give & dispose as she shall cause and my said wife to have ye best room in my Dwelling house at ye Wood end to dwell In so long as she remains my wife, and further my Will is y[t] my eldest son John Lewis shall provide corn, meat, firewood, and all things necessary for my Wife's comfortable subsistance so long as she remain my Widow.   My said Wife accepting of all as above in Lieu or consideration of dower or thirds in my Estate.   I give and bequeath to my eldest son John Lewis his heirs,. all my housing, lands, both upland, salt, and pasture and woodland of what kind soever, over and above what I have given him allready by Deed of Gift, my said son providing for my above Wife, his Mother, all things as above described and he paying all my just and honest debts at his own cost and charge.   I give and bequeath to my son Joseph Lewis and to my daughters Mary Mower, Abigail Lewis, Unice Lewis and Ruth Lewis all my movable Estate of what kind soever, to be equally divided between them, my said five children (excepting only so much of my said movable estate as I have, in this my Will already given to my Wife) said part to remain to her as aforesaid.   My son Joseph shall be put out to a trade as my Wife shall judge best.   I appoint my son John Lewis sole executor to this my last Will & Testament & for ye confirmation here of ye Thomas Lewis have hereunto affixed my hand & seale the day of date here of ye twenty seventh

day of January, Anno Do. One thousand seven hundred
thirteen, fourteen.

his

Thomas   X   Lewis.*

mark

Signed & sealed In yᵉ presence of us
    John Burrill
    Mich¹ Bowden
    Sarah Bowden.

On Jan. 13, 1713-14, 14 days before the execution of his
will, he deeded to his eldest son John, of Lynn, "one half
of all my dwelling house, barn & outhousing at Wood end
and one half of all my lands, salt marsh, pasture & woodland of all kind."†

Inventory of the estate of Thomas Lewis made Feb. 8,
1713-14.‡

Wearing apparell,	21 - 16 - 0
Arms,	3 - 0 - 0
two beds & bedsteads & all the furniture, be-	
longing to them in ye great chamber,	15 - 0 - 0
Three beds with bedsteads & all furniture, be-	
longing to them in ye kitchen chamber,	23 - 0 - 0
one bedstead, bed & furniture in ye porch	
chamber,	7 - 0 - 0
two bedsteads & furniture in ye garrit,	8 - 0 - 0
nine pare sheets,	5 - 5 - 0
six pare pillowberes,	12 - 0
five dozen napkins,	2 - 0 - 0
six table clothes,	1 - 0 - 0
Powder,	6 - 0 - 0
Ironware in ye house,	8 - 0 - 0
one chest of Drawers 25s three old chests 20s	2 - 5 - 0
table forms & chears,	3 - 0 - 0
old barrils & lumber in ye house,	2 - 0 - 0
about 100 bushels of oats 2ˢ a bushel,	10 - 0 - 0
weges, axes and tools,	2 - 5 - 0
plow, cart wheels, sleads, yoaks & chaines,	5 - 5 - 0

*Essex County Probate Records, Vol. 311, f. 104.
†Essex County Deeds, Vol. 26, f. 260—2.
‡Essex Court Probate Records, Vol. 311. f. 105.

nine cows, three pound ten apece & with other, 31 - 10 - 0
five oxen & two bulls,   24 - 0 - 0
two yearling steers,   3 - 10 - 0
forty sheep,   14 - 0 - 0
one horse, one young mare & two horse colts,   18 - 0 - 0
ten swine,   3 - 10 - 0
a hundred gallons of rum at 3ˢ a gallon,   15 - 0 - 0
fifteen gallons Madare Wine 4ᵃ a gallon,   3 - 0 - 0
one pipe of green wine & fifteen barrels of cider 22 - 10 - 0
a smal lsloop with all appurtenances,   20 - 0 - 0
Saddle & pillians,   1 - 10 - 0
plate and money,   16 - 1 - 0
a negro man   30 - 0 - 0
                                        _____
                                               329 - 5 - 0

Out of the personal estate the widow was allowed best bed & furniture belonging to it   £13 - 0 - 0
One chest of drawers,   1 - 5 - 0
one pott & one kettel,   19 - 0
pewter & cheers,   1 - 15 - 0
one cow,   3 - 10 - 0
                                           _____
                                              £20 - 9 - 0

	£	s.	d.
To house & homestead & land adjoining,	131	5	0
To a Lott in the general field,	8	5	0
To common Lott £58, To salt marsh £24,	82	0	0

                                              £221 10 0

By ye Personal Estate
To Inventory on file in Quick Stock   £329 05 0
                                           _____
                                              £550 15 0

                To the said Estate Dr.

	£	s.	d.
Sundry Creditors as per list on file,	435	02	0
Allowing ye Widow necessary,	20	9	0
Allowing Admr. Extra trouble,	15	0	0
Expenses Admr. &c.	21	10	9

                                              £492 1 9

Children of Thomas and Mary, born in Lynn :

43. JOHN, b. Aug. 2, 1687.
44. THOMAS, b. Dec. 2, 1689; d. young.
45. MARY, b. Aug. 4, 1691; m., Nov. 13, 1711, Thomas Mower. Adm. on the est. of Thomas Mower, late of Lynn, deceased, was granted to his wid., Mary Mower, on 8 March, 1730-31. Youngest child was then 2 yrs. old.
46. REBECCA, b. Mar. 18, 1693-4; d. June 11, 1694.
47. BENJAMIN, b. June 26, 1695; d. young.
48. ABIGAIL, b. Oct. 14, 1696; m. (int. Sept. 30, 1716), John Stocker, b. Nov. 13, 1693, son of Ebenezer and Sarah (Marshall) Stocker of Lynn. He was a shipwright, and resided in Boston, where several children were born. Had: (1) Thomas, b. Mar. 25, 1715. (2) John, b. Oct. 1, 1717. (3) Thomas, b. Mar. 25, 1719. (4) Abigail, b. Mar. 29, 1721. (5 Sarah, b. Dec. 1, 1723. (6) William, b. July 30, 1726.
49. JOSEPH, b. April 28, 1699; cooper; d. Nov. 23, 1726.
50. EUNICE, b. Nov. 18, 1701; m., Mar. 26, 1720, Thomas Pearson, a cooper, of Boston.
51. BENJAMIN, b. Jan. 16, 1703; d. young.
52. RUTH, b. Jan. 18, 1705; m., April 12, 1725, Thomas Copp of Boston, who d. soon after.

23 Thomas Lewis, born April 29, 1668, at Lynn. He bought land of the Trustees of the Province of Massachusetts Bay, in the northeastern corner of Swansea, 5 Sept., 1715 (Bristol County Deeds, Vol. 9, f. 478). He also bought land of Zachariah Eddy, of Peletiah Mason, and Thomas Brooks. He bought a farm in Rehoboth of Ephraim Pearce on July 5, 1717 ; 20 acres in Metapoiset of Thomas Bowen, on Mar. 28, 1718; and 27 acres in Rehoboth of John Martin, on Oct. 21, 1718. He is called a weaver. His will, dated 12 Aug., 1717, probated Nov. 4, 1717, is as follows :

Imprimis :—I give and Bequeath to Elizabeth my Dearly Beloved Wife The one halfe of my household goods to be at her dispose allso I give to my said wife the one third part of the use or profit of both my ffarms, the one in Swansea and the other in Rehoboth and the use of the best room in each house on said ffarms During her being my widow, but if she marry again to Dismiss her Right to housing and lands to my two sons hereafter named, they paying to her the sum of three pounds in money yearly during her natural life.

It. I give and bequeath unto my eldest son James Lewis all that my ffarm situate in Swansea containing about seven score acres as it is butted and bounded with ... improvements and all appurtenances belonging to him his heirs and assigns forever, he allowing to his mother that abovesaid.

It. I give and bequeath to my son Timothy Lewis the one half of my ffarm situate in Rehoboth with the Dwelling house being the South end of said ffarm that I bought of Ephraim Peirce with the appurtenances belonging to the said South halfe part of said ffarm, to him and his heirs and assigns forever, he allowing to his mother as aforesaid :—

It. I give and bequeath to my son Samuel Lewis the other half of my said ffarm situate in Rehoboth being the north end of said ffarm when he come to Twenty one years of age, to his heirs and assigns forever.

It. I give and bequeath to my daughter Mary the sum of fifty pounds, to be payed to her in money or Goods when she comes to age, or time of marriage.

It. I give and bequeath to my daughter Debora the sum of fifty pounds and also to daughter Tabitha and daughter Lydia on the same terms. Also I ordain constitute my well beloved wife Executrix and my sons James and my son Timothy Executors of this my last Will and testament, And all the rest of my lands I give to my said Executors to pay my Debts and Legacies Also my movables.   Tho˙ Luis*

Inventory of his property shows £1604,19.0.

Extract from the will of Elizabeth Lewis, widow of Thomas Lewis, made 8th Nov., 1731. I? Elizabeth Lewis of Swansea, widow, and lately wife of Thomas Lewis of Swansea, deceased, being sick, etc. To daughter Mary, wife of Isaac Carter, my best and biggest bible, & to her two daughters Elizabeth & Sarah Carter. To daughter Deborah, wife of Samuel Eddy, to her daughter Abigail Eddy. To daughter Experience Mason and her two sons

*Bristol County Probate Records, Vol. 3, f. 36.

Nathan and Benjamin Mason. Equally. To daughter Tabitha Martin, wife of Daniel Martin, Hannah & Lydia Martin. To daughter Lydia, Sons Samuel & Timothy and James Lewis sole Executors; appointed 29 Nov., 1731.*

Thomas Lewis married in Swansea, Apr. 10, 1689, Elizabeth, daughter of Timothy Brooks of Swansea, formerly of Billerica.

Children born in Swansea, except Abigail :

53. NATHANIEL, b. Dec. 14, 1690.
54. ABIGAIL, b. Jan. 8, 1691, born in Bristol, R. I.
55. MARY, b. Jany. 2, 1694, m. Isaac Carter.
56. JAMES, b. Nov. 14, 1695.
57. TIMOTHY, b. Feb. 23, 1697-8.
58. DEBORAH, b. Mar. 4, 1699-1700; m. Samuel Eddy.
59. SAMUEL, b. Apr. 16, 1702.
60. EXPERIENCE, b. Apr. 27, 1704; m. Jan. 26, 1723, in Swansea, Samuel Mason, b. Feb. 24, 1700, in Swansea, son of Isaac and Hannah Mason. She was appointed admx. of his estate, Oct. 25, 1731, and married, 2d, Mar. 28, 1734, Ebenezer Martin. Children born in Swansea: (1) Nathaniel Mason, b. Oct. 9, 1724. (2) Nathan Mason, b. Nov. 12, 1726. (3) Hannah Mason, b. Feb. 4, 1728. (4) Benjamin Mason, b. Dec. 14, 1730.
61. TABITHA, b. May 8, 1706; m. Daniel Martin.
62. LYDIA, b. Mar. 2, 1708-9.

26 Samuel Lewis, born April 23, 1673, in Swansea, married Susannah Jones, Sept. 29, 1698, at Woodbridge, N. J.

Children of Samuel and Susannah:

63. SAMUEL, b. Jan. 1, 1702.
64. LEVI, b. Apr. 15, 1706.

28 Joseph Lewis, born in Swansea, May 13, 1677, removed to Haddam, Conn., where he died May 27, 1742. He married Elizabeth, daughter of John and Sarah Birge of Bristol, R. I. In the cemetery at Bristol, R. I., are two gravestones inscribed Mr. John Birge, died Sept. 5, 1733, in his 85th year. Sarah, wife of John Birge, died Jan. 25, 1716-17, in her 63rd year.

*Bristol County Probate Records, Vol. 7, f. 266—267.

(To be continued.)

NEWSPAPER ITEMS RELATING TO ESSEX COUNTY.

(Continued from Vol. XLII. page 345.)

There died in the first Parish in *Beverly,* from May 16, 1736 to the 30th of *September* next following, (being the Time when the *Throat-Distemper* prevailed most) Seventy Persons.

Boston Evening Post, July 8, 1754.

ALL *Persons desirous to Farm the Excise on* Coffee, Tea *and* China-Ware *in the County of Essex, are hereby Notified, That the Committee appointed for that Purpose, will attend that service on Tuesday the* 30th *Instant* July, *at* 3 *o'Clock Afternoon, at the Dwelling-House of Mrs.* Margaret Pratt, Innholder in Salem: *And all Persons who sell the above Commodities are Notified, that the Excise commences on them from the first Day of Instant* July.

By Order of the Committee, THOMAS BERRY.

Boston Evening Post, July 15, 1754.

On the 16th Instant, Mr. *Isaac Turner* of *Marblehead,* Housewright, with two other Persons, being at Work on a House in *Salem,* the Scaffold on which they stood gave way, and fell to the Ground, whereby Mr. *Turner* was so much bruised that he died the next Day.

Boston Evening Post, Aug. 26, 1754.

Wednesday last, at the Superior Court of Judicature, Court of Assize, &c. held here for the County of *Suffolk,* came on the Trial of *John Webb* late of *Salem,* but now of *Danvers,* indicted as a Common Cheat, when the Proof turned out so full and clear against him by a great Number of credible Witnesses, that the Jury declared him *Guilty,* without stirring off their Seats, and then the Court passed the following Sentence upon him, *viz.* To stand in the Pillory one Hour, with a Paper on his breast, having the Words COMMON CHEAT wrote thereon in Capitals, to be publickly whipped twenty five Stripes, to suffer one Year's Imprisonment, and after that to be

(89)

bound to his good Behaviour for five Years.   The former part of the Sentence was faithfully executed on Thursday, in the Presence of a great Concourse of People, who all expressed their Satisfaction at his Exaltation and Flagellation, and earnestly wished that an Amputation had also been added,— The Day of his Trial, *Joseph Verry* of said *Danvers*, one of his great Cronies, and an Accomplice, commonly called by the Gang, "*Squire Verry*," was committed to Goal for the same Crime; and we hear that several more of his Brethren in Iniquity are complained of, and will soon be prosecuted.

Boston Evening Post, Sept. 9, 1754.

About a Week ago, we had Advice by an Express from Fort *Halifax*, on *Kennebec* River, that a few Days before, as six Men belonging to that Fort were out upon Business at some Distance from it, they were fired upon by 8 Indians, who kill'd one (whose Name was *Newell*, of *Lynn*) took four Prisoners, and wounded the other, who notwithstanding some of 'em pursued him, threw their Hatchets after him, made his Escape to the Fort.

Boston Evening Post, Nov. 11, 1754.

TO *be sold at publick Vendue at the House of Mrs.* Hannah Pratt, *in* Salem, *on the Eleventh Day of* December *next, a Farm lately belonging to* Benjamin Marston, *Esq; deceased, containing about* 170 *Acres, Scituate on* Manchester *great Neck, at the Mouth of the River, very convenient for carrying on a Fishery and has Fish Stakes already erected, with a Fish House, a large handsome Dwelling House, and a good Barn, Well, a Garden and a Good Orchard, consisting chiefly of young and growing Trees, and makes now about thirty Barrels of Cyder, the Pasturing good, scarce ever failing on account of Drought, and cuts enough to keep all the Stock.   Any person minded to purchase, may do it before the Time of Sale, if they like the Conditions, which they may know by applying to* Benjamin *and* Elizabeth Marston, *Executors, who have full Power to dispose of the same.* N. B. *A sum equal to the Value of the Buildings, &c., to be paid at or in a short Time after the Sale, would give Content, the remainder on good Security.*

Boston Evening Post, Nov. 18, 1754.

Notice *is hereby given to the Proprietors with Haskins in* Coxhall (*so called*) *in the County of York, that at their Meeting held at* Ipswich *the* 21*st of October Instant, they ordered a Tax of eighteen Shillings to be raised on every* 100 *Acre Right in that Tract of Land, and paid to Mr.* Francis Goodhue *their Treasurer, and appointed a Committee to sell the Lands of Delinquents for Payment thereof according to Law; of which Tax each original Proprietor is to pay as follows, viz.* Roger Haskins, 36*s.* Edward Bishop 36*s.* William Baker 36*s.* George Herick 18*s.* Thomas Edwards 18*s.* Samuel Ingals, *Jun.* 18*s.* John Low, *Jun.* 18*s,* William Dixey 36*s.* Thomas Shepard 36*s.* William Goodhue 90*s.* Samuel Giddings 36*s.* Barnard Thorn 18*s.* Michael Farlo 36*s.* Meshech Farlo, 36*s.* Moses Bradstreet 36*s.* Matthew Perkins 36*s.* John Giddings 36*s.* Paul Thorndike 36*s.* Isaac Fellows 54*s.* Richard Walker 54*s.* Nathanael Brown 54*s.* Zechariah Herick 18*s.* Thomas Higginson 18*s.* John Staniford 36*s.* Robert Lord *Jun.* 18*s.* Robert Bradford 18*s.* Mark Haskol 18*s.* William Cleaves 18*s.* John Harris £5.8*s.* John Burnham £5.8*s.* Nathanael Rust 36*s.* Andrew Eliot 18*s.* John Brown 54*s.*
Marblehead, October 28th, 1754. NATHAN BOWEN.
Boston Evening Post, Dec. 2, 1754.

These are to Notify the Proprietors of New Gloucester, *in the County of* York, *that the following Lots or Rights are to be sold at publick Vendue at the House of Mrs.* Mary Perkins, *Innholder, in* Gloucester, *in the County of* Essex, *on the* 30*th of* January *next, at* 10 *o' Clock in the Forenoon, viz.* 54, 19, 35, 23, 41, 63, 17, 58, 29, 46, 50, 14, 31, 49, 24, 47, 48, *unless the Owners of the said Lots or Rights, pay their respective dues on said lots or rights at or before the said Day of Sale.*

December 9th 1754 at Gloucester	Philemon Warner William Steven Nathaniel Allen	Committee.

Boston Evening Post, January 6, 1755.

Marblehead, January 15, 1755.
WHEREAS *the Shop of* Thomas Coes, *of* Marblehead, *Peruke-Maker, was broke open on Friday Morning last, from*

*which was stolen eight brown and three grey Wiggs, one of
the last had a feather'd Top, some were bordered with narrow red Ribband and some with purple, and silk Cauls.
And also the same Morning, the Shop of* Nathaniel Reynolds,
Cordwainer, *adjoining to the other was broken open, and three
Pair of Shoes stolen, one Pair finished, the other not:—If
any Person will make discovery of the Thief or Thieves, so
that he or they may be brought to Justice, and be thereof con-
victed, shall have* FIVE DOLLARS *Reward, and all nece-
sary Charges paid by*

Thomas Coes.
Boston Evening Post, January 20, 1755.

Salem, Jan. 25. Last Week a Gentleman of this Town
received a Quantity of Cheese from *Rhode-Island,* recom-
mended to him for extraordinary good ; but having
parted with a few of them to some of his Neighbours, all
that eat of them were very severely purged ; upon which
several others had the Curiosity to try if it would have the
same Effect upon them, and were soon after satisfied,
for they vomitted and purged to such a Degree for some
Hours, that Life was almost despaired of. The Cheeses
that were thus poisonous, were marked E. B.

Another *Salem* Person of good Credit, after giving
some Account of this Affair, says, *As to the Truth of it,
being a near Neighbor, I was an Eye-Witness to it in more
than 2 or 3 of the Persons who eat of it, and saw the Opera-
ion.*

Boston Evening Post, January 27, 1755.

Boston, Feb. 1, 1755.
To *be sold by* John *and* William Stickney, *at* Newbury
*a Schooner almost new, between thirty and forty Tons, a
prime Sailor.*

Boston Evening Post, Feb. 3, 1755.

We hear, that in the late Storm, a Brigantine inward
bound from *Oporto* in *Portugal,* having put into *Cape
Anne,* was drove on Shore from her Anchors, and bilged.
That some Piecies of a Vessel are come ashore in *Ipswich*
Bay, and that a Snow is ashore on the Back of *Cape Cod.*

Boston Evening Post, Feb. 10, 1755.

These are to give publick Notice, That the Committee for farming the Duties of Excise on Spirituous Liquors, &c. for the County of Essex, *will attend that Service at the Dwelling House of Mrs.* Margaret Pratt, *Innholder in* Salem, *on Thursday the Third Day of* April *next, at 3 o'Clock in the Afternoon.* By Order of the Committee,
Salem, Feb. 22, 1755. Benjamin Lynde.
Boston Evening Post, Feb. 24, 1755.

Marblehead, March 17th, 1755.
On the first Instant died here, very suddenly, in the 59th Year of his Age, Cap't. *David Le Gallais.* He was a tender Husband, a good Neighbour, a chearful Companion, a sincere Friend: In him the Gentleman and Man of Business were happily blended, not to add, that if Humanity, Honesty, Integrity and Benevolence can render a Character amiable, his was truly so.— As he was justly esteemed in Life, his Death is greatly regretted by his Friends here.
Boston Evening Post, March 17, 1755.

The Proprietors of the common and undivided Lands in the Township commonly called New-Marblehead *in the County of* York, *are hereby notified and warned to assemble and convene at the Townhouse in* Marblehead *in the County of* Essex, *on Saturday the twenty-ninth Day of* March *Instant, at Two of the Clock Afternoon, then and there to recieve and adjust all their Accounts: To chuse a Clerk and all other Officers (as shall be thought needful) for the Year ensuing: To enquire into the State and Condition of the Home-Lots, in order to, and make some suitable Allowance to such Proprietors as have been at extraordinary Charge in making and encouraging the first Settlement of said Township (agreeable to former Votes of said Proprietors: To agree upon and order what Proportion of the Charge the said Proprietors will be at in calling and settling another Minister in said Township (the former being deceased). To take under their Consideration the present Condition of the Bridge at* Saccarippy *Falls, and agree upon some proper Method for repairing the same: To take and pursue all lawful Means to prevent the Obstruction of the natural Course of*

Salmon and other Fish in Presumscot River; *and to raise such Sums of Money on said common Lands, as shall be thought needful for defreying the necessary Charge of what shall be then and there agreed on, and pass orders for assessing and collecting the same.*

Marblehead, March the 14th, 1755.   By Order of the Committee, *William Goodwin,* Clerk of said Proprietors.

Boston Evening Post, March 17, 1755.

By a Person from *Salem,* we hear that Capt. *Orne,* who sail'd from that Place (about two Months since) for *Bilboa,* after being a few Days at Sea, met a Mountain of Ice, which gain'd so fast upon him that he could not weather the same, by Means of which his Vessel founder'd.   Capt. *Orne* with the rest of his Crew (being 6 in Number) took to their Boat, in which deplorable Condition they remain'd 6 Days, when they were taken up by a *Frenchman,* who meeting with Capt. *Margery* bound for *Salem,* put them on board, at which Place they all arrived safe last Friday.

Boston Gazette, May 26, 1755.

And we learn by other Letters that the New-England Troops behav'd to the Satisfaction of every Body.—That the only New-England Man kill'd was Joseph Pike, whose Friends belong to Newbury.

Boston Gazette, June 30, 1755.

On Wednesday last, the Rev. Mr. *Benjamin Adams,* was ordained to the Pastoral Office, over the 2d Church of Christ in *Lyn:* the Rev. Mr. *Carnes* Pastor of a Church in *Stoneham* began with Prayer; the Rev. Mr. *Hobby,* Pastor of the 1st Church in *Reading,* preach'd an excellent Sermon, and well adapted to the occasion ; The Rev. Mr. *Emerson* Pastor of the 1st Church in *Malden,* gave the Charge; and the Rev. Mr. *Leavitt* Pastor of the 1st Church in *Salem* gave the Right Hand of Fellowship : The whole of the Solemnity was conducted without the least Shew of Opposition ; and performed with an exemplary Regularity, Decency and good Order.

Boston Gazette, Nov. 10, 1755.

Salem, December 13th, 1755.
The Subscriber having purchased the Duties of Excise

arising on Tea, Coffee and China Ware, in the County of Essex, for one Year from the first of July *last, hereby notifies, all Sellers of the abovesaid Articles, that they render just Accounts of what they have sold the first of* January *next when the first half Year ends; and all those who have not settled for the last Year are desired to do it very soon, or they may expect Trouble.*

Peter' Frye, *Farmer.*
Boston Gazette, Dec. 15, 1755.

Ran away from his Master, Mr. Richard Meayberry *of* Salem, *on the* 12th *of this Instant* January, *an* Irish *Servant Boy named* James Clark; *about* 14 *Years of Age: He is pretty full faced, and Pock broken, and had on a homespun brown striped Cloth Coat, lined with red Bays, and Breeches of the same, lined with red Bays also, and had a dark coloured Yarn Cap on. Whoever shall take up the said Servant, and deliver him to his Master in* Salem, *shall have* TWO DOLLARS *Reward, and necessary charges paid.*
Salem, January 15, 1756.
Boston Evening Post, Jan. 19, 1756.

Whereas Nathaniel Lewis *of* Hartford *in* Connecticut, *who enlisted last Winter into Colonel* Winslow's *Regiment, was dismissed by Reason of Illness and came to this Town very ill, and was taken Care of, but died the 24th of De-cember last, and has left some Cloathing, with other trifling Things as also about* 40s Sterling *in Cash;* any of his Heirs who will send to Mr. *Joseph Elson* at *Salem,* Keeper of the Almshouse, may have the same paying the Charge of this Advertisement.
Salem, January 5, 1756.
Boston Evening Post, Jan. 19, 1756.

The Proprietors of the common and undivided Lands in the Township commonly called New-Marblehead, *in the County of* York, *are hereby notified and warned to assemble and convene at the Town House in* Marblehead *in the County of* Essex, *on Thursday the* 25th *Day of this Instant* March, *at Two of the Clock Afternoon, then and there to receive and adjust all their Accounts: to chuse a Clerk, and all other*

Officers as shall be needful for the Year ensuing; to impower and direct some suitable Person or Persons in the Name, and on the Behalf of the Proprietors to present a Petition to the Great and General Court, for a Confirmation of the Grant made them of the said Township, and any other Favours that may be thought needful at said Meeting, and agree upon and order a suitable Allowance for assisting the Inhabitants of said Township, to procure the preaching of the Gospel there for the present, and to raise such Sums of Money as shall be thought necessary for defreying the several Charges as shall be agreed for at said Meeting, and pass Orders for the assessing and collecting the same.

By Order of the Committee, William Goodwin *Clerk to said Proprietors.*

Marblehead, March 3d, 1756.

N. B. *Whereas several of the Proprietors are in Arrears for the several Taxes laid on their several Lots, these are to inform them, that if they do not pay the same at or before said Meeting, their Lands will be disposed of according to Law.*

Boston Evening Post, March 8, 1756.

To be Sold two large Schooners of 65 Tons each: Whoever inclines to purchase, may enquire of Col. Epes Serjeant *of* Salem, *or Mr.* Benjamin Bowdin *of Marblehead.*

Boston Gazette, March 1, 1756.

Last Friday Night Se'nnight, a coasting Sloop, Samuel Goodwin Master, bound to Newbury from the Eastward, was drove on Shore at Plumb-Island, and bilg'd : The Master and Men were sav'd, by being taken on board a Whaleboat that was sent from another Vessel to their Relief the next Morning, at which Time they had almost perish'd with wet and cold.

Boston Gazette, March 22, 1756.

(*To be continued.*)

SILVER PLATE OF THE FIRST CHURCH, SALEM.

The pieces made before 1800.

HISTORICAL COLLECTIONS

OF THE

ESSEX INSTITUTE

| VOL. XLIII. | APRIL, 1907 | No. 2 |

THE EARLY CHURCH PLATE OF SALEM.

BY JOHN H. BUCK.

With the exception of a flagon (1767), at the First
Church, a flagon (1773), and two mugs (1772), at the
North Church, made in London, the silver vessels belonging to the churches in Salem are by colonial silversmiths.
The earliest pieces are those marked I D with a fleur-de-
lis below, in a heart-shaped shield, undoubtedly the work
of Jeremiah Dummer, silversmith, of Boston (1645-1718),
an apprentice of John Hull, the mint master, who "served
his country faithfully in several Publick Stations." (Obituary in the "Boston News Letter," 2 June, 1718.) Plate
with this mark is to be found in many churches in New
England, from the First Church, New Haven, Conn., to
the First Church, Berwick, Me., and the South Parish
Church, Portsmouth, N. H. Next in order are the pieces
marked I C, fleur-de-lis below, heart-shaped shield, probably by John Cony (1655-1722), also of Boston, with whom
Apollos Rivoire, father of the patriot, served part of his
time as an apprentice. If John Edwards (1687-1743) of
Boston, made the baptismal bason presented to the North
Church by Benjamin Pickman in 1772, it proves how un-
safe a guide inscriptions are as to the date of vessels,
which were frequently presented for sacred uses after
years of domestic service. (Edwards: see "Curwin Papers;" "Records of the Church in Brattle Square;"
Weeden's Economic History of New England, p. 474.)
John Burt (1690-1745), maker of the loving cup bequeathed to Harvard College by "Col. Samuel Brown of

Salem, 1731," and his son Benjamin (1729-1804), both of
Boston, are also represented, the latter making the two
mugs for the Tabernacle Church, given four years after
his death.   Others of the old Boston silversmiths are:
Daniel Boyer, member of the Old South Church and Sergeant of the Artillery Co., 1762, whose mother was Mary
Ann Johonnot; Z. Brigden, born in Charlestown, 1734,
member of the West Church, d. 1787 ; D. Parker, who
advertised a sale of his tools and wares, 1763 ; Samuel
Minot (1732-1818), one of the Protestors in 1774 ; and
Paul Revere (1735-1818), the patriot, who is said to have
" frequently exchanged work " with Abijah Northey, a
goldsmith of Salem. (Boston Transcript, Jan. 20, 1900.)
    It is interesting to be able to identify the mark D. T.
on the alms basons of the East Church, from Dr. Bentley's
Diary, as that of David Tyler.   He appears as a goldsmith
in the Boston Directories of 1796-8.
    Of the early part of the last century are vessels by
Churchill & Treadwell (1815); J. B. Jones (1824): and
Baldwin & Jones (1820), all of Boston.   Jabez Baldwin,
of the latter firm, learnt his trade in Salem, possibly of
William Cleveland (grandfather of the Ex-president),
who, with Jedediah Baldwin, brother of Jabez, and Rufus
and Henry Farnum, were fellow-apprentices of a Scotch-
man named Harland, of Norwich, Conn.   Cleveland came
to Salem soon after his marriage in 1793, and on his returning to Norwich, was succeeded by Jabez Baldwin,
who, after the close of the War of 1812, established the
well-known firm of Baldwin & Jones of Boston. Baldwin
was the victim of a robbery which caused a sensation in
Salem and vicinity.   (See Salem Gazette, Oct. 29, 1805;
Dec. 6, 1805 ; April 21, 1807.)   The Farnums also set up
in business in Boston.
    The silverware marked Moulton is by William Moul-
ton, one of the family of silversmiths of Newburyport.
(See Currier's History of Newburyport.)   Local crafts-
men are represented by John Andrew at the sign of the
" Golden Cup," near Long Lane Wharf, 1769 (see Annals
of Salem, Felt), and Stevens and Lakeman (1825),
Eben K. Lakeman appearing in the Salem Directory as
late as 1850.

The communion vessels as a rule are plain and substantial, without ornamentation, with the exception of engraved coats of arms, or cartouches to hold the inscriptions, and many have been in use as domestic utensils. Some have unfortunately been made over into new forms, either to meet the changes of fashion or from becoming too dilapidated for use. In some instances, to the credit of those in charge (as in the case of plate belonging to the First and Saint Peter's churches), a record of the donors of the old vessels has been engraved upon the new.

THE FIRST CHURCH.

This church, the first in the Massachusetts Bay Colony, was established August 6, 1629.

FLAGON, height, 13 inches (jug shaped). Four marks, 1, lion passant; 2, leopard's head crowned; 3, black letter capital 𝕸; 4, maker's mark, $^{W.\,P.}_{J.\,P.}$ William and James Priest, London, 1767. Engraved with coat of arms, on a bend doubly cotised, three eagles displayed; crest, an eagle displayed; and this inscription:

> *The Gift of*
> *Saml. Browne Esqr.*
> *to the First Church of*
> *Christ in Salem*
> *1731*

Samuel Browne (1669-1731), in his day the greatest merchant in Essex county; for many years a representative at the General Court; the first town treasurer of Salem; a Judge of the Superior Court; colonel of the regiment, and a Councillor.

FLAGON, height, 13 inches (jug-shaped to match the flagon made in London in 1767, "The gift of Samuel Browne, Esq., 1731") One mark, **I. ANDREW**, twice repeated (silversmith of Salem at the sign of the "Golden Cup "). Inscription :

> *This Flagon belongs to the first*
> *Church of Christ in SALEM*
> *1769.*

CUP, two-handled, height, 5 3-4 inches. One mark, **J. BURT**, twice repeated (Boston). Inscription :

> *The Gift of Mrs. Mary Wolcot*
> *to the First Church In Salem 1728.*

Mrs. Mary Wolcott (Walcott) was the second wife of Josiah Wolcott, who died about May, 1729. She married, first, John Freke of Boston. She became a member of the First Church, Salem, May 6, 1722.

CUP, two-handled, height, 4 1-2 inches. One mark, **I D,** fleur-de-lis below, heart-shaped shield, twice repeated. (Jeremiah Dummer, Boston.) Inscription :

> *The gift of*
> *Francis Skerry*
> *to the Church*
> *in Salem.*

Francis Skerry, planter; freeman in 1637; will probated Aug. 20, 1684.

FIVE CUPS, two-handled, height, 5 inches. One mark, **I C,** fleur-de-lis below, heart-shaped shield, twice repeated. Inscription :

> *Ex dono Wm. Browne senr Esqur.*

William Browne (1608-1687), came to Salem in 1635 ; eminent merchant; benefactor of the schools of Salem and Charlestown, and also Harvard College ; representative at the General Court for several years ; an Assistant ; and a Councillor.

CUP, two-handled, height, 4 3-4 inches. One mark, **I C,** as before. Inscription :

*The Gift of Sarah Higginson To the
first Church in Salem 1720.*

Pounced on opposite side in a cartouche :

S

T M

Mrs. Sarah Higginson was the daughter of Thomas
Savage, and married, Oct. 9, 1672, John Higginson of
Salem, a merchant, who died Mar. 23, 1720, aged 73 years.
She was buried June 26, 1713.

BAPTISMAL BASON, diameter, 16 1-2 inches. No marks.
Engraved with a coat of arms ; three boars' heads couped;
crest, indecipherable; and this inscription :

The gift of Ichabod Plaisted Esqr 1762.

Col. Ichabod Plaisted (1700-1762), colonel of the Salem
company in the Crown Point expedition, 1755 ; representative to the General Court, 1724 ; Councillor, 1760-1761 ;
married, Oct. 20, 1720, Sarah Browne.

OVAL DISH, with cover; length, 11 inches. One mark,
CHURCHILL & TREADWELL (Boston). There
are similar dishes at Christ and Trinity churches, Boston
(1815), by the same makers. Inscription, on one side :

*The property of
the First Church in Salem
1815.*

On the other :

*Made by order of the Church:
of plate presented by
William Brown 2d Esqr. 1716
Samuel Barnard Esqr. 1763
Mrs. Rachel Barnard 1743.*

William Browne (1639-1715), successful merchant ;
Councillor ; Judge of the Court of Common Pleas ; and
benefactor of Harvard College.

Samuel Barnard (1685-1762), benefactor of the poor of Salem ; married Rachel (1686-1744), daughter of Timothy Lindall.

SPOON, length 10 inches, pierced.   One mark, **E B**, or **E R**, in script.

THE SECOND CHURCH.

The Second or East Church was organized in 1718. With this society the Independent Congregational Church at Barton Square, which was organized in 1824, united in 1897.

"Until 1798, the church owned but one silver cup, which was probably the one formerly called a tankard and came into the possession of the parish in 1747 under a process of distraint against Wm. Brown, Esqr., for non-payment of taxes. Two pairs of silver cups were procured in 1799, and two flagons and two plates in 1800."*

TWO FLAGONS, height, 13 1-2 inches.   No marks or inscriptions.   These flagons were purchased in 1800 at a cost of $120.00.

FOUR CUPS, two-handled, height, 5 3-4 inches.   No marks.   Inscriptions :

<blockquote>

East Church
Salem
1797.

</blockquote>

CUP, two-handled, height, 6 1-2 inches.   No marks. Inscription :

<blockquote>

For the Church of Christ in the
Lower Parish Salem T. Lindal.

</blockquote>

Timothy Lindall (1677-1760), eminent merchant in Salem and Boston ; representative to the General Court

*Essex Inst. Hist. Colls., Vol. XLI, July, 1905.

many times, and Speaker of the House, 1720-1721; Councillor; Judge of the Court of Common Pleas.

Two CHALICES, height, 7 inches.   One mark, **J. B. JONES** (Boston).   Inscription on each:

> *Independent*
> *Congregational Church*
> *Barton Square Salem*
> *from*
> *Joseph Coolidge*
> *Feb. 16th 1825.*

Joseph Coolidge.   Probably one of the Boston merchants of that name.

FOUR CHALICES, height, 7 inches (to match the above). No marks.   Inscription, on two:

> *The*
> *Church of Christ in*
> *Barton Square Salem*
> *from*
> *John D. Treadwell*
> *AD 1825.*

John Dexter Treadwell, M. D. (1768-1833), practised medicine in Marblehead and Salem with considerable celebrity.

On one:

> *The*
> *Church of Christ in*
> *Barton Square Salem*
> *from*
> *Jonathan Hodges*
> *AD 1825.*

Capt. Jonathan Hodges (1764-1837), merchant; commander of the Salem Cadets; treasurer of the town of Salem.

On one:

> *The*
> *Church of Christ in*
> *Barton Square Salem*
> *from*
> *Stephen White*
> *AD 1825.*

Stephen White (1787-1841), enterprising merchant; member of both branches of the Legislature; frequently called upon to hold positions of honor and trust.

EWER, height, 10 inches (with spout, gadrooned body). One mark, **STEVENS & LAKEMAN** (Salem). Inscription:

> *Presented to the Communicants of the Independent*
> *Congregational Church in Barton Square in*
> *Salem at their first celebration of the Supper*
> *by Willard Peele one of the Subscribers*
> *for the erection of said Church.*

Willard Peele (1773-1835), merchant; studied law before engaging in commercial pursuits; President of the Commercial Bank.

EWER, height, 10 inches (plain), to match above. One mark, **J. B. JONES** (Boston), Inscription:

> *The Church of Christ in Barton Square Salem*
> *from Mrs. L. G. Ferreira, a Roman Catholic*
> *and a native of Pernambuco, AD. 1824.*

TWO OVAL DISHES, 11 x 8 1-4 inches. No marks. Inscription on one:

> *The Church of Christ in Barton Square, Salem*
> *from Nathaniel West Esqr.*
> *A D. 1825.*
> *Henry Colman, Pastor.*

On the other, new inscription, the first three lines of above.

Nathaniel West (1756-1851), shipmaster and successful merchant ; commanded a privateer in the Revolution.

BAPTISMAL BASON, diameter, 13 1-2 inches.   No marks. Inscription :

East Church.

This bason, after having been missing for years, was found recently in a poultry yard, where it had been used as a pan for feeding chickens.

BAPTISMAL BASON, on stand ; diameter, 10 inches ; height, 6 1-2 inches,   No marks.   Recent inscription :

Presented by Stephen Phillips to the
Proprietors of the Independent Congregational
Church in Barton Square in Salem, February, 1825.

Stephen Phillips (1761-1838), shipmaster and merchant in the East India trade.

TWO ALMS BASONS, diameter, 11 inches.   One mark, **D. T** (David Tyler, Boston).   Inscription on one :

East Church, Salem.

On the other :

The Gift of Elizabeth West
Eldest Daughter of Elias Hasket Derby Esqr.
To the East Church Salem.

These alms basons were purchased in 1800, at a cost of $60.00 for the two, Mrs. West contributing $37.00 towards the amount. Dr. Bentley records in his Diary, under date of June 21, 1800 : "Had the silver plates from Tyler for our communion table."

TABLE SPOON, length, 7 1-2 inches.   One mark, **STEVENS & LAKEMAN** (Salem).   Inscription :

From Geo. Nichols, 1825.

George Nichols (1778-1865), master mariner, and engaged in the stock brokerage business in Salem.

ST. PETER'S CHURCH.

St. Peter's Church was established in 1733.

FLAGON, height, 14 inches. One mark, much worn, **BALDWIN & JONES** (Boston, founded 1812). Inscription:

A. D. 1820.
This Flagon is the gift of Eleanor
F. Carlile wife of the Rev. Thomas
Carlile to the Ecclesiastical authority
of the Protestant Episcopal Church in
the state of Massachusetts to be by said
authority appropriated to the Sacred
use of any church in Massachusetts
Subject to their discipline: preference
to be given to St. Peters Church in
Salem under the above named restrictions.

Rev. Thomas Carlile was rector at St. Peter's Church from 1817 to 1822.

The flagon was originally a two-handled cup or vase, with cover. One handle has been removed and a spout substituted, the cover being fastened with rings and surmounted with a cross.

OVAL DISH, with cover. No marks. Inscription, on the cover:

A Gift to the Protestant
Episcopal Church in Salem, Massachusetts,
from the Members of said Church A. D. 1817.

On the dish:

A Gift to the Protestant
Episcopal Church in Salem, Massachusetts,
A. D. 1817.

TWO CHALICES, melted down to make a new one (1881). The inscriptions read:

Presented by Mifs Susan Hathorne
to St. Peters Church March 1817.

Miss Susan Hathorne (1759-1818) was the daughter of William and Mary (Touzel) Hathorne.

Two ALMS BASONS, no mark (modern), inscribed as follows :

> *These plates were made from two cups*
> *and a small plate bearing the folowing*
> *inscription:*
> *A Cup "By the Rev. Wm Mc Gilchrist*
> *a gift to St Peter's Church in Salem 1757"*
> *A Plate "The gift of John Touzell to*
> *St Peter's Church Salem 1785"*
> *A Cup "The Bequest of Capt Andrew*
> *Woodbury of Beverly to St Peter's Church*
> *in Salem A. D. 1771"*

Rev. William McGilchrist was rector of St. Peter's Church from 1747 to 1780. John Touzel was a goldsmith and jeweller in Salem as early as 1756. Capt. Andrew Woodbury, a master mariner of Beverly, died in 1757, and bequeathed to St. Peter's Church, " where I was used to worship, a Piece of Plate for the use of the Table." The bequest was not executed until 1771, after the death of his widow.

THE TABERNACLE CHURCH.

The Tabernacle Church was established in 1735, and was known as The Third Church.

Two FLAGONS, height, 11 1-2 inches, One mark, **DAVIS PALMER & CO. BOSTON, PURE SILVER COIN.** Inscription on each :

Bequest of
Miss Abigail P. Lawrence
to the
Tabernacle Church, Salem, Mass.
of which
She was a beloved member.
1841.

THREE MUGS, height, 5 inches. One mark, **BOYER** (Daniel Boyer, Boston). Engraved with a coat of arms; ermine, three increscents; crest, a sun in splendor. (The arms are those of Sims; the crest of ?). Inscription:

The Gift of Edwd. Kitchen Esqr. to the Church of Christ of which ye Revd. Mr. John Huntington ws Pastor-1766.

MUG, height, 5 1-4 inches. No marks. Inscription (modern?):

The Gift of Madam Kitchen
to the First Church of Christ in Salem
1766.

Two MUGS, height, 5 3-4 inches. One mark, **BENJA-MIN BURT** (Boston). Engraved in front in a wreath,

$$J \quad B$$
$$to$$
$$J \quad T$$

and underneath the inscription:

Presented by the Hon. John Treadwell Esq.
to the Tabernacle Church in Salem
1808.

John Treadwell (1738-1811), ordained minister of the First Congregational Church in Lynn, 1763; representative to the General Court; State Senator; Judge of the Court of Common Pleas.

There are ten other mugs similar to the above, without marks or inscriptions, probably by local makers.

BASKET. No marks. Inscription :

Presented by Mr. Nathaniel Knight
to the Tabernacle Church, 1808.

Nathaniel Knight (1754-1839), shipmaster, and afterwards wharfinger of Derby wharf.

BASKET. No marks. Inscription :

Presented by Deacon Nehemiah Adams
to the Tabernacle Church, 1808.

Nehemiah Adams (1769-1840), cabinet maker, with a shop on the corner of Williams street and Washington square.

TWO BASKETS. No marks or inscriptions.

BAPTISMAL BASON, diameter, 12 1-2 inches. One mark, **J. R.** Engraved with a coat of arms ; on a bend doubly cotised, three eagles displayed ; crest, an eagle displayed ; and this inscription :

The Gift of
Benja. Browne Esqr.
to the now Tabernacle Church of Christ
in Salem
1708.

Benjamin Browne (1648-1708), representative to the General Court ; Councillor ; benefactor of Salem schools and poor.

See notes on the South Church plate.

THE NORTH CHURCH.

The North Church was formed from the First Church in 1772.

FLAGON, height, 16 1-2 inches (jug-shaped). Four marks : 1, lion passant ; 2, leopard's head crowned ; 3,

black letter capital 🅢 (London, 1773) ; 4, maker's mark,
I. K. Inscription:

Property
of the
North Church
SALEM
1772.

TANKARD, height, 8 1 2 inches (with mid-band).   One
mark, **D. PARKER** (Boston). Engraved with the Pickman arms, and inscription:

The Gift
of BENJN PICKMAN ESQR to the
First Church in Salem, 1759.
Transfered to the
North Church
SALEM
1772.

Benjamin Pickman (1708-1773), successful merchant;
representative ; Councillor; Judge of the Superior Court;
colonel of the Essex county regiment; member of the
Committee of War in 1745.

TANKARD, height, 8 inches (restored, new finial).   One
mark, **I C,** fleur-de-lis below, heart-shaped shield.   Engraved with the Clarke arms, and inscription :

The Gift of Mrs. ELIZth CABOTT
TO THE NORTH CHURCH in SALEM
1784.

Mrs. Elizabeth (Clarke) Cabot (1716-1785), was the
wife of Francis Cabot, an eminent Salem merchant.

TANKARD, height, 9 1-4 inches (with mid-band).   Two
marks, **MINOTT, M.** (Boston).   Inscription :

The GIFT of
Edward Augustus Holyoke M. D.
To the North CHURCH of CHRIST
in SALEM
1805.

Edward Augustus Holyoke, M. D. (1728-1829), practised his profession in Salem for eighty years; first President of the Massachusetts Medical Society; one of the founders and President of the American Academy of Arts and Sciences; President of the Essex Historical Society, the Institution for Savings, and the Salem Dispensary.

Two MUGS, height, 5 inches. With the marks and maker of Flagon, but the date-letter for the previous year, 1772, London. Inscription:

The Gift of
WILLIAM PICKMAN
Esqr.
to the North Church
in
SALEM
1772.

William Pickman (1748-1815), merchant and naval officer of the port of Salem.

Two MUGS, height, 5 5-8 inches. One mark, **REVERE** (Boston). Inscription :

The Gift of
Mrs. Mary Pickman
to the
NORTH-CHURCH OF CHRIST
IN SALEM
under the Pastoral care of the
Revd. Thomas Barnard DD.
1802

Mrs. Mary (Toppan) Pickman (1744-1817), wife of Benjamin Pickman the eminent merchant.

FOUR MUGS, height, 5 1-2 inches. One mark, **MOULTON** (Newburyport). Inscription:

Property
of the
North Church
in
Salem
1805.

Two MUGS, height, 6 3-8 and 8 1-2 inches. One mark, **MOULTON** (Newburyport). Inscription:

Property of
the NORTH CHURCH in
SALEM
under the Pastoral care of the
Revd. Thos Barnard DD.
1805
THE GIFT OF
Mrs. JOHANNA WARD.

Mrs. Joanna (Chipman) Ward (1761-1831), wife of William Ward, master mariner and merchant.

Note. All the foregoing mugs have modern covers.

Two BREAD TRAYS (with gallery). One mark, **Moulton** (Newburyport). Inscription:

Property of
the NORTH CHURCH in
SALEM
1805.

BAPTISMAL BASON, diameter, 10 inches. One mark, **I. EDWARDS** (Boston). Inscription:

The Gift of BENJAMIN PICKMAN ESQr.
to the North Church in SALEM,
1772.

Benjamin Pickman (1708-1773), successful merchant; representative; Councillor; Judge of the Superior Court; colonel of the Essex county regiment; member of the Committee of War in 1745.

THE SOUTH CHURCH.

The South Church was organized in 1774.

TANKARD, height, 11 inches. Domed top, no marks.

TANKARD, height, 9 1-4 inches. Domed top, no marks.

CUP, two-handled; height, 6 inches. One mark, **I. D.** fleur-de-lis below, heart-shaped shield (Jeremiah Dummer, Boston). Inscription :

> *Elizabeth Brown*
> *gave this for the Churches use*
> *1686.*

THREE MUGS, height, 5 inches. One mark, **BOYER** (Daniel Boyer, Boston). Engraved with coat of arms (Sims), crest (?), and inscription, as on the mugs at the Tabernacle Church :

> *"The Gift of Edwd. Kitchen Esqr," 1776.*

MUG, height, 5 1-4 inches. One mark, **Z. BRIGDEN** (Boston).

MUG, height, 5 inches. One mark, **J. V.**

There are three other mugs similar to the above, without marks or inscriptions, probably by local makers.

BAPTISMAL BASON, diameter, 12 1-2 inches. One mark, **J. R.** Engraved with a coat of arms (Browne), as on the bason at the Tabernacle Church, and this inscription :

> *The Gift of*
> *Benja. Browne Esqr.*
> *to the now Third Church of Christ*
> *in Salem*
> *1708.*

Benjamin Browne (1648-1708), representative to the General Court; Councillor; benefactor of Salem schools and poor.

The original and much larger bason was melted down and made into two basons at a division of church stock between the Tabernacle and South churches, Dec., 1785, one for each church. That division included ten other pieces, five to each church, and in this division are two pieces that came from a previous one, probably in 1762, of church plate between the First and Third Churches, the South Church receiving one Tankard, the three Mugs, " The Gift of Edwd. Kitchen, Esqr.," and the two-handled cup given by Elizabeth Brown, by agreement of the committee chosen by the said churches, 1785.

THE FIRST BAPTIST CHURCH.

This Society was organized in 1804.

Two EWERS, height, 16 1-2 inches. One mark, **R. & H. FARNUM** (Boston).

EXTRACTS FROM THE INTERLEAVED ALMANACS OF WILLIAM WETMORE* OF SALEM, 1774-1778.

COPIED FROM THE ORIGINALS NOW IN POSSESSION OF HON. GEORGE PEABODY WETMORE OF NEWPORT, R. I.

1774. About ye middle of May I was in Boston and Govr H. then lived at his seat in Milton. There was so great fears at that time (real or pretended) that ye Govr w^d be assassinated if he attempted to come to Boston that his friends dissuaded him from it. Once in particular he was met upon ye road to Boston and desired to return, for ye people were so incensed y^t nothing c^d withstand y^r violence. He was persuaded to return where he lived till he sailed for England. Addresses were presented to him at Milton from various quarters procured at ye importunity and by ye artifice of his friends, and forwarded by ye inconsideration, and impetuosity of others who did not wish success to his political opinions, but wished to engage him to assert himself against ye tyrannical and oppressive acts of ye Brittish Legislature; and tho' ye language and stile of the Addresses were far from being agreable to many gent^m w^o signed y^m yet, for ye reason I have ment^d & because y^r was not time to form new ones, & because y^y esteemed those better y^n none, they were persuaded to sign y^m — these reasons prevailed on many, to my certain knowledge. It was suspected (and with great justice) that those gent^m w^o promoted the Addresses & draughted y^m had direct views to y^r own sinister purposes & private Emolum^t.

---

*William Wetmore, the son of Jeremiah and Abigail (Butler) Wetmore, was born Oct. 30, 1749, in Middletown, Conn.; married, 1st, Nov. 5, 1776, Catherine, daughter of William Pynchon of Salem, Mass.; married, 2d, Oct. 8, 1782, Sally, daughter of Samuel Waldo, of Falmouth (Portland), Me.; and died in November, 1830. He was graduated at Harvard College, 1770, and settled in Salem where he practiced law and represented the town at the General Court in 1777. He removed to Boston in 1785 and was Judge of the Court of Common Pleas for a number of years, and also one of the founders of the Massachusetts Historical Society. He was very successful in his profession from the active practice of which he retired in 1792.

This was most certainly the Case with several y_t came within my observat^n.

Aug. 7. On Friday or Saturday last a Ship arrived from Engl^d with dispatches for his Ex^y & this day we hear y^e bills for regulating ye Gov^t have arrived— On Monday y^e 8th a new Council was summoned & met, some were sworn—& some desired time for consideration. On ye 11—Three Transports arriv^d in this Harbour with a Brig^t from Halifax under ye Command of Col^o Hamilton, landed near the fort & pitched their tents upon ye rising ground on this side & about 6 o'Clock the Col^o politely entertained several gent^m from town with his band of music— 16th, a meeting of Council this day when it is thought many will refuse from timidity, from prud^e and from Principle—17th—only one refused viz Mr. Russell— Col^o Worthington considers further.

Sept. 10. Ab^t 5 o'clock this morn^g ye Reg^t at ye Fort marched thro' ye town wt^h fife & drum to Boston ye heavy Baggage being transported yesterday by water to ye same place.

Oct. 6. About 3 o'clock this morning a fire broke out in Col^o Frye's Wood house whereby his Store & dwelling house, Dr. Whitaker's Meeting House, Coats' house & shop, Northey's Shops, Field's, Bartlet's, Cheever's, Appleton's, Britton's, Hathorn's & Ropes' Dwelling houses & outhouses were burnt to ashes, the Town house took fire but by the activity of ye M'head people it was stopped tho' ye house is ruined.

1775. Feb. 26. Col^o Leslie's Reg^t from ye Castle landed at M'head marched to Salem & caused an alarm among ye people. It is supposed y^t they came for one or two pieces of Cannon y^t y^y heard of.

April 3. Bad news from England for ye Colonies if they persist in y^r opposition—Treason, rebellion, Sedition, Whiggishm, Bugbears to fright Children.

April 28th. Mrs. Pynchon, Mrs. Orne, Miss Katy, Sally, John, myself & Mr. Bean's family, set sail for Nantucket, to avoid ye continual Alarms to wch ye town is liable by being upon ye sea coast, and exposed to the K . . . s Ships, and the ignorance of a c . . . y P.

May 3.   We arrive at Nantucket after a most tedious &
disagreable passage; the Women being continuously sick,
the weather rainy & blustering, no conveniences, & destitute of some of ye necessaries of Life.   We are received,
and kindly entertained by hospitable People, upon a peace-
able island.   Nantucket is 15 miles long from East to
West & generally 4 miles wide.   There are 10,000 sheep
upon ye Island & above 600 cows.   This y^r ye town laid
out 100 acres for ye poor to plant potatoes.

June 17.   I sail from Nantucket ab^t 1 o'clock P. M. and
arrive at a little harbour above Wood's hole in Buzzard's
bay ab^t sun sett^g. Battle at Charlestown.

June 19.   Set out upon my journey by land from
Falm^o thro' Camb^e to Salem in Comp^a with Mr. Bunker of
Nantucket.

June 23d. I arrive at Salem at Sun Sett^g wearied out
with the journey and ye Difficulties met with upon it.   I
tarried at Camb^e & Roxbury from 20th inst^a to 23^d.

June 30th.   'Tis reported that ab^t 400 Reg^m marched
over y^r lines at Roxbury & were fired upon by our Cannon 13 times.   A Capt Mascot bound to ye W. I. had all
his men pressed by a Tender.

Aug. 8.   Capt Lyndsey chases two schooners belonging
to Salem into Cape Ann & is fired upon by ye people—
ye report is y^t he has lost many of his men ye whole N^o
being 150—3 dead men were drove ashore it is said in one
of his boats—& 28 taken prisoners—Capt L. fired upon
ye town thro ye meet^g house & 8 houses—& killed 2 men.

Sept. 9.   Dr. Warren informs me y^t ye Kings Troops
came out of B. ab^t 10 Days ago to intrench near Browne's
house but were repulsed by our Cannon from ye forts, y^y
came out ag^n ye next day in a thick fog & held possess^n.
Our Troops have advanced upon ye ground w^r ye Gun
Tavern stood and intrenched—About 14 days ago our
Troops at C. intrenched upon ye plow'd hill.   Bombs, &c.
fired upon y^m ev^y day—2 men killed ye first day & none
hurt since.

October 10.   The Nautilus of 14 or 16 guns (6^lb
chased ye Bev^y* Privateer in to Bev^y harb^r—& fired upon
*Beverly.

her after she had run aground and was stripped for ab^t 4 hours. The Salem people, to ye n^o of 200 or more went down upon Salem Neck & were preparing to fire upon ye Ship with their field pieces when she fired ye first shot among a party of y^m w^o were collected upon a hill. I was myself present. Our men then began to play their 4 lb guns & after making 8 or 10 shot apiece they levelled them well. The Ship fired several times at us but after our Guns began to play she fired but seldom, and hoisted sail to go off—when she got aground—she got off ag^n ab^t 1/2 after 7 P. M.—for 4 hours we fired upon her constantly & tis supposed y^t she rec^d some of our shot—We fired very badly many times.

Oct. 11. A barn burnt in Bev^y. The people of Salem began to throw up a small breast work at Juniper point. I was present & assisted, walked home at noon & fatigued myself very much.

Oct. 18. Reports that ye Troops are to attack Bost^n— Gun bursts & kills 2 & wounds 10 at C.

July 21, 1776. Capt. Lander took a ship with a valuable cargo from Jamaica, put 12 of his men on board & ordered her into ye eastw^d—she has not yet arriv^d

July 25. As this ship was going into Newbury near ye barr she was retaken by a sloop of 16 guns, ye above 12 men escaped in y^r boat.

Aug. 24. A prize ship sent to M'head.

Aug. 25. A prize snow retaken near Bl^y* shore.

Sept. 15. New York abandon^d to ye Enemy in haste— most of ye Stores being first remov^d—tis said we left go pieces of heavy cannon owing to ye cowardice of a body of Connecticut troops, stationed at Harlem.

Oct. 16. Capt. Forrester has taken 4 prizes—2 very valuable—3 have arrived into port—ye 2 valuable ones among ye n^o.

Oct. 18. News that Capt. Carleton is taken near Nova Scotia. He deserves it—as he went down to rob ye very men of y^r property w^o forwarded his escape from Halifax to Salem, some time ago.

1776. Feb. 29. A very cold day, Mr. Burke, Capt

*Beverly.

Laurea, &c, sail this night for Antiqua. The Vessell went out by M'head & was fired at by ye King's ship.

March 2. A heavy Cannonade at night from ye Camp at Cambridge & Roxbury wch was returned from Boston.

March 3. At night it was again renewed.

March 4. I ride to Cambridge wth Verrey. A heavy Cannonade began this Ev^g at Seven o'Clock from ye forts at Cobblehill & Lechmore's point & from Roxbury wch continued all night, and was ret^d from Boston. We lost two men.

March 7. I return from Cambridge on foot. Our troops advanc^d to ye hills in Dorchester ye 4th inst^a at ye very mom^t ye cannonade began & fortified ye ground, ye kings troops did not molest y^m except by a few Cannon shot ye next morning.

March 5. An uncommonly stormy night wch it is supposed prevents ye troops in Boston from landing to annoy our men at D.

March 9th. It is said y^t our Troops advanc^e to D. point this night & were repulsed wth ye loss of 4 men. Reports that ye troops are ab^t to leave Boston directly.

March 11. At night a Cannonading at ye Camp.

March 17. The King's Troops left ye town of Boston ab^t 9 o'clock in ye morning unexpectedly to y^r fr^ds there— & in haste. In ye cannonade of Boston 6 persons (soldiers) had y^r legs fractured as y^y lay in bed wth a can^n ball & some of them died of y^r w^ds & others had y^r legs taken off.

June 8. A prize bro't into M'head having 95 Highlanders on board. Y^e Yankee hero undoubtedly taken.

July 12. Capt. Lander brings in a Sloop wi^th dry goods & salt. A provis^n ship comes to an anchor in Bostn harb^r & is seiz^d. A meeting of ye train^g band & alarm list to raise men for Canada to make part of ye 1500 —this town to raise 20.

July 18. Capt Fiske brings in a prize one of ye kings tenders—two men killed in ye tender & 7 wounded. Capt. Fiske lost 1 man killed, 1 w.

Aug. 11. Capt. Fiske sends in a prize brig bound from a French isl^d to Halifax &c—but owned as is said at Newport—he took also a schooner belonging to ye Pitt's in ye Halifax trade—She is supposed to have gone into ye s^o shore—She went to Dartm^o.

Aug. 16. Col⁰ Carleton & one Comp march from hence to Crown p.

Aug. 31. The Milford in y Bay takes severall vessells —burns some & keeps others. Capt. Burke of y Constitut Schooner is one of y number taken.

Sept. 17. Maritime Court at Salem condemned y foll vessells—The Ships Anna Maria, Isaac, Nancy, Polly; Brig, Perkins; Schooner Deborah.

Dec. 4. The Militia met at y Meeting house, being rainy, to raise 1/4 part as a Reinforcement to y Continental army—y proposition for this town being 87. 70 Volunteers turned out & followed y Drum—either to go in person or to procure a hearty strong man. y Rem being 17 to compleat y n were draughted as y Law requires. The Meeting was y adjourned to y 5th at 8 o'clock P. M. When y Col⁰ inform y Comp y 39 only had enlisted to march, for y bounty of £10—w sum was p into y Committee's hands by every man, 10 turned out as a Volunteer yesterday in order to hire men. After an animating & encouraging speech y Drums turned out for Volunteers—none turned out. y Drums then went round for those w inclined to turn out for £10 bount. Only 3 or 4 appeared. Y most of those w were now enlisted were persons of Character & property such as Masters of Vessells, Shop Keepers, &c. Y Col⁰ w also turned out again addressed y People. Y drums went round & 92 persons enlisted on y spot—marchd 17th inst.

Apr. 6, 1777. The Cabot Brig drove ashore at y Eastw by y Milford, y people escaped. Y Brig tis said bilgd before she was abandon. Capt. Fiske in y Mass & Capt. Harriden in y Tryannicide, Brigs, were in comp with y Cabot, & thinking it imprudent to attack y M. y stood off. Y M. out sail y Cabot upon y wind & so took her. Many people blame Capts. F. & H. I think y did right not to attack.

July 28, 1778. Ab 12 o'clock in y day my beloved wife died.

Oct. 6. The F. Officer* w was wounded in y Sailors affray at Boston dies & is buried privately at night.

*Count de Sauveur.

EDMUND LEWIS OF LYNN AND SOME OF HIS DESCENDANTS.

BY GEORGE HARLAN LEWIS OF LOS ANGELES, CAL.

(*Continued from Vol. XLIII, page 88.*)

Children of Joseph and Elizabeth:

65. SARAH, b. 1703-4; m., Nov. 16, 1725, Thomas Beckwith of Lyme, Conn., born there July 1, 1702, son of Capt. Joseph and Marah (Lee) Beckwith.
66. ELIZABETH, b. 1705-6; m., Nov. 24, 1027, Hezekiah Shailer of Haddam, Conn.
67. REBECCA, m., June 24, 1730, Joseph Lee of Guilford, Conn.
68. HANNAH, m., Mar. 6, 1734-5, Simon Arnold of Haddam, Conn.
69. DEBORAH, b. April 16, 1721, at Haddam; m. Daniel Clark of Haddam, Conn.
70. JOHN, b. April 14, 1723, at Haddam.

32 Joseph Lewis, born in Swansea, June 6, 1672, was brought up with the family of his stepfather, Obadiah Jenkins, in Malden. After his marriage, in 1700, to Hannah Jones of Malden, he settled in Woburn, in that part which was set off to Wilmington, Sept. 25, 1730, on or near the Billerica line. In 1733 he was of Wilmington. He disposed of his father's lands in Swansea, for £6, to Thomas Lewis (23) of Swansea (Bristol Co. Deeds, Vol. 14, f. 34). He also sold to John Luther of Swansea, land at Mattapoisett (Middlesex Co. Deeds, Vol. 99, f. 668). These deeds identify him with his father Joseph (6). His sister Sybil was an heir to her grandmother, and they both were heirs of Obadiah Jenkins, Jr., a half-brother. Joseph Lewis died in Wilmington, July 25, 1755, and his will, made July 1, 1751, gives to his wife Hannah £7 lawful money, with all my provisions and live stock to improve and dispose of during her life, the dwelling house and barn, and all household goods of all sorts. Thomas Pearson, a son-in-law, is made executor, and ordered to fence lands, get in hay, make cider, and put it in the cellar, care for cows, winter and summer, drive and fetch them, provide a horse for meetings, etc.; also 20 bushels

(121)

of meal (12 indian, 8 rye), 140 pounds of meat (100 pork, 40 beef), one bushel of malt, and firewood. Care for the widow tenderly in sickness, and bury her decently after death. To son Benjamin £20, also a £50 bond he owes his father is his portion. To son Joseph, 20 shillings. To son John, 20 shillings. To daughter Abigail, and to her husband Thomas Pearson, all lands and meadows of all sorts, homestead and outlands. To 4 grandchildren, children of daughter Hannah Durant, £7. All wearing apparel to Benjamin, Joseph and John.

The will of the widow, Hannah Lewis of Wilmington, made June 13, 1757, and probated May 25, 1761, gives to son Benjamin Lewis £10, who is appointed executor. To son Joseph Lewis £10. To daughter Abigail Pierson £10. To son John Lewis, if living, £50. In case of his death, to his two children, John Lewis and Susannah Lewis. To children of son Joseph Lewis, " which he hath by his first wife Lydia Lewis," remaining estate.

She died Nov. 6, 1760, in Wilmington.

Children of Joseph and Hannah, born in Woburn:

71. HANNAH, b. Oct. 13, 1700; m. —— Durant.
72. MARY, b. Feb. 22, 1702.
73. BENJAMIN, b. June 5, 1705.
74. JOSEPH, b. Jan. 1, 1707.
75. ABIGAIL, b. April 11, 1710; m. Thomas Pearson.
76. JOHN, b. June 9, 1713.

39 Edmund Lewis, born in Lynn, Dec. 8, 1695, was a yeoman. He came into possession of his father's lands by purchase of the rights of the other heirs. He also obtained possession of most of his uncle Thomas' land by purchase from his son John (43). Nov. 10, 1736, he also bought of John Lewis (43), tanner, for £600, a certain messuage, or tenement, consisting of upland and meadow, with one dwelling house and barn, situate in Lynn, bounded northerly on land of Nathaniel Ingalls, easterly on land of Edmund Lewis (39), and partly on Bassett's land, southerly on said Edmund Lewis' land, and westerly on Lynn commons, containing about 20 acres (Essex Co. Deeds, Vol. 73, f. 179). This was the house and barn of Edmund (1) which John (43) inherited from his father Thomas (9), who inherited it from John, Sen (2).

Edmund Lewis re-conveyed this property to his brother Thomas, the following month, for £250. Together with Hannah, his newly married wife, he conveyed to his eldest son John, for £19. 18s., " the east end of my Dwelling House, and one half my barn, and one half my salt marsh, wood and upland," on Dec. 8, 1756 (Essex County Deeds, Vol. 178, f. 172). He died intestate, and Sept. 29, 1777, Samuel Ingalls was appointed administrator (Essex Co. Prob. Rec., file 16,745). The widow's dower was set off to her by the court on May 4, 1779, viz.: The west end of the dwelling house, the line running through the centre of the chimney, with a privilege to use the front and back doors, entry and stairs. The east end of the barn containing two Bays, and is 20 feet in length. 100 poles of land, on part of which the dwelling house stands, the east line running through the centre of the chimney. One acre, 96 poles of land in the field by the house. Seven acres, 136 poles of land, part tillage, and part fresh meadow. Four acres of pasture land near the house. Four acres of woodland laid out to John Lewis on town common, it being part of a ten acre lot, the total being appraised at £870. 6. 8.

John Lewis, eldest son of said intestate, having received as advancement of his father certain real estate fully equal to a single share, his heirs desired that only one share be set off to them. The estate was divided into seven lots, and apportioned to Jonathan Blaney Lewis (148), representative of Nathaniel Lewis, deceased, to Lydia Ingalls, Elizabeth Ingalls, Joseph Lewis, Edmund Lewis, Sarah Newhall, and to the legal representatives of John, the eldest son, deceased. The portions were each valued at £248. 13s. 4d.

Edmund Lewis married, Jan. 8, 1723-4, Hepsebah, daughter of Allen, 3d, and Elizabeth (Ballard) Breed of Lynn. She was born June 19, 1697, and was buried Mar. 15, 1756. He married, second, Nov. 25, 1756, Mrs. Hannah (Prince) Fuller, widow of Capt. John Fuller* of Lynn, son of Hannah (8) (Lewis) Fuller. She died in 1795.

Children of Edmund and Hepsebah, born in Lynn:

77. JOHN, b. Oct. 16, 1724. Called "Junior."
78. SARAH, b. Oct. 25, 1726; m., April 10, 1746, John Newhall, son of John and Lydia (Scarlett) Newhall of Lynn. He was b. May 12, 1721, and d. Jan., 1810. She d. about 1793. (See Newhall genealogy, No. 338.)
79. LYDIA, b. Aug. 7, 1729; m. Samuel Ingalls, son of Samuel and Sarah (Ingalls) Ingalls, born in Lynn in 1720. He was a cordwainer. His will was dated July 10, 1794.
80. NATHANIEL, b. Oct. 30, 1731.
81. JOSEPH, b. March 15, 1733-4.
82. ELIZABETH, b. July 8, 1736; m., Nov. 27. 1758, Eleazer Collins Ingalls, born 1731, in Lynn, son of Joseph and Rebecca (Collins) Ingalls. He was a shipwright, and lived in Lynn.

Child of Edmund and Hannah, born in Lynn:

83. EDMUND, b. June 20, 1757.

42 Thomas Lewis, born in Lynn, May 10, 1708. He was the first of the family to learn the trade of shoe-making. He lived in the old Edmund (1) Lewis house, which he bought of his brother Edmund on Dec. 23, 1736 (Essex Co. Deeds, Vol. 73, f. 179.), until he sold it to John Ingalls on Jan. 26, 1758. Afterwards he lived in East Saugus on land bought of the Stockers, and others. His will made Nov. 5, 1774 and probated Jan. 2, 1775, is as follows:

Item—I give and bequeath unto my beloved Wife Elizabeth Lewis the whole use and Impovment of the one half of my Estate both real and personal so long as she shall remain my Widow and all my Household Furniture, to her own Disposal, her Improvement in the House to be the Westerly end & one half of the barn.

I give and bequeath unto my son Amos Lewis and unto his Heirs & Assigns forever the Easterly end of my

*Capt. John Fuller, m., Sept. 15, 1746, Hannah Prince, and had two children, born in Lynn: Millicent, b. Sept. 7, 1748; James, b. June 7, 1752.

Dwelling House & half an acre of land lying on the northerly side of sd Dwelling house also one half my Barn.

I give unto my three sons, Amos Lewis, Thomas Lewis & Nathaniel Lewis and unto their Heirs and Assigns forever the other half of my Estate both real and personal in equal Proportion.

I give and bequeath unto my daughter Elizabeth Johnson, the wife of Timothy Johnson, twenty four shillings yearly & every year to be paid her by my Executors out of my Estate so long as my Wife's Improvement continueth and at the end of my Wife's Improvement I Will, give & bequeath unto her children forty pounds to be paid unto her, if living, or her children if Providence so do order that she dieth before my Wife.

After the Improvement of my Wife is ended, I give unto my sons Thomas & Nathaniel the west end of my House.

I give and bequeath unto my three sons Amos, Thomas & Nathaniel the whole remaining part of my Estate both real and personal unto them, their Heirs and Assigns forever, to be equally divided betwixt them.

Constitutes wife Elizabeth and son Amos as executors.

Dec. 10, 1779, Amos Lewis (85), cordwainer, of Lynn, Elizabeth Lewis, widow, of Lynn, and Thomas Lewis (87) of Boston, cordwainer, for £12,750 (depreciated currency) conveyed to Jacob Newhall of Lynn, a farm of 120 acres in Lynn, also two lots of salt marsh, 7 acres, and 2 lots of woodland, 5 acres. (Essex Co. Deeds, Vol. 138, f. 51.)

May 16, 1777, Ephraim Rhodes and wife Mary, conveyed to Thomas (87) and Nathaniel Lewis (88) of Plymouth and Amos Lewis (85) of Lynn, 5 acres land in Lynn. (Essex Co. Deeds, Vol. 123, f. 278.) On July 19, 1777, John Batt of Lynn for £186 conveyed to Amos Lewis (85) of Lynn, and Thomas (87) and Nathaniel Lewis (88) of Plymouth, 80 acres land in Lynn, bounded on Amos, Thomas and Nathaniel Lewis and Thomas Stocker. (Essex Co. Deeds, Vol. 123, f. 278.)

Thomas Lewis married Dec. 8, 1741, in Lynn, Elizabeth Carder. He was buried in Lynn, Nov. 12, 1774.

Children of Thomas and Elizabeth, born in Lynn:

84. ELIZABETH, b. May 6, 1744; m. Nov. 27, 1766, Timothy Johnson. 3rd church records say m. Jan. 12, 1767. Had: Nathaniel Lewis, b. Oct. 18, 1774.
85. AMOS, b. Sept. 26, 1746.
86. THOMAS, b. Sept. 14, 1748; d. Jan., 1749.
87. THOMAS, b. Nov. 1, 1750.
88. NATHANIEL, b. Nov. 14, 1751.

43 **John Lewis,** born in Lynn, Aug. 2, 1687. He was an innholder succeeding his father and grandfather. Later he became a tanner and owned a tannery on the Boston road. He was elected deacon for life in the 3d church in 1757. He owned about the last slave, owned in Lynn, and to whom he gave his freedom. The slave was brought from Africa when a boy. John Lewis died in 1778 at the ripe age of 91 years. Alonzo Lewis says he died 1775, aged 92 years, whereas, he was alive in 1778. (History of Lynn, 2d Edition, p. 215.) In 1720 he kept the grammar school. (History of Lynn, 2d Ed. p. 196.) The next year he opened a tannery, for Dec. 21, 1721, Theophilus Burrill of Lynn, tanner, conveys to John Lewis "my tan house and tan yard and 26 poles of land near said Lewis' dwelling house, beam house, mill stone, horse, cart, 2 sleds, 1/3 of Malt house given me by my Father." (Essex Co. Deeds, Vol. 38, f. 278.) He bought considerable land that had formerly belonged to his wife's father Samuel Burrill, and her grandfather John Burrill, and about 1747 he retired from the tannery business, as May 12, 1747 he is "John Lewis, Gentleman," in a deed to John Lewis, jr., schoolmaster (his son) of a dwelling house, barn, several out buildings, and one-half acre of land in the body of Lynn, late in the possession of Joshua and Lydia Ward of Salem, and conveyed by them to John Lewis (Essex Deeds, Vol. 44 f. 49), late enjoyed by Col. Burrill deceased and conveyed to said Lydia, by said Burrill in his will. (Essex Co. Deeds, Vol. 101, f. 89.) There are over 30 deeds on record bearing his name. His father Thomas gave him one-half his house, barn, outhousing and lands, two weeks before his death, and left him the other half if he would pay his debts, care for his widow, etc.; which he declined, but the

Judge of Probate appointed him Administrator of the Estate, and he worked it out of debt, and paid the other heirs £30 each.   His will probated Oct. 5, 1778, contains the following items:

Constitutes his son-in-law, Revd. Mr. John Carnes, executor.

Item.   I give and bequeath to my daughter Lydia Henchman, widow of the late Rev. Nathaniel Henchman, the sum of ten shillings she being entitled to her proportion of that part of my Estate that came of her Mother, and having my note of hand for a sum to make her equal to my other daughters, as to her fitting out at the time of marriage, and her circumstances in several respects being so much better than those of my other heirs. But I dont do this for want of affection for my dear daughter, for whom I bear a great regard.   Item   I will, give & bequeath to my daughter Mary Carnes, and to her heirs and assigns, forever, one just and equal third part, in all regards of my remaining Estate, which with what I have already given to and done for her is her full portion in my Estate.

Item: I will, give and bequeath to my three grandchildren, Samuel Lewis, Sarah Lewis and Mary Lewis, children of my deceased son John Lewis, two just and equal third parts of my remaining Estate as . aforesaid, that is to say, to the said Samuel, Sarah and Mary Lewis in just and equal parts, or shares, being one third part of the said two thirds of my said Estate to each of them, and their respective heirs and assigns forever, and my will and pleasure is that my said Grandson Samuel Lewis have my Tan house and Tan yard with all the appurtenances & utensils for the Tanning Business belonging, if the said Samuel shall choose the same, and receive them in part of his interest in my Estate aforesaid, which with what I have already given to and done for their deceased Father in his lifetime is their portion in my Estate.

Item: I will and order that the division of my said Estate between my said daughter and grand children be made according to the appraisal & Inventory of my said Estate.

His second wife's estate was settled by Joseph Ballard
in 1790, and among the charges was one for nursing since
1778.

The inventory of his estate amounted to £1508. 8s.
old tenor. The inventory of the estate of his wife Mary,
amounted to £612. 10. old tenor. In the division of her
estate, to John and Mary Carnes was set off one-half of
the homestead, viz. house and barn, and a third of the old
malt house, with other small buildings, together with land.
To Samuel Lewis was set off the tan house and yard.
To Sarah Newhall and the heirs of Mary Newhall, the
whole of the brick yards. Deeds were given by the heirs
Sept. 19, 1782.

John Lewis married, first, Nov. 10, 1715, Mary Burrill,
born Aug. 24, 1698, the daughter of Samuel and Margaret
(Ruck) Burrill. She died Aug. 31, 1754. He was published, second, in Boston, Apr. 25, 1756, with Jane (Ballard) Hunting, widow of Joseph Hunting of Boston, the
daughter of John Ballard. They were married in June,
1756. She died about 1790. Administration was granted on her estate July 15, 1790.

Children of John and Mary, born in Lynn :

89. LYDIA, b. Aug. 20, 1716, became the 2d wife of Rev. Nathaniel
Henchman, b. Nov. 22, 1700, and d. Dec. 23, 1761.
She m. 2d, Russell Trevett, a merchant of Marblehead, and d. before Mar. 26, 1799, when her will was
proved. Had: (1) Anna, b. Feb. 25, 1735-6 ; d. Sept. 6,
1736. (2) Lydia, b. Apr. 20, 1740; d. Sept. 19, 1761. (3)
Anna, b. May 18, 1742; m. Humphrey Devereaux, jr. of Marblehead.

90. SARAH, b. Jan. 5, 1717-18; m. Mar. 20, 1748-9, Dr. Jonathan
Fuller. She died July 1, 1751 and he m. 2d, Apr. 15, 1755,
Mary Wyman.

91. MARY, b. Apr. 19, 1720; d. June 15, 1798; m., July 16, 1747, Rev.
John Carnes, b. in Boston July 11, 1723, and d. in Lynn Oct.
23, 1802, son of John and Sarah (Baker) Carnes of Boston.
John Carnes, sen., was a Colonel in the English army, com-
manding artillery in Boston in 1748. Rev. John Carnes
graduated at Harvard College in 1742, was pastor at Stoneham from 1746 to 1757, at Rehoboth from 1759 to 1764, and
lived in Boston during the seige of 1775, corresponded

with General Washington, was suspected by General Gage, had his house and papers searched, and was ordered to leave, which he did. Was chaplain in the army during the Revolution; Justice of the Peace; Representative in the Massachusetts Legislature, 1784 to 1790, 1794, 1795; and delegate to ratify the constitution of the U. S. in 1788. He lived on the John Lewis place, Boston street, Lynn. Children: (1) Dorothy, b. Apr. 25, 1749, in Stoneham; m. Jonas Walsh. (2) John, b. July 17, 1751, in Stoneham. (3) Lewis, b. Oct. 31, 1753, in Stoneham; d. Aug. 1, 1799, in Demarara, W. I.   (4) Thomas, b. July 12, 1755, in Stoneham; d. Aug. 5, 1755, in Stoneham. (5) Thomas, b. Oct. 11, 1756, in Stoneham. (6) Burrill, b. July 24, 1761, in Rehoboth. (7) Edward, b. Feb. 12, 1765, in Rehoboth. (8) Joseph. (9) Mary; m. Rev. Benj. Wadsworth, b. in Milton, July 29, 1750 (second wife). He d. Jan. 28, 1826. Her will was recorded in Suffolk County, May 6, 1845.

92. LOIS, b. July 17, 1722; d. Nov. 7, 1750; m. May 7, 1750, in Boston, Capt. Richard Mower, jr. He d. before March 1, 1761. Their daughter Sarah died Oct. 30, 1750, aged 7 days (g. s.), a premature birth, that probably caused the mother's death. See Henchman tomb in Western Burying Ground.

93. JOHN, b. Nov. 7, 1724.

56 James Lewis, born Nov. 14, 1695, at Swansea; received by his father's will the farm in Swansea, consisting of about 140 acres. On May 8, 1723, he conveyed to his brother Samuel 60 acres in Metapoiset (Bristol County Deeds, Vol. 16, f. 336), and on June 25, 1725, he conveyed to his brother Timothy, a house, barn, outhousing, and 80 acres of land in Swansea (Bristol County Deeds, Vol. 16, f. 337). He was executor of his mother's will, Nov. 29, 1731, and was then of Rehoboth. On June 7, 1742, Hannah Lewis of Greenwich, Providence Co., R. I., widow of James Lewis, for £1000, conveyed to Nathan Pierce of Warwick, 100 acres of Oak swamp in Rehoboth (Bristol County Deeds, Vol. 31, f. 74).

57 Timothy Lewis, was born in Swansea, Feb. 23, 1697-8. He received by his father's will one-half of his farm, with the dwelling house, it being the southern end of the farm formerly purchased of Ephraim Pearce, and June 25, 1725, he bought of his brother James 80 acres of land in Swansea, with the buildings thereon.

Administration on his estate was granted to Anne Lewis, his widow, Feb. 18, 1754.

Children of Timothy and Anne, born in Swansea :

94. THOMAS, b. Mar. 22. 1726; m. Jan. 14, 1753, Hannah Martin. Lived in Rehoboth.
95. ELIZABETH, b. Nov. 20, 1728; m., Jan. 22, 1756, Benjamin Mason. Lived in Swansea.
96. ANNE, b. Jan. 11, 1730; d. 1806.
97. HEPZABETH, b. Feb. 14, 1732; m. July 18, 1751, Gideon Cornell.
98. ABIGAIL, b. Feb. 3, 1734; m., 1766, Elisha Cornell; lived in Swansea; and d. Dec. 2, 1769.
99. DEBORAH, b. Feb. 23, 1736; m., Nov. 4, 1787, Richard Hale.
100. MARCY, b. Nov. 6, 1739; d. 1811; will proved Mar. 5, 1811.

59 Samuel Lewis, born April 16, 1702, in Swansea, received by his father's will the northern half of his farm in Rehoboth. He married Hannah ——, and died in 1763.

His will, made March 13, 1762, and proved Oct. 10, 1763, appointed Hannah, his wife, executrix, and gave to her the improvement and profit of all the farm, house and buildings during her life, together with all the stock and household goods. His son Benjamin received the housing and land in Diton (Dighton). This he afterwards sold and gave him the money, as appears by a codicil dated Sept. 16, 1763. His son Joseph received all the land that laid south of what he had sold him, he paying his mother £12 yearly during her widowhood. Samuel received 50 acres on the north end of the home field, he allowing his mother firewood and timber for rails for use on the place during her widowhood.

His sons Benjamin, Joseph and Samuel received his wearing apparel, arms, all his tools and tackling. His daughter, Betty Cornell, one cow and £20. His daughters, Tabitha, Mary, Hannah and Phebe, "all the land between the land I have given to Samuel and to Joseph after their mother's death divided equally." To the daughters that remained single at their mother's death all the household goods and stock that remained after her death, and use of two lowermost rooms so long as they remained single, then all buildings to go to Joseph.

The inventory, filed Oct. 5, 1763, amounted to £128. 11. 6.

Children of Samuel and Hannah, born in Swansea:

101. BETTY, b. Mar. 29, 1729; m. April 13, 1752, Elisha Cornell, and d. Dec. 28, 1765.
102. TABITHA (twin), b. Dec. 21, 1733(?); m., Sept. 24, 1764, William Baker.
103. BENJAMIN (twin), b. Dec. 21, 1733(?); m., Aug. 22, 1754, Ruth Norton.
104. SAMUEL, b. June 20, 1734(?); m., Jan. 12, 1758, Mary Martin.
105. JOSEPH, b. April 2, 1736; m. Patience Pierce.
106. MARY, b. Aug. 7, 1741; m. Joseph Fisk.
107. HANNAH (twin), b. Dec. 29, 1744.
108. PHEBE (twin), b. Dec. 29, 1744.

63 Samuel Lewis, born in Woodbridge, N. J., Jan. 1, 1702; married there Effie Davenport.

Children of Samuel and Effie:

109. JOHN, b. Oct. 16, 1727.
110. SUSANNAH, m. John Stout.
111. DOROTHY, m. Jeffrey Cooper.
112. SARAH, m. John Dow.

70 John Lewis, born April 14, 1723, at Haddam, Conn.; married there, June 21, 1744, Deborah ———, who died Feb. 1, 1813, in her 90th year. He died at Saybrook, Conn., Aug. 9, 1801.

Children of John and Deborah, the first eight born at Haddam, the last two born at Saybrook:

113. JOSEPH, b. Mar. 24, 1744-5.
114. JOHN, b. June 27, 1746; d. before 1765.
115. SIMON, b. 1749; d. Oct. 3, 1791, æ. 42 yrs. (Bible record)
116. SAMUEL, b. 1752-3; d. Sept. 10, 1780, æ. 27 y. (g. s.)
117. MARY, b. Aug. 16, 1758.
118. ANDREW, bapt. Oct., 1759.
119. ANDREW, b. Sept. 12, 1761.
120. SARAH, b. 1760-1762; d. June 29, 1806, æ. 45 y.; m., first, ——— Barker; second, ——— Jones.
121. JOHN, b. Mar. 23, 1764; d. Mar. 25, 1786.
122. ABNER, b. July 25, 1766.

73 Benjamin Lewis, born in Woburn, June 5, 1705, settled in that part that was set off to Wilmington Sept. 25, 1730. He was a yeoman and member of the church at Wilmington in 1735. He was of Billerica in 1744 and was a selectman in 1753-4 and 9. He was on the tax list Dec. 1776, for £2. 2. 5. as in the "Andover district near Salem Road." He was executor of his mother's will, and also was heir to a part of the estate of Obadiah Jenkins, a half-brother to his father.

Benjamin Lewis died Sept. 23, 1777. His will made Jan. 31, 1771, proved Nov. 10, 1777, gives to his wife Elizabeth the use of all household furniture during her natural life, a good cow, and three sheep to keep for her use during life, firewood, 8 bushels corn meal, 6 bushels rye, 120 weight good pork, 60 pounds beef, sufficient cider and molasses, and so much sauce as she needs, also the interest on £26. 13. 4. lawful money, to be paid her yearly. One half by the executor, and other half by son Benjamin. Also use of a horse to ride to meeting and when needed, all the use of such parts of the house as she chooses and all the conveniences during her life. "Sons Benjamin, Jonathan, John, Reuben and Samuel, each of them have received of me their full portions out of my real estate as will appear by their discharges." To son Ebenezer, £40 to be paid him in 3 months by executor, after decease of the widow.

All money, bonds, notes of hand, apparel, live stock, husbandry tools, to be equally divided between sons then surviving, except money, bonds, notes of hand, which shall be divided after wife's death. To daughter Elizabeth and daughter Esther, all that he gave his wife, also to Esther 40 shillings. "I have given to Elizabeth (125) her full portion out of my real estate." To son James Lewis all lands and buildings in Billerica and in Tewksbury, he to be executor.

Inventory filed Nov. 27, 1777, amounts to £317. 13. 2.

He was of medium height, thick set, inclined to corpulency, weight 180-200 pounds, of great humor and joviality of disposition. (Charles Lewis)

He married, June 5, 1728, in Woburn, Elizabeth Jaquith,

daughter of Abraham and Sarah (Jones) Jaquith of Woburn. She was born June 5, 1708 and died Oct. 1, 1777.
Children of Benjamin and Elizabeth:

123. BENJAMIN, b. Sept. 28, 1729, in Woburn.
124. JONATHAN, b. Apr. 10, 1731, in Woburn. (Family Bible, May 10, 1731.)
125. ELIZABETH, b. Jan. 8, 1733, in Woburn; m. Jan. 29, 1760, Jacob Baldwin of Townsend, Mass.
126. JAMES, b. Sept. 25, 1735, in Wilmington.
127. JOHN, b. Aug. 5, 1737, in Wilmington.
128. REUBEN, b. Sept. 25, 1739, in Wilmington.
129. MARY, b. Nov. 13, 1741, in Wilmington; d. June 6, 1749.
130. ESTHER, b. May 28, 1744, in Wilmington; m. Mar. 22, 1764, Abijah Wood.
131. SAMUEL, b. June 10, 1746, in Billerica; m. June 3, 1773, Betty Parker. He was then of Chelmsford.
132. SARAH, b. June 30, 1748, in Billerica; d. June 3, 1749.
133. EBENEZER, b. Dec. 4, 1750, in Billerica. (Church record, Nov. 4.)

74 Joseph Lewis, born in Woburn, Jan. 1, 1707, received 20 shilings by his father's will and was an heir to Obadiah Jenkins, jr. receiving part of his father's share.

He received £10 old tenor from his mother's will made June 13, 1757. She left all her residuary estate equally to his " children by his first wife, Lydia." He and his wife were members of the church at Wilmington in 1742.

He married in Wilmington, Oct. 22, 1731, Lydia Pearson, probably daughter of Deacon Kendall Pearson.

Children of Joseph and Lydia, born in Wilmington:

134. LYDIA, b. July 17, 1731; m. Oct. 15, 1751, Samuel Buck, jr. of Wilmington.
135. JOSEPH, b. Oct. 17, 1733.
136. TIMOTHY, b. May 24, 1736.*

76 John Lewis, born in Woburn, June 9, 1713, was in the army as Sergeant in Capt. Jonathan Butterfield's

---

*There may have been other children and another wife. His mother's will mentions the children of his first wife Lydia, from which it may be inferred that he had another wife in 1757 when the will was made.

company on the expedition against Crown Point in 1756 and was reported lost with Hodges.

His mother's will reads, viz : " If he shall be living and shall continue until time of payment [after her death] £50 old tenor, in case of death, his two children John and Susannah to enjoy it equally."

His wife was a member of the church at Wilmington in 1742, as were Benjamin Lewis (73) and wife, Joseph Lewis (74), and Thomas Pearson and wife (75). John Lewis died before Mar. 14, 1757 when Thomas Pearson was appointed administrator of his estate. Inventory was filed Feb. 22, 1760 amounting to £22. 18. 8. with debts of £29. 18. 2.

He married, first, Susannah, by whom he had John, born May 16, 1739 and died young. He married, second, Mar. 14, 1744-5, in Billerica, Phebe Walker, born May 5, 1723, daughter of Jacob and Hannah Walker of Billerica.

Children of John and Phebe :

137. SUSANNAH, b. Apr. 9, 1746; m. Apr. 7, 1768, Philip Peters.
137a. PHEBE, b. Nov. 14, 1747; probably d. in infancy.
138. JOHN, b. 1748, who chose his Uncle Benjamin (73) as guardian, Dec. 31, 1763, then in his 15th year.

77 John Lewis, born in Lynn, Oct. 16, 1724, was called junior, John (43) being senior. He was a yeoman and resided on the east half of his father's farm which had been given to him by his father, Dec. 8, 1756, a few days after his father's second marriage.

He added to his inheritance and was quite a land owner at the time of his death, which must have occurred but a few days after his father's, for the administrator of his estate was appointed Sept. 29, 1777 and the administrator of John, jr.'s estate on Oct. 7, 1777.

The inventory of his estate filed March 3, 1778, shows real estate valued at £1664. 9. 8.

Nov. 3, 1778 the same committee that divided his father's estate was appointed to appraise John, junior's and after setting off the widow's dower to Mrs Elizabeth Lewis, the remaining two-thirds were divided into 9 parts, the eldest son, John Lewis, receiving a double portion.

The other children were named as follows: Edmund, Hepzibah, Joseph, Elizabeth Ingalls, Martha Ingalls, Nathaniel, Benjamin.*

John was appointed guardian for his brother Benjamin, and Jacob Ingalls was appointed guardian for Joseph and Nathaniel, on March 3, 1778.

John Lewis, junior, married, Nov. 22, 1748, in Lynn, Elizabeth, born July 24, 1728, daughter of Joseph and Elizabeth (Potter) Newhall of Lynn.

Children of John and Elizabeth, born in Lynn :

139. MARTHA, b. Sept. 22, 1749; m. June 4, 1772, Jacob Ingalls, b. in Lynn, July 1, 1747, and d. Jan. 19, 1823, son of Jacob and Mary (Tucker) Ingalls of Lynn.

140. JOHN, b. Oct. 15, 1751.

141. EDMUND, b. Feb. 10, 1754.

142. HEPZEBAH, b. June 10, 1756; m. June 17, 1783, Ephraim Alley, who d. May 2, 1821. She died Feb. 4, 1828. Children: b. in Lynn: (1) Joseph (twin), b. May 6, 1784; (2) Benjamin (twin), b. May 6, 1784, d. May 23, 1821; (3) Lewis, b. Sept. 5, 1786; (4) Nathaniel, b. Mar. 24, 1789; (5) Mehitabel, b. Dec. 14, 1791; (6) Hepsibah, b. July 13, 1794, m. — Cheever; (7) Lydia, b. Mar. 27, 1797, m. — Batchellar.

143. ELIZABETH, b. Nov. 4, 1758; m. Oct. 8, 1778, her cousin Daniel Ingalls, b. 1760, son of Samuel and Lydia (Lewis) Ingalls. He was a cordwainer and lived in Lynn.

144. BENJAMIN, b. Jan. 31, 1761.

145. SARAH, b. Jan. 25, 1763; d. Aug. 12, 1765.

146. JOSEPH, b. Feb. 4, 1765.

147. NATHANIEL, b. 1768.

80 Nathaniel Lewis, born in Lynn, Oct. 30, 1731, was a cordwainer and lived in Lynn where he died May 23, 1767. (g. s.) He married, Sept. 22, 1757, Abigail, daughter of Jonathan and Hannah (Grey) Blaney of Lynn. After his death his widow married, second, Jan. 13, 1774, Capt. Joseph Felt of Salem, and had a daughter Molly Felt, b. June 6, 1779, who married John Lewis (152). Capt. Felt died and she married, third, Nov. 25, 1790, John Watts of Lynn, and died his widow about 1800.

*Essex County Probate, Vol. 354, f. 70-73.

Children of Nathaniel and Abigail, born in Lynn :

147a. A child, d. in infancy.
147b. A child, d. in infancy.
148. JONATHAN BLANEY, b. 1760 ; d. 1780. In the settlement of
the estate of Edmund (39) he drew his father's share. His
uncle John was appointed his guardian, Jan. 4, 1774 and
administration on his estate was granted July 12, 1780 to
his mother, Abigail Felt.

81 Joseph Lewis, was born in Lynn, Mar. 15,
1733-4. By his marriage, he came into possession of the
old Edmund (1) Lewis house, John Ingalls having
bought it from Thomas Lewis (42) on Jan. 26, 1758.
Joseph Lewis was a cordwainer and died· between
Sept. 12, 1799, when he made a deed, and 1805, when his
widow's dower was divided. He married Dec. 19, 1765,
Mrs. Sarah (Alley) Ingalls, widow of John Ingalls who
was drowned in " ye Pines River " Sept. 30, 1762.
Children of Joseph and Sarah, born in Lynn :

149. JAMES, b. 1766.
150. NATHANIEL, b. 1768.
151. WILLIAM.
152. JOHN.

83 Edmund Lewis, born in Lynn, June 20, 1757,
was a private in Capt. Wm. Farrington's Co. which
marched from Lynn to Concord on the alarm of April 19,
1775. He married Nov. 25, 1779, Rebecca, born Sept. 7,
1760, daughter of Robert and Mary (Newhall) Mansfield
of Lynn. He died in 1789, and his wife's brother, Robert
Mansfield, was appointed guardian of his two sons, April
6, 1795. After his death his widow married, second, Nov.
29, 1792, his nephew Benjamin Lewis (144). Her sister
Martha, married John Lewis (140).
Children of Edmund and Rebecca, born in Lynn :

153. JAMES FULLER, b. Feb. 20, 1781.
154. EDMUND, b. Feb. 8, 1784.

85 Amos Lewis, born in Lynn, Sept. 26, 1746, was
a cordwainer and executor of his father's will. He removed to Boston and resided on Sun Court street leading

into North Square. He applied for a license as a retailer
at a town meeting held Aug. 11, 1786. On the 14
March, 1796, he was elected constable for the year and
from 1803 to 1810 inclusive. He died July 23, 1812, aged
66 years (Boston Records). His will made May 29,.
1812; proved Aug. 10, 1812, appoints his wife Lydia,
executrix, and mentions his children : Sally, wife of
Joshua Ellis, cordwainer, of Boston, Amos, John's two
children, Lydia, Betsey, Sukey, Asa, Joshua and Charlotte.
He married Dec. 25, 1768, Lydia Newhall, born in Lynn,
Sept. 11, 1750, died in Boston, May 24, 1837, (Copps
Hill Epitaphs) daughter of Moses and Susanna (Bowden)
Newhall of Lynn.

Children of Amos and Lydia :

155. SALLY, m. in Boston, Dec. 25, 1791, Joshua Ellis. He was a
cordwainer with a dwelling house on North Square, Boston, which was burned in March, 1812. He was b. in Sand-
wich, May 4, 1769 and d. July 29, 1829.
156. AMOS, b. 1771; d. of fits, July 13, 1816, æ. 45 y. (Boston Records)
He was licensed as an auctioneer in Boston in 1805 and 1808.
157. JOHN, b. 1773; d. Apr. 7, 1811, æ. 38 y. (Boston Records) leaving
two children.
158. LYDIA.
159. BETSEY.
160. SUKEY.
161. ASA.
162. JOSHUA.
163. CHARLOTTE.

87 Thomas Lewis, born in Lynn, Nov. 1, 1750,.
was a wharfinger in Boston, and held wharf property near
the foot of Fish, now North street. At that time the
water of the bay or harbor came up to Fish street, and it
was some time later when the improvement was made of
filling in the harbor and building Quincy Hall market. He
lived on Fish street, near North square, at that time a
residential part of the town. He had large interests in
that quarter. After his death there was litigation over
his affairs, and his children did not agree.

In addition to his Boston property he owned a farm, in
the south part of Malden, now Everett. He died May 9,
1813.

Administration on his estate was granted to his wife
Sarah, on July 12, 1813.   Inventory :—

Household furniture,	$618.30
Malden, farming utensils and stock,	217.75
Pew in New Brick Meeting house,	200.00

$1,036.05

Real Estate :

Lewis Long Wharf (so called) in North end of Boston, incumbered by two mortgages, one to Samuel Dexter, and the other to Jno. Merry,	$60,000.00
Lewis Short Wharf,	7,700.00
Mansion house and land,	6,000.00
Brick house at corner, incumbered by a mortgage to Jonathan Merry,	5,000.00
Brick block on land in Fish St. adjoining mansion house, undivided half, incumbered,	7,000.00
One piece of flats, south side Lewis Wharf, incumbered,	13,000.00
Farm in Malden, incumbered,	2,800.00
One-half Lewis & Watts Wharf, incumbered,	4,000.00
Land and house in Hallowell, Me.,	800.00
9 shares in 100 of Lewis & Dexter's Wharf,	963.00

Total,	$107,263.00

List of Debts :

Thomas Lewis, claim,	$57,376.40
Abiel Smith's claim,	19,200.00
John and Samuel Willis, Samuel Spear & Abiel Wood, Jr.,	17,944.50
Isaac Warren,	1,700.00
Dr. John Warren,	150.00
Elijah Nickerson,	867.00
John Lewis,	12,551.11
W. A. Fales, as trustee of Polly Lewis,	1,155.86
Jonathan Merry,	131.40
Others,	519.35

$111,595.62

Thomas Lewis married, April 19, 1770, in Lynn, Sarah Merry, born in Lynn Nov. 19, 1750, daughter of Ralph and Sarah (Noah) Merry. She died in Boston, May 22, 1835. Children of Thomas and Sarah, born in Boston:

164. THOMAS, b. ——, 1771.
165. DAVID, b. June 18, 1776. He was a portrait painter, and d., unm., Dec. 6, 1807.
166. JOHN, b. Aug. 27, 1779. (g. s.)

88 Nathaniel Lewis, born in Lynn, Nov. 14, 1751, was a cordwainer, and removed to Plymouth, Mass. He was lieutenant in Capt. Abraham Hammett's company, which marched on the alarm of April 19, 1775; also a subaltern in Capt. Thos. Mahew's company, in Col. Cotton's regiment, stationed at Roxbury; also lieutenant in the same company and regiment on a muster roll dated Aug. 1, 1775; also in Capt. Lathrop's company, Col. Freeman's regiment, probably in 1778, guarding prisoners belonging to the (British) ship Somerset. The will of Lucy Lewis, his widow, made Dec. 9, 1852, mentions, Mary Elizabeth Edmunds, wife of J. Lincoln Edmunds; Georgianna Shaw, wife of George Shattuck Shaw; and Cornelia and Grace Henshaw, children of her daughter Mary Ann Henshaw, wife of John Henshaw, deceased. John Andrew Henshaw, son of her daughter Mary Ann Henshaw, also received a legacy. To her daughter-in-law, Mary C. Lewis, wife of her son Charles H. Lewis, is given the miniature likeness of her sons, Charles H. and George A. Lewis, which are set in one frame. All the rest of her property to her children, Hannah Lewis, wife of John Lewis; Lucy S. Danforth, wife of Joseph Danforth; Edmund H., Samuel S., Charles H., and George A. Lewis (Middlesex County Probate, file 28,984). She was a pensioner of the United States, at the rate of $106.66 a year.

Nathaniel Lewis married, first, Hannah Drew, born 1752, and died May 29, 1790, in her 38th year (Plymouth Epitaphs), daughter of James and Mary (Churchill) Drew. He married, second, Sept., 1791, Lucy Shaw, born in Plymouth, June 2, 1773, and died in Malden, June 2,

1859, daughter of Ichabod and Priscilla (Atwood) Shaw, of Plymouth. He died Feb. 25, 1818 (Boston records).
Children of Nathaniel and Lucy, the first six born at Plymouth:

167. HANNAH, b. Oct. 12, 1792; m. John Lewis (166).
168. LUCY SHAW, b. Sept. 8, 1794; m., Oct. 22, 1815, Joseph Danforth of Louisville, Ky. Had: (1) Joseph Lewis, b. April 19, 1822; (2) Julia.
169. EDMUND HUTCHINSON, b. Nov. 22, 1796.
170. SAMUEL SHAW, b. June 19, 1799.
170a. INFANT, b. and d. Dec., 1801.
170b. INFANT, b. and d. Feb., 1803.
171. CHARLES HENRY, b. June 26, 1804.
172. MARY ANN, b. July 29, 1806, at Hallowell, Me.
173. GEORGE ATWOOD, b. Mar. 8, 1809; d., unm., at Louisville, Ky.
174. NATHANIEL, b. Aug. 10, 1811; d. June 3, 1813.

93 John Lewis, born in Lynn, Nov. 7, 1724; graduated from Harvard College in 1744, and was a practicing physician. His father called him schoolmaster in a deed dated May 12, 1747. He died Oct. 21, 1754.

In the inventory of his estate, taken Nov. 4, 1754, is listed 1 small fish house, 1-2 shed by brick yard, 1-2 small schooner, 1-4 of a lighter, 1 old horse, 1-2 a Gundalo, 1-2 a boat, 1 pump in brick yard, gun & swords, books valued at £10. 5. 1., dwelling house, barn and several small buildings, 2 acres land. Total, £630. 18. On April 16, 1755, his widow and administratrix, far £150, current lawful silver, conveyed to Zaccheus Norwood, innholder, a dwelling house, barn, and several other buildings in the body of Lynn, and about two acres of land (Essex County Deeds, Vol. 102, f. 56). This was the same property conveyed to him by his father, May 12, 1747, and is now situated on the corner of Boston and North Federal streets, formerly Hart's Lane (Essex County Deeds, Vol. 101, f. 89).

He married, in Woburn, July 2, 1751, Abigail, born Oct. 2, 1729, the daughter of Timothy and Abigail (Wyman) Brooks of Woburn. She removed to Woburn, Oct. 17, 1757, and married, second, Dec. 15, 1757, Samuel Belknap of Woburn, and there she died, Oct. 16, 1761.

Children of John and Abigail, born in Lynn:

175. SAMUEL, b. June 6, 1752.
176. SARAH, b. Nov. 15, 1753; m. Dec. 3, 1772, Thomas Newhall, son of Joseph and Elizabeth (Hodgman) Newhall of Salem and Danvers. She d., and he m., second, Nov. 27, 1806, Sally Hudson.
177. MARY, or POLLY, b. Mar. 6, 1755 (posthumous): m. Dec. 12, 1776, Charles Newhall, son of Allen and Love (Breed) Newhall. She d. Mar. 27, 1780, and he m., second, Mar. 15, 1781, Lois, daughter of James and Lois (Burrill) Newhall of Lynn, and d. Oct. 11, 1817, æ. 65 y. Had: (1) Polly (Martin), b. Oct. 17, 1777; d. Oct. 11, 1800; (2) Charles Newhall, b. Dec. 27, 1779. Child by second marriage: James Newhall, b. Feb. 16, 1782.

94 Thomas Lewis, born in Swansea, Mar. 22, 1726, received by his father's will 19 acres of land and half the house. His sister, Marcy or Mercy (100), left part of her property to his son Thomas, on condition that he provide and care for his parents during life. Jan. 4, 1763, he sold to Benjamin Lewis (103) of Dighton, 44 acres of land in Swansea, lying westerly on land of Abigail Lewis (Bristol County Deeds, Vol. 57, f. 102). He married, Jan. 14, 1753, Hannah Martin, in Swansea.

Children of Thomas and Hannah, born in Swansea:

178. TIMOTHY, b. Oct. 21, 1753; m. Dec. 17, 1778, in Swansea, Elinor White.
179. NATHANIEL, b. Aug. 18, 1755; m. Jan. 9, 1783, in Swansea, Candace Peirce.
180. ELIZABETH, b. July 12, 1757.
181. DANIEL, b. Aug. 1, 1760.
182. THOMAS.

103 Benjamin Lewis was born in Swansea, Dec. 21, 1733(?). He received money from his father for his portion of the estate. He bought, Jan. 4, 1763, 44 acres, 144 rods of land, from Thomas (94) (Bristol County Deeds, Vol. 57, f. 102). He married, Aug. 22, 1754, Ruth Norton. His will, made April 9, 1767, proved April 27, 1767, contains the following bequests: " Being sick," etc. To beloved wife, two cows and all household goods and movables, income and profit of all estate that remains after debts and funeral charges, so long as she remains his widow, to enable her to bring up children. To five sons : James, Aaron, Benjamin, Timothy and Reuben, all real estate equally after their mother's decease, they paying £4 each to their sister Betty. To daughter Betty £20. Appoints wife and brother Joseph Lewis (105), executors.

Feb. 6, 1792, Timothy Lewis of Swansea, yeoman, Aaron Lewis of Rehoboth, yeoman, Reuben Lewis of Rehoboth, cordwainer, Nathan Goff, yeoman, and Betsey, his wife, of Rehoboth, for £30, paid by Benjamin Lewis of Rehoboth, cordwainer, convey all right, title and interest " we have or ought to have in 28 acres 144 rods in Swansea, and buildings thereon, being ye dwelling house whereof our honored father, Benjamin Lewis, deceased, dwelt, and is all the Real Estate our father died seized of, except 12 acres sold by his Executor, bounded as may appear from deed of Thomas Lewis (94) to our father, that is all ye right we had to said house and land by our sd father's Will and as Heirs to ye share that did belong to our brother James Lewis " (Bristol County Deeds, Vol. 72, f. 5).

Children of Benjamin and Ruth, born in Dighton :

183. JAMES, d. between Apr. 9, 1767, and 1792.
184. AARON.
185. BENJAMIN, b. Feb. 16, 1761.
186. TIMOTHY.
187. REUBEN.
188. BETTY, m. at Rehoboth, April 9, 1782, Nathan Goff of Rehoboth.

105 Joseph Lewis was born in Swansea, April 2, 1736. He was a private in Capt. Peleg Peck's company, Col. Thomas Carter's regiment, Aug. 3 to Aug. 9, 1780 ; also named twice for warrant for pay, dated July 7, 1784 ; marched to Tiverton, R. I. ; also again on roll of same date (Mass. Rev. Rolls). He was a cordwainer and yeoman, and married Patience Pearse in 1770. His will, made 16 Nov., 1798, and proved Apr. 2, 1799, contains the following bequests :

I give and bequeath to Patience Lewis, my beloved wife, the use and improvement of all my real estate, except what I shall hereafter mention, until my son Joseph Lewis shall arrive at lawful age, and afterwards the use and improvement of one-half of my Real Estate as long as she remains my widow and no longer. I also give to my wife all my household goods and indoor movables, except what I shall otherwise dispose of . . . as long as she is my widow. Also all the Provisions that I have by me at my death. What I have herein given to my said wife is in lieu of Rights or Thirds. If my wife Patience shall marry then I only give her one feather bed furniture, one riding horse, one cow, one set of copper plate, curtains, and my brass kettle.

Item. I give to my son Joseph Lewis all my Real Estate except what I shall herein otherwise dispose of after the use & Improvement for the term that I have herein disposed of to my wife.

Item. I give to my daughter Sarah Pearse in addition to what I have already given to her, one cow at my death and £20 in 3 years.

Item. I give to my daughter Mary Lewis one cow at lawful age or marriage day and household goods and indoor movables to be equal to what I have given my daughter Sarah and £20 in 6 years, and use of my great chamber while single.

Item. I give to my two daughters Sarah Pearse and Mary Lewis a lot of land equally, a lot I bought of mother Hannah Lewis late of Swansea deceased.

Item. I give to my son Joseph Lewis my saddle and bridle, desk and all my wearing apparel, with all farming tools and utensils. Finally, I give my said wife all my living stock that I haven't given away to enable her to pay the legacies, debts and charges, and lastly constitute and ordain my wife Patience Lewis my sole Executrix.

Children of Joseph and Patience:

189. SARAH, m. May 15, 1784, Preserved Pearse.
190. MARY.
191. JOSEPH.

109 John Lewis, born in Woodbridge, N. J., Oct. 16, 1727 ; died in 1773, in London, Eng.   He married, in 1751, Mary Gifford.
Children of John and Mary :

192. WILLIAM, b. 1752; d. 1774.
193. SAMUEL, b. Sept. 29, 1754, in New York, N. Y.

122 Abner Lewis, born July 25, 1766, in Saybrook, Conn.; married, June 19, 1794, Lois, b. June 5, 1772, daughter of Daniel and Jemima Kelsey of Killingworth, Conn. A family Bible in the possession of Mrs. Daniel Levan of Middleport, N. Y., contains a record of the birth of eleven children, of which six were born at Saybrook, Conn., two at Chester, Conn., two at Homer, N. Y., and the last child at Solon, N. Y.
Children of Abner and Lois :

194. JOHN, b. July 26, 1795.
195. REBECCA, b. Dec. 30, 1796; m. July 3, 1823, Zimri Augur, and
       d. at Mt. Auburn, Ill.
196. LOIS KELSEY, b. June 9, 1798; m., 1825, at Cambria, N. Y.,
       Samuel Boynton Crosby, b. Aug. 30, 1795, at Andover, Mass.,
       son of John and Hannah (Boynton) Crosby. She d. at Cam-
       bria, N. Y., Jan. 16, 1837, and he m., 2d, her sister Achsah.
197. NANCY, b. Feb. 11, 1800; m. Orsemus Braman; d. at Rome,
       Wis.
198. DAN KELSEY, b. Oct. 15, 1801.
199. ELECTRA, b. Aug. 19, 1803; m. Amos Jones; lived at Medina,
       N. Y.
200. ORPHA, b. Feb. 1, 1805; m. Herman Fox; lived at Homer,
       N. Y.
201. WARNER, b. Jan. 15, 1807; m. Achsia Bradley of Solon, N. Y.
202. ACHSAH, b. Oct. 16, 1808; m., 1st, Allen Skinner; m., 2d, Sam-
       uel B. Crosby.
203. RICHARD, b. July 27, 1810.
204. TRUMAN, b. Nov. 15, 1812.

(*To be continued.*)

Chosen to Serve on the Jury of trials

M^r Jn° Browne sen^r   Mr Rich^rd holingworth
Mr Joseph hardy   ffrancis nurce
Mr Sam^{ll} Pickman   Samuell Beadle
Mr Samuell Gardner Junr

voated upon Jn° marston his Request to the towne that the fine Laid on Wm Courtis and Jn° marston by the Select men is Remited

voated vpon henry Reinolds his Request for Land to be Laid out y^t was formerly granted that Its Left to ye select men to make him Satisfaction according to his former grant

[191] June 1673 the whole Sum of the ministers Rate Is	li	s	d
	182	14	2
the whole Sum of the single Country Rate Is	72	01	4
Constable Jn° marston his p^rt of the ministers Rate Is	76	06	06
his part of the Country Rate Is	29	12	02
Constable Christopher Babbage his p^t of the ministers Rate Is	76	15	08
his part of the Country Rate Is	23	07	08
Constable Jn° Pease his pt of ye ministers Rate Is	29	12	00
his part of the Country Rate Is	19	07	08

At a meeting of the Comitee of militia and the select men the 4th da of august 1673

ye Com^t of militia
maj^r hauthorne
Capt Corwin
& Capt Price

we having Received ord^r from the major generall and the majo^r of the Regiment spedily to Repair our fort mend the platforme and fit up the great

*Copied from the original by Martha O. Howes and verified by Sidney Perley, Esq.

(145)

y⁰ Select men
maj' hawthorne
m' Edm Batter
Lev' Joseph Gardner
m' Jn⁰ Corwin
Serg' Jn⁰ Pickring
Bartlemew Gedney

artilary and make such provitian as this Juncture of time Requires doe Conclude all of us, to take our turns. two of us at a time upon Each day to oversee the worke and to Imploy workmen to Cary on the worke as the Cafe Requires and doe desire m' Bartlemew to be asistant with us In his turn In Carieng on of this worke

At a meeting of the select men the 15ᵗʰ day of August being present as In the margent

maj' Hawthorn
m' Batter
Lev' Jos : Gardner
Jn⁰ Pickring
Bartlemew Gedney

Agreed that ther shall be a generall towne meeting warned for the Inhabitants of the towne to meet together on the 22ᵗʰ da of this Instant mo to Chuse an eight man to Joine with the Select men In making the Country Rate 2ly to Chuse a grand Jury : 3ly to Consider about paieng the towns fine to the marshall and to take Care of Sarah Lamberts Child 5ly to make Choice of sum parsons to Run the Line betwen the farmers and the towne

[192] At a me‖e‖ting of the Select men the 18 August 1673 Being present as In the margent

m' Batter
m' Jn⁰ Corwin
Lev' Joseph Gardner
Serj Jn⁰ Pickring
Bartlemew Gedney

wee having made enquiry after the town stock of powder and musket Bullets : doe find att Capt Corwins two Barrills of powder which we have Comited to m' Batters hands to keepe for the towne and of Bullets we find in m' Brown Sen' his hand 1ᶜ : 3/4ᵃ : 0ᵉ : and In Capt Price his hands about 60ᵘ the wholl Is about 2ᶜ : 1ᵃ : 4ᵘ : thes we have put Into Capt Price his Costodie to ‖be‖ kept as town stock and alsoe that yᵉ towne stock may Be Compleat according to Law : wee have provided each of us as foloweth m' Batter one Barill of powder m' Jn⁰ Corwin one Barrill ditto and Capt Price & Leivtenant ‖Jo Gardner‖ Each of them one Barrill of powder and Jn⁰ Pickring and Bartlemew ‖Gidny‖ Each of them 100 li of muskett buletts all which we Engadge to keep for the towns use untill march next : and Shall after Remaine towne Stock provided we abov-

named be paid In Specie according to o^r disbursments :
for s^d powder and Bulletts

Wee Appoint Capt Price Sirueier of the high way from
the meetinghouse to m^r Ruckes to take Care speedily to
Repair thatt Broken way neer m^r Rucks and thatt by Jn°
horns house

We allsoe Appoint deacon prince Surveier of the high
way from timothy hix his hous downe to ould goodman
Rumbals

At a generall towne meeting held the 22th day of August 1673

   ther was Chosen to Serve on the grand Jury

Tho ffuller Senr	Edward fflint
m^r Jn° Ruck	Thomas Roots
ffrancis Scery	John Ingersoll
Sam^{ll} Eaborne Senr	

Capt Georg Corwine Is Chosen Eight man or Comis-
sioner to Joine with the Select men In making the Country
Rate

Voated that the fine of five pound which the towne Is
to pay to the marshall shall be paid out of o^r next
towne Rate.

[193] 22 August 1673
Chosen To Run the Line Betwene the ffarmers and us
Betwen this and the Last of Octob^r next

m^r Jn° Corwin	m^r Wm Brown Junr
Levt Jos Gardner	m^r Benja Browne
Serj^t Jn° Pickring	Bartlemew Gedney
	Anthony needham

Voated that the Select men shall aggre with greansled
as they shall thinck fitt for the keeping Sarah Lamberts
Child : and In ord^r to It they have power to dispose of
Land to the valew of five pounds

vpon the motian of Sum for the ful prosecution of the
Last Law made about horses

It is Left to the Select men and they are desired to
draw up wt they Judg meet In that Case and present It
att the Next towne meeting to be Confirmed by the towne

Nathaniell Beadle Is dismist from being sealer of
Leather : and Ishack williams Is Chosen in his Roome

vppon Jn° higginsons Request for a houselott Next to
goodman Rumbals Its Left to the select men to veiw the
place & make Returne att the Next towne meeting w^{th}er
any or how much may be Conveniently spared for thatt
End

Att a meeting of the Select men 29 August 1673

maj^r hawthorne
m^r Batter
m^r Jn° Corwin
Levt Gardner
Jn Putman
Jn° Pickring
Bartlemew Gedney

Agreed with m^r Batter to pay the marshall five pounds for the towne which
the towne was fined att the County
Court for Neclecting to fitt up the Bridg
neer Wils hill & he Is to have one q^{rtr}
of an acre of Land next to the End of
Jn° neals ground neer old m^r gednys
pafture to be laid out by : m^r Jn° Corwin Left Joseph
Gerdner and Bartlemew Gedney

[194]　At a meeting of ye Select men the 12^{th}day of
7 ^{br} 1673 Being presen As In the margent

Maj^r hawthorne
m^r Batter
Leff^t Jo Gardner
m^r Jn° Corwin
Bartlemew Gedney:

Wee Appoint & Impower peeter Chevers
and Jn° Lander to make up the Draine
for Conveieng the water thorough all
those Lotts thatt were Granted to Severall persons on the Comon below good-
man Rumbals & to warn the severall p^rpriato^rs to Asist In
the doing of the whole In Case any Refuse or Neclect they
above named are to disburse for the doing of It and Each
propriator that doth soe Neclect Is to pay them Againe
the Charge of their part of the worke

Constable Jn° Williams Is D^r

	^{ll}	^s	
ffor his part of ye ministers Rate	71	14	06
ffor his p^{rt} of the Country Rate	22	18	06
for his part of the towne Rate	25	06	01
	119	19	01

The acc^t Above Is Cred^r

pd ‖of‖ m^r Higinsons Rate to m^r Browne	60	00	00
pd the Country tresurer			
pd m^r Epps	06	05	08
pd ffrancis Scerry	06	08	00
pd ffrancis Scerry more	04	00	00

p Alowed him for Charge About ye french
woman   00 08 00
By Abatement of Severall mens Rates that
Could not be gathered 41^s   02 01 00
by a bill to m^r Norrice   10 00 00
by m^r Bartholmew   03 14 05
by feverale men gone out of towne before he
had ye Rate   01 07 06
by tow men wch was In his Rate y^t Nik^o
manning Refd   00 13 00
by his own Rate   00 10 00

                                                   95 07 07
Reft to ballance this Accompt   01 13 00
Res^d of Mr Batters to ball aboves^d acc^{tt}
agreed p Selectmen   00 15 00

we Appoint and Impower m^r Samuell Gardner francis
Nurce and Bartlemew Gedney & Jno Putman to Bound
out the Comon Lieng neer beverly and to Require the
neighb^rs bordering upon It to shew their bounds that y^t
land may be bounded out In ord^r to the Sale of It to pay
m^r Higinsons debts

[195]   At a meeting of the Select men the 24th day of
September 1673 Being present as In marg^t

Maj^r hawthorne
m^r Batter
m^r Jno Corwin
Leift Jo: Gardner
Jno Pickring
Bartlemew Gedney

m^r Batter Leift Gardner m^r Rucke &
m^r Jno Hawthorne are appointed to
finish the high way at mordecays Cut
that It may bee a Suffitient way for Cart
and horse to Goe to the ffort we Alsoe
Joine with them m^r Jno Turner

Jno Gilman Is alowed to Live in the towne a 12 month
upon triall : not to have any privelidg on the towns
Comon Exept to Cut sum timber for making of wheeles

Its ordered thatt W^m dounton shall build up the west
End of the two formost womens seats as he hath begun
the East End of the Said Seats   Nothing being ffuly Con-
cluded In o^r forme^r meeting but Refered for the finishing
untill another time and to be done upon the towne Charg
and Capt Corwine & Ed Batter to pay w^m dounton for his
worke

*m^r Batter is d^r to the towne as ffoloweth
Inp^r By Joseph Grey 5^{ll} & by Joseph

prince 5^{ll}	10	00	00
to paid him by Thomas Beadle	5	00	00
paid him by Jno Land^r	5	00	00
more paid to him by Peeter Chevers	5	00	00
mor by Nath Silsby	5	00	00
more In Lead 1^c 0^{qr} : 7^e	2	00	04
	32	00	04
m^r Batter Is Cred^r for severall disbursments	33	09	07

Rest due to him to Balance 1^{ll} 9^s : 3	01	09	03
*Wm Lord Is debt^r for wine had of m^r Gardner	0	08	00
by m^r Corwin 3^s	0	03	00
By Bartlemew Gedney 2^s 6^d mony	0	02	06
Pr Jno Pickring 1 buſhell of Corne	0	03	00
P^r m^r Batter 5^s 8^d	0	05	08
	1	02	02
to a bill to Nath Ingersoll for 6^{ll}	6	00	00
to a bill to John marston	0	18	00
	8	00	02

Wm Lord Is Cred^r for Ringing nine and 5 a clock bell and sweeping the meeting-howse	8	00	00

[196]   A meeting of the Select men 4th of Novemb^r
1673 Being present as In the margent

Majr Hawthorne
Mr Batter
Mr Jno Corwin
Jno Pickring
Lev^t Jos Gardner
Bartlemew Gedney

Its ord^{r}ed thatt a generall towne meeting be warned for the Inhabitants of
the towne to meet together on Saturday
Come Sevennight being the fifteenth
day of this month at 9 aclock that
those to whoum the towne Is Indebted
may Bring In their Seveverall accompts of the townes debts
In ord^r to making the towne Rate and to ffinish the agreement with Tho Greansla^t about Sarah Lamberts Child

*This account between the asterisks is crossed out in the original.

Agreed that the select men are to meete together the next tuseday after the towne meeting y⁰ 18ᵗʰ of this month to Receive the severall accompts about the fort : Cut & great artilary

Aggreed that the Laiers out which are Chosen By the towne Shall Lay out & Bound that 200 Acres of Land that was fformerly Granted to mʳ Peeters

& alsoe that quarter of an acre that was Grantᵈ to old mʳ Gedney

At a generall towne meeting held the 15 of November 1673

Chosen to Serve on the Jury of Trialls

Nathaniell Putnam   Steven hasket
John Graffton   Thomas Jeggles
John Turner   John Procter
Edward wooland

Voated that the Select men have powʳ to dispose of halfe an acre of Land to Thomas Greenslat provided that he doth Engadge : In Consideration of It to Keep Sarah Lambrts Child till It be eighteen years old : and that the said Land be Security to the towne for the *the* performanc of It.

[197] 15 Novembʳ 1673. Its Voated that mʳ. Edward norice Shal have ten pounds Alowed him out of the towne Rate this year In Consideration of his Keeping Skoole as a Gramer Skoole master the year to begin the 17ᵗʰ day of July Last.

It is voted that It is Left to the Select men to vew that Land which Niclis Bartlet would purchase of the towne & make Returne to the Next towne meeting how much It is or what may be Spareed.

Its alsoe voted that the Same persons that were Chosen the Last towne meeting to Run the Line Betwene the farmers and us : have their power Continued and are desired to Run that Line as soone as they Can Conveniently : not to exeed the first of January next

At a meeting of the select men : 18ᵗʰ day of November 1673 Being pʳsent as In y⁰ marjent

Constable francis Nurce Is D^r to his part of the min-
isters Rate   40^{li}-14^s-00
Major hawthorn
m^r Batter   his part of the town Rate is   18-06-03
m^r Jno Corwin   Thee Above acc^t. Is Cred^r.
Lev^t Jos Gardner   By m^r Browne for ye minis-
Sarj^t Jno Pickring
Jno Putman   ters Rate   31-08-00
Bartlemew Gedney pd to m^r Norrice   04-17-00
                  pd to John Putnam   01-15-00
pd to William fflint   02-04-00
pd to John Smith   00-03-00
pd to Josiah Southrick   01-07-00
more paid to m^r Browne as p^r. Receipt   00-04-08
more paid to m^r Bartlemew 30^s 6^d 01-16-00
more by 7 months abated of the ministers Rate
to the farmers   05-05-10
pd to Lt Gard^r 01-16-00

---

posted the other fid pd   50-19-02

At a meeting of the ffree men 1 day of decemb^r 1673
m^r. Batter was Chosen to serve as a deputy at the Generall Court for the Reft of the year untill the Next Generall
Court of Election

[198]   At a generale towne meeting held the 4th day of
decemb^r 1673

accompt of Debts brought In for the Raising of a towne
Rate

By Captaine Price   02-13-06
by Wm Lord for Ringing the bell 7^{li} 07-00-00
more for Ringing att 5 a clock   00-10-00
p^r Jno Pickring o^r part of marble bridge
to m^r Gidny select men expences   0-18-5
to his seruant work on high wais   0-04-0
diat of Jno Baker w^n about ye fort   0-04-0
to provitions at Raising the metin houfe 17-00-0 } 18-06-05

                                        18-06-5

By deacon prince mending the highway   01-17-00
to m^r Bartlemew for his servis at the Court as a
deputy 56 dayes att 2^s: 6^d p da and ffor whatt he
shal Spend Next Sesion as deputy   9-00-00

ffranc Nurce Crd. on other fide	50-19- 2
p Jno Phelps out of Towne	00-05-00
p Thom Gofey	00-05-00
p John Hebbert	00-01-06
p Ifack Meacham	00-01-06
p his payns about gatheringe Rats & other labour for comig to towne	01-00-00
	52:12:02

Acc^{ted} : 30: (11) 73: Rest to ballance is fixe \
pounds eight shillings w^h the faid Nurce doth \
Ingage to pay to the felect men at or before the }06-08-00 \
last of the 4th moneth next enfuinge as witnes \
his ‖Land‖ the day & yeare above written \
figne

ffranc Nurce   I

[199] 4th day of decemb^r 1673
Voated that the select men that are the next year shall
make a Rate ffor to pay Capt Corwin and others for ther
worke and charg on the ffort In the ffirst building of It
according to the towne order the 18th of 4th mo 1666

vpon Jno Higginsons ‖Junr:s‖ Request to the towne to
sell him a peece of land next to good man Rumbals: It is
voated that Leaving the way four Rod wide att the ffront
and soe wide In the Reare. as the groand will give. Leaving for him ther 3 Rods in Breadth: that he Shal have It
home to good man Rumballs fence he payeng for It aftter
the same Rate or proportion that other men have paid for
their Lots further downwards and that the select men are
to Lay It out

Voated that maj^r hawthorne and m^r Wm Browne Junr
are desired and Impoured to Agre with the doctor for the
Cure of thomas Robinson and alsoe to take Care for his
accomodation In ord^r to It and the towne to pay the
Charge

Its voated that the select men have pow^r to dispose of
Sarah Lamb^{r}t according to their best discretion and allsoe
of her Child: But not to dispose of above 30 Acres of
Land although It be very Rocky

At a meting of the select men and the Comition[r] to make
the Adition to the Country Rate 9th decem 1673 Being 3/4
of a single Country Rate

Constable Christopher bab- [li]   s   d

Maj[r] Hawthorne   badg his pt Is   19 : 01 : 5
Capt Corwin Comtn[r]
m[r] Batter   Constable John marston
Leifft Gardner   his pt is   21 : 19 : 0
Jn[o] putnam   Constable Jn[o] peas his pt is 15 : 12 : 3
Jn[o] pickring
Bartlemew Gedney   ————————
Is In all   56 : 12 : 8

It is agreed that the Layers out of Land shall Lay out
and Bound that Lott which was formerly granted to William bowdish : according to thee townes Grant

[200]   At a meeting of the Select men 26 decemb[r] 1673
being present as In the margent

Nicho maning Is d[r] for the Rates Comit-
major hawthorne   ted to him the yeare In which he was
m[r] Batter   Constable
Leift Gardner
Jn[o] Putman   to his part of the ministers   [li]   s   d
Rate   75 : 09 - 00
to his part of the town Rate   31 : 12 : 11

————————
107 : 01 : 11

the Abov Accompt Is Cred[r]

By M[r] Browne pd him of the ministers Rate 43 : 03 : 01
27 : 1[mo] : 74 : more as p Recept of m[r] brown 04 : 05 : 00
more by a Recept from m[r] Brown payd in
Cafh   10 : 00 : 00

————————
57 - 8 - 01

his pt of towne Rate C[r]
by a bill w[ch] old m[r] Gidny hath excepted 03 - 00 - 00
by a Recept from m[r] bartholmew   01 - 16 - 09
by a Recept from old flint   02 - 07 - 00
by Nath[o] Pickman   00 - 04 - 00
by Jo[s] buffum   00 - 19 - 06
by M[r] Batter his one Rate   01 : 04 : 00
by Capt Curwine his one Rate   03 : 15 · 00

by m^r Browne fen^r by his one Rate   04 : 10 : 00

by Capt Price for his one Rate   00 : 15 : 00

       18 - 11 - 03

by feveral men Allowed & his own Rates   03 - 18 - 00

       22 - 09 - 03

Constable Jno marston his p^t of the towne

Rate Is   49^{11} : 08 : 09

Constable Babbadg his part of the town

Rate Is   39 : 19 : 05

Constable John Pease his part of the towne

Rate   32 : 09 : 06

Its ordered that w^m Smith shall have a bill for 9^s to steven hasket ther being mony due to the towne from him: and this his to have for his Charge In entertaineng Tho Robinson

[201] At A meeting of the Select men 27 decemb^r 1673 being present as In the margent

Maj^r hawthorne
m^r Batter
Leift Gardner
m^r Jno Corwin
Jno Putman
John Pickring
Bartlemew Gedney

John dodge Is dismist from being an overseer of the towne Comon on Riall Side: and Cornel: Baker and Jno Leeche: Richard Leech his son: to Execute the towne ord^{r}s formerly made for the pre-servation of wood and timber on the towne Comon :

we Appoint and Impour Jno Clifford Edward wooland sen^r and Joseph Phipen Senr to take Care for the preser-vation of the wood ‖& timb^r‖ upon Bakers Iland and moltons misery and to seaz upon and bring away Such wood as they shall find Cut by men of marblehead and al-soe to enfforme the select men of any such trespas which they find done att any time by any person of any other towne and to have the wood they soe seaz for their own use and themselvs and all other persons are prohibeted from falling any trees on Said Ilands withowt Licenc from the select men only have Liberty to Cut up the wood already ffalen : and herby ffrancis Colins Is dismist from having any pow^r or Care over thos Islands

vpon Infformation thatt w^m Traske hath within his
ffence : Som of the townes Comon Land we Apoint and
Impour m^r Batter m^r Jno Corwin and Leift Jos Gard^r
speedily to see to It and Cause It to be Laid open to the
Rest of the towne Comon

The Select men having Considered what the Law
directs and Inioines as the select mens duty Concerning
Children and youith that are not brought up In sum honest Caling and taught to Read as the Law directs : we
finding seveall men Neclecting their dutyes In thatt Kind
we ord^r thatt these severall Children & ||youth|| underneath
mentioned shall he placed out as the Law directs to such
persons as are able and will undertake to bring them up In
sum honest Caling and teach them as the Law directs and
thatt this ord^r be Publisht By seting ||it|| up on the meet-
ing ||houf|| that those that are disposed to take such Chil-
dren may Repaire to the Selectmen to treat with them about
It and we alsoe Intend to *To* take the Like Cours with
all such Children and youth as we shall ffind In the Like
Condition : those which wee At present shall take Care
about are As foloweth —John Blith his Children And
alister mackmalys and w^m Smiths : and John Glovers
Children and Tho Greanslads

m^r norris hath a Bill Granted to John Williams for the
10^{li} he hath given him by the towne

[202] the select men being Impoured to take Care of finding out and setling ffor this town all such Land as belongs
to the towne as Common : that Is Claimed of any; and held
by any : beiond what Is their Right according to the
townes Grants we theirfore desire and Impowr ffrancis
nurce Richard Leech and Israell porter and m^r John hawthorne to examin and state ffor the towne what Land they
shall find of the townes In thees Severall Claimes viz
Joshua Raies farm wch was Gra||n||ted to m^r holgrave and
Jacob barnies 50 Acres : on the back side of Leeches hill
and his other granted to barnie and Ingerson determined
with a strait Line from Leeches bounds on the top of the
hill and allsoe Thomas smals ffarme Granted to Capt Cor-
win at Iswich Riv^r and Nath feltous thatt his son Jno
Lives upon : and Nathaniell putmans 50 : Acres Granted

first to w^m Jegles and Capt Corwins farm ||of|| 100 Acres
Granted to Capt traske and that Land of Capt Corwins
that was Avryes Land

wee alsoe Joine with the Above mentioned : Sarjant
John pickring they or any three of them have pow^r fuly to
act In the Premises and make Returne to *to* the select men

m^r Bater Is d^r for the paym^t 6 house for	li s d
Lots pd by each man 5^u	30 : 00 : 0
to Lead used by w^t was bought for ye meetingh^s	02 : 17 : 2
the 1/4 pt added It being mony	00 : 19 : 0
	33 16 - 2
tt Deptt^r to Nech° manning for his Rate towne Rate	01 : 04 : 0
	35 : 00 : 02

m^r Batter Is Cred^r to seveall disbursm^ts for the towne as pr acct	33 : 01 : 00
pd Rich holingworth for wood for the Cut	00 : 06 : 00
more 2 dayes worke of his man	00 : 04 : 00
to Richd addams pd him	00 : 05 : 00
to Ely Giles for a Load of brush	00 : 08 : 00
pd John bulock for 1 days worke	00 : 02 : 06
	34 : 06 : 06

[203] At a meeting of the Select men this 1 day of
January 1673 being present as In the
margent

m^r Batter
Leift Jo Gardner
Sarj^t Jn° Pickring
Bartho Gedney

Bills Granted to pay the
townes debts
pd by m^r batter 6^s_*] tto
Jno marcey work about the fort 02 :
02 : 00   02 : 08 . 00
& pd by m^r Brown 24^s_*] to w^m Curtis w^t
Remaines due to him for worke about
the wheels, the Iron worke 16^s : 11^d   02 : 00 : 11
& pd by m^r batter 4^s 6^d _*] francis Colins for
work about fort & Cut 3^u : 13 : 6^d   03 : 18 : 00

*Entered in the margin.

& pd him by m^r Batter 9^s *] to John be‖c‖k-
  ett for wheels for the Guns 9 : 15 : 0   10 : 04 : 00
& pd him In Iron 14^s *] to manaseth marston for Iron worke 5 : 05 : 06   05 : 19 : 6
to m^r Jno Hawthorne ‖20^s‖ & for w^t he pd
  to bealle × 20   2 : 00 : 0   02 : 00 : 00
to . J^{o}nathan walcut for making wheels
               3 : 00 : 6   03 : 00 : 06
to . John marston for towne & fort bill
               7 : 04 : 0   07 : 04 : 00
to . Tho fflint making wheels for guns
               2 : 01 : 3   02 : 01 : 03
th . Richrd Hide for worke on ye wheels
               0 : 18 : 9   00 : 18 : 09
pr . m^r Jno Corwin   6 : 00 : 0   06 : 00 : 00
pr . Jno Ormes for worke upon the whels
               0 : 17 : 0   00 : 17 : 00
pr . Capt price   2 : 13 : 6   02 : 13 : 06
pr . Goodman Rumball work on ye ffort
               1 : 04 : 0
pd by m^r Batter 6^s *] to nath pickman &
  Company   5 : 15 : 9   06 : 01 : 09
to George Keyser team & men 1 : 16 : 0   01 : 16 : 00
to Nath pease and Company for Lights
               2 : 12 : 0
pd already as on booke 23^s *] to w^m Lord
  w^t Remaines due to him   6 : 18 : 0   08 : 00 : 00
pd of this out of his meetinghouf Rat
  5^{ll} : 11^s : 10^d *] to m^r Gedney sen^r
  for provitions about Raising the
  meetinghous : 17^{ll} : and other Cr.
  12 : 08 : 7 18 ^{ll} 6^s : 5^d 18 : 06 : 05
to Sarj^t pickring   05 : 01 : 06   05 : 00 ; 00
pd by m^r Bater 6^s *] Ito w^t Remaines due
  to Jonath Ager   00 : 06 : 6   00 : 06 : 06
pd by Jno Corwin 6^s *] to Antony needham . for : Carting : fort 01 : 10 : 0   01 : 16 : 00
to bill for payment for 174 days worke In
  Conft babadge his ward 2^s pd
              17 : 01 : 00   17 : 01 : 00

*Entered in the margin.

to 184 days worke done In Jn° mastons
marstons ward at 2ˢ p d : on fort
                  19 : 13 : 06   19 : 13 : 06
& 2ˢ alowed mʳ Gidney ₊] to deacon prince
for his waies   01 : 15 : 00   01 : 17 : 00
pd In Corne by mʳ battʳs 6ˢ ₊] pd wᵐ
Smith & ben Afhby for sawing
                  00 : 18 : 00   00 : 18 : 00
to wᵐ traske for 4 Inch plancke 00 : 16 : 00   00 : 16 : 00
paid already by Jn° Higginson 3¹¹ : 8ˢ : 0ᵈ
₊] for Laieng the platform In the fort
& the plank and worke & Speekes
                  16 : 11 : 02   19 : 19 : 02
to mʳ Browne for Iron & nailes 01 : 19 : 05   01 : 19 : 05
for Riched Richards for Lightering
01 : 10 : 00   01 : 10 : 00
to 37 dayes worke In John peas his ward
and 3 teames 17ˢ 6ᵈ 04 : 11 : 06   04 : 11 : 06
to Capt Corwine 4¹¹ 04 : 00 : 00   04 : 00 : 00
to mʳ Phipen 30ˢ 6ᵈ 01 : 10 : 06   01 : 10 : 06
to ffrancis Scery for keeping Sarah Lamberts child 05 : 00 : 00   05 : 00 : 00
to mʳ Gedney Senʳ for yᵉ select mens
||Expenses|| 01 : 00 : 04   01 : 00 : 04
more 56 dais work. In babadg his ward
at 2ˢ p day 05 : 12 : 00   05 : 12 : 00
Caried to the other sid

[204] att a meeting of the select men the 16 day of
January 1673 being present as In the margent
                  Its ordʳed that mʳ Norice shall have a
majoʳ hauthorne bill of teen pounds to John Williams we
mʳ Batter
Leift Gardner ffinding ther is mony of the townes In
mʳ John Corwin his hands
John Pickring
Bartlemew Gedney Is ordered that Bartlemew Gedney Is
                  Appointed to Recon with Constable Inger-
son and ordʳ him Speedily to make payment of what Is
due to the towne from him
    Its agreed that mʳ phipen Senʳ shal have a Bill to the
Constable for 18ˢ : 9ᵈ : pᵗˢ due to him ffrom the towne

*Entered in the margin.

Its Agreed that m^r Ruck shall be abated ten shilings out of this ministers Rate

23 January 1673 Constable John marston his part of the meeting house Rate Commited to him to Gather is 164^{li}: 05^s: 00

Constable Christoph^r Babbadge his pt of the meting hous Rate Comited to him to Colect is 150 : 00 : 00

Constable John pease his part of the meetinghouse Rate Comitted to him Is 155 : 07 : 00

Att a meeting of the Select men the 30th day of January 1673 being present as In the margent

maj^r hawthorne
m^r Batter
m^r John Corwin
Leift Jo^s Gardner
John Pickring

Licence Is Granted to Nathaniell Ingersoll Senr to sell Beere and Sider by Retaile for one year ensuing

Granted to ffrancis scery for work at ye fort	00 : 13 : 00
pd Leift Gardner 5^l: 10: 10^d by Jacob barnie & 20^s 10^d pllp Cromwell and bill to the Constable 2^s 2^d	06 : 14 : 00
for 27 & 1-2 days worke In John marstons ward and 1 teame	02 : 15 : 00
to the widow suthrick 5^s for her team	
22 : 4mo : 74 Allowd Jno Normon by a bill to Jno marfton for planks for ye ffort wch is In ye lew of mony 20^{ts}	01 : 00: 00

[205] At A meeting of the select men the 24th day of february 1673 being present as In the margent

maj^r hawthorne
m^r Batter
m^r Jos: Gardner
m^r Jno Corwin
Bartlemew Gedney

wee Abate 5^s out of deacon prince his ministers Rate for the year past

It is Agreed that two of peeter Joyes Children Shall Bee placed out at Servis & we being Enformed that farmer porter Senr Is wiling to tak the boy and Josep porter Is wiling to take the Girle as an Aprentic Its theirfore Agreed that they shal be soe placed to the Above mentioned parties

(*To be continued.*)

INSCRIPTIONS FROM THE OLD BURYING GROUND AT SAWYER'S HILL, NEWBURYPORT, MASS.

COPIED AND ANNOTATED BY MRS. ANNA BARTLETT BOYNTON, OF WEST NEWBURY.

(*Continued from Vol. XLIII. page 32.*)

Here lyes buried the body of Mr John Huse who died August ye 3th 1736 & in the 42^d year of his age
Son of Abel and Judith (Emery) Huse.

Here lyes buried the body of Mrs Sarah Huse the wife of Mr John Huse who died May ye 2nd 1730 & in ye 33rd year of her age.
Daughter of Jacob and Sarah (Kent) Tappan; m. Oct. 25, 1716.

Mr. Ebenezer Huse who died July 31st 1792 in the 97th year of his age.
Son of Thomas and Hannah —— Huse, born Jan. 16, 1696.

John Huse son of Mr John & Sarah Huse who died Nouember the 25, 1736 aged 8 months

Here lyes buried the body of John Huse ye son of Mr John and Mrs Sarah Huse who died July ye 9th 1733 in ye first year of his age with his brother who died August the 17th 1734 being 6 days old

William Huse son to Mr William & Mrs Mary Huse he died May ye 13 ——

In memory of Mrs Sarah Huse consort of Mr Thomas Huse who died April 23^d 1777 aged 31 years
Thomas Huse m. Sarah Moody, Jan. 2, 1777.

Here lies buried the body of Mrs Elizabeth Huse the wife of Mr Abel Huse Junr who died March ye 7, 1735 & in ye 25 year of her age
Elizabeth (Little), wife of Abel Huse; m. April 29, 1729.

Here lyes buried ye body of Elizabeth Huse who died Nouember ye 3ʳᵈ in 1734, aged 25 year.

Joseph N. Jackman, died Nov. 12, 1851, aged 74 yrs. & 6 mos.

Mary M. wife of Joseph Jackman, died June 24, 1874 aged 85 yrs. & 5 mos.

Hannah the wife of Iohn Iones who decd yᵉ 4 mo 30 day, 1710.

John Jones m. Hannah Hoege of Amesbury (1st wife), April 27, 1706.

In memory of Caleb Kimball who died Jan. 1, 1795, Æt. 88.

Son of Caleb and Lucy (Edwards).

Sarah, wife of Caleb Kimball who died April 16, 1793, Æt. 83.

Daughter of Abel Huse and Judith (Emery).

Hannah wife of Capt. Caleb Kimball died Dec. 2ⁿᵈ 1820, aged 77 yrˢ

Caleb Kimball, jr. m. Hannah Noyes, Nov. 25, 1766.

Abel Kimball, died July 4ᵗʰ 1787, aged 13 yrˢ

Judith Kimball died March 17ᵗʰ 1787, aged 1 yʳ

Sacred to the memory of Mr. Leonard W. Kimball who died Sept. 16, 1828, aged 28 years.

Thomas N. Kimball died Oct. 5ᵗʰ 1833, aged 25 yrˢ

Here lyes buried the body of Mʳ Iohn Knight who died April the 6 1723 & in the 26 year of his age.

Son of Joseph and Deborah (Coffin) Knight.

Here lyes interred body of Mrs. Iudith Huse who was formerly ye wife of Mʳ John Knight & afterwards the wife of Mʳ Daniel Emery deceased the wife of Mʳ Stephen Huse September yᵉ 5, 1770 & in the 72ⁿᵈ year of her age.

Judith Greenleaf, dau. of Tristram and Margaret (Piper), b. Sept. 28, 1698; m. (1) John Knight, Jan. 9, 1721; (2) Daniel Emery, Nov. 29, 1723; (3) Stephen Huse, June 30, 1727.

In memory of Mrs Judith Lewis wife of Mr Frederick Lewis died Octr 28th 1775, in ye 28th year of her age.

Frederick Lewis of Deerfield, N. H., m. Judith, dau. of Moses and Judith (Rogers) Bartlett in South Hampton, N. H., Dec. 24, 1774. He m. (2) Sarah, dau. of Benjamin Bartlett, Sept. 22, 1777.

Here lyes buried the body of Mrs Mary Little the wife of Capt Joseph Little who died Nouember 28, 1725 in the 69th year of her age.

Mary (Coffin) Little, dau. of Tristram and Judith (Greenleaf) (Somerby) Coffin.

Here lyes buried the body of Mrs Edna Little the wife of Mr Gorge Little who died October ye 15 1732 & in the 48 year of hr age.

Daughter of Capt. Thomas and Sarah (Northend) Hale; 1st wife of George Little (son of Joseph and grandson of George).

In memory of Mary Relict of Dea^{n} Stephen Little, who died Octr 4th 1798 in the 75th year of her age.

Sacred to the memory of Mehetable Little wife of Ezekiel Little Esq. of Boston and daughter of Saml & Ruth Emery, she died June 26, 1821, Æt. 57.

Son of Moses and Lydia (Coffin) Little. Married Sarah dau. of Sergt. Stephen and Deborah Jaques, Feb. 12, 1716.

Erected in memory of Mr Moses Little of Newbury and Mrs Sarah his wife. Mr Mofes Little departed this life Octr 17th 1780, in the 90th year of his age.

Under this Monument is deposited what was Mortal of Mrs. Sarah Little Confort of Mr Mofes Little, who departed this life in the 66th year of her age on the 12th of Novr in the year of our Lord 1763.

Erected in memory of Mifs Anna Little Daught of Col^{n} Moses & Mrs Abigail Little, who died Augt 14th 1775 in the 19th year of her age.

In memory of Josiah Little Esq. who died Decr 26th 1830, aged 83 yr^{s} 10 mo^{s}.

Col. Josiah Little, son of Col. Moses Little and Abigail, dau. of Joshua Bailey (sister of Gen. Jacob Bailey) born Feb. 16, 1747. Married, Nov. 23, 1770, Sarah, dau. of Edward Toppan of Newbury. Representative in General Court nearly 30 years.

In memory of Mrs. Sarah Little wife of Josiah Little, Esq. who departed this life Oct. 11ᵗʰ 1823, aged 75.

Moses, son of Josiah & Sarah Little died March 7ᵗʰ 1802, aged 27 years.

Sally Little died Dec. 26, 1777, aged 11 mo.

Judith Toppan Little died April 16, 1791.
Daughters of Josiah and Sarah Little.

Moses Little Esq, died April 28, 1857, aged 90 yrs. 3 mos. 8 days. He held the commission of Justice of the Peace 50 years ; he represented the Town of Newbury in the Legislature of Mass. 19 years, also a member of Mass. Convention for altering her constitution, Deacon, of the Belleville Church 36 years.
Youngest son of Col. Moses and Abigail (Bailey) Little, born Jan. 20, 1767; m. Aug. 6, 1786, Elizabeth, dau. of Shubael and Deborah (Moody) Dummer.

Elizabeth Dummer wife of Moses Little Esq. born Sept. 13, 1763, died Nov. 21, 1840, aged 77.

William D. son of Moses & Elizabeth Little, died January 21, 1868, aged 79. An honest, upright man.
William Dummer Little, son Moses and Elizabeth (Dummer) Little.

Caroline G. wife of Wm. D. Little, died July 29, 1873, aged 73.
Daughter of Thomas Bell and Mary (Gardner) Stevens.

Abigail daughter of Moses & Elizabeth Little, died May 14, 1871, aged 84 yrs. 7 mos.

Elizabeth D. daughter of George & Jane Little, born at Littleton, N. H. Sept. 30, 1827, died Dec. 19, 1852, aged 25 yrs.

Albert, youngest son of Moses & Elizabeth Little, born Aug. 14, 1800, died Dec. 6, 1852, aged 52 yrs. 84 ds.

Erected in memory of Jacob Little Esq. who died Feb. 22, 1820, aged 57 yʳˢ. An eminent merchant.
Youngest son of Deacon Stephen and Judith (Bailey) Little. Married Hannah, daughter Moses and Hannah Sawyer, Sept. 28, 1786.

Also, Joseph and Benjamin, infants, who died Nov. 19, 1789.

William, who died on his passage from Savannah to Boston, July 21, 1816, aged 16 y^{rs}

Alfred, who died in the City of New York, Feb. 8, 1819, aged 16 y^{rs}

Children of Jacob and Hannah Little.

Erected in memory of Hannah wife of Jacob Little, daughter of Moses & Hannah Sawyer, died Jan. 6, 1850, in the 86 yr. of her age.

Erected in memory of Hannah Little daughter of Jacob Little, Esq. and Hannah, his wife, who was born May 19, 1792, and died Oct. 16, 1876, in the 85th year of her age. She was a woman of great firmness powerful mind and untiring energy.

In memory of Judith daughter of Jacob & Hannah Little who died March 26 1842 in her 47th year

Caroline wife of John Phillips daughter of Jacob & Hannah Little died June 8, 1853, aged 46.

Harriet daughter of Jacob & Hannah Little died Feb. 4, 1847, aged 38.

Mich^L Little   [Small boulder.]

In memory of Michael Little Esq. who died March 16th 1830 ; aged 59 yr^s

Eldest son of Col. Josiah and Sarah (Toppan) Little; gr. Dartmouth, 1792; m. (1) Sarah Stover, (2) Elizabeth Ricker.

The family tomb of Joshua Little, Esqr erected 1818, in memory of his ancestors and of his wife and daughter who are deposited within.   George Little came from London in England, to Newbury, A. D. 1640, 5 years after its settlement: and lived until September 22, 1691.   Moses his son died March 8, 1691, Æt. 34.   Moses Little, son of s^d Moses died Oct 19th 1780 Æt. 90.   Judith, wife of Stephen Little, died Aug. 9, 1764. Æt. 41.   Dea^n Stephen Little, son of s^d Moses died Aug. 3, 1793. Æt. 74. Eunice, daughter of Joshua & Eunice Little, died Decr 9 ^{h} 1800, Æt. 16.   Eunice, wife of Joshua Little Esqr died Nov^r

9th 1816, Æt. 72. Joshua Little, Esqr died June 25th 1836: Æt. 98. Joshua L. son of Joshua L. & E. W. Newhall, died Sept. 5, 1836; Æt. 3 years.

In memory of Col. Moses Little who died May 27, 1798, aged 74 years.

Born May 8, 1724, son of Moses and Sarah (Jaques). King's Surveyor. Grantee of Littleton, N. H., 1750, and of the larger part of Androscoggin Co., Maine, 1768. Served at Bunker Hill as Col. and in N. Y. campaign till 1777. Declined naval command in 1779. He lost his speech in 1781 by a stroke of paralysis.

In memory of Mrs. Elizabeth Wigglesworth wife of Mr. William Wigglesworth, & daughter of Col. Moſes Little, who died Feby 22nd 1792 in the 38th year of her age.

Elizabeth Little m. Lieut. William Wigglesworth, March 20, 1786.

In memory of Mrs Abigail Little consort of the late Col. Moses Little who died Feb. 6, 1815, aged 91 years.

Abigail (Bailey), daughter of Joshua Bailey, twin sister of Mrs. Judith Little, m. June 5, 1743.

Here lies buried the body of Mr Beniamin Long Junr who departed this life Jenry 2nd 1760 aged 38 years.

Truman the son of Mr. Truman & Judea March who died October the first 1736 eged 6 years.

Russell son of J. P. & M. S. Marquand, born July 27, 1869, died July 13, 1894.

Russell Marquand son of Herbert Dudley & Margaret Marquand Hale, born Apr. 13, 1895, died Sept. 13, 1895.

Margaret Searle wife of John Phillips Marquand, born Apr. 28, 1828, died Feb. 18, 1898.

Daughter of Samuel and Margaret (Searles) Curson.

Joseph son of J. P. & M. S. Marquand, born Nov. 26, 1861, died Oct. 31, 1899.

John P. Marquand born Oct. 16, 1831, died June 3, 1900.

Son of Joseph and Sarah Winslow (Tyng) Marquand.

Here lyes the body of Abigail Merrill the wife of Deacon Abraham Merrill who died August y° 12 1712 aged yeres 70

Abigail Webster, daughter of John and Mary (Shatswell) Webster of Ipswich, m. Jan. 18, 1661, Abraham Merrill.

heyr ly buryed daborah Merril the wife of Iohn Merril died Ianuary the 2ᵗʰ 1727 in the 49 year

Deborah (Haseltine) 1st wife of John Merrill, m. in 1708.

Heyr ly buryed farah Merril ———

Daughter of John and Deborah, b. Oct. 22, 1721; d. Nov. 25, 1727.

Sarah Merrill died Feb. 6, 1806 Æ 88. Widow of Enoch Merrill.

Enoch Merrill died Dec. 28, 1812, Æt. 58. Also Joseph Merrill died Oct. 13, 1811 Æt. 23

Temperance relict of Enoch Merrill died June 11, 1842; aged 85 yrs.

Daughter of Stephen and Judith (Bailey) Little, m. Enoch Merrill jr. 1778.

Judith daughter of Enoch & Temperance Merrill, died May 1, 1805 Æ. 19.

Temperance daughter of Enoch & Temperance Merrill, died July 16, 1805 Æt. 18.

Elizabeth daughter of Enoch and Temperance Merrill died July 14, 1815, Æt. 19.

Mary daughter of Enoch and Temperance Merrill died Nov. 28, 1822; aged 44 yrs.

In memory of Paul Merrill, who died Jan. 2ᵈ 1813 in the 31ˢᵗ year of his age.

Son of Henry and Rebekah (Moulton) Merrill, b. Jan. 25, 1782.

In memory of Miss Abigail Merrill who died July 24, 1813 aged 37 years.

Daughter of Henry and Rebekah (Moulton) Merrill.

In memory of Rebekah Merrill, wife of Henry Merrill, who died Decʳ 10, 1823 aged 73.

Daughter of Samuel Moulton, bapt. Jan. 20, 1750-1.

Deacon Henry Merrill died April 3, 1844 ; aged 92.
Henry, son of Henry and Priscilla Merrill, bapt. Oct. 6, 1751.

In memory of Hannah [2nd] wife of Henry Merrill who died Dec. 30, 1836; aged 73

In memory of William son of Henry & Rebecca Merrill, who died Nov. 12, 1811, aged 17 years.

Capt. Samuel Merrill born March 1, 1786, died November 5, 1882.

Mary wife of Samuel Merrill and daughter of Samuel Chase died Jan. 2, 1815 ; aged 56 yrs & 8 mos.

John Merrill M. D. son of Samuel & Mary Merrill, died March 4, 1851, aged 29 yrs. 8 mos.

In memory of Rebekah daughter of Henry & Rebecca Merrill, who died Nov. 22, 1811, aged 20 years.

Hannah wife of Samuel Merrill died April 22, 1879, aged 76 yrs 11 mos. 28 days.

Enoch Merrill born Jan. 1783, died May 1855.
Son of Enoch Merrill and Temperance (Little), m. June 24, 1822.

Mary wife of Enoch Merrill born Jan. 1783, died May 1856.
Daughter of Benjamin Morse of Bradford.

Benjamin son of Enoch & Mary Merrill born Jan. 1822 died Feb. 1863.

Olive Morse daughter of Elbridge and Abigail E. Merrill died Aug. 18, 1838, aged 7 weeks.

Elbridge Warren son of Elbridge & Abigail E. Merrill died Sept. 2, 1845, aged 6 yrs.

Hannah Merrill died May 28, 1865, aged 22 yrs. She was for several years superintendent of the North End Mission School " and her assiduous labors have been greatly blest in the conversion of many children. Visiting the abodes of want and suffering she did not her alms to be seen of men but clothed the naked fed the hungry and pointed the sinner to the Lamb."

Here lyes buried the body of Mrs Abigail the wife of Mr William Molton who died Iuly ye 24 1723 aged 62 years

Abigail Webster, b. Mar. 16, 1662, daughter of John Webster and Ann (Batt). Married May 21, 1685, William Moulton.

Here lyes buried the body of Jonath n Moulton who [ ] January th[ ] 1718 & in the [ ]ear of his age.

Son of William and Abigail (Webster) Moulton, born Sept. 7, 1692; m. Rebecca Chase.

In memory of Mr. Joseph Moulton who died Augft 24 1795 in the 72 year of his age.

Grandson of William and Abigail (Webster) Moulton. Probably son of Joseph and Mary (Noyes) Moulton, b. Aug. 4, 1724. A goldsmith of Newburyport.

Here lyes the body of Hannah Mor ison who died Iune 18 1716 in the 22nd year of her age

Daughter of Daniel and Hannah Morrison, b. Jan. 27, 1696.

Here lyes buried the body of Dea^c: Caleb Moody who died May 2nd 1741 in the 75th year of his age.

Son of Caleb and Judith (Bradbury), his 2d wife. Born Sept. 9, 1666. Imprisoned for resisting Andros in 1688.

Here lies buried the body of Mrs. Ruth the wife of Deac : Caleb Moody who died Iune 26th 1748 in the 79th year of her age.

Daughter of Benjamin and Ruth (Sawyer) Morse, b. Dec. 8, 1669; m. Caleb Moody, Dec. 9, 1690.

In memory of Mr Caleb Moody who departed this life in ye 17th 1776 ye 71st year of his age.

Son of Caleb and Ruth (Morse) Moody; b. Nov. 4, 1705; m. Elizabeth Emery, June 15, 1727.

Here lies buried the body of Mrs Elizabeth the wife of Mr Caleb Moody who departed this life Sept 14th 1754 in the 47th year of her age.

Daughter of Ens. Stephen and Ruth (Jacques), Emery b. Feb. 2, 1708.

Elizabeth the daughter of Mr Caleb and Elizabeth Moody died Octr 6 1749 aged in ye 15^h year.

Elisabeth the daughter of Mr Caleb and Abigail Moody who died June 1st 1760 aged 3 years old.

Here lies buried the body of Mr Stephen Moody who departed this life April ye 8^h 1768 Ætat 23 years.

Son of Caleb and Elizabeth (Emery) Moody, baptised April 7, 1745.

In memory of Lieut. Caleb Moody who died July 24th 1795 Æt. 61.

Son of Caleb and Elizabeth Moody.

In memory of Mrs Dorothy Moody, who died March 18th 1826. Aged 89. She was the mother of 15 children of whom she buried 11, and in repeated afflictions, submitted without a murmur to the dispensations of Heaven. She was a professed member of the Church of Christ over 40 years, & uniformly exemplified her profession by her walk in life. She lived greatly beloved and esteemed and died much lamented.

Dorothy Sargent of W. Amesbury, pub. to Caleb Moody, Nov. 9, 1754.

Joshua Moody who died Nov. 29th 1781 Aet. 22.

Joseph Moody who died at St. Pierre, Martinico, May 7th 1805. Aet. 24.

In memory of Moses S. Moody Esq. who died January 1st 1817 aged 60 years.

Caleb Moody who died Jany 27th 1784 Aet. 19.

The four preceding were sons of Caleb and Dorothy (Sargent) Moody.

In memory of Mrs. Susannah Moody, wife of Mr. Moses S. Moody who died Jany 21st 1784 Aet. 18.

In memory of Ruth relict of Moses S. Moody, Esq. who died Feb. 17, 1839 aged 73.

Daughter of Joshua Ordway, bapt. Nov. 17, 1765.

In memory of Mrs. Sarah Moody wife of Mr. Moses S. Moody who died Dec. 13, 1789 Aet. 25.

Charles Moody died Feb. 21, 1875 aged 84 yrs.

Samuel Moody died June 15th 1801 Æt. 39.
Son of Caleb and Dorothy (Sargent) Moody. Baptised June 17, 1762.

Mrs. Hannah Moody, relict of Mr. Samuel Moody, died Aug. 12, 1847, aged 81.
Samuel Moody, jr. m. Hannah Emery, April 24, 1790.

Here lies buried the body of Mrs. Mary Morss the wife of Mr Philip Morss who died December ye 29 1727 in the 83 of her Age.
Daughter of Ephraim and Sarah Brown of Salisbury, m. in 1707, Philip, son of Benj. and Ruth (Sawyer) Morss.

Here lies buried the body of Mr Benjamin Morss who died Oct 26 in 1743 in ye 76h year of his age.
Son of Benjamin and Ruth (Sawyer) Morse, m. in 1692, Susanna daughter of Abel and Priscilla (Chase) Merrill.

Here lieth buried the body of Mrs Susannah the wife of Mr Benjamin Morss who died Octobar 23 1733 aged 60 years.
Daughter of Abel and Priscilla (Chase) Merrill, m. Benjamin Morse, Jan. 28, 1692.

Here lyes buried the body of Mr Anthony Morss who died February the 7th 1729 & in the 40 forst year of his age.
Son of Joshua and Hannah (Kimball) Morse; m. Judith, daughter of Caleb and Judith (Bradbury) Moody, pub. April, 1710.

Ruth Morss the daughter of Anthony & Iude Morss who died December ye 10th 1728 being 8 weeks old.

Here lies buried the body of Mr Stephen Mors died March 6 1740 in ye 38 year of his age.
Deacon Stephen, son of Anthony and Sarah (Pike) Morse, m. Elizabeth Worth in 1725.

Here lies buried the body of Elisabeth ye wife of Samuel Mors who died Apral ye 20th 1723 & in ye 32nd year of her age.
Samuel Morse, b. Dec. 7, 1688; m. Elizabeth March, Feb. 1713.

Here lyes buried the body of Mrt Bethiah Morss the wife of Samuel Morss who died Iune ye 13 1726 in the 29th year of her age.
Bethiah Dalton m. Samuel Morse, in Sept. 1725.

Here lyes buried the body of Mr Joshua Mors who departed this life April 12 1756 in the 43 year of his age
Son of Anthony and Judith (Moody), m. Prudence Ordway, Aug. 19, 1741.

Here lies interrd Mr Isaac Morss who departed this life Sept. ye 27th 1754 in the 40th year of his age
Son of Wm. and Sarah (Merrill) Morse, m. Jane (Lunt) in 1739.

In memory of Humphrey Morse died Oct. 12, 1816, aged 72
Born Dec. 11, 1743, m. Elizabeth Lunt.

In memory of Mrs. Elisabeth Morse, wife of Humphrey Morse, died Nov. 4, 1806, aged 67

In memory of Mr. David Morse who died Aug. 19 1801 in the 55 year of his age.
Son of Moses and Anne Morse, m. Abigail Bailey, d. of Dea. Edmund and Abigail (Bartlet) Bailey.

In memory of Abigail wife of David Morfe who died May 22, 1802. In the 54 year of her age.
Daughter of Edmund Bayley.

Joseph Morse died July 15, 1851 aged 73.
Joseph Morse, b. Apr. 30, 1778, m. Olive, daughter of Benjamin Morse of Bradford.

Mrs. Olive wife of Joseph Morse died May 31, 1838; aged 52.

Moses Atkinson died Feb. 2, 1816 aged 20 months. Edwin died Aug. 21, 1816, aged 1 day. Children of Mr. Joseph & Mrs. Olive Morse.

Charles son of Mr. Joseph & Mrs. Olive Morse died Nov. 10, 1810, aged 9 months

In memory of Humphrey Morse who was born April 6 1808 died April 4, 1836; aged 28. He graduated at Amherst College Aug. 25, 1834. At his death he was a member of the Theological Seminary at Andover preparing to become a missionary to the heathen.
Son of Joseph and Olive Morse.

Joseph W. Morse died March 24, 1849, aged 28.

Walter Scott infant son of Joseph W. & Judith E. Morse, died Aug. 1, 1849, aged 7 mos.

Mary Olive Morse wife of David Jackman, died March 16, 1845, aged 33

Born Sept. 24, 1811, daughter of Joseph and Olive Morse.

In memory of Mr. Henry Mowatt who died Oct. 10, 1840, aged 64.

Walter youngest son of Joshua L. & Elizabeth W. Newhall, died January 14, 1872, aged 20 yrs.

Joshua Little Newhall died Jan. 9, 1874, aged 65 yr. 7 mos. 21 days.

Elizabeth wife of Joshua L. Newhall died Sept. 10, 1863, aged 54 yrs.

Joshua L. son of Joshua L. & Elizabeth W. Newhall, died July 15, 1865, aged 23 yrs.

To the dear memory of my husband Preston son of Joshua L. & Elizabeth W. Newhall, died April 22, 1867, aged 30 yrs.

Little Preston only child of Preston & Mary Newhall born Aug. 8, 1867, died Sept. 20, 1870.

In memory of Mrs Lucy Noble, the amiable consort of the Revd Oliver Noble of Newbury: Who departed this life May 28th 1781. In the 46th year of her age.

Sacred to the memory of Mrs. Sarah Noyes, relict of Mr. Nathaniel Noyes who died Dec. 14th AD. 1827. aged 48.

In memory of Rebecca Noyes daughter of Cutting Noyes, who died Febr^y 24th 1794; Æt. 21.

In memory of William son of Cutting Noyes who died Aug. 29, 1797. Æt 22.

Here lyes buried the body of Sargent Iohn Ordway who died February ye 2 1718 in the 60 year of his age

Son of James, the immigrant. Born Nov. 17, 1758, m. Hannah, daughter of Richard and Hannah (Emery) Bartlett, Dec. 28, 1706.

Here [lies] the [body of] Hann[ah Ordway] who [departed this life] the 24 [in the 30ᵗʰ year of her age]

Here lyes buried the body of Mrˢ Hannah the wife of Mr Iohn Ordway died Octʳ 2ⁿᵈ 1741 in ye 58 year of her age

Here lyes buried ye body of Iohn ye son of Mʳ Iohn Ordway & Mʳˢ Hannah who died Oct. yᵉ 13ᵗʰ 173[ ] in year

Hear lyes buried the body of Hannah Ordway the daugh. of Mʳ Iohn Ordway and Hannah his wife who died August the 4 1729 in the 22 year of hur age

Miss Sarah Ordway died April 17, 1820, æt. 83.

Marcey Ordway dau——— Iohn & Mrs Han——— his wife who died Oct 1735 i— ye 11 year of her age

Richard Ordway ye son of Mʳ Iohn Ordaw y & Mᴿˢ Hannah died Octob yᵉ 6 1735 in the 9 year of his age

Miss Judith Ordway died Feb. 10, 1821, Æt. 44.
Daughter of David and Lois Ordway.

Mr. David Ordway died Sept. 26, 1826, Æt. 81.
Son of Nathaniel and Sarah (Hale) Ordway, bapt. Sept. 22, 1745.

Mrs. Lois wife of Mr. David Ordway died June 2, 1818 Æt. 75.

Rebecca daughter of Mr. David & Mrs. Lois Ordway died May 25, 1814 Æt. 28.

Mrs. Mary wife of Mr. David Ordway died Oct. 21, 1819, Æt. 36.
Daughter of Stephen and Hannah (Little) Emery, m. David Ordway, jr. Aug. 9, 1802.

Here lyes buried the body of Lieu Nathanail Ordway who departed this life August 30 1765 in the 71 year of his age
Son of Hananiah and Abigail (Merrill) Ordway, b. July 8, 1695; m. Sarah Hale, Apr. 13, 1736.

Here lies buried the body of Mrˢ Joanna Ordway who dec Sepʳ yᵉ 16ᵗʰ 1772 in the 75ᵗʰ year of her age.

Mrs. Betty Ordway wife of Mr. Enoch Ordway who departed this life Dec'r 28th 1783 in the 19th year of her age.
Daughter of Abiel Rogers.

In memory of Mr. Joshua Ordway who died Feb. 27, 1826 in his 88th year.
Son of Nathaniel Ordway, bapt. August, 1738; m. Sarah Downe Oct. 9, 1759.

In memory of Mrs. Sarah Ordway wife of Mr. Joshua Ordway who died April 9, 1811, in the 72nd year of her age.

Mr. Nathl Ordway died March 24, 1824, Æt. 51.
Son of Joshua Ordway, bapt. Nov. 8, 1772.

In memory of Hannah Ordway who died Jan.ʸ 15, 1810 in her 48th year.

James Ordway born Nov. 15, 1803, died Jan. 19, 1893.

Judith, wife of James Ordway died Feb. 18, 1861 aged 70 yrs. 6 m.

Here lies buried the body of Mrˢ Hannah the wife of Samuel Poor who dep—— life April — 1767 in ye 83ʳ —ar of her age.

Here lies buried the body of Mr Samuel Poor who departed this life July the 11ʰ 1769 and in the 87ʰ year of his age.
Son of Samuel and Rachel (Bailey), born June 3, 1682.

In memory of Mrs Judith Poor the wife of Mr Benjamin Poor who deceased August the 7th A. D. 1776 in the 61st year of her age.

Judith Poor died Dec. 21, 1837, aged 86.

Abigail Poor Obt. Dec 14, 1830, Aet. 77.

In memory of Ruth Poor who died Novʳ 5th 1802 in her 84 year.

Mr. Benjamin Poor died March 18, 1817 ; Æt. 93.

Mrs. Catharine relict of Mr. Benjamin Poor; died July 2, 1827, Æt. 95.

Catherine Gerrish m. 1st, Henry Adams ; m. 2d, Dec. 4, 1774, Benjamin Poor.

Joseph Ridgway died May 21, 1802; aged 34 yrs.

Elizabeth Ridgway died Feb. 20, 1860 ; aged 88 yrs.

Daughter of Caleb and Dorothy (Sargent) Moody; bapt. 1771.

Here lies buried the body of Mr Thomas Rogers who died April 29th 1744 in ye 41st year of his age.

Thomas Rogers, 3d, m. Hannah Morse, Sept. 30, 1729.

Here lies buried the body of Mrs Anna the wife of Mr Abiel Rogers died Agust 1st 1747 in the 24 year of her age.

Here lies buried the body of Mr Iohn Rogers who died Jany 17th 1740 in ye 54th year of his age.

Son of Thomas and Ruth (Brown) Rogers, b. July 11, 1686.

Here lies buried the body of Mrs Esther Rogers the wife of Mr John Rogers who died Octr ye 21st 1774 & in ye 87th year of her age.

Daughter of James and Mary Ordway; m. John Rogers in 1713.

Here lies buried the body of Edmand Rogers who departed this life December ye 25 1747 aged 21 years 8 [?] mo. & 11 days.

Nathan Rogers died Aug. 21, 1837, aged 88.

Mrs. Hannah, wife of Nathan Rogers, died Sept. 8th 1830; aged 76.

In memory of Enoch, son of Nathan & Hannah Rogers who died Sep^t 9th 1812, in his 30th year.

Caleb Rogers died Sept. 4, 1847, aged 75.

Oliver Rogers, died Oct. 8, 1826 ; aged 67 years.

Abigail relict of Oliver Rogers died May 8, 1838; aged 79.

Abigail Ordway, m. Oliver Rogers, Nov. 1, 1795.

Here lyes buried ye body of leftenent Samuell Sawyer who died February the 11 1718 in the 72 year of his age.
Son of William and Ruth (Bidfield) Sawyer.

Hear lyes ye body of Mr^s Mary ye wife of Mr Iohn Sawyer who died Febr^y ye 21 1707: 8 & in ye 35 year of her age.
Daughter of Isaac and Rebecca (Bailey) Brown; m. (1) Peter Merrill; m. (2) John Sawyer, Dec. 25, 1700.

Here lyes buried the body of Iohn Sawyer the son of Mr Iohn Sawyer who died April ye 17, 1723 aged 19 years & 12 days old.

Here lyes buried the body of Samuel Sawyer who died Apral 20 forst 1723 & in the 49th year of his age.
Son of William and Mary (Emery) Sawyer.

Here lyes buried the body of Abigail ye wife of Samuel Sawyer who died Octobe ye 14, 1722 in y 48 year of her age.
Daughter of Joseph and Martha (Moores) Goodridge; m. Dec. 17, 1702, Samuel Sawyer.

Here lies buried the body of Mr Josiah Sawyer who departed this life April 4 1756 in the 76 year of his age.
Son of William and Mary (Emery) Sawyer.

Here lies buried the body of Mr^s Tirzah Sawyer wife of Mr Iosiah Sawyer died Sep^t 2 1739 in ye 56 year of her age.
Daughter of Samuel and Elizabeth (Titcomb) Bartlett; m. 1707.

Erected in memory of Mr Moses Sawyer who departed this life Auguft 29th 1778; in the 67th year of his age.
Son of Josiah and Tirzah (Bartlet) Sawyer.

In memory of Hannah relict of Mr. Mofes Sawyer who died May 19, 1802 in the 76 year of her age.

Erected in memory of Mr Matthias Plant Sawyer who departed this life July 29th 1777; in the 24th year of his age.

Here lyes Buried the body of Hannah Sawyer who died Agust 6 1739 in ye 24 year of her age.

Here lyes buried the body of Israel Sawyer who died Agust 2 1739 in ye 22 year of his age.

Son of Josiah and Tirzah (Bartlett) Sawyer.

Here is enterred the body of Mrs Abigail Sawyer the wife of Mr Abel Sawyer who departed this life Sep^t ye 22^d 1778. In the 59th year of her age.

Abigail Ordway, m. Abel Sawyer, Apr. 24, 1744.

Sacred to the memory of Joseph Sawyer, who died April 22nd 1831 : aged 73.

Son of Moses and Hannah Sawyer.

In memory of Sarah, wife of Joſeph Sawyer, who died March 26, 1791 Æt. 38.

Mrs. Sarah, wife of Mr. Joseph Sawyer, & only daughter of Mr. Nathan & Mrs Naomi Long died Jan. 18, 1813 Æt 51.

Doct. Moses Sawyer died Aug. 5, 1799, aged 43 yrs.

Hannah Burnham died Nov. 25, 1849 aged 87 yrs. She was widow of Doct. Moses Sawyer.

Daughter of Moses Little, m. Dr. Moses Sawyer, July 25, 1781.

Hannah daughter of Moses & Hannah Sawyer died May 30, 1801 aged 8 yrs.

Here lyes buried the body of Insin Beniamin Smith who died May ye 14 1723 & in the 42 year of his age

Son of Lieut. James and Sarah (Coker), b. Aug. 21, 1681.

In memory of Mary Tomb daughter of Rev. Samuel and Mehitabel Tomb, who died June 25, 1800, Ætat 7.

Capt. Daniel Toppan, died Nov. 18, 1800 Æt 53. Daniel his son died at Port de paix April 5, 1792 Æt. 19.

Here lyes the body of Iohn Tufts the son of the Rever^d Mr Iohn & Mrs Sarah Tufts who died March the 10th 1727, being just nine weeks

Abbie K. wife of Charles A. Whiting and daughter of Thomas K. & Susan T. Bartlett, born Nov. 19, 1850, died Jan. 22, 1883.

Charles oldest son of Nathan & Caroline Whiting of Stow, Me. Died March 29, 1876 aged 41 yrs.

Hear lies buried the body of Mr^s Ruth the wife of Mr Thomas Wilimars who died —— 16th 1745 —— 3rd ——

Here is interrd Dc^n Archelaus Woodman who departed this life March ye 17th 1766 in the 95th year of his age.

Son of Edward and Mary (Goodridge) Woodman, b. June 9, 1672; m. ab't 1695, Hannah ——.

Here lies buried the body of Mr^s Hannah the wife of Deackon Archelaus Woodman died April 25 1749 in the 75 year of her age

Here is interred MR Edward Woodman who departed this life Nov^R ye 1st 1762 in the 64 year of his age

Son of Archelaus and Hannah Woodman, b. May 12, 1698; m. Mary Sanders, Nov., 1729.

Here is interred Mary Woodman consort to MR Edward Woodman who des March ye 19th 1771 in the 67th year of her age.

In memory of Miss Meriam Woodman who died June 9 1816 aged 75 years.

This stone is erected to the memory of Mr. Nathan Woodman who died Decr 13th 1786 in the 41st year of his age.

PUBLIC HOUSES IN SALEM.

A LETTER FROM REV. JOHN HIGGINSON TO THE
COUNTY COURT, JUNE 25, 1678.

To the Honoured Magistrates now prefent at the County Court at Salem, June 25, 1678.

Being credibly informed that there are at this time belonging to Salem about 14 Ordinaries & publick drinking Howfes, fome of them licenfed others of them vnlicenfed, (viz. 1 m^r Gidny, 2 m^r King, 3 Capt More, 4 Ellin Hollinwood, 5 Jo: Procter, 6 Nath. Ingerfoll, 7 Darling, 8 m^r Croad, 9 Will: Lake, 10 Edw: Bridges, 11 Gilbert Taply, 12 Fra: Collins, 13 Goodie Kippin, 14 Ruben Guppa, & that there are 4 more y^t now at this time defire & endeavour to get approbation & licenfe, viz. 15 John King, 16 John Peaf, 17 Sam: Eburn, 18 John Clifford.

And being fet in this place by God & men as a watchman by office, I dare not but difcharge my duty in giving warning agſt ye fin of Drunkennes & ye excefiiue number of drinking howfes in this place; & having libertie by Law (as title Common Liberties) vpon confideration of many things in ye fear of God, I find it to be my duty at this juncture of time to prefent this information to ye Honoured County Court: That though the continuance of thefe & ye adding of more may be a gratifying of fuch as are too much given to drinking & not so well affected to Sobriety Law & good order, yet I believe it is a very great grievance to ye generallitie of ye church members freemen & Sober people of Salem, af well af to my felfe & I doubt not if there be need upon enquiry your Worfhips would finde it fo) not feeing how fuch a multitude of drinking howfes can poffibly ftand with ye law made in 75 for a Reformation of exceffive drinking vnder ye title of provoking Evils, when it is well known y^t till within this few years 2 ordinaries were judged fufficient for Salem, & y^t divers of thefe haue fet up fince ye making of ye Law in 75 & moft of them are known to be frequented by town dwellers, to ye great impoverishing of ye town, ye encreas of tipling drinking & company keeping the difhonor of God & further provoking of his wrath.

Therefore it is humbly propounded to ye ferious confideration of the Honoured County Court, whether by ye Exercife of & Emprovem^t of your wifdome Integrity authority & zeal for God, againft fin (according to the forementioned Law & as an act of reall reformation of fuch a provoking evill) whether there may not be a putting down of all fuch publick howfes as are found vpon mature deliberation not to be abfolutely neceffary for ye entertainment of travailers & ftrangers, & a reducing them to fome few wch may be sufficient for y^t end, as in former times.

And in particular y^t you would pleas not to License Edw : Bridges, He being not approved by ye moft of ye Sober people of this place, either for his Sobriety, or for his Fidelity to Law & good order.

The Lord give you ye Spirit of Wifdome & Counfell & of ye Fear of God to make you of quick vnderftanding in ye fear of ye Lord, y^t you may doe in this & all things elf, as may be for ye glory of God, ye Reformation of growing Evils, ye difcountenancing of Prophanes & encouragm^t of Godlines in this place, y^t it may turne to your own comfortable account in ye great day of ye Lord.

Your humble & affectionate
fervant

Salem June 25, 1675.   John Higginfon

Essex County Court Files, Vol. XXIX—leaf 39.

LETTER FROM REV. JOHN HIGGINSON TO HIS SON NATHANIEL HIGGINSON,* AUGUST 31, 1698.

Salem, Avgvst the 31ˢᵗ 1698.

My Beloved Son

Although my Self & yʳ Brothʳ Jnº. haue written to you Seueral times Since you went to yᵉ Indiaˢ Yett we know not yᵗ Euer you Receiued any one from us, & though I Question not but you haue written diuers Times to vs Yett we have not Refᵈ any one from you, Except yᵉ first Year when you ſent vs yʳ Journal, wᶜʰ I doe not Impute to any want of affection In yᵒ but to ſome Unknown Accidents, as Intercepting of Lettʳˢ &c Yett I am not diſcoraged from writting to yᵒ again becauſe (if ye lord pleaſe) this may come to yᵒ though never any did before, I know yᵒ are willing to heare from yʳ Relations & Native Country. In yᵉ last lettʳ I Refᵈ from yᵒ befor yᵒ wentto yᵉ Indiaeˢ yᵒ Informed me that one Reason why yᵒ left England was, you was willing for a time to be out of yᵉ way of yᵉ Troubles wᶜʰ yᵒ Saw coming vpon Englᵈ & yᵗ yᵉ Same Troubles would Reach us In N: Engᵈ wᶜʰ has most sadly come to paſe for Sʳ Edmund Androſe being ſent over from K: Jeames to be Gouernʳ here wᵗʰ a compᵃ of ſobjects nedy pʳſons Lawyers &c by yᵉ Exerciſe of an arbitrary Government, yᵉ foundation of all our Good things ware destroyᵈ, yᵉ wicked walked on Euery Side & yᵉ Vilest of men ware Exalted, yᵉ Opreſsions & Sufferings of yᵉ multitudes ware such, yᵗ yᵉ as Sone as they heard yᵗ yᵉ Prince of Orange was Gone for England, yᵉ Country Roſe in Armes Impriſioned ye whole Crew & Sent yᵐ for England, but in little more yⁿ a year yᵉ country was brought into a Sad condition being alſo diſtreſed by wars from yᵉ Indians & ffrench both by land & Sea wᶜʰ continues to this day & grate confusion in yᵉ time of

*For biographical note see Essex Institute Hist. Colls., Vol. V, p. 35.

(182)

ye comitte of peace till it pleafed god y^t King William
Gaue vs a new Chartt^r & Sent S^r Wm. Phip [a] Natiue
of N: England (ye last sumer) to be our Gouern^r wherby
we hope for Some Riuiueing By degrees, but ye nefsesary
Grate Taxations (30 000^{ll} one year), caufe much murmer-
ing among ye people & by ye concurrance of many such
caufes N: Eng^d is Gratly deminf hed & Impoueriſhed &
brought low & In noe place more y^n In Salem wch had
about 60 ffish^r K: & oth^r Trading Ships belonging to it
but is now Reduced to 15 ye whole fish^r Trade bing
ceafed & ye men Scattered & Gone & ye affliction of
this time hath fallen heauely vpon me & my familly
y^t whearas y^o know at first I had 160^{ll} p Annum
but because y^t was Troublesome I abatt^d 44^{ll} p^r An^o
y^t I might Rec^r 100^{ll} money & 40 cord of wood wch I
Enjoyed for many years till Sr Edmund Andros came y^t
ye way of Ratting was laid aside & left to a Voluntary
contribution wch hath proued from many nontribution it
hath ben for 6 years past but between 50 & 60^{ll} p an & it
is not for minifterf to conteft a maintinance Especially
in a time when ye people are inded Impoueriſhed. Your
broth^r Jno is a Justice p^o, Captt Horfe (He is lately made
Major of the Regim^t) & much vfed in publick Occasions
through ye bleſing of god one his prudence & Industry he
had attained a Competent Estate, he had fiue ffish^r K: &
p^{tt} of two oth^r Trading Ships & did thriue in ye world, but
by ye french taking his (& oth^r) K: he is now Reduced
to one K: & a ſmal Shop he is now 44 & has 5 child^r y^r
Broth^r Thos is now 38 a Single man & yett nott in any
settled way of Imployment haueing failed in y^t he was in,
I canott help him he is an object of pitty, & Soe is Especially y^r poor Sister Dolliuer being at last tottally deserted by her vnkind husband (after he had spent all y^t
they had or y^t I could doe for him) who was forced Severall years agoe She and her Children to returne home to
me and liue vpon me She is alas by ouerbaring mallon-
colly crazed in her vnd^{r}ftanding. She is 46 an object of
compafsion your Sister whartons two Daughterf Sarah &
Bethiah are alſo by ye afflicting providence of God Caft
vpon me. You know y^r Broth^r wharton was a ma[n] of
an Excellent Spirit when he married y^r Sister Sarah he had

an Eftate of a 5000ˡⁱ & in an Increasing way of marchan-
dizeing but since his second match yᵉ prouidence of god
frowned vpon him many ways he lost at once 2000ˡⁱ of his
Trading Estate by yᵉ Grate fire in Bofton, & a 1000ˡⁱ an-
othʳ time & Soe yᵗ he was forced to Borrow much & put
himself vpon a designe of a coopʳ mine here at Wooburne
by wᶜʰ means he hoped to Recouer himfelf, but in yᵉ Vig-
erous proficution of this designe at London it pleafed God
to take him out of this life he was much beloued & Lamented by all yᵗ knew him & yᵒ know he was a Good frenid
of yʳˢ. After his deceaf e his Estate proued Insoluent &
their is not a penny left for yᵉ Children they haue liued
wᵗʰ me diuers years & are vpwards of twenty being objects
of Grate compafsion haueing had Liberal Education &
now noe postions & I haue little or nothing to Giue vnto
yᵐ I suppose you haue heard your brothers Francis & Henry are dead.

Concerning yʳ self yᵒ haue ben by yᵉ especial prouidence
of god seperated from yᵉ Rest of yʳ Brothren & I haue
been bereaued of yᵒ this twenty years and wharas I intended you for yᵉ miniftrey & it was a Sore affliction to me yᵗ
you was Diuerted from it, & I have thought Sometimes
yᵗ it may be God Intended you should be as a Joseph to
preserue Relieue & Supply yᵉ nefeffeties of yᵒ fathʳˢ familly
& yᵒ owne flesh & blood of wᶜʰ alfo there hath been a Recent Excample, here in Nᵉ England not many Years since
Young Andʳson of Boston getting an Estate at Bantam
(before yᵉ change ther) he Sent fuch a considerable Supply
to his aged fathʳ Brothʳ & Sisterˢ as Enabled yᵐ all to Liue
wel & Comfertably, when they ware but in a low condition
before. Yᵉ Truth is I Cannot wᵗʰ much confidence Propound this to you becaufe (though I doubt not of Josʳ
like andʳfon like child like Affection & brothʳly loue) I
know not whether indeed yᵒ have such an abillity yᵗ you
can doe as they did wᵗʰout wrong to yʳself & yʳ Imploy
yet being latly Informed by a neighbour In Salem coming
from Barbadof fᵗ yᵗ he there spake wʰ yᵉ Captains of 2
East Indʳ ships [&] they told him yᵗ they knew yʳ self
verry well & that you was Gouernʳ of Geoges forte from
if this be Indeed foe and yᵗ it may be wᵗʰout any wrong
whence they came & yᵗ you had a Greate Estate & Now

to your Viz y^t [you] can maintain your station cary on
your Trade & Injoy ye fruits of y^r owne Labour & yett
out of an Ouer plus y^t God has Granted you wch you can
spare y^t which may Reach to ye Supply of ye nefsesetys of
y^r ffath^r family & y^r owne flefh & blood: then Indeed I
propound to you ye Scripture Example of Jofeph & ye N:
Eng^d: Example of Anderson for y^r lmitation
    You may doe it Ether by sending from where y^o are, or
ordering from London iff y^o haue an Estate their or may
procure it to be done by ye East India Comp^a whome you
Serue as I haue heard of Some Examples of that Kind &
you know we have a cordial & tryed ffreind y^r Vnkle
whitefeild y^t will [be] Glad to be Imployed in Such a
Seruice as Res^{r}ing & transmitting ye Same vnto vs I am
not Ignorant of ye many difficulties & cafsualties in ye way
by Reason of ye distance of time & place & Interuening
accidents &c in all wch we must Submite to ye Prouidence
of God wating vpon in ye way of our Duty if he will
pleafe to profper Such a designe becaufe I am Aincient if
you Should Joyne Mr Noyce wth your Brother Jno to dis-
tribute to ye Reft ln cafe I Should be dead you may doe
well, I would pray you to Send a Particular Rememb^r to
y^r Moth^r her fformer hufband left her 30^{li} a year during
her Life (which) I Should haue had ffor my time but God
took it away by ye Great fire at Bofton. She hath been a
Good wife to me & a good mother to my Children & been
a prudent & Industrious manager of our ffamaly affaires.
Methinks I would not have you Stay much Longer where
you are but when you can come of wth honour & Safly &
wth ye Leaue & Good will of ye Eaft India Comp^a, y^t you
would Returne Either to Old or N England to Spend y^e
Reft of y^r days among y^r ffreinds & Relations diuers desire it here Especially y^r 2 Succefsiue chamber ffellows,
M^r. Noyce who hath ffully Anfwered ye Good carrected
you Gaue of him he is 45 & yet a single man & Cap^{tt}
Sewall who marring Mr Huls daughter of Boft^o he left
him a greate Estate, he hath been a good Brother Indeed
In Recruting & Raifing his Relations a good Ex^r for you
to Imitate they both p^{r}sent their Special Refpects & love
to your self I could defire it too & y^r Broth^r Jno but must
leaue it to god.

Though I am now 77 yet through mercy, I Enjoy a better Health then formerly preaching Preaching once a Sabbath & my turne at yᵉ Lecture Seldome failing my inwards are yet found & a pretty good Stomack, yet I feel yᵉ crazines & decares [?] of old age gradually Growing Vpon me I would be Glad if yᵉ Lord pleafe to see this which I haue propounded accomplished before I dye, yᵗ I may fee yᵐ in a better way to Liue when I am Gone but I leaue your Self & them & this whole buiffinef, to my gracious god & father in Christ who takes care of yᵉ children of his Seruant when they are dead & gone—. & now I shall tell you (in a word) wᵗ are yᵉ Cheife brathing desires of my Soul, O Lʳᵈ my God in they fauer is ye life of my foul, thy sauing Kindnes is bettʳ then liffe & to be wᵗʰ Christ is best of all O yᵗ I may find Grace in they Sight & yᵗ Christ may be they couenant wᵗʰ me and my covenant wᵗʰ the yᵗ I may win Christ & be found in him yᵗ I may be accepted of him & yᵗ I may be Sincere & wᵗʰout offence till yᵉ day of Christ my dear Child let thefe be yᵉ Chiefe defires of yᵒ Soul alfo & Remembʳ Mattʳ 6 19: 20: 21 Mark 8: 34 to yᵉ End 1 Timᵒ 6: 17: 18: 19 then Shall wee affuredly meet in heauen tho͵ we Should neuer more fee on another here vpon Earth Soe I Comend you t[o] yᵉ Grace of God in Christ Jesus & Rest

yʳ Loueing ffather
John Higginfon

When you write to me Informe of thefe three things

1 how yᵉ breach betwene yᵉ Englifh & Indians is made Vp & whethʳ be like to hold

2 whethʳ their be any track or footsteps of Christianity in thofe parts fom authʳˢ haue writtin of yᵉ Christians of Saint Thomas

3 What Reallity & progrefs of Christianity by yᵉ dutch in yᵉ Ile of Ceylon not far from you fome years ago we heard their had been 300000 Baptized

This is a 3ᵈ letter written by one of your bro : Johns Sons.

Essex Institute Manuscript Collections, Misc. MSS.

THE SEACOAST DEFENCES OF ESSEX COUNTY IN 1776.

Report of a Com^{tee} appointed to view ye Sea Coaſt.

A Report from the Committee who were ordered to Newbury

The Committee appointed to view the Sea Coasts from Boston to Newbury Port and examine their State of Defence &c. having attended that Buiſneſs, report as follows. There are two Forts erected on the Point of Land in Salem Harbour No. 1 & No. 2 or old Fort, No. 1 contains 10 ambozeurs has 2 twelve pounders 2 nine pounders with three small pieces, fit for use, which with the Cannon in No. 2 or old Fort we judge sufficient as these Forts are overlooked by another Fort which is now erecting on an eminence not far distant from those already mentioned, which commands Beverly & Salem Harbour in a very advantageous manner, in this Fort there is one 12 pounder only. This Fort we must own, does Credit to the gent^n of the Town of Salem, and with the addition of some heavy pieces and ordinance stores would enable them to make no dispicable Figure in the common Defence.

The Situation and Importance of the Harbour of Marblehead with the Strength & Beauty of their Works, are equally conspicuous, they have 18 pps. of Artilery in their Fort and is in one of their Batteries viz 2 of 24. 2 of 18. 2 of 14. 4 of 12 the remainder nines Sixes & fours, four of the four pounders are expected to go on Board the armed Schooner Tyrannicide and a part of the 14 & 12 pounders answer better for an ornament to the Fort than for use, besides there they have a six gun Battery well situated & very advantageous for the Defence of their Sea Coast but destitute of Guns, they are also erecting a five gun Battery at a Place called Hewetts Head and propose erecting another on the Back Part of the Town. These Fortifications We judge Sufficient if well manned & Sup-

plied with Artillery & ordinance Stores for the Defence
of the Harbour, unlefs it should be judged best to take
Pofsession of a Height of ground called Noggshead, which
would be of advantage to Salem & Beverly equally with
Marblehead.

At Beverly they have erected a Sand Bank Battery laid
out for five Ambozears in which they have two borrowed
field Pieces.   This Battery appeared to the Committee of
no great Importance.   The Situation of a Seven Gun Battery, nearly opposite Salem Fort, in Woodbury's Point
and a four Gun Battery erecting on Thorndicks Point together with a five Gun Battery erected at Barnetts Point
and a three Gun Battery at West Beach are of such a
nature as to demand an immediate attention for the Pre-
servation & Security of the Sea Coast.

They have a Part of Coll Glover's Regiment stationed
here, have one 18 pounder & two 12 pounders borrowed
of Gen^{ll} Ward and four small borrowed field Pieces of
little Consequence, they have 150 w^t of Powder belonging to the Town with 200 w sent there by a Committee.

At Manchester, they have no Works except a small one
near Glass Head, as their men are out in the Service of
the Continent and they naked & Defenceless they petition
for two or three Cannon and a Sea Coast Company, being
obliged to keep several watchers and lying more than six
mile on the Sea Coast.

The Importance of the Harbor of Gloucester is so great
as in the judgment of your Committee to demand a very
early and serious Consideration.   They have a Fort erected called Fort Anne with ten Ambozeurs in which they
have 12 ^{llders} 4 ^{llders} with three nine pounders, havey comb'd
and not fit for use if possible to be avoided.   No. 2 is a
four gun Battery in which is one 9 ^{llder} that is not good
and one 6 Pounder fit for use.

No. 4 is a four Gun Battery lying on a neck of Land
between No 1 & No 2 and not of so much Importance as
No 1 which is a five Gun Battery & has one 2 pounder
& 1 nine pounder.   Besides these there is a Battery erected which has no Guns but in which a Field Piece or two
might be of great Service, they have about 240 men 100

Shot for the large Cannon and one thousand w^t of Powder for the whole.

The Town of Newberry Port is fortified in such a manner as to do Honour to the gentlemen concerned. The Noble Exertions that have been made by that Town for the Defence of such an important Part of the Colony demands the most gratiful Returns from every Well Wisher to American Liberty, they have ten nine pounders 8 sixes and two fours belonging to the Town, but have no Guns nor ordinance Stores belonging to the Colony and have been able to procure but very little of the latter at their own, and a very great Expense.

The above being a State of Facts your Committee beg leave to report as their opinion, that Cape Ann, be immediately supplied with thirty two and —— Pounders with ammunition and ordinance Stores suitable therefor and that some Measures be adopted for the speedy filling up the Sea Coast Companies stationed there in the Room of those who have enlisted or shall enlist on Board any of the Continental or Colonian armed Vessells.

We beg Leave also to observe it as our opinion, that some heavy Pieces be sent to Salem, Marblehead & Newbury Port, that the State of Manchester be taken into Consideration, that a Sea Coast Company & a *Matross* Company be raised at Newbury Port, and that they be supplied at Newbury Port with ordinance Stores & ammunition proper for the Cannon already there and such other as shall be sent there that Beverly also be supplied with a proper Proportion of Cannon & ordinance Stores

Recd June 19th & committed to the Committee on ye State of ye Sea oast.

Massachusetts Archives, Vol. 137, pp. 93-5.

THE CHILDREN OF MORDECAI LARCOM OF BEVERLY.

COPY OF AN UNRECORDED QUIT CLAIM DEED NOW IN THE
POSSESSION OF WILLIAM F. ABBOT OF
WORCESTER, MASS.

This document throws much documentary light upon
the children of the emigrant Mordecai Larcom, in that it
proves absolutely that Mordecai[2], Thomas[2], Daniel[2], Rebecca[2], and Elizabeth[2] were his children and as the heirs
quit claim to David[3] (son of Cornelius[2]) it is practically
conclusive that Cornelius[2], the ancestor of the Beverly
Larcoms, was another son although documentary proof is
wanting. Mordecai[2] lived in Wenham and had many
daughters and one son, John[3], who grew up. This son John
removed to Enfield, Ct., where he died leaving two sons who
are the chief source of Larcoms outside of Essex County.

"Know all men By these Presents that We Daniell
Larcom of Beverly in the county of Essex in New Eng-
land Brother & one of the Heirs of the Estate of Elizabeth
Whitahar Late of Manchister in s[d] County dec[d] John
Bradford of s[d] Beverly & Hannah Bradford his wife Mark
Morse & Jemima Morse his Wife & Phebe Patch widow
representatives of Thomas Larcom Late of s[d] Beverly dec[d]
Brother & also one of the Heirs of the s[d] Eliz[a] Whitahar
William Stanley Bethiah Stanly & Elizabeth Patch all of
s[d] Beverly Representitives of thare mother Rebeckah
Stanley dec[d] Sistor & also one of the Heirs of the s[d] Eliz-
abeth Whitahar Robert Sallows of s[d] Beverly & Elizabeth
Sallows his wife William Burroughs of Ipswich & Mary
Burroughs his wife George Toppin & [   ] Toppin
his Wife [   ]

"Representatives of thare father Modecai Larcom Late of
Wenham dec[d] Brother & also one of the Heirs of the aforenamed Elizabeth Whitahar dec[d] In consideration of the
sum of forty nine pounds money of New England to us in

190

hand paid at the delivery hereof By David Larcom of s^d
Beverly husbandman Have Remised Relesed Quit claimed
& do By these presents Remise Release & Quit claime
unto him the s^d David Larcom & his Heirs & Assigns for
Ever all the Right Share & Intrest Portion Preportion
Divident & Inheritance Whatsoever which we the s^d Daniell Larcom John Bradford & Hannah his wife Mark
Morse and Jemima his wife Phebe Patch William Stanley
Bethiah Stanley Elizabeth Patch Robert Sallows & Elizabeth his wife William Burroughs & Mary Burroughs his
wife George Toppin & [   ] his Wife [[
have or ought to have in & unto the Estate Reall Parsonall
or mix^d of the Above named Elizabeth Whitahar dec^d Late
of s^d Manchistor To Have & To Hold unto him the s^d
David Larcom & his Heirs & Assigns forever without Any
after challeng Lett—Hindrance or molestationfrom By or
under us or any of us our Heirs Exec^rs Admin^rs or Assigns
In Witness Whar of we do hereunto Set our hands &
seals this second day of June one Thousand seven hundred
& forty Eyght & in the 21 year of this Majesteys Reign

" Signed sealed & delivered	his Daniel X Larkcum [seal] mark
In Presents of	John bredford [seal] hir hanah U Bredferd [seal] mark
his robert D Sallows [seal] mark	hir Phebe V Patch [seal] mark
her elezebeth D Sallows [seal] mark	William Standly [seal] hir Bethiar ◯ Standly [seal] mark
	hir Elezebath O Patch [seal] mark
	Mark Mors [seal] her Jemima 10 Morse [seal] mark

[On the back of deed] " The Within Instrewment Was Signed Seled & delivered In Presents of us Whose names are under Ritten
    James Taylor
    Theophilus Hull
    John Prince
    John Standly Juner
    Peter Pride
    James Thissel "

REQUEST FOR PREACHING AT METHUEN, 1787.

Methven September 8 day 1757
To the Re[nd] Mr. John Cleavlend of ipswich and the Church of god under your pastorl care as we Suppose to them that are renewed By the Spirit of Grace and hold the doctren of faith in word and practis Grace Be vnto you and peas from god the father and the Lord jesus Christ Amen

Whareas it hath Pleased the father of all marcies to begit the hop of Eternal Life in vs through jesus Christ his son and finding ovr selves Bound to Evidence the Same By a Godly life and conversation and to vse all Lawfull means to promot the Spritall Wellfare of ovr Selues and ovr fellow men——

We writ vnto you greting being at present withovt a paster and ovr Souls Longing for the gospel that we might be Edified and taught more and more in the Doctrings of the gospel of trvth and seing Scores of ovr neighbovrs whos ears are opned to hear the desire of ovr sovl is that you would consider ovr Case and Spare that Gift of preaching we vnderstand yov are fauoured with at Som Convenent time And to the paster we writ not in perticeler beleiveng ovr brethren Shall make known ovr Case vpon the Delivery of this Leatter brethren pray for the Prosperity of Sion Amen——

Sined by the desire and in the behalf of the Church now present   Joseph Gutterson
                            Caleb Richardson

Essex Institute MSS. Colls. Rev. John Cleaveland MSS., Vol. I, leaf 49.

NEVV-ENGLANDS
PLANTATION.

OR,
A SHORT AND TRVE
DESCRIPTION OF THE
COMMODITIES AND
DISCOMMODITIES
of that Countrey.

Written by a reuerend Diuine now
there resident.

LONDON,
Printed by *T.C.* and *R.C.* for *Michael Sparke*,
dwelling at the Signe of the *Blew Bible* in
Greene Arber in the little *Old Bailey.*
1 6 3 0.

HISTORICAL COLLECTIONS
OF THE
ESSEX INSTITUTE

| VOL. XLIII. | JULY, 1907 | No. 3 |

LITERARY SALEM.

BY REV. JOHN WRIGHT BUCKHAM.

If the question were asked, " what was the first published work written in New England, who wrote it, and where?" very few persons could answer correctly. Many would venture, as a guess, Bradford's " History of the Plymouth Plantation," but this was not written until some ten years after the settlement of Plymouth and was not printed until 1856. If we except Robert Cushman's " Plymouth Sermon," published in London, 1622,—which, although it is well worthy to be classed as literature, was not in book form—the honor of publishing the first book written in New England seems to belong to Francis Higginson of Salem, whose volume " New England's Plantation " was published in London in 1630. Although the manuscript of the little volume was not originally written for publication, there is in this glowing description of the New World " a delicate felicity of expression and a quiet imaginative picturesqueness," as Moses Coit Tyler characterizes it, which gives it a unique and worthy place in American literature. It went through three editions in a single year, and although it has now lost that timeliness which made it popular when so many in old England were wondering what New England was like, yet one finds it most readable and delightful still.

From the time of this earliest literary production onward, Salem has been prolific of authors and is worthy to rank with Cambridge and Concord as a cradle of American literature. Many of the successors of Mr. Higginson in the pulpit of the first church have been men of literary talent as well as pulpit power. Roger Williams and Hugh Peters did not make their contributions to literature until after leaving Salem, but Nicholas Noyes, of witchcraft fame, was a noted versifier in his day, after the style of the school of Donne and Herbert, and his verses, conceits and epitaphs in rhyme were much admired and sought after. The broad-minded and beloved John Higginson, a son and successor of Francis, also possessed true and substantial gifts as an author. Professor Tyler writes of his " massiveness of meaning, seer-like earnestness of tone and quaint dictions as of dead sages and saints " in his " attestations to Mather's Magnalia " and has warm praise for his Election Sermon on " The cause of God and his people in New England."

But although the literary instinct came with the Cambridge scholars and thoughtful Puritans across the sea, and the tender plant of literature was kept alive here through all the hardships of wilderness life, it was not until after the Revolution that it blossomed and began to bear fruit which had the unmistakable flavor of genuine literature, slowly but surely ripening. In the period comprising the last decade of the eighteenth century and the first decade of the nineteenth, Nathaniel Bowditch, the most brilliant mathematician and astronomer of earlier American science, completed his " American Practical Navigator " and began his famous translation of Laplace's " Mechanique Celeste ;" Dr. William Bentley, the genial and progressive parson, linguist and observer, was writing his pithy comments on current events ; Timothy Pickering, Salem's distinguished Revolutionary General and representative on Washington's cabinet, composed his admirable state papers and addresses ; Joseph Story was cultivating in verse and public address that literary talent which afterward made his Supreme Court decisions so notable ; Dr. Edward Augustus Holyoke, the centenarian, the first man who received the Medical degree from Harvard College, was making his noteworthy contributions to the medical journals, and John Pickering was carrying on those linguistic studies which made him one of the leading scholars of his time and which issued in his Greek Lexicon, his works on the Indian languages and other books of great scientific value.

This outburst of literary activity in Salem in the opening years of the nineteenth century in the direction of scientific and professional literature was followed by an almost continuous literary productiveness along many divergent lines. Fiction shyly lifted its head above the rocky soil in Nathaniel Hawthorne's "Fanshawe," published in 1826. Poetry, in purest raiment, appeared about ten years later, when verses began to come out in the papers by that true child of the Spirit, Jones Very. Salem gave birth to William H. Prescott, but before his boyhood was past the talented author of the "Conquest of Mexico" left his native place to shed the lustre of his fame over Boston. Historical work of high character was done by Joseph Felt, Charles W. Upham, Daniel Appleton White, and many others. Samuel Johnson and Josiah Willard Gibbs maintained the high standard of oriental scholarship set by Dr. Bentley and John Pickering, while the Worcesters, father and son, Thomas Brazer, Thomas Barnard, James Flint, and Elias Cornelius, kept up the best literary traditions of the Salem pulpit.

Salem has been the birthplace, or the home, for a longer or shorter period, of many authors distinguished in all fields of literature. Of poets there were born here Charles T. Brooks, the eminent translator of Schiller and author of many poems of grace and delicacy (among them a fine tribute to the city of his boyhood), and William Wetmore Story, who inherited that talent for poetry which his distinguished father, Chief Justice Story, possessed. Justice Story, published a poem entitled "The Power of Solitude," but afterward secured all the copies he could find of this, his only published poem and consigned them to the flames. His son, the sculptor, has been kinder in leaving to posterity "The Poet's Portfolio" and other volumes of thoughtful and musical verse. Salem was the birthplace, too, of

Samuel Johnson who was the author, not only of "Oriental Religions" and of several essays of great literary charm, but of a number of hymns of the first rank, such as the well known hymn, "Father! in thy mysterious presence kneeling." Together with his friend and biographer, Samuel Longfellow, he made the collection of hymns that Theodore Parker used to call the "Book of Sams."

From the time that Anne Bradstreet, the "Tenth Muse lately come to America," first of American poets, struck the rock from which issued the stream of poesy, the waters ceased not until the wilderness of the New World blossomed as the rose. One name stands out as the poet *par excellence* of Salem, Jones Very, the mystic, friend of Emerson, whose essays and poems Charles Eliot Norton well described as "the work of an exquisite spirit." Never was a poet who had a deeper conviction of Divine inspiration. As James Freeman Clark said of him, "he came and went, spoke or was silent, as the Spirit directed him." Jones Very's "To the Humming Bird," "The Old Road," "To the Painted Columbine," "The Voice of God," "The New World," and "Beauty," breathe a love of God and nature, an insight, an artless purity and serenity that insures them a permanent place in American literature. They touch the deep things of life. It is well for Salem that the house where he lived, by will of his sister Lydia, is to be kept as a memorial of the gifted singer and of his talented brother and sisters. No one who loves the woods and hills and shores of old Salem can well forget the gentle poet who has made them the more beautiful by the touch of his own pure and elevated spirit.

Salem has been the harbor and home, for a time, of many beside those already mentioned, whose names are familiar in American Literature. Edwin P. Whipple resided in Salem for a time, as librarian of the Salem Athenaeum. Elizabeth Peabody lived in the old Grimshawe house on Charter Street, Maria S. Cummins, the author of that famous novel, "The Lamplighter," was born and passed her early life in Salem. Dr. George B. Cheever, while pastor of the Howard Street Church, began here his literary career by publishing the famous pamphlet, "Deacon

Giles' Distillery," destined to outlast his later and more elaborate work. James Hoppin, O. B. Frothingham, Rufus Choate, George B. Loring, "D. R. Castleton," Henry W. Foote, Alpheus S. Packard, and scores of other writers are associated with Salem, either by birth or residence and helped to keep alive the literary spirit in the old city by the sea.

But the bright particular star in the firmament of Salem literature, whose name, even if she possessed no other, would make the literary fame of Salem secure, was Nathaniel Hawthorne. He was, like Jones Very, the son of the typical Salemite, a ship-master. The blood of a Salem ancestry going back to the very beginning of the town flowed through his veins. The very atmosphere and flavor of Salem is in all his work. It is difficult, to be sure, as one looks at the unattractive house of his birth and the streets of his boyhood, to realize how this exquisite orchid of literary genius could have sprung from this unimaginative environment and antecedents. But genius is unaccountable. It knows no laws. Or, at least, if it has laws, they are too subtle and refined for complete analysis. It springs up here or there in the spot of God's appointing and no man knows its genesis or can fathom its nature. Hawthorne was of Salem; his roots went deep into her soil; he breathed her air and drank in her life and interpreted her to herself. And yet the flower of his genius opened far above her narrow streets and confined conceptions in an atmosphere of eternal truth and light. And Salem did not wholly understand him. Nor did he bear with her as a son should bear with his mother.

Hawthorne felt, even when he resented it, the strength of Salem's hold upon him. He knew that he was bound up in the bundle of life with her, and wherever he went Salem went with him, coloring all his imaginations, his ideas, his thoughts. His first great novel grew out of Salem soil and in his last he returned to Salem for his scene. But if Hawthorne owed much to Salem, Salem owes still more to Hawthorne. What, if he did hold himself aloof from his fellow-citizens and, once at least, dipped his pen in vitriol when he wrote of Salem,—has he not done more than enough for his native city to atone for

this? Has he not traced with that wizard power of his
the evolution of her main street? Has he not immortal-
ized her town pump? Has he not made forever famous her
penny shops? Can one sit in one of Salem's old gardens
at twilight without thinking of that immortal garden of
the House of Seven Gables? The spell of the genius of
this man is over the old town like that of a magic wand,
held by a hand that death has not paralyzed ; while through
him Salem has become famed and familiar wherever American literature is known.

SALEM FIRE ENGINES IN 1797.

Names of the Fire Engines belonging to Salem, with the
Names of the Commanders thereof, and where Stationed
viz. :—

Union, Stationed in Washington Street, near Mr Jno Daland's store. Joseph Henfield Captain—but now removed behind the Courthouse. Old one with the Essex.

Salem, Stationed on the Common. Near the Town pump
there—Joseph Vincent Captain. Old one.

Reliance, Stationed at the Head of Long Wharf, the one
imported from Phil^a Joshua Phippen Capt.

Friend, Stationed near Buffums Corner. One of the old
Engines—Caleb Buffum Captain.

Essex, Stationed a little North of the Courthouse. Commanded by Mr Jno Hill. (New one from London.)

Federal, Stationed Near the Church, Samuel Sweetser
Captain. New one from London.

Alert, Stationed in Washington Street near the Store of
Mr John Daland. Mr Henry Rust Captain. Old One.

Exchange, Stationed in Essex Street, Near the House of
Mrs Rebecca Cabot,—Nathl Knight Captain. (New one
from London.)

To the Gentlemen, The Fire Wards for the Town of Salem, sent them ℔ order of the Selectmen of Salem.

                    Attest.   E. NORRIS Town Cler.

Salem, Nov. 1797.

REVOLUTIONARY LETTERS
WRITTEN TO COLONEL TIMOTHY PICKERING.

BY GEORGE WILLIAMS OF SALEM.

(*Continued from Vol. XLIII. page 16.*)

Salem, Sepr 12th 1778

Dr Sir

Received yours of 1st, 7th of Augt at Road Island, and also yours of 18th & 28th came to my hand Two days past, which I Thank you for. You ask advice of your Friends consarning your carring your wife to Pheledelphia. I find many are against your carring her. If you desire to continue at the war office, I should, if I was in your case, carre her with me. Some of your Friends asks how will you due for your Furniture. I say to them I would Live at Board, as many due that Travel, have a room or Chamber. One Trouble has come to your wife, y^r Son has bin Sick some Time past, but has got the better of it, and is not I Judge, fit to have the Small pox as you mentioned, and you may make provision before y^o Set of for Home, in case you bring your wife you may have a place to board at, at your return. Many of your Friends wishes you was clear of the publick, and thay Judge you might due as well here for Intrest. I due not no what your income is so I dont give y^o my opinion. As for the camppaine to Road Island it would Take more than the compas of a letter. This I can say, never was greater Spirit seen in America for the expidision, and greater disappointment, when Mr Frenchman Left us on a Island in the Lurch, all of us mad that there Stay only was 8 hours, and one third part of there Ships to Lay before the Town, and Two or three more to cover the Landing of Some Troops on Brintens point, was I as informed by some General officers & others that was a Judge, that one day after

(199)

thay halled before the Town & Troops Landed on s[d] point, would have compleated the Busness, and I beleve it might have bin don. We went up y[e] hill, and down again, and then got home to Salem Safe. Farewell following French man. If I can find a good oppertunity, shall send you my old money to exchange. I and severel others desired to have come to Philedelphia, but the Burning of part of Bedford,* will prevent us, for fear thay should Take a Turn hear after M[r] French man.—If you have Time Cap[t] Mason & I would have you employ a good man to sell our old Schooner as she Lays for the most she will fetch and bring the neat proceeds with you, and will pay you for expence & Trouble. All Friends well and hope to See you soon. yours of 28th came to my hand by M[r] Alcott from Maj[r] Biglow, and he inform[d] me of his disappointment as well as you. You may informe any member of Congres that the goods he bought of the owners of said goods as thay was for the publick & for the use of y[e] Army he had the preffrance, and if I had not given my Intrest he would not have had them. I was Obliaged to one of the owners to pay him £1500 in Four weeks if the money did not come. It did not, and I was obliaged to pay the said Am[o].— and we could have had the money for s[d] goods at the de- livery from privet men, and no goods have bin sold hear cheaper. Many have bin sold dearer, and many of the goods he had could have had 300 to 1500 ℔ ct. none un- der 1100 ℔ ct. so you may see the publick has bin better sarved then privet men, and I have suffer'd by my Intrest in the affare. I have offen wondred that delays in our publick affares was so many, when I have it from one that has bin, and acquainted the rulers that he wantd money to pay for Cloathing for the Army, so he may have the Army Cloath'd in Season to be detained allmost a month's Time, I say fare well publick busness. I wish for a Honorable peace and Soon.

Pickering MSS. Vol. 17, p. 216.

*New Bedford, on Sept. 5, 1778.

At Boston Jany 19 1779.

Dr Sir

This is to Informe you all Freinds is well, and we have had no Acco^t of your Arrival. We Judge you had a very Bad Journey after I Left you, for we have had very cold & Bad weather, and more misfortune then I ever now'd of on this coast. Nothing new only what you may see in our papers. The prise currant of goods as below. please to Informe if any alterrasions Should Take place in the money, as the resolve of Jany 2^d, will be a great damage to the seeport Towns as the countrymen will not sell any provisions for the money that is order^d out of surculation, and if any News you may have of the enemy's going off or any Likeways of a peace, so I may regulat my affares accordingly. Give my Love to Sister & Littel John.

P. S. prise Current. Flouer 15 to 18£ ⅌ Ct. Sugar 50 to 60£ Rum 90 to 100/ ⅌ g^l Moll^s 54/ Wine at 300, to 320£ p^r pipe Beef 2/6 pork 4/ have no oppertunity to Send y^r wine yet. You have in our Lottery Two 10 dol^{rs} prizes.

To Timothy Pickering Esqr. member of the Board of war. Pheledelphia.

Pickering MSS. Vol. 17, p. 235.

Salem Feby. 28, 1779

Dr Sir

Received yours pr. Millet and the enclosed three hundred doll^{rs} for John Gardner J^r. Shall send it to him the First opportunity. We are Glad to hear of you &c giting safe and so well Accomedated, and so well supplied with Bread. In this State on the Sea Coast the Inhabbitants will not have any to eat. A Bisket is sold for 6^d. What shall we doo for Bread, as the State of York has Answered a Letter from Council, say they can't spare any. The General Court has appointed a Committee to go on from State to State Till thay git as far as Meryaland, to ingage Flour &c. If we are not releived many will not have Bread to eat. The cry is great allready. We was in hopes to have had some by the way of Priverteering. None come as yet. No prizes only from the Pelgrim & Franklin. The dead money has made the poor in great distrest, and Many Marchants intirely Stoped as all there money is dead. One more such Move will intirely destroy all Faith for the money. Moll⁸. for Live Money sold at 45ˢ/ pʳ Gallᵒ for dead 60ˢ/. The Country men for provitions to the poor in proportion as Moll⁸. This State has Ordered a Tax of one Million pound, for the Two Million dollers order'd by Congres & the Remainder for States use, to be paid in the dead Money for the 20ᵗʰ May next. The reason of this Large Tax so sudden was to help the poor & midling people, so thay may not give away one third of the whole to have it exchanged, & to save what thay can spare for said Tax. Marchants of this Town has 7/8 of there Money of this dead Sort. It is supposed some Gentlemen 20 Miles westward of us knew of this, & put of all the dead money. The whole money from Mʳ. Bigelow to the Owners of the Montgomery's was paid in that Sort. 1 became bound for Mʳ. Bigelow, to one of the Owner's that he would pay in a month for £1500, before he would Let the goods go, and was Obliaged to pay it in current money. When I was repaid 1 had for Serving the public Sheets of April. So much for serving the publick for nothing. I Remember the saying of your Good Farther—no Faith in paper money. The Makers of Money sent it to there servants to purchas goods and thay knew it was to be out of circulation in a few months. It would be called by some Jockeing. If any Alteration in State Affairs you will much oblige me to Let me know, by post or any other way. It may be of Service to me. 1 am Sorry the Tea came to a bad Market. No opportunity as yet to send yʳ wine. Shall not Fail of sending it if any good Opportunity serves. You will see the prise current of goods: &c. as pʳ other side. All Freinds well. As for Newes hear nothing more than you see in the Boston papers, my wife joins me in kind Affection to you, wife & John.

prise current Wine, @ £300 to 400. Moll⁸. @ 45 / to 60/ pʳ Gallᵒ. Rum @ 72 to 96/ pʳ dᵒ. Sugar Brown £40

to 78 ℔ Ct. Bohea Tea 72/ pʳ ˡᵇ. Beef 4 to 5/ dᵒ.
Mutton 4 to 6/ dᵒ. Pork 5 to 5/3 dᵒ. Flour, 20 to 24
£ ℔ Ct., none to be bought now. Corn, 17 to (some say)
25 dollʳˢ pʳ bush. English goods, 15 to 20 for one 1ˢ/
Sterling, cases.

Pickering MSS. Vol. 17, p. 24.

At Boston March 15ᵗʰ 1779

Dʳ Sir,
   Yesterday at Salem received yours of 21 Febʸ, and
the inclosed which I delevered. All Freinds is very well,
and are glad to hear of you &c. being well. Am sorry you
mentioned John being inoculated for it gives pain to our
good mother for fear he will not due well. Hope you will
soon Acquaint us of his recovery. The Secret great good
news I hope will soon arrive, if Some Thing dont, to put
a Stop to the Farmers extorsion. I beleive the poor of the
Sea ports, in case of the enemys appearing thay would not
Turn out. You will see by the prise current the reason
of the poors complaint. Privertering has by Bad conduct
Turned out Badly. The Brig Harreden & Benson, has
Taken 3 Valuable prises and sent them for Martinico &
are retaking. The Ship Black prince no Accot of. I am
glad to hear you have a prospect of geting mine & Masons
money exchanged. Stoping the money has bin one means
of the great rise of provisions, for the poor would offer 10
to 25 pʳ Ct. to the Farmers for provision to git of the dead
money. The marchants with us had 7/8 to 4/8 of that
sort. If congres had put on a Tax of 30 million the sea
ports would have gladly paid it for this reason. Some got
all Live money thay could, & put of the dead and now
make a marchandize of it, at 10 to 25 pʳ Ct. If congres
should strike dead one more emission, I beleive no Faith
for money any Longer this way. To hear the poor in the
Markets Dam the makers of it, thay would not Take Such
a step again. Write me if any News should Turn up so I

may Take care of my self & Freinds. Pray Let me know by any way you may have.

N. B. prise current. Beef, 5/ Mutton, 5 to 6/ pork 5 to 6/ Indian Meal 20 to 25 dolrs. Flour none to be bought (Last sold 27 to 30£) Sugar 50 to 60 p^r Ct. Moll^s 50 to 54/. N. E. Rum, 60/ West Indies d^o 96/. Wine 3 to 400£. No oppertunity to send y^r wine as yet.

Pickering MSS. Vol. 17, p. 247.

Salem April 6 1779

Dr Sir

Received yours yesterday p^r Mr Hendley with the inclosed note, and he has promised me he would discharge it soon. I am Glad you have exchanged Mason and mine money so far. We are Glad to hear of John so far well advanced in the Small pox. We are Longing for the great News to Transpire for we are in great distress hear for the want of Bread. Many Famely's has none to eat. Our wicked Farmers has the modesty under a good grace to Ask for Flour the small prise of £45 to 50 p^r Ct. Veal 6/ 7/ p lb. Beef 5/ to 6/ p lb. Many hear that had a good Liveing must be reduced to Beggery on Acco^t of the above prises. The Sea port Inhabitants are all most discouraged with the Loss of all most all of their marchant Vessells &c and those that arrives at the southern ports are stop-[ped] and wont Let them have corn &c. Privertering is in much the same way. The ship Bunker hill gone away. The Montgomery & the Pickering coming home in the Latt. of 36 N. in a very hard gale of wind the Montgomery Sprange a Leak, & the next day thay was obliaged to Leave her, and she is gone, and all the men saved by the pickering, and all their prises retaken, and the ship Black prince no Acc^o of, so you may see what a fine Winters work I shall make. Am fearfull we shall not be able to send the priverters out for the want of Bread. I have about £5000 of the dead money by me. It is to be exchanged by a resolve of congres from the 1st June to Augs^t. Many are fearfull it wont be exchanged. I Took it from the Gent^m that was employed by congres, and in a few months after made dead. The expences of Living Obliage me to have current money for it. If I had a safe oppertunity I would Send it to you, to have it exchanged after the 1st of June next, as you have the Bank by you. I am fearfull there wont come a Long any hear in season to exchange it. Please to Let me know by the First oppertunity. Y^r Affectioned Freind, etc.

P. S. prise Current Rum Jamaca, £6 p G^n W. I. d^o 4.16 N. E. d^o 3.6 Brown Sugar 50 to 70 p lb. Loaf d^o 24/ p lb. Coffee, 14/ p lb. Tea, p Chest £44 p lb. English goods sold at Vandue of the prise Goods of sloop providence, Linin that cost 1/6 starling sold at 60/ p yard, which is double the prise that was sold out of ye shops at retale. So much for Vandues. Beef 5 to 6/ p lb. Veal 6 to 7/ Indian Meal £9 p bushell Flouer £45 to 50 p Ct. Madera wine a £500 p pipe. Your wine no oppertunity to Send it.

Timothy Pickering Esqr member of the Board of war. Pheledelphia.

Pickering MSS.   Vol. 17. p. 253.

At Boston, April 17 [1779]

Dr Sir

This is to Informe you of the succes of our State Vessels & the Ships Warren, Ranger & Queen of France. The Hazard took a 18 Gun Brig priverteer after a Bloody ingagement. The Brig Tyranicide took a Brig of 14 Guns, also after a Bloody ingagement. Thease Two Captors I beleve it may be called as Great a Battel by Sea as ever was in any war. Great Honour to the Commanders

of Boath Sides is due. The Ships Warren &c. has Taken
a privertur of 8 Guns 45 men, the 6th Instant. The 7th
do fell in with a Fleet, of 9 Saile under Convoy of a 20
Gun Ship 150 men Bound from York to George, Took her
and 6 others. The report per the Warren which arrived
Last night say thay are worth £130,000 Sterling. The
perticulers I suppose will be at Congres soon. He Lost
them Last Monday in a fog on St. George's Bank. All
the continental Ships was out before the Warren Arived.
If thay would Keep out I make no doubt that thay will
due good, as this Capture will I hope give them Spirrit.
Nothing New sence my Last. Yr Affectionate Freind.

Pickering MSS. Vol. 17, p. 259.

Salem, May 17, 1779

Dr Sir

Received yours by Millet. Many of us are Sorry you
are at Pheledelphia on account of Living. You mention'd
you have Spent your Salary, Waggon, horses, & part of
my money, the residue with my premission go the same
way. You have my premission to use it. Your note by
Dr Hendley he has not paid me nor cant. I complained
to his Br Colo Hendley and yesterday he promised me to
pay me soon. Please to remember don't trust the young
Bucks. Some Time past I wright you of the Success of
the continaltel Ships. Hoped that thay would have spirit
to go to Sea again. When they all Arrived with all there
prises all tho thay had been out but 5 or 6 weeks thay
sayed the Cruse was out and all hands discharged, to the
great Damage of the States, and disgrace to officers. Our
Two State Brigs will sail again in a few days. Hope thay
will due honour to them selves again. Thay are bound out
after the English priverteers on this coast. You have
inclosed a List of priverteers out of Salem. Hope thay
may have Success this Spring if not many will be ruined.

A List of priverteers of Salem & Beverly, mostly owned in Salem.

Ship	pilgrim	.	.	.	.	.	16 Guns	9 lb
do	Black prince	.	.	.	.	18	—	6 lb
do	Pickering	.	.	.	.	16	—	6
do	Oliver Cromwell	.	.	.	.	16	—	6
do	Harlequin	.	.	.	.	18	—	4
do	Hunter	.	.	.	.	18	—	4
Brig	Franklin	.	.	.	.	18	—	6
do	Fame	.	.	.	.	14	—	4
do	Monmouth	.	.	.	.	12	—	4
Sch^r	Roback	.	.	.	.	12	—	4
do	Jewett	.	.	.	.	12	—	3
do	Grey hound	.	.	.	.	8	—	3
do	Santepe	.	.	.	.	4	—	2
Dolphin		.	.	.	.	.	10 Swivels	

All at Sea, ye above.

Ship Lyon	.	.	.	18 Guns 6 lb & 2 4 lb
Brig Tyger	.	.	.	8 — 3
do Wildcat	.	.	.	12 — 4
do Macarona	.	.	.	14 — 4

Will be at Sea soon.

We have a number of others new built, no provisions for them, and are now go^s Letters of marque on a Voyage. All the List of priverteers is new. Last year & this, only the Dolphin. I am conserned in Black prince, pickering [both] at Sea, [and] Lyon, not at Sea.

The high prices of provisions and Cloathing will destroy about 2/3 of the inhabitants on the Sea coast. A report a few days past that the emission of Sep^t was Struck dead. Many that had that money to get it off gave a doller a gallon more for moll^s. If Congras should order that or any other emission to be taken out of Surculation Judge no body would sell goods for any of there money. I hope it will never be the case. The money men that had Surculation money got 10 to 25 p^r Ct. for exchanging April & May, & the Cuntry man for his provissions got in the Same proportion. Nothing will

Answer but Taxing & Sinking a sum every year or wait
Till the war is Over, or a Foreign loan. The Grand Secrit
we so much heard of, is supposed hear as a hum[bug] you
mentioned. Am Sorry our rulers will have out such reports. The pepol sayes no Faith for there money, nothing
in there report of a Grand Secrit. God send us peace
that the Sea coast inhabbitants may be saved from ruin.
Pray dont for get to Acquaint me if any Thing extraordinary Turns up, so I may have an Opportunity to prevent
my not suffring by a sudden change. We have plenty of
Fresh Fish & Meat. Bread very much wanted, you will
See by the prise current. As for the wine, Should send
you a quarter cask if I had a good Oppertunity, if not
Shall Sell it Soon. Brother John S. Ward & myself is
chosen to go to our Genl Court again. As for my self I
Told my Townsmen I would not Accept to go to court
again, only on the condission, I would be at Liberty to
Stay at home the whole year if I pleased. Y^r Affectionate, &c.

P. S.   prise current Beef 6 to 7/ p^r lb.   Veal 4 to 6/p^r
lb. Flour £50 p^r Ct. Corn £10 p^r bus. Moll^s 13 doll^r p
g^l. N. E. Rum 15 doll^{rs} W. I. do. 20 doll^{rs}.   Sugar £55
to 65£ p^r Ct. Coffe 15/ Tea 22 doll^r English goods 40.
for 1/ Sterling. Butter 12/ (at Boston 24).

N. B.   Capt Nickolls ask'd me if you had wright con-
serning him as he say'd he had wright to you on business
and had no Answer. I Told him I supposed his had mis-
carr'd. Dont for get to Acquaint him.

To Tim^o Pickering Esqr member of the Board of war,
Philadelphia.

Pickering MSS. Vol. 17, p. 266.

(*To be Continued.*)

MARBLEHEAD TAX LIST FOR THE YEAR 1748.

COPIED FROM A RECORD BOOK NOW IN POSSESSION OF

J. J. H. GREGORY OF MARBLEHEAD.

CONSTABLE ISRAEL PHIPPEN'S LIST OF RATES FOR THE
YEAR 1748 IN MARBLEHEAD.

	Poles.	R. Estate.	P. Estate.	
John Andrews & man.....39s.		21s.	39s. 3	£4.19.3
Eben^r Allen Junr.........19. 6		4.11	7.	1.11.5
Eben^r Allen.............19. 6				19.6
Joseph Ashton..........19. 6		4.11	4.3	1.7.9
Jedediah Blaney & Son....39.		10.6	7.	2.16.6
Joseph Banister & Son....39.		8.6	8.6	2.16.
John Blackler............19. 6		10.6	14.	2.4.
John Burd...............19. 6		4.3	4.3	1.8.
Thomas Bartlett.........19. 6		70.	7.	4.16.6
Joseph Bowden..........19. 6		4.3	4.	1.7.9
Francis Bowden & Son....39.		28.	7.	3.14.
John Bassett Junr.........19. 6		4.3	5.8	1.9.5
John Bassett............19. 6		24.6	92.6	6.16.6
John Boden.............19. 6		5.	7.	1.11.6
Humphrey Bartlett.......19. 6		4.3	3.6	1.7.3
John Brooks & Son......39.		70.	5.8	5.14.8
Daniel Conant.............			35.	1.15.
Sand Chapel.............19. 6		4.3	3.6	1.7.3
Joshua Coombs & Son....39.		35.	19.8	4.13.8
William Chapel & Son....39.		5.	19.	3.3.
Osmand Clark & Son.....39.		5.	8.6	2.12.6
Stephen Chapman.......19. 6		5.	3.6	1.8.
Stephen Chapman 19. 6			7.	1.6.6
Wid^o Chapman for Son....19. 6		4.3		1.3.9
Isaac Colyer...............19. 6		20.	56.	4.15.6
Samuell Chapman Junr....19. 6		4.3		1.3.9
Capt. Moses Calley & 2 Sons 58. 6		64.6	71.6	9.13.6
Capt. Thos Calley.........19. 6			35.	2.14.6
John Deverix.............19. 6		78.6	14.	5.3.6
Ralph Deverix.............19. 6		78.6	14.	5.3.6
Robert Deverix...........19. 6		78.6	14.	5.3.6
Capt Humphrey Deverix..19. 6		112.	56.3	9.11.9
Joseph Davis.............19. 6		4.3		1.3.9
Joseph Davis Junr.........19. 6				0.19.6

(209)

	Poles.	R. Estate.	P. Estate.	
Samuell Dennis	19s. 6	4s. 3	4s.	£1. 7. 9
Andrew Denniss	19. 6	4. 3	4.	1. 7. 9
Joseph Doliber	19. 6			19. 6
Sand Doliber	19. 6	4. 11	5. 8	1. 10. 1
John Fowler	19. 6		5. 8	1. 5. 2
William Furness	19. 6	5.	5. 8	1. 10. 2
Henry Flurey	19. 6	5.	7. 6	1. 11. 6
David Furniss	19. 6	14.	22. 6	2. 16.
Jeremiah Gatchel	19. 6	138. 2	14.	8. 11. 4
Elisha Gatchel	19. 6	8. 6	7.	1. 15.
Increase Gatchel	19. 6	5.	21.	2. 6. 6
Samuell Gatchel	19. 6		29. 5	2. 8. 11
Capt. John Gardner			25.	1. 5.
Bengm Gatchel	19. 6	4. 3	5. 8	1. 9. 5
Robert Gray	19. 6	4. 3		1. 3. 9
Nicholas Girdler	19. 6	5.	7.	1. 11. 6
Thos. Grant & Son	39.	14. 3	54. 8	4. 7. 11
Thomas Horton	19. 6	5.	4. 3	1. 8. 9
Benjm Hammond & Man	39.	5.	8. 6	2. 12. 6
William Hake	19. 6	4. 3	5. 8	1. 9. 5
David Howard	19. 6	21.	4. 3	2. 6. 9
John Harris & Son	19. 6			19. 6
Joseph Hollett	19. 6	8. 6	5. 8	1. 13. 8
Richard Hawley	19. 6	8. 6	5. 8	1. 13. 8
John Hill	19. 6	5	5. 8	1. 10. 2
John Ingalls	19. 6		3. 6	1. 3.
Widow Rackwood		21.		1. 1.
John Johnson	19. 6		3. 6	1. 3.
Thomas Jarvis & Son	39.	7.	7.	2. 13.
Saml. Lee Esq	19. 6	68.	532.	30. 19. 6
Phillip Lewis	19. 6	4. 3	5. 8	1. 9. 5
Elias Lodge	19. 6	5.	5.	1. 9. 6
Phillip Mason	19. 6	12.	4. 3	2. 14. 6
Dixey Morgan	19. 6	80. 6	56.	7. 16.
Thomas Morgan	19. 6	4. 3	2. 10	1. 6. 7
Robert Moulton	19. 6	35.		2. 14. 6
John Maybody	19. 6	4. 3	2. 10	1. 6. 7
James Morgan	19. 6		3. 6	1. 3.
William Nicholson	19. 6	5.	2. 10	1. 7. 4
Saml Nicholson	19. 6	22. 6	32.	3. 14.
William Nick	19. 6	7.	12.	1. 19. 1
Robert Nicholson	19. 6	4. 3		1. 3. 9
Jonah Nicholson	19. 6		8. 6	1. 8.
Benjm Oaks	19. 6	4. 3	3. 6	1. 7. 3
Benjm Oakes Junr	19. 6		7.	1. 6. 6
Jacob Oakes	19. 6	4. 3	5. 8	1. 9. 5

	Poles.	R. Estate.	P. Estate.	
Richd Pedrick & Son	39s.	9s. 2	7s.	£2 . 15 . 2
Joseph Procter	19 . 6	5 . 8	8 . 6	1 . 13 . 4
Pierce Poor	19 . 6	4 . 8		1 . 3 . 9
Thomas Proctor	19 . 6	5 .	4 . 3	1 . 8 . 9
Jonathan Proctor & 2 Men.	58 . 6	50 . 6	131 . 8	12 . 0 . 8
Samuell Parsons	19 . 6	4 . 3	4 . 1	1 . 7 . 9
Peter Pollow	19 . 6	8 . 6	4 . 3	1 . 12 . 3
John Proctor	19 . 6	5 .	5 . 8	1 . 16 . 2
Willm Pickett	19 . 6	5 .	7 .	1 . 11 . 6
Richard Pearce	19 . 6		4 .	1 . 3 . 6
Willm Quiner	19 . 6	5 .	5 . 8	1 . 10 . 2
Will Quiner Junr	19 . 6			19 . 6
John Reading & Son	39 .	31 . 6	72 . 2	7 . 2 . 8
Benj^m Reading	19 . 6	4 . 3	3 . 6	1 . 7 . 3
John Reading Junr	19 . 6	8 . 9	7 .	1 . 15 . 8
Abraham Roundy	19 . 6	12 .	52 . 6	3 . 4 .
Edward Roles	19 . 6		4 . 3	1 . 3 . 9
Joseph Roads	19 . 6	7 .	5 . 8	1 . 12 . 2
Thos Richards	19 . 6	4 . 3	3 . 6	1 . 7 .
John Roundy & Son	39 .	21 . 2	54 . 9	5 . 14 . 11
Samuell Read & Son	39 .	21 .	48 .	4 . 8 .
Nehemiah Skillions	19 . 6	73 . 6	30 . 2	6 . 3 . 8
Thomas Sandin	19 . 6	4 . 3	2 .	1 . 5 . 9
Thos Swan Jun	19 . 6	19 . 8	53 . 10	4 . 13 .
John Spinney	19 . 6	4 . 3	4 .	1 . 7 . 9
Sand Stephens	19 . 6	4 . 3	4 .	1 . 7 . 9
John Shepherd	19 . 6	4 . 3	7 .	1 . 13 . 6
Thomas Swan	19 . 6	5 .	3 . 6	1 . 8 .
Tobias Jones	19 . 6	4 . 3	3 . 6	1 . 7 . 3
Russell Trevett	19 . 6	26 .	90 . 10	6 . 16 . 4
John Tasker Esqr	19 . 6	53 . 10	322 .	19 . 15 . 4
Watton Thorne	19 . 6			19 . 6
Thos Tucker & Son	39 . 6	5 .	5 .	2 . 9 .
Thos Tucker Junr	19 . 6	5 . 8	5 . 8	1 . 10 . 2
John Tucker	19 . 6	5 .	7 .	1 . 11 . 6
Richd Trevett	19 . 6	8 . 6	5 . 9	1 . 13 . 8
James Vinson	19 . 6	5 .	5 . 8	1 . 10 . 2
John Vinson	19 . 6		5 . 8	1 . 5 . 2
Richard Webben	19 . 6	39 . 2	12 . 7	3 . 11 . 3
Robert Wallis	19 . 6	4 . 3	4 .	1 . 7 . 6
William Wallis	19 . 6	4 . 3	4 .	1 . 7 . 6
Calley Wright	19 . 6	8 . 6	7 .	1 . 15 .
Thomas White	19 . 6	4 . 3	8 . 6	1 . 12 .
Micheal Wormstead	19 . 6	5 .	5 . 8	1 . 10 . 2
John Warkes & Son	39 .			1 . 19 .
John Wormstead 2 Sons 2 Sev^{ts}	97 . 6	14 . 6	35 . 8	7 . 7 .
Micheal Wormstead Junr	19 . 6		5 . 8	1 . 5 . 2

CONSTABLE ROBERT HARRIS'S LIST OF RATES FOR THE YEAR 1748.

Name	Poles.	R. Estate.	P. Estate.	£ s. d.
John Allen	19s. 6	4s. 6		£1. 4.
Ephraim Ashton	19. 6	5.	5s. 8	1.16. 2
John Andrews Junr	19. 6		7.	1. 6. 6
Saml Ashton	19. 6		7.	1. 6. 6
John Bridges	19. 6	6.	4.	1.11. 6
Obadiah Bridges	19. 6		7.	1. 6. 6
Thos Brimblecome	19. 6	5.	4.	1. 8. 6
Richard Bowden	19. 6	8.	5. 6	1.13.
Giles Burrows	19. 6	5. 3	5. 8	1.10. 5
Joseph Blany Esqr & Son	39.	45. 6	82. 3	8. 6. 9
Nathl Bartlett	19. 6	51.	37. 6	5. 8.
Benja Boden & Son	39.	40.	46.	6. 5.
Martin Broughton	19. 6		8. 6	1. 8.
William Burroughs	19. 6		5. 8	1. 5. 2
John Bartol	19. 6	21. 6	21. 6	3. 2. 6
Christopher Bubier	19. 6	26.	120.	8. 5. 6
Saml Bowden	19. 6	5. 3	4. 3	1. 9.
Simpson Bowden	19. 6	10. 6	4. 3	1.14. 3
Benja Brown	19. 6	5. 3	4. 3	1. 9.
Benja Brown Junr	19. 6	4. 5	3.	1. 6.11
John Broughton	19. 6	5. 3	5. 8	1.10. 5
John Bartlett	19. 6	19. 3		1.18. 9
Phillip Craw & Son	39.	5. 3	8. 6	2.12. 9
Francis Cavendish	19. 6	4. 5	4. 3	1. 8. 2
Thomas Cavendish		5.		5.
Micheal Coombs & Son	39.	7.	25. 6	3.11. 6
William Craw	19. 6	5. 3	4. 3	1.19. 6
Gurdler Cavendish	19. 6	5. 3	4. 3	1. 9.
Daniel Carr	19. 6	4. 5	4. 3	1. 8. 2
John Dixey	19. 6	4. 5		1. 3.11
Saml Dixey & Son	39.	5. 6	5. 6	2.10.
Joseph Devereux	19. 6	4. 5	4. 3	1. 8. 2
Thomas Dove	19. 6	4. 5	4. 3	1. 8. 2
John Doliber	19. 6	4. 5	5. 8	1. 9. 7
John Dodd	19. 6	5. 3	5. 8	1.10. 5
John Dixey Junr	19. 6	5. 3	7.	1.11. 9
Samuell Dixey Junr	19. 6	4. 5	4. 3	1. 8. 2
Thomas Dodd	19. 6	5. 3		1. 9.
Thomas Denniss & Son	19. 6			19. 6
Daniel Felton & 2 Sons	58. 6	8. 6	5. 8	3.12. 8
Thomas Frothingham	19. 6	17. 6	34.	3.11.
Jam Farewell	19. 6	4. 5	4. 3	1. 8. 2
Benga Furniss	19. 6	4. 5	4. 3	1. 8. 2
Phillip Follett	19. 6		4. 3	1. 3. 9
William Furniss Jun	19. 6		4. 3	1. 3. 9

	Poles.	R. Estate.	P. Estate.	
John Hooper	19s. 6	12s. 8	4s. 3	£1 . 16 . 6
Benja Hendly	19 . 6	59 . 6	30 .	5 . 9 .
George Hendly	19 . 6	5 . 3	4 . 3	1 . 9 .
John Hind & Man	39 .	20 .	56 .	5 . 15 .
Sam¹ Hitchins	19 . 6	8 . 6	21 .	2 . 9 .
Sharpley Hawley & Son	39 .	5 . 3	5 . 8	2 . 9 . 11
Willm Humphreys	19 . 6	4 . 5	5 . 8	1 . 9 . 11
Natha Hooper	19 . 6	24 . 6	70 .	5 . 14 .
Richa Harris & Son	39 .	4 . 5		2 . 3 . 5
Dr. Robert Hooper & Man.	39 .	24 . 6	73 . 6	6 . 17 .
Thomas Horton	19 . 6	4 . 3	5 . 8	1 . 9 . 7
Joseph Howard	19 . 6	33 . 3	54 .	5 . 6 . 9
Rich Hubbard	19 . 6	5 . 3	7 .	1 . 11 . 9
John Hooper	19 . 6	4 . 5	4 . 3	1 . 8 . 2
Robert Harris	19 . 6	8 . 6	8 . 6	1 . 16 . 6
James Harris & Son	39 .	5 . 3	4 . 3	2 . 8 . 6
Phillip Hye	19 . 6	4 . 5	5 . 8	1 . 9 . 7
C. W. Hylager & Man	39 .	25 .	130 .	12 . 4 .
Peter Knap	19 . 6	4 . 5	4 . 3	1 . 8 . 2
Joshua Kimball & Man	39 .	17 . 6	58 .	5 . 14 . 6
Capt. Sam King & Sevt.	39 .	10 . 6	46 .	4 . 15 . 6
Sam Killey	19 . 6	4 . 5	5 . 8	1 . 9 . 7
Thomas Kinsman	19 . 6	4 . 5	4 . 3	1 . 8 . 2
Peter Leecraw	19 . 6	4 . 5	4 . 3	1 . 8 . 2
Thos Loois Jun	19 . 6	5 . 3	7 .	1 . 11 . 9
John Lee	19 . 6		5 .	1 . 4 . 6
Joseph Lindsey	19 . 6	10 .	8 .	1 . 17 . 6
Andrew Lee	19 . 6	5 . 3	7 .	1 . 11 . 9
Richd Lee	19 . 6	9 .	25 .	2 . 13 . 6
Capt. David Leegallan	19 . 6	78 . 6	312 .	20 . 10 .
John Lapthron	19 . 6	5 . 9	7 .	1 . 11 . 9
Willm Messor	19 . 6	5 . 3	7 .	1 . 11 . 9
John Mame	19 . 6	4 . 5	5ᵘ. 8	1 . 9 . 7
Thomas Martin	19 . 6	36 . 6		2 . 15 . 6
Joseph Majory	19 . 6	24 . 6		2 . 4 .
Knott Martin	19 . 6	9 .	8 . 6	1 . 17 .
Dr. Joseph Lemmon & Man	39 .	54 .	192 .	14 . 5 .
George Newmarsh	19 . 6	13 .	9 .	2 . 1 . 6
John Nut & Man	39 .	10 . 6	42 .	4 . 11 . 6
John Neal	19 . 6	5 . 3	8 . 6	1 . 13 . 3
Henery Oliver	19 . 6	4 . 5	4 . 3	1 . 8 . 2
Jacob Oliver	19 . 6	4 . 5	4 . 3	1 . 8 . 2
Willm Orne	19 . 6	10 . 6	35 .	3 . 5 .
John Oliver	19 . 6	4 . 5	5 . 8	1 . 9 . 7
George Oakes & Son	39 .	4 . 5	5 . 8	2 . 9 . 1
Aaron Oakes	19 . 6	5 . 3	5 . 8	1 . 10 . 5
Thos Oliver	19 . 6			19 . 6 .

	Poles.	R. Estate.	P. Estate.	
Henry Pain	19s. 6	5s. 3	10s. 6	£1 . 15 . 3
Dr. John Pearce	19 . 6	35 .	90 .	7 . 4 . 6
Benjᵃ Persons	19 . 6	4 . 5	5 . 8	1 . 9 . 7
Joseph Pickitt	19 . 6	9 .	16 . 6	2 . 5 .
Joseph Pickitt Jun	19 . 6	10 . 6	10 . 6	2 . 6 . 6
Andrew Peltrow	19 . 6	4 . 5	3 . 8	1 . 7 . 7
Thomas Pimour	19 . 6	4 . 3	3 . 6	1 . 7 . 3
John Palmer	19 . 6	78 . 6	70 .	8 . 8 .
Stephen Phillips & 3 men.	.78 .	13 .	10 . 6	5 . 1 . 6
Thomas Procter Jun	19 . 6	5 .	7 .	1 . 11 . 6
Samˡ Parker		17 . 10	49 .	3 . 6 . 10
Peter Polt	19 . 6	4 . 3	4 . 3	1 . 8 .
Thoˢ Skinner	19 . 6	12 . 7	14 .	2 . 6 . 1
Joseph Swett	19 . 6	35 .	91 . 6	7 . 6 .
Thoˢ Stephens Jun & Son.	39 .	8 . 6		2 . 7 . 9
Frances Salter & Sevt.	39 .	12 . 9	59 . 6	5 . 11 . 3
Joseph Sinecross	19 . 6	5 .	7	1 . 11 . 6
Samˡ Sanders	19 . 6		2 . 2	1 . 1 . 8
Isaac Turner & Son	39 .	24 . 6	10 . 6	3 . 14 .
Willᵐ Vinson	19 . 6	4 . 3	7 .	1 . 10 . 9
John Vickroy & Son	39 .	5 .	5 . 8	2 . 9 . 8
John Vickroy Jun	19 . 6	5 .	7 .	1 . 11 . 6
John Vickroy 3ᵈ	19 . 6	5 .	8 . 6	1 . 13 .
Jacob Vickroy	19 . 6	5 .	8 . 6	1 . 13 .
Benjᵃ Wilkins	19 . 6	4 . 3	4 .	1 . 7 . 6
John Webber	19 . 6	13 .	49 .	3 . 1 . 6
William Weber	19 . 6	12 . 6		1 . 12 .
William Widger	19 . 6	4 . 3		1 . 3 . 9
Richᵈ Weber Jun	19 . 6	4 . 3	2 . 2	1 . 5 . 11
Charles Wheden & Son	39 .	17 . 6	14 .	3 . 10 . 6
William Webb	19 . 6	4 . 3		1 . 3 . 9
Thomas Widger	19 . 6	4 . 3	4 . 3	1 . 8 .

CONSTABLE WILLIAM DOLIBER'S LIST OF RATES FOR THE YEAR 1748.

	Poles.	R. Estate.	P. Estate.	
Jacob Allen 2 Sons	58 . 6	5 . 8	3 . 6	3 . 7 . 6
Capt. Jno Addams 3 Servtˢ	78 .	22 . 6	84 .	9 . 4 . 6
John Allen junʳ	19 . 6	4 . 3	3 .	1 . 6 . 9
John Barker	19 . 6	5 .	5 .	1 . 9 . 6
George Barker & Son	39 .	7 .	3 . 6	2 . 9 . 6
George Barker jun	.19 . 6	5 . 1	7 .	1 . 11 . 7
Samˡ Bowden	19 . 6	11 . 3	5 . 8	1 . 16 . 5
Edward Boden	19 . 6	5 . 3	5 . 8	1 . 11 . 5
Joseph Brimblecomb	19 . 6			19 . 6
John Bartlett junʳ	19 . 6	5 . 3	3 . 6	1 . 8 . 3
Samˡ Brimblecome	19 . 6	24 .	21 . 8	3 . 5 . 8
Samˡ Bushop	19 . 6			19 . 6

	Poles.	R. Estate.	P. Estate.	
Nathan Bowen	19s. 6	132s. 4	86s. 10	£11 . 18 . 8
Palmer Bushop	19 . 6	17 . 6	17 . 6	2 . 14 . 6
George Batchelder	19 . 6	2 . 3	14 .	1 . 17 . 9
Benjᵃ Bacon	19 . 6	8 . 6	6 . 5	1 . 14 . 5
Nathan Bowen junʳ	19 . 6			19 . 6
Edward Bowen	19 . 6		7 .	1 . 6 . 6
John Bray	19 . 6	5 . 3	14 .	1 . 18 . 9
John Brown	19 . 6	3 . 6	7 .	1 . 10 .
Thomas Brown & Son	39 .	5 .	7 .	2 . 11 .
John Boen	19 . 6	5 . 3	7 .	1 . 11 . 9
James Bowden	19 . 6	4 . 5	2 . 10	1 . 6 . 3
Michael Bowden	19 . 6	5 .	5 .	1 . 9 . 6
John Brimblecome	19 . 6	7 . 9	4 . 11	1 . 12 . 2
Phillip Curney	19 . 6	7 . 8	7 .	1 . 14 . 1
Willᵐ Cruff Junʳ	19 . 6	5 .	4 . 3	1 . 8 . 9
Wido Mary Chapman		14 .		14 .
Matthias Collins	19 . 6	7 . 8	7 .	1 . 14 . 2
Wido Susannah Coleman		20 . 4		1 . 0 . 4
Richard Cowell	19 . 6	9 .	45 .	3 . 13 . 6
William Cruff & Servt	39 .	5 . 3	8 . 6	2 . 12 . 9
Phillip Cross	19 . 6	5 . 3	4 . 11	1 . 9 . 8
Richard Curtias	19 . 6	5 . 3	7 .	1 . 11 . 9
Thoˢ Cloutman & Son	39 .	14 . 6	7 .	3 . 0 . 6
Widd Crab & Son		10 .		10 .
John Caine	19 . 6	4 . 5	1 . 5	1 . 5 . 4
Wido Elizabeth Carden		7 . 8	36 . 6	2 . 4 . 2
John Corney	19 . 6		8 . 6	1 . 8 .
Elias Conal	19 . 6	10 . 6	7 .	1 . 17 .
John Cloue	19 . 6	4 . 5	1 . 5	1 . 5 . 4
Timothy Curtis	19 . 6	5 . 3	5 . 8	1 . 10 . 5
Willᵐ Curtis & Son	39 .	8 . 7	10 . 6	2 . 18 . 1
Joseph Carder	19 . 6	27 . 4	105 . 1	7 . 11 . 11
Issaac Card	19 . 6	5 . 3	7 .	1 . 11 . 9
Adoniram Collins	19 . 6	10 . 6	1 . 5	1 . 11 . 5
Micajah Collins	19 . 6	13 . 3	75 . 10	5 . 8 . 7
Amos Dennis & Son	39 .	7 .	7 .	2 . 13 .
William Diamond & Son	19 . 6	8 . 7	5 . 3	1 . 13 . 4
John Doake	19 . 6	4 . 5	1 . 5	1 . 5 . 4
James Darlin	19 . 6	28 .	33 .	4 . 0 . 6
William Tucksbery	19 . 6			19 . 6
Devereux Dennis	19 . 6	5 . 3	5 . 8	1 . 10 . 5
Issaac Dehoman	19 . 6	10 . 6	7 .	1 . 17 .
John Doliber	19 . 6	4 . 5	3 . 6	1 . 7 . 5
Peter Doliber & Son	39 .	5 . 3	8 . 6	2 . 12 . 9
Thomas Doliber	19 . 6	12 . 7	21 . 9	2 . 13 . 10
Thomas Doliber Junʳ	19 . 6		8 . 7	1 . 8 . 1
—— Denniss	19 . 6	5 . 3	5 . 8	1 . 10 . 5
William Doliber	19 . 6	4 . 5	7 .	1 . 10 . 11
James Denniss & Son	39 .	10 . 6	8 . 6	2 . 18 .
Jones Denniss	19 . 6	5 . 3	2 . 10	1 . 7 . 7
John Denniss	19 . 6	4 . 5	5 . 8	1 . 9 . 7
Amos Denniss 3ᵈ	19 . 6			19 . 6

	Poles.	R. Estate.	P. Estate.	
Sam¹ Dodd & Son	39s.	5s. 3	7s.	£2 . 11 . 3
Joseph Doliber Junʳ	19 . 6	4 . 5	5 . 8	1 . 9 . 7
Thomas Dixey	19 . 6	12 . 8	7 .	1 . 19 . 2
Thomas Disemore	19 . 6	8 . 7	28 . 2	2 . 16 . 3
Sam¹ Dixey & Son	39 .	4 . 5	42 .	4 . 5 . 5
William Dixey	19 . 6	35 .	10 . 6	3 . 5 .
Sam¹ Dixey Junʳ	19 . 6	4 . 3	5 .	1 . 8 . 9
Nathᵃ Evins	19 . 6	12 . 6	5 .	1 . 17 .
John Eletrap	19 . 6	8 . 6	5 .	1 . 13 .
Thomas Elkins	19 . 6	8 . 6		1 . 8 .
David Flury	19 . 6	5 .	7 .	1 . 11 . 6
Edward Fetteplaice & Servt	39 .	5 .	10 . 6	2 . 14 . 6
David Furniss	19 . 6	8 . 6	5 . 8	1 . 13 . 8
Elizabeth Finch		17 . 6	7 .	1 . 4 . 6
Thomas Foot	19 . 6	5 .	7 .	1 . 11 . 6
John Felton	19 . 6	37 . 6	100 .	7 . 17 .
John Felton Junʳ	19 . 6	7 .	7 .	1 . 13 . 6
Francis Felton	19 . 6		5 .	1 . 4 . 6
John Fetteplace & Servt	39 .	5 .	8 . 6	2 . 12 . 6
Nicholas Gourdon	19 . 6		8 . 6	1 . 8 .
Amos Grant	19 . 6	5 .	4 .	1 . 8 . 6
John Gale	19 . 6	5 .	4 . 3	1 . 8 . 9
William Green		17 . 4		17 . 4
Joseph Gallison	19 . 6	21 .	3 . 6	2 . 4 .
John Grandy	19 . 6	8 . 6	7 .	1 . 15 .
Benjᵃ Girdler	19 . 6	8 . 6	7 .	1 . 15 .
William Goodwin	19 . 6	16 . 6	31 . 6	3 . 7 . 6
William Goodwin Junʳ	19 . 6	5 .	4 . 6	1 . 9 .
Timothy Goodwin	19 . 6	5 .	4 .	1 . 5 . 6
Sam¹ Graves	19 . 6	10 . 6	4 . 6	1 . 14 . 6
John Grant & Son	39 .	5 .	5 .	2 . 9 .
Francis Girdler	19 . 6	24 . 6	75 . 8	5 . 19 . 8
Thomas Gale	19 . 6	4 . 6	8 . 6	1 . 12 . 6
Widᵒ Girdler		5 .		5 .
William Gale 3 Servt	78 .	18 . 6	20 .	5 . 16 . 6
Robert Girdler Junʳ	19 . 6		3 . 6	1 . 3 .
Robert Gifford & Son	39 .	8 . 6	8 .	2 . 15 . 6
William Girdler	19 . 6	5 .	7 .	1 . 11 . 6
Thomas Gilbord	19 . 6	5 .	14 .	1 . 18 . 6
John Grist & Son	39 .	8 . 6	32 .	2 . 19 . 6
John Grist Junʳ	19 . 6		3 .	1 . 2 . 6
Capt. Thomas Gerry	19 . 6	84 .	137 . 2	12 . 0 . 8
John Ingalls	19 . 6	4 . 3	5 . 8	1 . 9 . 5
Richard Ireson	19 . 6	4 . 3	4 .	1 . 7 . 9
Capt. George Jackson	19 . 6	10 . 6	3 . 6	1 . 13 . 6
John Jackson Junʳ	19 . 6	5 .	5 . 8	1 . 10 . 2
Giles Juimy	19 . 6	59 . 6	88 . 6	8 . 7 . 6
John Jackson	19 . 6			19 . 6

	Poles.	R. Estate.	P. Estate.	
John Knight	19s. 6	4s. 3		£1. 3. 9
Thomas Kimball	19. 6	10. 6	35s.	3. 5.
Willm Knight	19. 6	4. 3	14. 3	1. 18.
George Kirk	19. 6	4. 3		1. 3. 9
William Laskin	19. 6	5.	5. 8	1.10. 2
John Laskin	19. 6	4.	5. 8	1. 9. 2
Joseph Leelgrow	19. 6		2. 6	1. 2.
Thomas Leefavour	19. 6	5.	5. 8	1.10. 2
John Leecraw	19. 6	7.	2. 6	1. 9.
Calab Lindall	19. 6	18.	10. 6	2. 8.
Nicholas Lamprell & Man.	39.	8. 6	28.	3.15. 6
Thomas Luke	19. 6	4. 3	2. 10	1. 6. 7
James Lyon	19. 6	4. 3	7.	1.10. 9
Saml Lavis	19. 6	4. 3	5. 8	1. 9. 5
Seward Lee	19. 6	15. 6	56. 8	4.11. 8
Jeremiah Lee & Man	39.	48.	462.	27. 9.

CONSTABLE THOMAS CALLEY'S LIST OF RATES FOR YE YEAR 1748.

	Poles.	R. Estate.	P. Estate.	
Samuell Andrews	19. 6	4. 3	5. 8	1. 9. 5
John Andrews ye 3d	19. 6	5.	6. 5	1.10.11
Joseph Abbut	19. 6	5. 7	5. 8	1.10. 9
John Andrewson	19. 6	5. 7	5. 8	1.10. 9
James Andrews		5. 7		5. 7
Joseph Bubier	19. 6			19. 6
Faithfull Bartlett	19. 6	13. 1	29. 2	3. 1. 9
Nicholas Bartlett	19. 6	9.	42.	3.10. 6
Saml Beal	19. 6	5. 7	5. 8	1.10. 9
Willm Broughton	19. 6	4. 4	5. 8	1. 9. 6
Aaron Beal	19. 6	5. 3	2. 10	1. 7. 7
Robert Bull	19. 6	13. 2	7.	1. 19. 8
Joseph Bigsbey	19. 6	4. 5	4. 3	1. 8. 2
William Bartlett	19. 6	29. 6	10. 6	2. 19. 6
John Bartlett ye 3d	19. 6		5. 8	1. 5. 2
Suard Brimblecom	19. 6	4. 3	5. 8	1. 9. 5
Peter Briggs	19. 6	4. 3	1. 5	1. 5. 2
John Brockett	19. 6	4. 5	5. 8	1. 9. 7
Saml Brimblecom	19. 6	9. 8	28.	2.16. 6
Michael Bowden Jun	19. 6	4. 5	5. 8	1. 9. 7
Richd Crafts	19. 6	4. 5	3. 6	1. 7. 5
Phillip Cross	19. 6	4. 5	5. 8	1. 9. 7
Saml Chamblits & Servt	39.	17. 8	65. 6	6. 2. 6
John Caswel	19. 6	5. 3	7.	1.11. 9
Saml Cook	19. 6		5. 8	1. 5. 2
William Crafts	19. 6	9.	8. 6	1. 17.
William Curtis Junr.	19. 6	4. 5	5. 8	1. 9. 7
John Chapman	19. 6	10. 6	10. 6	2. 0. 6
Elias Cook	19. 6	4. 5		1. 3. 11
John Caradge 2 Sons	58. 6	4. 5	7.	3. 9. 11

	Poles.	R. Estate.	P. Estate.	
John Carrell	19s. 6		4s. 3	£1 . 3 . 9
John Curtis	19 . 6			19 . 6
Robert Coleny	19 . 6		5 . 8	1 . 5 . 2
Saml Colyer & Servt	39 .	12 .	54 . 7	5 . 5 . 7
William Curtis	19 . 6	18 . 4	7 .	2 . 4 . 10
John Chambers	19 . 6	4 . 5	4 . 3	1 . 8 . 2
James Denniss Jun	19 . 6	4 . 5	4 . 3	1 . 8 . 2
John Davis	19 . 6		4 . 3	1 . 3 . 9
Benja Darlin 2 Servts	58 . 6	20 .	63 . 3	7 . 1 . 6
John Dodd	19 . 6			19 . 6
Micheal Dodge	19 . 6		3 . 6	1 . 3 .
Nicholas Edgcome Jun	19 . 6			19 . 6
Nicholas Edgcome	19 . 6	24 . 6	10 . 6	2 . 14 . 6
Samuell Fortine	19 . 6	5 . 3	7 .	1 . 11 . 9
Willm Foster	19 . 6	4 . 5		1 . 3 . 11
Major Jacob Fowler	19 . 6	58 . 4	308 .	19 . 5 . 6
Joshua Foster	19 . 6	22 . 6	14 .	2 . 16 .
James Freeto	19 . 6	5 . 3	8 . 6	1 . 13 .
William Fabins	19 . 6	4 . 5	3 . 6	1 . 7 . 5
Daniel Gould	19 . 6	13 . 6	7 .	1 . 19 . 6
Hutton Goldsmith	19 . 6	4 . 5	3 . 6	1 . 7 . 5
Nathl Goldsmith	19 . 6	4 . 5	5 . 8	1 . 9 . 7
Peter Green	19 . 6	4 . 5	7 .	1 . 10 . 11
Nicholas Girdler Junr	19 . 6	5 . 5	5 . 8	1 . 10 . 5
Will Gray	19 . 6	7 .	2 . 10	1 . 9 . 4
Thos Girdler	19 . 6		5 . 8	1 . 5 . 2
William Goss	19 . 6	5 . 3	12 . 7	1 . 17 . 4
Robert Hooper Esq.& Serv.	39 .	229 .	4347 .	230 . 11 .
John Harmond	19 . 6	7 .	8 .	1 . 7 . 2
Edward Humphreys	19 . 6	5 . 3	3 . 6	1 . 8 . 3
Willm Haydon & Servt	39 .	5 . 3	3 . 6	2 . 7 . 9
Stephen Heyton	19 . 6	5 . 3	5 . 8	1 . 10 . 5
Nathal Homan & Son	39 .	13 . 4	7 .	2 . 19 . 4
Thomas Hollet	19 . 6	4 . 5	5 . 8	1 . 9 . 7
George Johnson	19 . 6	4 . 5	4 . 3	1 . 8 . 2
Wido Eliza James for man.	19 . 6	9 .		1 . 8 . 6
Capt. Batha Jackson	19 . 6	17 . 6	10 . 6	2 . 7 . 6
Benja James Junr	19 . 6	5 . 3	5 . 8	1 . 10 . 5
Richard James Jun		13 . 6		13 . 6
John Merritt	19 . 6	5 . 3	5 . 8	1 . 10 . 5
Peter Martin	39 .	5 . 3	5 . 8	1 . 10 . 5
Thos Muguire & Son	39 .	7 .	5 . 8	2 . 11 . 8
Isaac Mansfield & man	19 . 6	27 . 5	33 . 6	4 . 19 . 11
Micheal Murre	19 . 6		2 . 10	1 . 2 . 4
Abraham Morse	19 . 6	13 . 4	28 .	3 . 0 . 10
Thomas Mullett	19 . 6	5 . 3	8 . 6	1 . 13 . 3
Willm Messor Junr	19 . 6	5 . 3	5 . 8	1 . 10 . 5

	Poles.	R. Estate.	P. Estate.	
Thos Mullett Junr	19s. 6	5s. 3	7 .	£1 . 11 . 9
Bonnel Merifield	19 . 6			19 . 6
Sarah Martin for Son	19 . 6	5 . 3		4 . 4 . 9
George Melzard	19 . 6	4 . 5	7 .	1 . 10 . 11
Abraham Mullett	19 . 6	8 . 9	22 . 6	2 . 10 . 3
Lewis Russell & Son	39 .	8 . 9	8 . 6	2 . 16 . 3
Willm Revell	19 . 6	8 . 9	7 .	1 . 15 . 3
John Roads Junr	19 . 6	5 . 3	5 . 8	1 . 10 . 5
Peter Renew	19 . 6			19 . 6
John Read	19 . 6	25 . 10	28 .	3 . 13 . 4
Richard Ringe	19 . 6	5 . 3	5 . 8	1 . 10 . 5
John Raynold Junr	19 . 6	4 . 5	4 . 3	1 . 8 . 2
John Raynold & Son	39 .	7 .	2 . 10	2 . 8 . 10
John Road & Son	39 .	27 . 6	109 . 2	8 . 15 . 8
Thomas Pickett	19 . 6	4 . 5	7 .	1 . 10 . 11
Joseph Procter	19 . 6	8 . 9	7 .	1 . 15 . 3
Nicholas Procter	19 . 6	5 . 3	3 . 6	1 . 8 . 3
Israel Phippin	19 . 6	5 . 3	5 . 8	1 . 10 . 5
Joseph Potter	19 . 6		1 . 5	1 . 0 . 11
Robert Pearce	19 . 6	4 . 5	4 . 3	1 . 8 . 2
John Pearce Junr	19 . 6	4 . 5	8 . 6	1 . 12 . 5
John Pickitt	19 . 6	4 . 5	5 . 8	1 . 9 . 7
Joseph Pickworth	19 . 6	5 . 3	7 .	1 . 11 . 9
John Scarlot	19 . 6	5 . 3	7 .	1 . 11 . 9
Thomas Seal	19 . 6	4 . 5	8 . 9	1 . 12 . 8
Saml Selman	19 . 6		7 .	1 . 6 . 6
William Stevens	19 . 6	21 .	32 . 9	3 . 13 . 3
Thomas Smith	19 . 6	5 . 3	7 .	2 . 11 . 3
Saml Stacy Junr	19 . 6	4 . 5	5 . 8	1 . 9 . 7
Joseph Stevens & Son	39 .	5 . 3	7 .	2 . 11 . 3
Richard Sharply	19 . 6	4 . 5	2 . 8	1 . 7 . 7
Saml Severit & Son	39 .	5 . 2	7 .	2 . 11 . 3
John Stephens	19 . 6	4 . 5	14 .	1 . 17 . 11
Robert Whicher	19 . 6			19 . 6
Joseph Whicher & Son	39 .	9 .	8 . 6	1 . 17 . 0
John Williams Junr	19 . 6	9 . 6	14 .	2 . 2 . 6
Richard Williams	19 . 6	4 . 5	7 .	1 . 10 . 11
Saml West	19 . 6		3 . 6	1 . 3 .
John Williams	19 . 6	9 .	10 . 6	1 . 19 .
Saml Whicher	19 . 6	4 . 5	5 . 8	1 . 9 . 7

CONSTABLE WILLIAM HOMAN'S LIST OF RATES FOR THE YEAR 1748.

	Poles.	R. Estate.	P. Estate.	
William Homan & Son	39 .	31 . 6	54 . 8	6 . 5 . 2
John Harris	19 . 6		7 .	1 . 6 . 2
Edward Hayles	19 . 6	17 . 6	32 . 3	3 . 9 . 3
Edward Hayles Junr	19 . 6	5 . 3	5 . 8	1 . 10 . 5
Richard Homan	19 . 6	24 . 6	75 . 8	5 . 19 . 8
Clattery Homan	19 . 6	4 . 5	5 . 8	1 . 9 . 7

	Poles.	R. Estate.	P. Estate.	
Joseph Hinds	19s. 6	10s. 6	5s. 8	£1 . 15 . 8
John Hundson	19 . 6	4 . 5	5 . 8	1 . 9 . 7
Peter Homan	17 . 6	28 . 1	74 . 9	6 . 2 . 4
Willm Homan Junr	19 . 6		19 . 8	1 . 19 . 2
Willm Hickey & Son	39 .	5 . 3	5 . 8	2 . 9 . 11
William Hinds	19 . 6	5 . 3	7 .	1 . 11 . 9
John Huy	19 . 6	5 . 3	7 .	1 . 11 . 9
Moses Hooper	19 . 6	5 . 3	5 . 8	1 . 10 . 6
Saml Haulman	19 . 6	7 .		1 . 6 . 6
John Hendly	19 . 6	4 . 5	7 .	1 . 10 . 11
Phillip Hammond	19 . 6	5 . 3	46 . 10	3 . 11 . 7
John Hooper	19 . 6	4 . 5	5 . 8	1 . 9 . 7
Joseph Homan	19 . 6	35 . 10	54 . 8	5 . 10 .
Joseph Hendly	19 . 6			19 . 6
Joseph Hendly junr	19 . 6	4 . 5	4 . 3	1 . 8 . 2
John Homan Junr	19 . 6	4 . 5	7 .	1 . 10 . 11
Wido Ann Herrick & Servt.	19 . 6	7 .		1 . 6 . 6
Ebenr Hawks 2 Servts	58 . 6	105 .	63 .	11 . 6 . 6
Timothy Jackman			20 .	1 . 0 .
Daniel Merro	19 . 6	4 . 5		1 . 3 . 11
James Murry	19 . 6	4 . 5	3 . 6	1 . 7 . 5
Phillip Messervy	19 . 6	5 . 3	6 . 8	1 . 11 . 5
Thomas Martin Junr	19 . 6	7 .	59 .	4 . 5 . 6
John Mailey	19 . 6	4 . 5	7 .	1 . 10 . 11
Nicholas Merritt	19 . 6		4 . 5	1 . 3 . 11
Daniel Mailey	19 . 6		7 .	1 . 6 . 6
Thos Meden	19 . 6	8 . 10	36 . 6	3 . 4 . 10
James Mugford	19 . 6	7 .	8 . 6	1 . 15 .
Ebenr Nutting	19 . 6	7 . 6		1 . 6 . 6
Ebenr Nutting Junr	19 . 6	4 . 5		1 . 3 . 11
Joshua Orne Esq	19 . 6	50 . 10	55 . 3	6 . 5 . 7
Simond Orne	19 . 6	8 . 10	5 . 8	1 . 14 .
John Orne	19 . 6	12 . 3	5 . 8	1 . 17 . 5
Samuell Orne	19 . 6	5 . 8	54 . 10	4 . 0 .
Thomas Owens	19 . 6	5 . 3	3 . 6	1 . 8 . 3
John Owens	19 . 6	5 . 3	7 .	1 . 11 . 9
James Oakes	19 . 6	5 . 3	3 . 6	1 . 8 . 3
Joshua Orne Junr 2 Sons	58 . 6	55 .	156 .	13 . 9 . 6
Joshua Orne Junr for Sand Sweet		21 .	84 . 5	5 . 5 . 5
Benja Pritchett	19 . 6			19 . 6
Joseph Pedrick	19 . 6	23 . 10	33 .	3 . 16 . 4
John Phillips	19 . 6	4 . 5	7 .	1 . 10 . 11
Cornelious Phillips	19 . 6	5 . 3	7 .	1 . 11 . 9
Mark Pittman	19 . 6	4 . 5		1 . 3 . 11
Capt. Robert Parimore	19 . 6	49 .	101 . 10	8 . 10 . 4
Thos Peach	19 . 6	75 . 3	196 . 2	14 . 10 . 11
John Pattin	19 . 6	4 . 5	5 . 8	1 . 9 . 7
John Peach	19 . 6	4 . 5		1 . 3 . 11

	Poles.	R. Estate.	P. Estate.	
John Pittman............		25s.		£1 . 5 .
Moses Pittman............		10 .		10 .
Willm Peach..............19 . 6		17 . 6	5 . 8	2 . 2 . 8
Benja Pittman............19 . 6		4 . 5	3 . 6	1 . 7 . 5
Willm Peach Junr.........19 . 6		8 . 10	8 . 6	1 . 16 . 10
Mathew Pennel...........19 . 6		5 . 3	7 .	1 . 11 . 9
David Poor...............19 . 6				19 . 6
Nehemiah Pribble........19 . 6		5 . 3	5 . 8	1 . 10 . 5
Capt. Richard Reed.......19 . 6		36 . 6	25 . 10	4 . 1 . 10
Capt. Richard Reith......19 . 6		38 . 6	51 . 2	5 . 9 . 2
William Reith.............19 . 6		4 . 5		1 . 3 . 11
Charles Reading & Son....39 .		5 . 3	5 . 8	2 . 9 . 11
Freeborn Reaves..........19 . 6		4 . 5		1 . 3 . 11
Capt. Giles Russell.,......19 . 6		33 . 8	140 .	9 . 13 . 2
William Robison..........19 . 6		4 . 5		1 . 3 . 11
Richard Russell & Son....39 .		4 . 5	8 . 6	2 . 11 . 11
Patrick Reading..........19 . 6		4 . 5		1 . 3 . 11
Saml Smith...............			11 . 2	11 . 2
John Shappon Junr........19 . 6				19 . 6
John Swettland...........19 . 6		4 . 5	3 . 6	1 . 7 . 5
Andrew Stacy 3 Sons......78 .		10 . 6	10 . 6	4 . 19 .
William Smith & man.....39 .		7 .	14 .	3 . 0 .
Sand Standley & man.,.....39 .		5 . 3	19 . 6	3 . 3 . 9
Sand Standley Junr........19 . 6			4 . 3	1 . 3 . 9
Richard Stephens.........19 . 6		8 . 10	19 . 6	2 . 7 . 10
Saml Swettland...........19 . 6			5 . 8	1 . 5 . 2
Archibald Selman & man..39 .		5 . 3	10 . 6	2 . 14 . 9
Joseph Selman Junr.......19 . 6		4 . 5	7 .	1 . 10 . 11
George Salkins............19 . 6		5 . 3	5 . 8	1 . 10 . 5
Capt. Benja Stacey 2 men..58 . 6		33 .	35 .	6 . 6 . 6
Dr. Edward Stacey........19 . 6		17 . 6	10 . 6	2 . 7 . 6
Ebenr Stacey 2 Sons.......58 . 6		32 . 9	70 .	8 . 1 . 3
Capt. John Stacey & Son..39 .		17 . 6	14 .	3 . 10 . 6
Benja Stacey 2 Sons.......58 . 6		10 . 6	10 . 6	3 . 19 . 6
Samuell Stacey............19 . 6		7 .	7 .	1 . 13 . 6
John Smith...............19 . 6			5 . 8	1 . 5 . 2
Nicholas Severy..........19 . 6			5 . 8	1 . 5 . 2
William Tompkins........19 . 6		10 . 6	4 . 3	1 . 14 . 3
Saml Tompkins............19 . 6			5 . 8	1 . 5 . 2
John Treffery............19 . 6		7 . 6	6 . 6	1 . 13 . 6
James Treffery & Servt....39 .		4 . 5	7 .	2 . 10 . 5
Jonathan Thompson & Son 39 .		10 . 6	8 . 6	2 . 18 .
Jona Thompson junr......19 . 6		4 . 5	5 . 8	1 . 9 . 7
John Thompson Junr......19 . 6		4 . 5	5 . 8	1 . 9 . 7
Benja Thompson..........19 . 6		4 . 5	4 . 3	1 . 8 . 2
William Treffery..........19 . 6		16 . 10	35 .	3 . 11 . 4
Andrew Tucker 2 Servt....58 . 6		8 . 10	45 . 6	5 . 12 . 10
George Thompson........19 . 6		4 . 5		1 . 3 . 11
Phillip Thrasher & Son....39 .		7 .	8 . 6	2 . 14 . 6
Thos Treffery...........19 . 6		4 . 5	5 . 8	1 . 9 . 7
ChristopherTwisden 2 Sons 58 . 6		8 . 10	42 .	5 . 9 . 4

	Poles.	R. Estate.	P. Estate.			
James Thompson..........19s. 6		4s. 5	5s. 8	1 .	9 .	7
Thomas Treffery Junr.....19 . 6			5 . 8	1 .	5 .	2
Roger Vickroy............19 . 6		5 . 3	5 . 8	1 .	10 .	5
Stephen Vickroy..........19 . 6		5 . 3	33 . 3	2 .	18 .	
John Vickroy.............19 . 6		5 . 3	7 .	1 .	11 .	9
Alexn Watts 2 men........58 . 6		55 . 7	195 . 1	15 .	9 .	2
Saml Webber & Son.......39 .		8 . 6	7 .	2 .	14 .	6
Wido Hannah White......		20 . 9		1 .	0 .	9
Willm Wittey.............		5 . 3			5 .	3
Isaac Williams............19 . 6		17 . 6	7 .	2 .	4 .	
Daniel White.............19 . 6		5 . 3	7 .	1 .	11 .	9
George Wills.............19 . 6		4 . 5	5 . 8	1 .	9 .	7
John Waddon.............19 . 6		4 . 5	5 . 8	1 .	9 .	7
William Wouldrige........19 . 6		4 . 5	5 . 8	1 .	9 .	7
Lattimen Warters.........19 . 6		5 . 3	8 . 6	1 .	13 .	3
Abraham Williams........19 . 6		5 . 3	2 . 10	1 .	7 .	7
Thos Wood & Servt........39 .		32 . 11	14 .	4 .	5 .	11
John Wouldrige..........19 . 6			3 . 6	1 .	3 .	
William Hammond........19 . 6		4 . 5	5 . 8	1 .	9 .	7

Marblehead, May 30th, 1749.

The foregoing is a true Copy for the last year Rates.

Examined per

(Signed) Thos Gerry, Benja Hendly, Ebenr Stacy, Robt Laramore.

Total number of Names, 620. Total number of Poles, 730.

(*Continued from Vol. XLIII, page 64.*)

[122]   Depositions of Jonathan Ager, shipwright, aged 77, Daniel Bacon, shipwright, aged 75, and John Masters, mariner, aged 62, all of Salem, that "they were nigh Neighbours to & well acquainted with Moses Vouden formerly of y⁰ Island of Jersey more Lately of Salem aforesd & that he was Married to one Mary Ormes of Salem aforesd who is yet living & remains A widow & that by her he had Issue only Two Daughters viz Mary Voden & Elizabeth Voden who are Married as followeth Mary to one Richard Palmer & Elizabeth to John Presson & that y⁰ aforenamed widow & her Two Daughters with their husbands are all aliue & well at ye taking of these affidavits." Salem, Oct. 29, 1716.

Franc: Willoughby, town clerk, certifies that Mary Voden, daughter of Moses and Mary Voden, was born April 6, 1677. Franc: Willoughby, town clerk, certifies that Elizabeth Voden, daughter of Moses and Mary Voden, was born July 9, 1679.

Protest. Capt. William Scott, commander of the Princess Galley, made declaration that by a charter party made between the said Scott on one part, and Disney Staniforth of London, merchant, on the other part, it was agreed that said Scott should stay in New England 26 days and might be kept 30 days at 25s. per day demurrage, and that the ship should be loaded with fish by the factors of said freightors but although he waited the 25 days, as mentioned in a former protest and then waited the 30 days allowed for demurrage he still needed 200 quintals of fish to complete his loading. Salem, Nov. 20, 1716.

[123]   Protest. Eleazer Collins of Lynn, master of the sloop Seaflower, made declaration that on a voyage from New Hampshire to Boston on Nov. 24, 1716, "to y⁰ Eastward and Northward of Cape Anne they met with a

great Storme of Wind at y^e —— which raised such a great Sea that broke vpon them & fill'd them so y^t a considerable p^t of thier Loading all being boards were floated & carryed ouerboard into ye Sea which by no means could be Saved by them having a Narrow Escape of thier lives & that on ye 26th Instant a Glocester Sloop releiued them by towing them into Marblehead harbour." Salem, Nov. 27, 1716.

Bill of loading. Shipped by Thomas Hebb Senr of St. Georges, Maryland, by the Sloop Tiger of Salem, William Brown, master, 157 bu. of wheat to be delivered to John Conant of Marblehead, freight to be paid at the rate of 18d. per bushel. St. Georges, April 5, 1716.

Indorsm^t { "Marblehead ye 1st December 1716 Agreed wth M^r Wm Browne for ye within menconed Bill if it be a Bill p John Conant."

[124]   Decr 25th 1716. Major John Turner Esq. owner, or part owner of the Brig Olive branch of Salem, made declaration against Daniel Bray that on the 17th of this [unfinished]

Deed. John Osbourne of Salem, husbandman, and Hannah Osbourne his wife, formerly Hannah Buffum, to Caleb Buffum of Salem, yeoman, in behalf of Jabez Tucker of Westerle, Rhode Island, in consideration of £50 for "two Certain Messuages pieces or parcelle of land" situated in Westerle, which were formerly mortgaged by said Jabez Tucker to Hannah Buffum, before her marriage to John Osbourne. Salem, Nov. 7, 1716, Witnesses: Richard Kimball, Richard, Newcombe.

Brandford, March 30, 1714. Receipt by John Russell to Wm English for two hogsheads of molasses to dispose of for said English. Recorded, March 22, 1716/17.

"An Inventory of ye Goods and Estate of Richard Oake of Salem Shopkeeper declared a Bankrupt done by ye desire of ye Comissioners & Shewn to us by ye s^d Oakes. Feb^{ery} ye 1st 1714.

	2 old trunks 8s. Mault 3s.	£0	11	0
In ye	a Small quantity of Hops & a Kegg		2	.
Garret	a few beans & Casque		3	.
	1 old Saddle & box		5	.

£1 . 1   0

	A Small pcell of old Iron	. 2	.
K. Chamb[r]	Some Sheeps Wool & an old box	. 1	6
	A Small pcell fethers & an old Casque	. 4	.

	12 high back Colour'd Chairs 3s. p	}	2 . 1	.
Best	1 Great Ditto 5s	}		
	1 Large Trunk 11s. 6d. 1 Small[r]			
	Ditto 5s. 6d.		17	.
Chamb.	1 Looking Glass		14	.
	Glasses on y[e] Mantle Shelfe		1 . 6	

4 . 1 . 0

[125]   20 pr pewter buckles together   £0 . 2 . 0
In y[e] Shop A pcell Buttons of Sev[ll] Sorts

in a box with some Necklaces	12 . 0
Wooden Ware	5 . 0
2 Small p[r] Scales & w[ts] in a box	
wth two Graters	3 . 6
1 Pewter Tankard & funnell	3 . 6
1 Old hat Some old Knives & Some	
white cord	4 .
A Remnant of Stuff	2 . 6

£1 . 12 . 6

1 Round large Oak Table	£1 . 0 . 0
1 Old Trunk &c Sieve Bottoms	3 . 6
1 old warming pan & heet[r] Iron	5 . .
3 Rundlets 3s. 2 Sugar Boxes 6d	3 6
1 Tin pan & a Small pcell old pewter	13 .
1 p[r] Iron Dogs 8/. 2 old Iron Candle-	
sticks 9[d]	8 . 9
1 Chafing dish, hake Spit & old fire pan	11 . .

£3   4   9

```
2 Wedges 1 frying pan & brass Skillet     17   .
Some old Earthen Ware                       1 . 6
1 pr Small Stilliards 2s. Old Iron 5s.      7 . 0
1 old Cow 70s. 2 pigs 24s.                4 . 14 . .
1 old horse & Mare                          4     . .
                                        ─────────────
                                        £19 . 8 . 9
```

Examd   John Pickering
             Benjᵃ Gerrish."

Form of the oath administered to Richard Oakes, a
bankrupt debtor, taken March 9, 1716/17. " You do Solemnly Swear that you have already or now forthwith will
make a full true & Certain discovery & Declaration of all
& Singular yᵉ money goods Chattels Credits wares Mer-
chandizes Effects & things whatsoever belonging to you
Either in your own Custody use occupation or possession
or in ye custody keeping use occupation or Possession of
any other person or persons Whomsoever & that you
have also Surrendered up to yᵉ Commissioners all your
books of accounts bills bonds & other papers whereby they
may have a full knowledge of & thereby Ability to Re-
cover all yᵉ Debts due to your Estate & Further You do
Swear that you neither do nor have directly or Indirectly
Sold Leased or otherwise Conveyed Disposed of or In-
trusted any part of Your Estate thereby to Secure yᵉ
Same or to receive or Expect any profit or Advantage
thereof to defraud or deceiue any Creditor or Creditors
Whatsoever to whom you Stand Indebted & this you do
Swear Solemnly & plainly without any Mental Reserva-
tion or Equivocation whatsoever So help you God.
Sworne forma (Quakers) yᵉ abovesᵈ

Essex   Attest } Stephen Sewall   { Justices of yᵉ
       Coram }   John Turner   { peace for
                        { yᵉ County aforesᵈ
                        { & Commissioners."

Bond.   James Bryant Junʳ of Younhur, County of
Albermall, husbandman, to John Green of Salem, mariner,
for £9. 12s. 6d. Sterling,   Mehering, April 26, 1717.
Witnesses: John Dutting, Edward Hewcott.

[126] Decision of Sam¹ Collins of Lynn, blacksmith, Thomas Choat of Chebacco, and Walter Newberry of Boston, merchant, arbitrators, chosen "by Mary Sanders of Glocester, widow, administratrix to yᵉ Estate of Joseph Sanders of Glocester, Deceased," and Capt. John Calley of Marblehead, to put a final end to a difference between them & John Maule of Salem, Executors to Jonathan Springer of Glocester, Deceased, having heard both parties and examined the books of said Springer, decided that the "said John Calley hath already paid what yᵉ said Mary Sanders demands being Twenty Nine pound 12/6 to yᵉ said Jonathan Springer who haueing included what he Receiued of sᵈ Calley in yᵉ Inventory of yᵉ Said Joseph Saunders his Estate & made an equal Dividend thereof as appeares by sᵈ Springers booke folio 206 & haueing also seen the accompt between yᵉ said Joseph Saunders & Jonathan Springer signed by yᵉ sᵈ John Maule Doe also declare that it is our opinion yᵉ said Mary Sanders as admˣ to ye sᵈ Joseph Sanders hath no right to demand or receiue any money of ye sᵈ John Calley or John Maule on accompt of yᵉ sd Joseph Sanders of Glocester Deceased." Salem, 30ᵗʰ 3ᵈ month "called May," 1717.

Bond given by Mary Sanders of Glocester, widow, and administratrix of the estate of Joseph Saunders, and John Calley of Marblehead, for himself and on behalf of John Maul, for £50. Salem, April 14, 1717.

[127] Protest. Capt Samuel Rodham, commander of the ship Mary & Johanna, made declaration that by a charter party made in London, April 15, 1717, between Joseph Lopus of London, merchant, on the one part and the aforesaid Samuel Rodham on the other part, it was agreed that the latter should sail from the River Thames to Boston there to load such fish as shall be supplied by the agent of said Lopus to the full amount of the ship's loading and to remain in Boston or Marblehead until Aug. 10, with provision made that they may be kept 20 days after the time agreed at the rate of 25s. per day demurrage to be paid on the return of the ship to London. Freight to be paid on said fish at the rate of £4. 15s. per ton. And

said Capt. Samuel Rodham affirmed that he arrived in Boston, July 15, 1717 and according to the directions received of Isaac Lopus, agent of said Joseph Lopus, he went to Marblehead and there waited ready to received the fish but up to the date of protest he had received only one-half of his loading.

Sworn to by John Bell, Alexander Arburthues.

Witnesses Geo. Morris, R. Newcomb.

"To Sam Horris Deputy Sheriffe in Marblehead to publish this protest by reading it to Isaack Lopus or Abraham Goutey & make me return thereof Stephen Sewall No^t pub." Salem, Aug. 10, 1717.

[128]   Protest.   Capt. Ellis Huske, commander of the ship Riga Merchant, made declaration that on a voyage from Lisbon to New England, being laden with salt, on June 21, 1717 about 80 leagues westward of Fyall, " he met with a great & Sudden calm Imediatly after a hard Storm yt had causd a great Sea & Just before another Storm yt Speedily came vpon them So that it was betwixt Two Storms when thier ship rowld at Such a dangerous rate that carried away *both* her Topmast & the mainmast & started or loosnd Some butt head in ye Garbord Streak Whereby wee were so very leaky yt wee had 4 foot Water in ye Hold & Expected Nothing but Sinking insomuch y^t wee wasted much of our Lading of Salt tho wee kept ye pumps going for our lives till all ye Company were almost Tyrd out."

Sworn to by Humphrey Hutchins, Math. Ridett, James Dejon, Thomas Kelley, officers and sailors of said ship. Salem, Aug. 19, 1717.

Protest.   Capt. Renatus Curtis, commander of the ship Tyson Frigatt of London, made declaration that by a charterparty made in London, March 22, 1716-17, between Thomas Halsey, Samuel Crispe, Henry Noale, John Kiggell, and Solomon Merrill on the one part and the said Capt. Curtis on the other part, it was agreed that the said Curtis should sail April 10, 1717 from Graues End to Boston, Salem, or Marblehead, and there stay for 60 running days to receive on board merchantable dry fish to the amount of thirteen hundred quintals and after loading he should sail to Alicant, allowing, 30 days demurrage, at the rate of "six dollers" per day.   The said Capt. Curtis affirms that he arrived in New England, June 24, 1717, and according to directions received from Henry Franklin, merchant in Boston, factor of said freightors, he went to Marblehead with directions to several persons about the fish, and although he was always ready and waiting to receive the fish, he received, within the 60 days agreed upon but 800 quintalls of fish.

Sworn to by Wm. Righton, boatswain and Edward Knight, carpenter.

Witnesses: Samuel Rodham, Richard Newcomb.

Salem, Aug. 26, 1717.

Protest.   Thomas Karslake, resident of Salem, merchant, made declaration that by a certain charterparty made Apr. 30, 1717, at Livorne between Capt. James Harlow, master of the ship Cowe Tree, and the said Karslake. it was agreed that the ship's boat should load on board said ship such goods as Karslake should see fit and also if the ship staid in one port, for repairs, for more than four days, the time over four days should not be counted in the freightors charges.   Karslake affirmed that Harlow would not let his boat carry on board and on shore the goods Karslake saw fit to send and moreover that he kept the ship from Aug. 3-17 for repairs " & Graving " to the great detriment of the freightor.   Salem, Oct. 3, 1717.

[130]   Letter of attorney given Oct. 22, 1717, by Benjamin Jones, of Swansey, Bristol County, yeoman, and Elizabeth his wife, daughter of John & Colete Vorden, deceased, formerly of the Island of Jersey, and later of Salem, to Richard Palmer of Salem, friend and kinsman, to collect money, goods, etc. in Jersey.

Signed by mark by Benjamin & Elizabeth Jones.

Witnesses : John Higginson jr., John Marsters.

Protest.   Capt Nathaniel Brooke, commander of the

ship Restoration, made declaration that the summer before
he was sent by his owner, Joseph Lopus of London, merchant, to New England, where he arrived Aug. 17, 1717
and there applied to Abraham Gutterns, merchant in Boston, to whom he was consigned, who sent him to Marblehead to load fish, which he had done but said Gutterns
neglected to give him " his dispatches & Sayling orders."
    Witnesses: Richard Newcomb, Nicholas Lyddjard.
Salem, Nov. 19, 1717

    [131] " Capt Hollister's Credentiall Letter, Recorded,
Nov. ye 29 1717.
    Capt Jacob Hossester   Bristol 24 Decem^r 1716
    " Whereas By our Direction and Appointment thee art
possast Mas^r of y^e Good Ship y^e Royall Guardian of Bristoll we direct thy repairing on Board Said Ship wth a
Sufficient Crew of hands Take y^e first Opportunity of wind
and wether & Saile as Direct as possible for y_e Gum
Coast called Portendyrick on y^e Coast of Affrica Keeping
Company for y^e Better Security wth our Ship y^e Bensworth Gally Nicho^s Gardner Commander and as A Cargo
proper for that Coast herewith we diliver y^e Invoice of
Sundry Goods and Merchandize Amounting to £ ———.
    " When it shall please God You ariue There we would
have thee do ye Utmost for our Advantage in ye disposall
of our Cargoe and purchasing Thy Loading of Gum or
what part thereof thee Canst gett Butt Should it So happen y^t Between ye Bensworth & thy Self You Should pur-
shace thy Loading or at Least one hund^r and Thirty Tons,
Then we direct that ye Same Be Loaden on Board Thy
Ship and when you think it not worth yor while to Stay
Longer on ye Coast of Affrica for Both ye Royall Guardian & Bensworth to proceed To ye Island of May But If
ye Guardian Get 130 Tonns or upward & ye Bensworth
50 Tonns or upwards Then in Such case & ye Season over
You are Both to make ye Best of Your way for this Port
of Bristoll with your Loading as Afforesaid likewise should
Both Ships Gett But fifty Tonns or not Exceeding The
Bensworth Loading we direct that ye Same to put on
Board her whither you do it on ye Coast or Leave it Till

you Come to ye Isle of May we Referr To Your Discretion When You ariue at ye Isle of May if should Be your fortune To Go There & Neither Ships has ye Quantity of Gum Stipulated Before That you do Your Utmost to Gett a Loading of Salt and when Done make ye Best of your way for New England In this cas we don't Tye You to Saile Together or keep Company Believeing it may Be a disadvantage To ye Sale of ye Salt In New England The Reasonableness of this Case you are Judges of But to return ye Isle of May if Either of ye Ships has ye Quantity Stipulated yett we Direct that Shee Stay there Till ye Other can be Loaden wth Salt to ye intent That Both Ships Crews Be Imploy'd in making a Loading ye Same.

"In Case y^t Salt Cannot be had at ye Isle of May which has happened we order You to Proceed to St Iubes. That Ship as Goes to New England to have all ye Peices of 8-8 That shall Remain of Both Ships undisposed of If it Be thy fortune to proceed to New England wth a Loading of Salt dispose of ye Same for most w^{ll} yeild & wth ye Produce Thereof ye peices of 8-8 & w^t may Be Left of they other Cargoe that will Sell to advantage purchase thy Loading of well Cured & marchentable fish which we Conceive cant Be a great Deal Less Then 3000 Quintells what money thee mayst want to Compleat thy Loading Thee art to Draw at the Highest Exchange wch Bills Shall Be Duly honoured we are inform^d its now about 80 p cent when thy Ship is Loaden make ye Best of thy way for Cadiz and Apply to John Russell The English Consull There where we intend to Lodge letters for your Government But should it happen That thee dost not find our Letters There and Thy Cargoe of fish w^{ll} Sell att 5 dollers p Quintell or upwards on Board Dispose of ye Same but If not Gett what advise thee Canst of ye Markets in ye Streights and do thy Best for our Advantage at all or Any of ye Poarts According to w^{ht} Time ye mayst Be there In Short do ye Best thee Canst. This Seemes To Be ye Chiefest we have now Say Respecting ye Voige as Yett Except y we intreat and desire that there may be no misunderstanding Between thee and Capt Gardner knowing how much our Interest may Suffer thereby and how much advanced by Your Unanimity and Agreement we dont mention This as Being doubtfull it w^{ll} happen otherwise only by way of Caution one Thing very Necessary that is freequent advice when any opportunity of Conveyance when Need not Mention to Be a Good husband of thy Ships Stores Tackel &c or Thy Care of fire we Conclude wishing of thee a prosperous Voiage and Safe Return to thy Assured friends and partners

" For James Maund & ourselves W^m & John Reeve Neh^h Champion Caleb fLoyd John Teague In^o Parkin Edwd Lowe Walter Grimes

Examd.   Willm Ball "

[132]   Protest. Dec. 21, 1717. Capt. Edward Dennet, commander of the ship Loyal George, made declaration that by a charterparty made in London, July 26, 1717, between the said Edward Dennet on the one part and Thomas Halsey, John Barnes, Jonathan Perrie, Solomon Merrett and Henry Neale, freightors, it was agreed that the said Capt. Dennet should sail from the River Thames to Boston and there stay, or go to some other port as the agent of said freightors might direct, for 50 running days to unload and reload with fish, fifty days' demurrage at the rate of 55s. per day to be allowed. After loading, the ship was to proceed to Alicant. He affirms that he arrived in Boston, Oct. 31, and the agent of said freightors, viz, John Barnes, sent him to Marblehead, where he went and was always ready to load fish, but up to the date of protest had not received any. The respective shares were to have been Thomas Halsey 800 quintals, John Barnes, 800 quintals, Jonathan Perry, 600 quintals, Solomon Merret, 400 quintals, Henry Neal, 200 quintals. Witnesses: Nicholas Lydiard and Richard Newcomb. Salem, Dec. 21, 1717.

(To be continued.)

EDMUND LEWIS OF LYNN AND SOME OF HIS DESCENDANTS.

BY GEORGE HARLAN LEWIS OF LOS ANGELES, CAL.

(Continued from Vol. XLIII, page 144.)

123 Benjamin Lewis, born in Woburn, Sept. 28, 1729; was taxed in Billerica in 1755, and was a soldier in the public service between 1745 and 1762. He was an early settler at Duxbury School Farm, later called Milford, N. H., where he had a farm on the north side of the Soughegan river, near the Wilton line (History of Milford, N. H.). He removed to Lyndeboro, N. H., where he and his wife were members of the church in 1780. He, his brother James, and his son Benjamin, jr., were taxed there in 1786. A large slate stone marks his resting place in the old cemetery, and is inscribed, " died Jany. 13, 1796, aged 67 years." His wife died and was buried at Milford, N. H., her gravestone having the inscription, "died Oct. 24, 1777, in her 46th year." He married, April 9, 1752, Mary Brown, born in Billerica, Dec. 9, 1731, daughter of Samuel and Mary (Davis-French) Brown of Billerica.

Children of Benjamin and Mary, born in Billerica:

205. BENJAMIN, b. May 6, 1753.
206. MARY, b. Jan. 19, 1755; m., Nov. 20, 1779, Amos Boardman of Reading, b. 1775, son of Amos and Elizabeth (Smith) Boardman of South Reading. They had a large family.
207. ASA, b. Oct. 22, 1756. He was one of the first who enlisted for three years in the Revolutionary war. His head was shot off by a cannon ball at the battle of Bennington, Aug. 16, 1777.
208. SARAH, b. June 14, 1758; m., 1st, Dec. 23, 1784, Zebadiah Holt of Andover, b. July 28, 1759, and d. Mar. 15, 1817; m., 2d, Jotham Blanchard. Mr. Holt was in the Revolutionary war from the Concord fight, April 19, 1775, until Dec. 20, 1783, when he was discharged at headquarters in New York, with the rank of sergeant major. He often remarked that he did

(233)

not receive to the value of fifty dollars in silver for his services. Children of Zebadiah and Sarah: (1) Amasa, b. Dec. 30, 1785; d. at Lynn. (2) Zebadiah, b. Apr. 25, 1787. (3) Sally Lewis, b. April 5, 1789; d., unm., Oct. 19, 1837. (4) Asa Lewis, b. June 1, 1791. (5) Jonathan, b. June 17, 1793. (6) Elizabeth Gould, b. June 13, 1795. (7) Charles, b. April 30, 1797.

209. HANNAH, b. Jan. 12, 1761; d. April 10, 1844; m. Elias Boardman of Reading, who d. May 16, 1844, æ. 89 y.
210. PATTY, b. March 8, 1763; m. Jonathan Holt of Boscawen, N. H.
211. KEZIAH, b. June 22, 1766; m. —— Hinckley.
212. MOSES, b. April 17, 1770.
213. BETSEY, m. —— Gould.

124   Jonathan Lewis, born in Woburn, April 10, 1731 (also recorded at Wilmington), was taxed at Billerica in 1755, and was a soldier in the public service during the period between 1745 and 1762. He removed to Pepperell, where he died Nov. 10, 1776. He was a yeoman, and married, April 3, 1755, Persis Crosby, born Aug. 9, 1733, daughter of Lieut. Simon and Abigail (Kidder) Crosby. After his death, she married, second, John Green of Pepperell, and had a son Benjamin.

Children of Jonathan and Persis, the first six born in Billerica:

214. PERSIS, b. Dec. 15, 1755; m. Benjamin Hatch.
215. JONATHAN, b. Mar. 20, 1758.
216. MARY, b. Apr. 3, 1761; m. Sept. 16, 1784, Elijah Noyes, b. Oct., 1758, at Chockermouth, son of Deacon Enoch and Elizabeth Noyes (Hollis, N. H., records).
217. RHODA, b. Oct. 17, 1763; m. Nathan Nutting.
218. ISAAC, b. Feb. 4, 1766; m. Elizabeth Cram.
219. DAVID, b. May 7, 1768; m. Mary Boynton.
220. ANNA, b. July 17, 1770 ; unm.
221. ABIGAIL, b. Oct. 2, 1773; m. Nov. 13, 1793, Samuel Perley, of Harrison, Me., son of Samuel and Hepzibah (Fowler) Perley of Gray, Me. (Fowler Genealogy, p. 113).

126   Capt. James Lewis, born in Wilmington, Sept. 25, 1735, was an officer in the militia during the whole of the Revolutionary War, and also was at Concord bridge on the 19 April 1775. His name is on the tax list at Billerica, Dec., 1776, for £2 15ˢ 1ᵈ, as of the Andover district near Salem road. He was a selectman in 1781 and 1785 and from 1787 to 1790. He removed from Billerica to Groton on May 24, 1796, where he was highly respected and died lamented June 12, 1810. (See obituary in Groton Historical Series.) He married Jan. 3, 1760, Rebecca Brown, born Feb. 18, 1738-9, daughter of Samuel and Mary (Davis-French) Brown, who died Jan. 1, 1814, æ. 75 years (g.s.)

Children of James and Rebecca, born in Billerica :

222. JAMES, b. Jan. 26, 1761.
223. REBECCA, b. July 15, 1762; d. June 21, 1809.
224. SETH, b. Jan. 1, 1764; d. Jan. 3, 1764.
225. RIZPAH, b. Mar. 13, 1765; d. Mar. 17, 1765.
226. SETH, b. Sept. 22, 1766.
227. RIZPAH, b. May 6, 1768; d. Jan. 9, 1776.
228. AARON, b. June 27, 1770; d. Jan. 12, 1776.

127 John Lewis, born in Wilmington, Aug. 5, 1737, was on the tax list in Billerica, Dec., 1776, for 13ˢ 9ᵈ. He was at Bunker Hill, Cambridge, Lexington, and at the siege of Boston. He was 2nd Lieutenant in Capt. Stickney's Co. Col. Bridge's regiment, and was also Ensign in Capt. Stickney's Company, and Lieutenant in Capt. Solomon Pollard's Co., Col. Samuel Denny's Regt. and marched to Claverack in 1779. There is no record of his marriage.

Children of John, born in Billerica:

229. HENRY, bpt. July 16, 1769.
230. MOLLY, bpt. July 12, 1772.
231. SARAH, bpt. Apr. 9, 1775.
232. BENJAMIN, bpt. June 21, 1778.
233. JOHN, bpt. Aug. 11, 1782.

128 Reuben Lewis, born in Wilmington, Sept. 25, 1739, was a corporal in Capt. L. Butterfield's Co., Col. Ebenezer Bridges' regiment, on Apr. 19, 1775. He was also a Lieutenant in the Continental Army, and served under Gen. Washington in his campaigns, and was at White Plains, N. Y., and at Valley Forge. He was a prayerful man, a Christian, a philanthropist and a patriot. He was one of the proprietors of Groton Academy. He

sold his farm in Dracut, Mass., taking Continental money
for pay, which became worthless, making him a poor man
with a large family to support. He possessed an independent spirit. A powder horn with his initials upon it was
presented by his son Reuben to the Groton Historical Society. He married, May 17, 1770, Abigail Shed, born Feb.
13, 1748, oldest child of Daniel and Abigail (Patten)
Shed, and died in Groton, May 4, 1804, where she also
died Oct. 20, 1817.

Children of Reuben and Abigail :

234. ABI, b. July 9, 1771; d. Apr. 21, 1863. For over 30 years she
        was a governess in the family of Hon. Josiah Quincy, the
        mayor of Boston.
235. REUBEN, b. Nov. 13, 1772; d. Sept. 29, 1773.
236. REUBEN, b. Aug. 6, 1774; d. Sept., 1777.
237. ZILPAH, b. Mar. 22, 1776; d. Sept. 25, 1777.
238. ZILPAH, b. June 17, 1778; m. John Vose, b. Nov. 5, 1780, in
        Boston, and d. there Sept. 3, 1824; she d. in Charlestown,
        Jan. 29, 1865. Had: (1) John Henry, b. June 16, 1811; d. in
        Walpole, Mar. 17, 1897. (2) Susan Ann, b. Aug. 22, 1813;
        m. 1st, Richard P. Cory; m. 2d, Geo. W. Palmer and d. Mar.
        18, 1898 in Charlestown. (3) Thomas Charles, b. Aug. 8,
        1818; m. June 22, 1845, Harriet Sophia Dayton; d. in Wal-
        pole, April 15, 1891.
239. BETSEY, b. July 18, 1780; m. David Torrey.
240. ANNA, b. Feb. 19, 1783.
241. AARON, b. Oct. 21, 1785; m. Ruth W. Dix who d. Jan. 5, 1823.
        No children. He was instantly killed Oct. 16, 1821, by
        falling out of a chestnut tree.
242. OLIVER PRESCOTT, b. July 10, 1787; d. July 29, 1820, leaving
        no children. He served in the War of 1812.
243. ASA SHEDD, b. June 25, 1790.
244. SUKEY HAMBLETT, b. Feb. 22, 1793; d. Mar. 4, 1793.

131 Samuel Lewis, born June 10, 1746, married
June 3, 1773, Betty Parker. He was then of Chelmsford,
Mass. The following record was furnished in 1898 by
his granddaughter Mrs. Nancy C. Robinson of Townsend,
Mass.

Children of Samuel and Betty (not in the order of
birth) :

244a. SAMUEL, b. Aug. 24, 1779.
244b. JOHN, b. 1781 at Washington, N. H.; m. 1806, Rhoda Baldwin.
244c. ISAAC, m. Mary or Polly Holt.
244d. SALLY, m. Samuel Currier of Concord, N. H., and had 8 children.
244e. HANNAH, m. Fred Reed and lived in Peterboro, N. H., had 2 children, a son and a dau.
244f. NANCY, d. at Henniker, N. H., of spotted fever when a young woman.
244g. DAVID, went to sea in the War of 1812; was wounded in the foot and had a sword cut. Swam the St. Lawrence river and never came home.
244h. DANIEL, a half brother to John, lived in Medford, Mass., was bitten by a mad dog and died.

133 Ebenezer Lewis, born in Billerica, Dec.4, 1750. (Nov. 4. family and church record), was married by Wm. Stickney, Esq. Sept. 29, 1772, to Ruth, born July 3, 1752, daughter of Benjamin and Mary (Corey) Parker. She was the first person buried in the new cemetery at Windham, N. H. He died 3 Oct., 1825 (Groton Records).

Children of Ebenezer and Ruth, born in Groton, now Ayer:

245. MARY, b. Sept. 20, 1774; m. Sullivan Davis.
246. JULIA, b. Jan. 8, 1777; m. Washington Davis.
247. ASA, b. July 19, 1778.
248. RISPAH, b. Sept. 7, 1781; d. Aug., 1800.
249. JOHN, b. Apr. 7, 1784; m. Nancy Childs; d. Mar., 1818.
250. SALLY, b. Apr. 3, 1786; d. Nov. 1808.
251. HENRY, b. July 5, 1788; m. Hannah Allen; d. June 18, 1832.
252. EBENEZER, b. July 25, 1790; m. Mary Hamblett; d. Nov. 12, 1869.
253. BENJAMIN, b. Feb. 1, 1793; d. unm. Nov. 1823.
254. LUTHER, b. Nov. 12, 1795.
255. LUCY, b. Nov. 12, 1795; m. June 5, 1814, Lewis Putnam of Cambridge.
256. ELIZABETH, m. Wm. H. Wait, b. Dec. 19, 1807, son of Phineas and Ruth (Bicknell) Wait of Shirley, Mass. (Groton Hist. Series, v. 13, p. 55.)

140 John Lewis was born in Lynn, Oct. 15, 1751. He was cordwainer and received parts 6 and 7 of his father's estate including one-half of a small dwelling house situated:

near the Friend's Meeting House which had been owned in
common by John Lewis (2) and his son John Lewis (7).
He died intestate Apr. 16, 1813, and his son Robert Lewis
was appointed administrator and guardian for John, Henry
Amos and George, minor children.

He married Feb. 4, 1773, Martha, daughter of Robert
and Mary (Newhall) Mansfield of Lynn. She died April
16, 1839.

Children of John and Martha, born in Lynn :

257. SARAH, b. Mar. 22, 1773; d. Mar. 3, 1793.
258. ROBERT, b. Apr. 3, 1774.
259. MARTHA, b. Mar. 25, 1777; d. Feb. 20, 1796.
260. JOHN, b. Feb. 15, 1779.
261. BLANEY, b. Oct. 7, 1780.
262. ELIZABETH, b. Oct. 7, 1780; d. Apr. 3, 1781.
263. NATHANIEL, b. Jan. 22, 1783.
264. HENRY, b. Jan. 20, 1785.
265. ELIZABETH, b. Sept. 7, 1787; d. Feb. 21, 1810; m. Nov. 15, 1807,
    Jacob Phillips. Had: (1) Walter, b. Aug. 15, 1808; (2) John
    L., b. Feb. 11, 1810. Mr. Phillips, m. 2d, Rebecca Farrington
    and 3d, Mrs. Martha (Ingalls) Atwell, daughter of Jacob and
    Martha (Lewis) Ingalls (139). She was the widow of Major
    John D. Atwell.
266. MARY, b. Sept. 4, 1789; d. Nov. 17, 1792.
267. ASA, b. Jan. 4, 1792; d. 1812.
268. AMOS, b. Oct. 17, 1794.
269. GEORGE, b. May 31, 1800.

141 Edmund Lewis, born in Lynn Feb. 10, 1754,
was a cordwainer and lived in Lynn. He marched on the
Alarm of April 19, 1775. He married Nov. 4, 1784 his
cousin Hepzibah, daughter of John (338 Newhall Gen.)
and Sarah (Lewis) (79) Newhall. He died Oct. 16, 1815,
and she died Jan. 19, 1837. All his children died without
heirs except Sarah, whose daughter Elizabeth Cloutman
lived with her grandmother Hepzibah Lewis and deeded
land with her as sole heir.

Children of Edmund and Hepzibah, born in Lynn :

270. SALLY, b. May 4, 1785; m. Sept. 25, 1805, Nathaniel Cloutman
    of Salem. Had: Elizabeth Cloutman (see 278).
271. ELIZABETH, b. Mar. 24, 1787.

272. HEPHSIBETH, b. Sept. 10, 1789.
273. ANNA, b. Mar. 30, 1792.
274. BENJAMIN, b. Apr. 9, 1795; d. June 9, 1813.

144 Benjamin Lewis, born in Lynn, Jan. 31, 1761, was a yeoman and cordwainer and lived in Lynn. He married, Nov. 29, 1792, Mrs. Rebecca (Mansfield) Lewis, widow of his Uncle Edmund Lewis (83). She died in 1794 and he married, second, Apr. 14, 1796, Mrs. Hannah (Richards) Lewis, widow of his brother Joseph (146). She died Oct. 14, 1813, and he died July 19, 1839.

Children of Benjamin and Hannah, born in Lynn:

275. BENJAMIN, b. Nov. 3. 1796.
276. LYDIA R., b. Apr. 9, 1798; m. Dec. 11, 1823, Joseph Lewis (307).
277. HANNAH, b. Feb. 15, 1800; m. June 19, 1843, William Watts, b. Nov. 29, 1810, son of William and Sally (Parrott) Watts.
278. BETSEY, b. May 20, 1802; d. May 18, 1836; m. Dec. 26, 1822, John M. Coombs and lived in Lynn. Had: (1) Eliza Jane, b. Aug. 14, 1823; d. Sept. 11, 1824. (2) Eliza Jane, b. Aug. 30, 1825; (3) Hannah, b. Aug. 17, 1827; (4) George, b. Aug. 10, 1829; (5) John M., b. June 25, 1832. John M. Coombs, sen. m. 2nd. Mar. 28, 1337, Elizabeth, daughter of Nathaniel and Sally (Lewis) Cloutman.
279. JOHN RICHARDS, b. June 20, 1804.
280. FRANCES B., b. May 20, 1807; m. July 30, 1837, Oliver Hall, and had (1) William Oliver, b. Mar. 17, 1844; (2) Mary Frances, m. Albert Lewis, b. in East Boston, Jan. 10, 1843, son of Oliver and Lydia (Bodge) Lewis of Reading. She d. Aug. 28, 1889.

146 Joseph Lewis, born Feb. 4, 1765, in Lynn, married April 13, 1786, Hannah Richards. After his death his widow married, April 14, 1796, his brother Benjamin Lewis (144). She died Oct. 14, 1813.

Children of Joseph and Hannah :

281. JOSEPH, b. Oct. 6. 1790. Was brought up in his uncle's family and often called his son.
281a. A daughter, d. in infancy.

147 Nathaniel Lewis, born in Lynn, in 1768, was a shoemaker and lived in Lynn, where he died Jan. 24, 1824. He married Mar. 13, 1791, Rebecca Richards, who died Aug. 7, 1821.

Children of Nathaniel and Rebecca, born in Lynn :

282. RICHARD, b. Sept. 26, 1791; d. July 15, 1792.
283. BENJAMIN RICHARD, b. May 26, 1793.
284. BETSEY, b. May 9, 1795; m. Sept. 5, 1816, Frederick Newhall,
  b. Aug. 1, 1795, son of William and Martha (Mansfield) Newhall. Lived in Lynn. Had: (1) Eliza, b. July 18, 1817;
  (2) Frederick Augustus, b. Sept. 13, 1818; (3) Nathaniel
  Cyrus, b. July 19, 1822; (4) Hester Ann, b. Mar. 31, 1826; d.
  Sept. 10, 1826.
285. REBECCA, b. Mar. 29, 1797; m. Edmund Lewis (154).
286. NATHANIEL, b. May 29, 1799; d. Dec. 30, 1822.
287. THOMAS, b. Jan. 7, 1801.
288. RICHARD, b. Nov. 6, 1802.
289. HEPZABETH, b. Sept. 16, 1804; m. in Malden, Nov. 8, 1827,
  Denison Gage of Malden, and d. June 20, 1885.
290. JOHN, b. June 6, 1806; d. Jan. 20, 1808.
291. LUCY ANN, b. Mar. 4, 1808; m. in Lynn, Apr. 28, 1830, Joseph
  A. Proctor, and d. Mar. 23, 1888. Lived in Lynn. Had:
  (1) Mary Elizabeth, b. June 5, 1831. (2) Joseph Warren, b.
  about 1836; d. young; (3) Joseph Warren b. Feb. 16, 1840.
292. JOHN, b. Sept. 5, 1812; m. June 21, 1835, Mary Jane Todd of
  Malden. Went to California and never heard from. 4 chn.

149　James Lewis, born in 1766, was a yeoman and
lived in Lynn. He was married four times. He used to
say he wore the same coat at each wedding and it was
still a good coat. He married, first, Dec. 7, 1791, Elizabeth
Newhall. He married, second, Aug. 1, 1797, Elizabeth
Thomas, who died Aug. 9, 1812. He married, third, Dec.
27, 1813, Betsey, daughter of Nathaniel and Abigail Tarbox, who was born in Lynn, July 9, 1787, and died April
22, 1825. No children. He married, fourth, Mar. 2,
1826, Hepzibah Tarbox, sister of Betsey, born in Lynn
Oct. 11, 1781 and died Dec. 1, 1835. He died Oct. 28,
1840, aged 74 years (g. s. in Western Burying ground).
Children of James and Elizabeth, born in Lynn:

293. SALLY, b. Dec. 20, 1791; m. Aug. 20, 1812, Joshua Bacheller,
  who d. Oct. 21, 1840. Children, born in Lynn: (1) Hannah,
  b. Mar. 25, 1815; (2) Joshua Warren, b. Mar. 27, 1817; (3)
  Sally Ann, b. Aug. 12, 1819; d. Sept. 17, 1820; (4) Sarah Ann,
  b. July 4, 1821; (5) George Augustus, b. Oct. 3, 1823.
294. STEPHEN, b. Jan. 4, 1794.

Children of James and Elizabeth, born in Lynn:

295. POLLY or Mary, b. Aug. 1, 1800; m. Sept. 24, 1818, in Lynn, Ephraim G. Taylor and d. Oct. 31, 1822. Had: (1) Sally, b. June 25, 1819; (2) Benjamin I., b. June 21, 1821.
296. NANCY, b. June 1, 1802.
297. BETSEY, b. Jan. 22, 1808; pub. Apr. 17, 1828, Nicholas Mailey. Children, born in Lynn; (1) Mary Jane, b. Sept. 18, 1828; (2) Nicholas James, b. Nov. 1, 1830; (3) Georgiana, d. Aug. 15, 1857; ae. 5 y. 2 m.; interred in Eastern Burying Ground.

150 Nathaniel Lewis, born in Lynn about 1768, was called "Junior" in deeds and birth records of his children. He was a laborer and lived in Lynn and was familiarly called "Turtle." He married, in Lynn, May 25, 1790, Rebecca Clark, probably born Apr. 2, 1771; daughter of Edmund and Elizabeth Clark of Lynn. She died Apr. 2, 1852, aged 81 years. (Lynn Records.) He died June 11, 1843, aged 75 years. (g. s.)

Children of Nathaniel and Rebecca, born in Lynn:

298. MARY, b. Sept. 29, 1790; m. in Lynn, May 5, 1811, Samuel Ashton, Jr., son of Samuel and Sarah Ashton. He was a shoemaker and lived in Lynn. She d. Nov. 29, 1841. Children, born in Lynn: (1) Otis B., b. Oct. 10, 1811; d. Oct. 2, 1817; (2) Warren, b. Oct. 17, 1813; (3) Mary Lewis, b. Oct. 13, 1817; (4) Hannah Phillips, b. Mar. 3, 1820; (5) Ann Jane, b. Feb. 19, 1822, m. Wm. D. Thompson; (6) Benjamin Franklin, b. May 9, 1827; d. Mar. 18, 1845, æ. 17 y. 10 m. (g.s.); (7) William Alden, b. Oct. 10, 1829; (8) Sarah Elizabeth, b. July 16, 1831.
299. HANNAH, b. May 25, 1793; m. Dec. 13, 1812, in Lynn, James Phillips, Jr., b. in Lynn, Mar. 5, 1790; son of Zacheus and Sarah (Ingalls) Phillips, shoe manufacturer; resided in Lynn. Had: (1) Eliza Jackson, b. Jan. 19, 1817, m. Thomas Collyer; (2) Sally Ann, b. July 25, 1822; (3) William Badger, b. Feb. 28, 1825; (4) Hannah Maria, b. Jan. 9, 1828.
300. EDMUND CLARK, b. Apr. 17, 1795; d. June 11, 1824.
301. REBECCA, b. Feb. 25, 1797; m. Dec. 25, 1817, Samuel G. Ashton. He d. Sept. 2, 1848, æ. 58 yrs. 10 mos. (g. s.) Painter; lived in Lynn. Had : (1) Samuel Gale, b. Apr. 21, 1819; (2) Benjamin Franklin, b. Nov. 5, 1820;(3) Elizabeth, b. Oct. 14, 1823; (4) James, b. Sept. 28, 1827; d. Oct. 19, 1828; (5) Sally Maria, b. Mar, 29, 1829.

302. NATHANIEL, b. Feb. 28, 1799.
303. PAMELIA, b. May 27, 1802; m. in Lynn, Dec. 12, 1822, Samue
    Haskell, Jr. of Gloucester. He d. May 9, 1868, æ. 68 y. 7 m.
    (g. s.) She d. Jan. 11, 1881. (g. s.) Shoemaker; lived in
    Lynn; Had: (1) Abigail Dennison, b. May 29, 1824; (2) Eliza
    Ann, b. Dec. 16, 1826; (3) Pamelia Augusta, b. Nov. 10, 1828;
    d. Apr. 1, 1832; (4) Hannah Maria, b. Jan. 3, 1831; (5) Sam-
    uel George, b. July 3, 1838.
304. SUSAN, b. Sept. 4, 1804; m. Oct. 10, 1824, Allen S. Rich, Jr.
305. MERANNE, b. Jan. 3, 1807.
306. BETSY MANSFIELD, b. Dec. 24, 1810; m. June 4, 1829, Samuel
    V. Spear of Philadelphia, Pa.

151 William Lewis, was a laborer and lived in
Lynn. He married Nov. 23, 1794, Ann, daughter of El-
eazer Collins and Elizabeth (Lewis) Ingalls. He died
Sept. 12, 1836. She died Nov. 4, 1856, æ. 82 years (g. s.).
Children of William and Ann, born in Lynn:

307. JOSEPH, b. Mar. 21, 1796.
308. BETSEY BLANEY INGALLS, b. Apr. 13, 1805; m. in Lynn, May
    29, 1822, Thomas Chapman. He d. Nov. 19, 1878, æ. 74
    yrs. (g. s.), and she d. May 5, 1890. Children born in Lynn:
    (1) William Ashton, b. Sept. 7, 1822; (2) Alanson Burrill,
    b. Aug. 28, 1825; d. Jan. 16, 1850.
309. ANN or NANCY, b. Oct. 7, 1812. In the will of her grandfather,
    Eleazer Collins Ingalls, she is called Ann but she signed her
    name Nancy. She m. Mar. 13, 1831 (as Nancy), Archibald
    Selman and had one child and possibly more, born in Lynn.
    (1) Nancy Ellen, b. May 20, 1831.

152 John Lewis, called "Junior," was a cordwainer
and resided in Lynn. He married in Lynn, April 9,
1797, Molly, daughter of Capt. Joseph and Abigail
(Blaney-Lewis) Felt of Salem (see No. 80). In the
Eastern Burial Ground her grave stone says she died Sept.
6, 1870, aged 91 years. He died in Lynn, Feb. 9, 1817.
Children of John and Molly, born in Lynn:

310. SARAH, b. Feb. 2, 1798; m. in Lynn, Dec. 3, 1815, John Seger.
    (His father and mother were of Marblehead.) He d. July 31,
    1852, æ. 60 yrs. and was interred in Swampscott cemetery.
    He was 64 years of age according to an old Bible record.
    His widow d. Dec. 13, 1879. Children, born in Lynn: (1)

John L., b. Oct. 5, 1819; (2) John Lewis, b. Oct. 10, 1823; (3) William, b. Nov. 1, 1826; m. Mary Standley and d. Feb. 6, 1899. (4) Henry, b. Nov. 2, 1829; m. 1st, Clara Standley, and d. 1896.

NOTE. The Standley sisters were daus. of Thomas and Sarah (Phillips) Standley of Swampscott.

311. JONATHAN BLANEY, b. Nov. 22, 1799.
312. ABIGAIL, b. May 22, 1802; m. in Lynn, Nov. 21, 1819, Samuel Atkins, fisherman; who died Mar. 19, 1864, æ. 70 years. Children, born in Lynn : (1) William, b. July 19, 1820; d. unm. (2) Caroline, b. Oct. 22, 1821; m. Rufus Questrom. (3) Warren, b. Dec. 10, 1823; (4) Samuel, b. Feb. 1, 1827; (5) Mary Jane, b. May 16, 1831; m. Apr. 16, 1848, Joseph Standley.
313. JOSEPH FELT, b. Sept. 2, 1804.
314. MARY, b. Aug. 30, 1806; m. in Lynn, Sept. 22, 1823, Abraham Perkins, son of Jonathan and Margaret Perkins of Lynn. Was a cordwainer. Children born in Lynn: (1) Shipley Wilson, b. Oct. 6, 1823; (2) Foster, b. Oct. 26, 1824; (3) Theodore, b. Sept. 16, 1826; (4) Margaret Maria, b. Mar. 1, 1828; (5) John, b. Sept. 7, 1829; d. July 31, 1830; (6) John, b. June 1, 1831; (7) Abraham, b. Oct. 6, 1837; (8) Hannah Maria, b. July 1, 1839; (9) Edward Augustus, b. Sept. 10, 1842; (10) Sylvester, b. Aug. 12, 1844; (11) Waldo, b. Sept. 26, 1846.
315. HANNAH (F.?), b. Jan. 22, 1809; m. Edward H. Lewis; his 2d wife. No children.
316. PERMELIA MERRIAM, b. Mar. 13, 1812.
317. HARRIET, b. Dec. 2, 1812?; the record of birth was filed after the death of her father, and may not be correct. She m. in Lynn, Mar. 5, 1834, Charles Harradon, who d. Nov. 5, 1843, æ. 31 yrs. Children born in Lynn: (1) Charles Oscar, b. Sept. 22, 1837; d. Feb., 1902; (2) Harriet Emily, b. Apr. 16, 1841; d. Aug. 23, 1853.

153 James Fuller Lewis, born in Lynn, Feb. 20, 1781, was a shoemaker and resided in that part of Lynn called Gravesend. He died Jan. 3, 1842. He married in Marblehead, Oct. 27, 1801, Abigail Humphreys, born Sept. 27, 1781, daughter of Benjamin and Jemima (Gale) Humphreys of Marblehead, who died in Lynn, June 27, 1852.

Children of James Fuller and Abigail, born in Lynn:

318. JAMES, b. Feb. 11, 1802.
319. REBECCA, b. Oct. 26, 1804 (Oct. 24. Family Rd.); m. May 29,
    1830 (May 9, 1829. Family Rd.), George Hobby, b. in
    Charlestown, son of William Hobby. She d. June 22, 1838.
    Children, born in Lynn: (1) George Henry, b. Mar. 8, 1831;
    d. Nov. 2, 1898; (2) Mary Ann, b. July 2, 1833; (3) Rebecca
    Ellen, b. Feb. 23, 1835; (4) Abby Green, b. May 6, 1837; d.
    Sept. 23, 1837.
320. SAMUEL HUMPHREYS, b. Jan. 26, 1807; m. July 5, 1833, in
    Lynn, Sally Parrott; d. July 26, 1873.
321. WILLIAM, b. June 8, 1809; d. Sept. 26, 1832; m. Nov. 20, 1831,
    in Lynn, Mary Newman. No children.
322. RUTHE, b. Feb. 17, 1812; d. Mar. 6, 1815.
323. NABBY, b. Nov. 8, 1813; d. Nov. 1, 1892; m. as Abigail, Dec.
    15, 1836, in Lynn, Abner Silsbee, b. in Lynn, Sept. 11, 1812
    and d. Aug., 1890, son of Henry and Mary (Chase) Silsbee.
    Farmer. Children, born in Lynn: (1) William Lewis, b.
    Sept. 12, 1837; (2) James Albert, b. Nov. 11, 1839; d. Apr. 17,
    1848; (3) Abbie Maria, b. Mar. 6, 1841; d. Sept., 1883; (4)
    Alden Burrill, b. Aug. 15, 1845; d. Mar. 22, 1849; (5) Sylves-
    ter, b. Jan. 24, 1848; d. Apr. 13, 1849; (6) Charles Albert, b.
    May 5, 1850.
324. RUTH VICKARY, b. Mar. 19, 1816; d. Sept. 21, 1843; m. in Lynn,
    May 15, 1839, James Grover Brown, b. in Danvers, Oct. 9,
    1812, and d. in Lynn, Oct., 1879. Children, born in Lynn:
    (1) James Otis, b. Feb. 7, 1840; (2) Melinda Ann, b. Mar. 2,
    1842; d. Nov. 2, 1842; (3) Emeline Ruth, b. Sept. 12, 1843.
325. EMELINE, b. Nov. 24, 1818, Family Rds. (Nov. 29. Lynn Rds.);
    m. in Lynn, Apr. 29, 1841, George Hobby, and died Aug. 30,
    1842; he d. April 7, 1879. Had: Lewis, b. May 6, 1842; d.
    Oct. 21, 1842.
326. THOMAS VICKARY, b. Sept. 3, 1820.
327. HORACE FULLER, b. July 23, 1827; d. Mar. 24, 1885. He m.
    1st, Nov. 30, 1848, Mary Angeline, dau. of Benjamin and
    Martha (Putnam) Ireson, b. July 16, 1830; and d. Sept. 12,
    1849, in Lynn. He m. 2nd, July 17, 1853; Martha Ann Ireson,
    sister of his first wife, b. May 29, 1827, Lynn Rds. (May 30,
    1827. Family Rds.); and d. Dec. 3, 1891, in Lynn.

154 Edmund Lewis, born in Lynn, Feb. 8, 1784,
was a shoemaker, lived on Lewis street, Lynn, and died
Oct. 8, 1870. He married in Lynn, Nov. 10, 1816, Rebecca Lewis (285), who died Dec. 18, 1861, æ. 64 years,
9 months.

Children of Edmund and Rebecca, born in Lynn :

328. EDMUND, b. July 20, 1817; farmer; removed to Rockford, Ill.;
d. there, unm., May 5, 1878. Interred in Eastern Burial
Ground, Lynn.

329. REBECCA, b. Dec. 26, 1818; d. Oct. 1, 1842; m., in Lynn, May
28, 1838, Jesse Smith Punchard, b. in Salem, Feb. 6, 1813,
and d. Feb. 12, 1864. Had: (1) Mary Lewis, b. May 15,
1839; m., 1st, Feb. 22, 1872, at Salem, Robert Henry Wilson
of Peabody; m., 2d, Charles H. Whipple of Peabody;
(2) Rebecca Pickworth, b. Sept. 25, 1842; m., Feb. 20. 1865,
William B. Cressy of Rowley, who d. July 21, 1873.

330. NATHANIEL, b. June 24, 1821; d. Sept. 1, 1821.

331. EDITH HANSON, b. Aug. 14, 1822; m. in Lynn, May 7, 1843,
George Whippen, b. Oct. 6, 1819, son of Joseph and Patience
Whippen. Had: (1) Eliza Jane, b. May 16, 1844, in Lynn;
(2) George Edmond, b. Feb. 1, 1846, in Lynn; (3) Louis
Ivers, b. June 15, 1848, in N. J.

332. OLIVE SAUNDERS, b. Mar. 8, 1825; d. Aug. 12, 1854; m. in
Lynn, Jan. 21, 1844, Jesse Smith Punchard. Had: (1) Olive
Delina, b. Mar. 21, 1845; d. April 15, 1845; (2) Olive De-
lina, b. May 31, 1846; d. young; (3) Emma Maria, b. June
30, 1849; m., in Salem, Jan. 26, 1871, George H. Symonds of
Salem; (4) Eliza Ellen, b. Aug. 29, 1853; d. Mar. 9, 1906;
m., Apr. 3, 1873, George P. Woodbury of Salem, who d.
Sept. 28, 1893.

333. BRIDGET, b. Apr. 13, 1828; d. June 18, 1856, unm. Death recorded as Hannah B.

334. CLARINDA, b. Oct. 13, 1830; d. Feb. 15, 1899; m. as Elizabeth
C., in Lynn, Oct. 15, 1853, Ephraim G. Ricker of Boston, æ.
25 y. Removed to Rockford, Ill.

335. HEPZIBAH MARIA, b. June 1, 1833; m. in Lynn, June 3, 1868,
Charles H. Carling, æ. 41 yrs., b. in England, son of Charles
H. and Elizabeth Carling, a glass blower, who d. in 1893.

336. LUCY ABBA, b. May 1, 1837; m. in Lynn, May 17, 1860, Edward A. Dickerson, b. in Lynn, Oct. 15, 1835; son of Edward
and Mary Dickerson. He d. in 1889.

164 Thomas Lewis, born in 1674, married, first, in
Boston, Jan. 1, 1794, Elizabeth Carpenter. He married,
second, in Boston, Jan. 6, 1806, Priscilla Nye. She died
in childbed, Sept., 1810, aged 29 years, and he married,
third, in Boston, Nov. 25, 1813, Polly Clapp, born in
Scituate Jan. 23, 1780, daughter of William and Priscilla

(Otis) Clapp. She' died in Framingham, Mass., Dec. 19, 1865. He was thrown from a carriage, his skull fractured and he died Aug. 18, 1824.

Children of Thomas and Elizabeth:

337. SARAH, bp. Mar. 22, 1795; m. Benjamin Scott; d. childless.
338. ELIZA, bp. Dec. 25, 1796; m. Edmund Hutchinson Lewis (169)·
339. CATHERINE L., bp. July 27, 1799, in Boston; m. Mar. 28, 1821, Jonathan Pratt Robinson of Roxbury. Had: (1) Henry Ware, b. Jan. 31, 1822 in Fredericksburg, Va.; d. Nov. 28, 1890; m. July 22, 1846, Sarah W. Ware; (2) Thomas Lewis, b. Sept. 26, 1823; d. Aug. 26, 1887, in Brighton, Eng.; m., Nov. 15, 1848, in Fall River, Hannah Valentine Durfee, b. Jan. 25, 1828; (3) Robert Lambert, b. May 7, 1827 in Boston; d. Aug. 23, 1866 in St. Louis, Mo.; (4) Catharine Augusta, b. Feb. 4, 1830, in Boston; d. Dec. 18, 1850, in Roxbury; (5) Hannah Hortense, b. Aug. 20, 1839, in Roxbury; m. Jules G. Tournade; d. Jan. 12, 1885, in Brooklyn; (6) Francis Kettell, m. Etta Stevens.
340. HANNAH BRACKETT, bp. Dec. 21, 1800; m. Samuel Shaw Lewis (170).

Children of Thomas and Priscilla :

341. THOMAS, b. May 24, 1808.
342. JOSEPH.
343. PRISCILLA NYE, bp. Nov. 25, 1810; d. in Boston, May 31, 1812.

Children of Thomas and Polly :

344. ABIEL SMITH, b. July 15, 1814.
345. WILLIAM GUSTAVUS, b. Aug. 21, 1816.
346. FRANCES MARY PRISCILLA, b. Nov. 5, 1819; m. John Little-john Wilson of Charleston, S. C. Living in 1907.

166 John Lewis, born Aug. 27, 1779 (g. s.), resided in Boston and Malden. He married, first, in Boston, Nov. 22, 1807, Mary Ann Ouvre (marriage intention Oliver), born in Guadeloupe, W. I. She d. June 30, 1814, æ 28 y. He married, second, in Boston, July 30, 1815, Hannah Lewis (167). She died in Malden, Jan. 16, 1862 (g. s.). He died in Malden, March 27, 1871, aged 91 years, 7 months (g. s.).

Children of John and Mary Ann :

347. MARY ANN, m., in 1832, David N. Badger, b. in Boston, July 16, 1799; d. in Malden, Dec. 4, 1878. Had: (1) David N.; (2) Mary Ann; (3) Sarah; (4) Elmer.

348. SARAH ELOISE, d. July 5, 1812, æ. 2 y. (Boston Rds.).

Children of John and Hannah :

349. JOHN, b. Apr. 29, 1816, in Boston; d. Apr. 30, 1816.

350. JOHN, b. Mar. 3, 1817, in Boston; d. Jan. 24, 1818.

351. JOHN, b. Jan. 21, 1819, in Boston.

352. HANNAH AUGUSTA, b. July 20, 1820, in Boston; d. Oct. 10, 1821.

353. CHARLES HENRY, b. Nov. 1, 1821, in Boston, d. in Malden, Jan. 12, 1877; m. Dec. 10, 1843, Almira Tufts, dau. of Joseph Tufts of Malden. No issue.

354. HANNAH AUGUSTA, b. Feb. 15, 1823, in Boston; m. in Boston, Aug. 18, 1843, Wm. Wilkes, b. Jan. 27, 1820, in Fredonia, Ind., s. of Henry and —— (Ballard) Wilkes. He lived in Louisville, Ky., and was of the firm of Lewis & Wilkes, wholesale hardware dealers. Later he removed to Alton, Ind., and engaged in agriculture. Was county commissioner of Crawford county, about 16 yrs.; and d. Aug. 3, 1891. She d. Aug. 27, 1893. Children, all but the first, b. in Alton, Ind.: (1) George, b. Oct. 7, 1844, in Louisville, Ky.; d. July 6, 1860; (2) Hannah A., b. July 24, 1846; m. John Birkla; res. at Alton, Ind.; (3) Alice G., b. Mar. 1, 1848; d., July 31, 1860, in Louisville, Ky.; (4) Louis, b. June 12, 1849; m. Cornelia M. Ridge; res. at Alton, Ind.; (5) John F., b. Jan. 16, 1851; m. Elizabeth Goad; (6) Thomas, b. Sept. 15, 1854; m. Eunice Carberry; res. at Alton,; Ind. (7) Benjamin, b. Sept. 23, 1858; m. Sarah E. Kemp; res. at Alton, Ind.; (8) William, b. Sept. 11, 1860; m. Amanda Culver; res. at Alton, Ind.; (9) Isabel, b. April 21, 1863; m. John Grubbs; res. at Skurry, Kaufman county, Texas; (10) Perry W., b. Nov. 10, 1865; m. Sally A. Pearson; res. at Alton, Ind.

355. LUCY DANFORTH, b. Sept. 5, 1824, in Malden; m. June 27, 1850, Paschal Paoli Pope Ware, b. in Wrentham, June 12, 1820; d. in Everett, Oct. 20, 1882. Children, b. in Malden: (1) Lucy Elizabeth, b. Nov. 15, 1855; m., Oct. 28, 1880, Theodore H. Pierce; (2) Paschal P. P., b. May 27, 1760; m., May 13, 1890, Lora D. Ward.

356. SARAH, b. Jan. 21, 1826, in Malden; m. Francis B. Wallis of Boston, and d. Nov. 8, 1894, in Everett. Children: (1) Arthur D.; (2) Mina.

357. NATHANIEL, b. Sept. 21, 1827, in Malden.
358. THOMAS, b. July 21, 1829, in Boston.
359. DAVID, b. Jan. 15, 1831; d. Jan. 18, 1831, in Boston.
360. GEORGE A., b. July 21, 1832, in Boston; d. May 8, 1843, in Malden.

169 Edmund Hutchinson Lewis, born in Plymouth, Mass., Nov. 22, 1796; married Sept. 5, 1819, Eliza Lewis (338). He resided in Louisville, Ky.
Child of Edmund and Eliza:

371. HENRY EDMUND, m. Margaret Clark. Had: Eliza, who d. childless.

171 Samuel Shaw Lewis, born in Plymouth, June 19, 1799; married in Boston, Nov. 3, 1824; Hannah Bracket Lewis (340).

He was a member of the Ancient and Honorable Artillery Co., 1845-1849. He was agent of the Cunard Steamship Co. and also various railroads, and originator of the project for filling in what is now Commercial Street, Boston. He was one of the principal promotors of the Grand Junction R. R.

His wife died June 4, 1859, and he died in 1869, in Boston.

Children of Samuel Shaw and Hannah:

362. FRANKLIN HENSHAW, b. July 20, 1825, in Boston.
363. LUCY ELIZABETH, d. Mar. 19, 1832; æ. 4 y. 4 m. (Boston Rds.)
364. CATHERINE AUGUSTA, d. Jan. 20, 1830, æ. 8 mos.
365. SAMUEL SHAW, d. Nov. 30, 1831, æ. 8 mos.
366. ANNA RICHMOND, b. 1833; unm., res. at 38 Norfolk Road, Brighton, Eng.
367. JOSEPHINE, b. 1835; m. Dec. 24, 1856, George Lyman Perry, and had one son, Lyman Lewis Perry.
368. FRANCES WILSON, b. 1837; d. 1885, unm. at Brighton, Eng.
369. SAMUEL SHAW, b. 1838; d. unm. in 1880 at London, Eng.
370. CAROLINE SUSAN, b. 1840; d. 1878; m. Frederick Smith, U. S. Navy, of Charleston, S. C., and had Rachel Gertrude, unm., who resides in Washington, D. C.
371. GERTRUDE MACIVOR. b. 1842; d. unm. Apr. 17, 1899, at Brighton, Eng.

171 Charles Henry Lewis, born in Plymouth, June 26, 1804; married in Cincinnati, Ohio, June 19, 1838, Mary Clark Anderson, born in Pittsburgh, Pa., daughter of Paul and Mary (Clark) Anderson of Pittsburgh, Pa. Resided at Louisville, Ky.
Children of Charles Henry and Mary Clark:

372. B. FRANKLIN.
373. CHARLES ANDERSON.
374. FANNIE CALDWELL, m. William Henry Kaye. Resides in Louisville, Ky. Had: William Henry, m. Mary E. Griffith and had one son, Lewis Griffith.
375. KATE CALDWELL.
376. MARY PAUL, m. David Edgar Park of Pittsburgh, Pa. and had one son, Lewis Anderson.

175 Samuel Lewis, born in Lynn, June 6, 1752, was a Mattross in Capt. Winthrop Gray's Co., Col. Craft's artillery regiment. His pay abstract, sworn to in Boston June 8, 1776, has his autograph signature. He received a tannery by will of his grandfather. He married in Lynn, Nov. 29, 1770, Susannah Meachum, born in Lynn, June 29, 1754, daughter of Isaac and Ruth Meachum of Lynn. She died Feb. 14, 1815 (g. s.). He died Apr. 25, 1806.
Children of Samuel and Susannah, born in Lynn:

377. JOHN, b. Feb. 15, 1772.
378. SUSANNAH, b. Mar. 24, 1774.
379. THOMAS, b. Sept. 29, 1776.
380. HENRY, b. Nov. 3, 1782.
381. ISAAC, b. Apr. 12, 1785.
382. SALLY, b. July 12, 1787.
383. SAMUEL, b. Nov. 3, 1789.
384. JESSE L., b. Apr. 16, 1792.

179 Nathaniel Lewis, born in Swansea, Aug. 18, 1755, was a private in Capt. Jonathan Danforth's Co., Col. D. Brewer's regiment, from May 7, 1775 to Oct., 1775; also in Capt. Peleg Peck's Co., Col. Carpenter's regiment, Sept., 1777, and again in Aug., 1780. He married in Swansea, Jan., 9, 1783, Candace Peirce.

Children of Nathaniel and Candace, born in Swansea :

385. ANNE, b. Aug. 26, 1785.
386. CANDACE, b. June 21, 1787.
387. MARCY, b. Apr. 14, 1789.
388. NATHANIEL, b. Feb. 16, 1791.
389. HIPSEY, b. Dec. 12, 1792.
390. AMOS, b. Jan. 14, 1795.
391. MASON, b. Dec. 21, 1796.
392. JESSE, b. Oct. 20, 1798.
393. POLLE, b. Aug. 4, 1800.
394. LEDIA, b. July 4, 1804.

184 Aaron Lewis, was a private in Capt. Peleg
Peck's Co., Col. John Daggett's regiment, on the alarm at
Rhode Island, Jan. 14, 1778, and was in the same company in the following August. On Nov. 6, 1820, the selectmen of Dighton complained that he was spending his
fortune in drink and on Nov. 10, Ebenezer Talbot was appointed as guardian. He married Apr. 4, 1779, Mary,
daughter of Noah Davis of Providence, R. I., who died
May 13, 1814.
Children of Aaron and Mary :

395. JOHN, b. 1780.
396. JOSEPH, b. Dec. 17, 1793.
397. MARY.
398. BETSEY, m. Henry Harrison.

185 Benjamin Lewis born in Dighton, Feb. 16,
1761, married, first, by Elder Jacob Hix, at Rehoboth,
Nov. 23, 1783, Lydia Bosworth, born Oct. 11, 1756, and
died July 29, 1795, the daughter of John and Lydia (Cap-
ron) Bosworth. He married, second, by Elder Hix, Mar.
27, 1796, Hannah, daughter of Joseph and Hannah Rounds
of Rehoboth, born Mar. 12, 1777, and died June 29, 1853.
He died Feb. 16, 1849, on his 88th birthday. Of his remarkable family of eighteen children, thirteen reached the
age of 66 years or upwards and possessed a marked degree
of individuality. Most of the men were masons, and they
ably carved out their way to success in life.
Children of Benjamin and Lydia, born in Dighton :

399. BENJAMIN, b. Feb. 14, 1785.
400. JAMES, b. Sept. 10, 1787.
401. LYDIA, b. Oct. 5, 1789; m. in Providence, in 1822, Benjamin Pidge, a widr. who d. Oct. 13, 1839, æ. 63 y. She d. May 1, 1867, in Providence, R. I. Had: (1) Charles W., b. May 11, 1823; (2) Sophia E., b. 1825? (3) Frances H., b. 1827? (4) Samuel J., b. Oct., 1832; (5) Henry C., b. Apr. 25, 1834; d. Oct. 7, 1835; (6) Henry P., b. May 7, 1835; d. Mar. 29, 1840.
402. A CHILD, buried at Swansea.
403. A CHILD, buried at Swansea.

Children of Benjamin and Hannah, born in Dighton :

404. SAMUEL, b. Mar. 24, 1797; m. 1st, Lydia R. West, daughter of Capt. John West, who d. June 10, 1859, æ 57 yrs.; m. 2d, Jan. 27, 1873, in Providence, R. I., Mary Ann, dau. of William and Ann Creswell of England. He endowed her with $700.00 a year during her life. He died Sept. 26, 1873, and she returned to England and m. again. He was a mason by trade and resided at Providence, R. I. where he accumulated quite a fortune.
405. CHACE, b. Nov. 1, 1798.
406. BOWERS, b. Mar. 13, 1801.
407. LEVI, b. May 24, 1803.
408. HANNAH, b. June 20, 1805; d. in Providence R. I., June 4, 1892; m. Charles Williams, b. July 4, 1804 and d. Nov. 8, 1877. Had: (1) Charles A., b. Oct. 8, 1828; d. Mar. 27, 1867; (2) Benjamin F., b. Sept. 22, 1831; unm; (3) Hannah E., b. May 29, 1835; d. Sept. 27, 1836; (4) Virgil C., b. Dec. 30, 1837; d. Apr. 7, 1862; (5) Hannah V., b. July 30, 1839; (6) Archelus A., b. Feb. 19, 1843; d. Feb. 6, 1856; (7) Alanson A., b. Feb. 19, 1843.
409. JEREMIAH, b. Dec. 2, 1806.
410. ALMIRA, b. Mar. 2, 1808; d. unm. June 12, 1876.
411. ALFRED, b. Feb. 28, 1810.
412. SYLVESTER, b. May 2, 1812.
413. CAROLINE, b. Nov. 26, 1813; d. Nov. 8, 1814.
414. CALEB MASON, Nov. 28, 1814; d. Jan. 29, 1815.
415. ANGELINE, b. Nov. 25, 1816; d. May 3, 1831.
416. ORIN JUDSON, b. Mar. 25, 1818; d. Sept. 15, 1883, in Dayville, Conn.; m. Hannah R. Sears. No issue. He was a hardware merchant and manufacturer of belts at Dayville, Conn.

186 Timothy Lewis, married May 9, 1788, Submit Bullock who died May 1, 1844. He died Nov. 22, 1821.

Children of Timothy and Submit, last six born at Dighton:

417. POLLY, b. Jan. 7, 1789; d. Aug., 1865.
418. BETSEY, b. Feb. 7, 1791; d. Oct. 12, 1854.
419. WILLIAM, b. Aug. 11, 1793.
420. RUTH, b. Nov. 3, 1794.
421. TIMOTHY, b. Dec. 18, 1795; d. Apr. 29, 1839.
422. SALLY, b. May 3, 1798; d. Feb. 21, 1865.
423. SUBMIT, b. June 18, 1800; d. 1887.
424. LEONARD, Dec. 31, 1802; d. Apr. 2, 1842, while serving in the Indian War.
425. NANCY VOCE, b. Nov. 27, 1804; d. Mar. 26, 1880, in Providence, R. I.; m. Apr. 7, 1826, Increase Sumner, b. Jan. 3, 1801, at Woodstock, Conn., d. Apr. 25, 1866. Had: (1) George Lowell, b. July 4, 1827 , in Providence, R. I.; d. July 21, 1827; (2) Eliza Ann West, b. Oct. 5, 1828, in Providence, R. I.; m. May 21, 1849, Edwin Blake Larchar, resides in N. Y. City; (3) Sarah Maria, b. Nov. 27, 1830; m. Aug. 25, 1855, Noble Warren DeMunn, in Providence, R. I.; (4) Timothy Increase b. Oct. 7, 1832; d. Mar. 17, 1849; (5) Nancy Lewis, b. June 24, 1835, in Providence, R. I.; d. Feb. 27, 1896, in Boston; m. Sept. 12, 1859, Charles Henry Crump; (6) Lydia Rand, b. Apr. 12, 1838; (7) Mary May, b. May 3, 1841; d. Jan. 27, 1893; m. Aug. 13, 1873, Wm. Woodward; (8) Julia DeEtt, b. Aug. 10, 1844; d. Aug. 2, 1848; (9) Julia DeEtt, b. June 1, 1848.
426. ISAAC, b. Dec. 5, 1807; d. July 10, 1872; m. 1st, Asea Ann Goff, who d. Jan. 13, 1863; m. 2d, May 22, 1864, Betsey J. West of Rehoboth, Mass.

187 Reuben Lewis, married by Elder Russell Mason, on Mar. 31, 1793, at Rehoboth, Luraney Brown of Swansea.

Child of Reuben and Luraney:

427. REUBEN, b. abt. 1797; m. in Providence, R. I., Sarah Borden of Fall River, Mass, and d. by suicide, in Providence, R. I. May 4, 1858, æ. 61 yrs.

193 Samuel Lewis, born Sept. 29, 1754, in New York city ; married, in 1778, Elizabeth Godfrey, and died Sept. 30, 1822.
Children of Samuel and Elizabeth :

428. SAMUEL J. N., b. Aug. 22, 1799; d. 1849.
429. MARYANA, b. Mar. 4, 1782; d. 1861.
430. FREDERICK, b. Nov. 22, 1784; d. 1786.
431. SARAH, b. Aug. 19, 1786; m. James Johnston.
432. HENRY, b. Oct. 4, 1788; d. 1822.
433. ELIZABETH, b. July 4, 1790; d. 1791.
434. JAMES, b. Mar. 29, 1792.
435. EDWARD SIMMONS, b. Nov. 26, 1794; d. 1829.
436. GEORGE, b. Aug. 27, 1798; d. 1883.
437. HARRIET, b. Feb. 26, 1800.
438. CHARLES, b. Feb. 27, 1803; d. 1863.
439. WILLIAM GIFFORD, b. Mar. 24, 1807; d. 1851.

194 John Lewis, born at Saybrook, Conn., July 26, 1795 ; married Emily Symonds, and died at Cambria, N. Y. Another report states that he died in Michigan.
Children of John and Emily :

440. JOHN.
441. LYMAN.
442. WILLIAM.
443. GERALDINE.

198 Dan Kelsey Lewis, born at Saybrook, Conn., Oct. 15, 1801 ; married at Hinsdale, N. Y., Nov. 2, 1828, Catherine, born Aug. 16, 1809, at Geneva, N. Y., daughter of John and Catherine (Foot) Conrad. He died Dec. 2, 1886, at Fontanelle, Neb., where his widow and family reside.
Children of Dan Kelsey and Catherine :

444. LOIS, b. Mar. 8, 1830, at Hinsdale, N. Y.
445. AUGUSTUS, b. Jan. 30, 1832, at Hinsdale, N. Y.
446. AUGUSTA, b. Jan. 30, 1832, at Hinsdale, N. Y.; d. Jan. 17, 1846, at Burlington, Iowa.
447. JOHN CONRAD, b. April 29, 1834, at Portville, N. Y.
448. CATHERINE, b. July 11, 1837, at Hinsdale, N. Y.; d. July 19, 1851, at Burlington, Iowa.
449. OSCAR, b. Oct. 25, 1840, at Portville, N. Y.

450. OSMAR, b. Oct. 25, 1840.
451. HELEN, b. July 24, 1849, at Burlington, Iowa; m., Nov. 28,
     1873, Frank W. Gibson, at Burlington, Iowa. Live at Lake-
     port, Calif. Had: (1) Birdie Amelia, b. Dec. 5, 1874; (2)
     Cora Helen, b. Aug. 8, 1878; (3) Osmar, b. June 27, 1881; d.
     June 23, 1884.
452. AMELIA JANE, b. Dec. 27, 1852, at Burlington, Iowa; m., Nov.
     28, 1876, Adrian Green, at Fontanelle, Neb.; reside at Mid-
     dletown, Iowa. Had: (1) Lewis A., b. Oct. 14, 1879; (2)
     Paul A., b. Dec. 11, 1881; (3) Roy W., b. Dec. 13, 1883; d.
     Oct. 31, 1894; (4) Bessie Helen, b. Jan. 20, 1885; (5) Inda
     Lois, b. July 6, 1889; (6) Eunice Amelia, b. May 6, 1892.

203 Richard Lewis, born July 27, 1810, at Homer,
N. Y.; married, Dec. 18, 1844, at Lockport, N. Y., Harriet Augusta, born May 31, 1818, at Darien, N. Y., daughter of George and Ruth (Clark) Hawley. He died at
Minneapolis, Minn., Oct. 5, 1886.

Children of Richard and Harriet Augusta, born at
Lockport, N. Y. :

453. LOUISA JANE, b. May 23, 1846.
454. GEORGE HAWLEY, b. July 23, 1847.
455. SOPHIE JANE, b. May 4, 1849.
456. CHARLES HINMAN, b. April 6, 1851.
457. RUTH CLARK, b. July 26, 1852.
458. JAMES RICHARDS, b. June 28 or July 5, 1855.
459. HARRIET AUGUSTA, b. May 23, 1861; m., Dec. 12, 1887, at Min-
     neapolis, Minn., Frederick Earle Dunn, b. March 6, 1859, at
     Shelby, Ontario, son of William and Adeline Olivia (Earle)
     Dunn. Had: (1) Lewis Earle, b. Dec. 4, 1888; (2) Helen, b.
     May 11, 1892.

204 Truman Lewis, born Nov. 15, 1812, at Solon,
N. Y.; married, March 11, 1838, at Pendleton, N. Y.,
Theresa, daughter of Benjamin and Naomi Simonds of
Homer, N. Y. He died Sept. 14, 1884, at Pendleton,
N. Y.

Children of Truman and Theresa:

460. PRUDENCE AMELIA, b. Aug. 25, 1840, at Cambria, N. Y.
461. EDGAR DAVID, b. Nov. 15, 1842, at Lewiston, N. Y.
462. RANSOM, b. Dec. 25, 1844, at Lewiston, N. Y.
463. EMMA SOPHIA, b. June 19, 1849, at Pendleton, N. Y.

205 Benjamin Lewis, born May 6, 1753, in Billerica, Mass.; was a farmer at Duxbury School Farm, now Milford, N. H., on the north side of the Souhegan river, near the Wilton line, before the settlement of Milford, N. H. He was a Revolutionary soldier, and was at Bunker Hill and Lexington. He removed to Greenfield, N. H., in 1814, and died there, and his gravestone in the cemetery in the centre of the town is inscribed : " Lieut. Benjamin Lewis, who died Feb. 1, 1817, aged 64 years." He married, July 18, 1775, in Billerica, Sarah, born in Billerica, Jan. 31, 1754, daughter of Samuel and Mary (Brown) Blanchard, who died Oct. 27, 1838, aged 84 years, 9 months and 27 days (Wilmington, Mass., Records).

Children of Benjamin and Sarah, born at Milford, N. H. :

464. SARAH, b. Feb. 4, 1776; m., July 25, 1793, Jacob Richardson, b. Aug. 10, 1769, in Billerica, Mass.; and d. Nov. 9, 1839, at Greenfield, N. H., æ. 70 yrs. She d. there Oct. 21, 1829. Had: (1) Jacob, b. Jan. 12, 1794; (2) Sarah, b. Feb. 25, 1797; d. unm. July 20, 1875; (3) Benjamin Lewis, b. Feb. 13, 1799; d. July 28, 1800; (4) Lewis, b. Aug. 3, 1801; (5) Albert Louis, b. Oct. 16, 1803; (6) Julia Ann, b. July 21, 1806; d. 1840; (7) Charles, b. July 30, 1809: (8) Cyrus, b. Aug. 23, 1812; (9) Mary Davis, b. Apr. 21, 1817; (10) Elizabeth. b. Mar. 22, 1819.

465. MARY, b. Nov. 25, 1777; m., April 20, 1804, Solomon Davis, b. July 31, 1776, in New Ipswich, N. H., son of Jonathan and Sarah (——) Davis. Lived at New Ipswich and Hancock, N. H., where she d. Jan. 4, 1809.

466. BENJAMIN, b. Sept. 21, 1779; d., unm., July 5, 1805, at Milford, N. H.

467. ASA, b. Sept. 14, 1781.

468. CYRUS, b. June 5, 1783; he taught school at Lyndeboro, N. H., in 1811, and it is stated that scholars came from other districts when he taught. He d. at Milford, Oct. 15, 1813. He was lieutenant of militia.

469. CHARLES, b. June 30, 1785.

470. HANNAH, b. July 10, 1787; m., Nov. 22, 1810, Henry Carter of Wilmington, Mass., b. July, 1785; s. of Jonathan and Lydia (Gowing) Carter of Wilmington, Mass. Resided at Wilmington, Mass.

212 Moses Lewis, born April 17, 1770, in Billerica, Mass., settled in Bridgewater, now Bristol, N. H. He was a man of wealth in 1812, with large business interests, but the war used up his means and he was imprisoned for debt. He was a selectman in 1801 and 1802, and paid taxes on a tannery in 1810. He removed to Gainesville, Ala., where he died Jan. 10, 1852. He married, Aug. 15, 1794, at Alexandria, N. H., Sally, born in Pembroke, N. H., July 21, 1776, daughter of William and Jane (McDonald) Martin of Pembroke, N. H.

Children of Moses and Sally, born in Bridgewater, N. H.:

471. MARY, b. Oct. 20, 1796 (Oct. 14, family records); d. Nov. 6, 1827, of consumption.
472. WILLIAM MARTIN, b. Aug. 29, 1798.
473. RUFUS GRAVES, b. Sept. 14, 1800.
474. HIRAM, b. Aug. 14, 1802; d. March 14, 1803 (Feb. 18. town records).
475. ELIZA WEBSTER, b. June 26, 1804; d. Oct. 1, 1843, at Kempner Springs, Miss.
476. SARAH, b. Sept. 1, 1807; m., May 28, 1835, at Springfield, Ala., Dr. Samuel Smith; d. Aug. 29, 1844, at Lowdonville, Ohio.

215 Jonathan Lewis, born March 20, 1758, in Billerica, Mass., was a Revolutionary soldier, and was at the battle of Bunker Hill and at the surrender of Gen. Burgoyne near Saratoga, N. Y. He was of Pepperrell, and removed to Harvard, Mass., where, according to his family Bible, he married, first, widow Hannah (Willard) Turner, daughter of Dr. Lemuel Willard, who died Aug. 1, 1785. (She had one child by her first marriage.) He married, second, Sept. 28, 1786, Sarah Warren, who died July 2, 1795, at Concord, Vt. He married, third, March 22, 1796, at Royalston, Mass., Lucy Stockwell, who died Jan. 1, 1841. He removed from Harvard, Mass., to Concord, Vt., March 20, 1788, and from thence to Kirby, Vt., March 20, 1806, where he was the first town clerk and an influential man. He died at Kirby, Vt., Aug. 1, 1841.

Children of Jonathan and Sarah:

477. JONATHAN, b. July 6, 1787, at Harvard, Mass.
478. SALLY, b. Aug. 1, 1789 (first female child born at Concord, Vt.); m. John Bates, and d. at Mooers, Clinton Co., N. Y.
479. CALVIN, b. June 8, 1791, at Concord, Vt., where he d., unm., Nov. 23, 1872.
480. LUTHER, b. July 27, 1793; m. Elethea Streeter; d. Feb. 12, 1843, at Burke, Vt.

(To be continued.)

SALEM TOWN RECORDS.

TOWN MEETINGS, VOLUME II.

1659—1680.*

(Continued from Vol. XLIII. page 160.)

upon m^r Gedneys motion for the setling of m^r Clarks ffarme according to the townes grants both to m^r Clarke and Affter to himself for Alowing him what was taken away by Lin Line   Its agreed that when the Line Is Perfected between Lin and us that It shall be done by the Laiers out according to the townes grants.

Its ordered that a generall towne meeting be warned for the Inhabitants of the towne to meet together on munday Next being the Second day of the month at nine of the Clock In the morning ffor the Choice of select men and Constables

At A generall towne meeting held the second day of march 1673 thees persons presented themselves and took the oath of fidelity

John Nurce	henry wilkins
John ffoster	Samuell Steevens
Richard Richards	John green

Chosen for Select men for the year Ensueng

major hawthorne	m^r Henry Bartlemew
Capt Corwin	m^r Grafton Senr
Capt Price	m^r Rich^rd Prince
m^r Jn° Corwin	

Constables Chosen to Serve for the yeare Ensuing

John Clifford	
w^m Lake	and: Tho ffliut sen^r

[206]   At a meeting of y: select ||men|| Salem: this 3th of march 1673/4

It is ordred that the same order: made in the yeare 71: 72: about swine shall stand in force for the yeare enfuing

*Copied from the original by Martha O. Howes and verified by Sidney Perley, Esq.

Att a meetting of ye felect men being prefent 17th:1mo 7 3/4

It is Agreed thore fhall be a Gene^{al}

major hathorn
Capt Curwin
Capt Price
m^r bartholmew
decon prince
m^r Graffton
Jno Curwin

town metting on tuefday next being ye 24th of march 1673/4 for to Confider of ye way of m^r higinfons mayntenence for this yeer and Alfo to know ye mind of ye towne for m^r Nicoletts onti neuance with us Another yeere & fome other things y^t may then ffall In

Jno Curwin Is Choffen to Keepe ye towne Booke for ye yeere Infueing

Att a meetting of ye felect men 20th 11mo 7 3/4 being prefent as p margentt

Jno Pickering & fam^{ll} Gardner ‖Junr‖

major hathorn
Capt Price
m^r Grafton
m^r Bartholmew
m^r Prince
Jno Curwin

are Choffen furvey^rs of fences for ye north ffeeld for this yeere

Jos buffum & Thos Robins are Choffen furuey^rs of ffences for ye fouth feeld:

Danell futherek & Jos boyce ‖Ju^r‖ are Choffen furuoy^{rs} of ffences for ye Glaff houfe ffences & all ye ffences without

Phelip Cromwell & Thos Rootts are choffen furuey^{rs} of ye ffences from ye town bridge to mordykay Creffords Neke

It is ordered y^t all ye ffences be mayd up In ye towne at or before ye 9th of Aperell Next 1674 & Inclofed

Capt Prece & m^r Jno Ruke ‖ & Ed fflint ‖ are Choffen to take Care for ye mendeng off ye ways from Thos Cromwell Corner to ye town bridge

m^r Grafton & m^r Prince are Choffen to take Care for ye mending of ye highways from Thos Cromwells to ye lower end of ye towne

Henery fkery fen^r is Choffen feayler of Leether for this yeer

Thomas Iues Is Choffen Clerk of ye market for this yeer & ye Conftable to prefent him to ye major to be fworn In this offic

[207]   20th: 1mo 7 3/4

Natha Prece Is Allowed fix fhillings for a fpade & work done at ye fortt & to haue a Note to ye Conftable

Rubin Guppy and william Reeus are Apoynted to take Care yt all fwine be fuffeciently Ringd & yokd according to ye order mayd In 67 & 68 upon ye faym forfeture formerly & yokd by ye 7th of may

' m^r Endycott Ifrell Porter & fergeatt Leach are Apoynted to Lay out a highway Throw ye land fformerly Granted to old Goodmon hutchefon for wch ye fayd hutchefon hath Recd fatiffaction for formerly The fayd way to be layd out foe af may be moft Convenient for ye Inhabitants * to Come to there meetting howfe

Leftenent Putnam Jno Putnam and Jofeph Porter are Apoynted to goe In pembulation between us & topffeld to Renew ye bounds formerly fetled this to be done fometime In ye 1mo or 2mo 74

The felectt men Confidering how yt by ye prouedence of God Capt more Is brought Very low, they Judg It meett to Grant him Liberty for ye keeping of a publick howfe of Entertaynmentt ffor ye felling of beer wine & fyder This to be done for ye ffereft yeer upon tryall & foe to be left to ye difcretion of ye felect men for time to Come

Major hathorn m^r henery ‖ bartholmew ‖ & m^r Jofeph Gardner are Apoynted ffor to fetle ye bounds betwen us & Marblehead

It Is ordered That all fwine aboue tow months old fhall be fuffetiently Ringd by ye 20th march and foe to be kept Ringd on ye penelty of twelue pence p day for euery neglect and to be fuffetiently yoked by ye feirft of may on ye fayme penelty & Ruben Gupy & william Reeus are Appoynted & Impowred to fee ye Execution of this order & Impowred to deftrayne any that fhall Refufe this order

[208] Att a Generall towne meetting ye 24th of ye 1th mo 1673/4 The motion with Refp^{tt} to ye way of M^r higefons mayntanence is Refferd to fome other time

A motion being mayd by feuerall of ye towne for ye Abaytment of fome pt of there meetting howfe Rate It is wholly left to ye felect men to Act In It by a vote of ye towne

*" Ye ffarmers " written in the margin.

Mᣵ Charlls Nickolett is Called by ye towne to Continew with us a Nother Yeere for to helpe Carry on ye worke of ye meneftry as formerly

In Anfwer to a petetion of ye ffarmers to abate fome pt of ye meeting howfe Rate It is left wholly to ye felect men to Act In It as they fhall fee meett

In Anfwer to Nathanell ffelton for fix ffoote of land In lenght & twenty ffoott In bredth It is Granted and ffranfis Nurce & Ifak Cooke are Apoynted to lay It out & make Return

Rubin Guppy hath foe much land Granted him at ye end of ye howfe where Obedyah Rich lius as ye felectmen fhall Judg meett to fpare Not exeeding thre or foore pole

Voted yt ye felect men haue liberty to difpoffe of farah Lambertt

Voted yt ye felect men In beeng haue ye fayme power yt ye felect men had ye laft yeer

[209]   Att a meetting of ye felectmen 27ᵗʰ march : 74

majoᣵ hathorn
Capt: Curwine
mᣵ Grafton
Good Prince
mᣵ Prece
Jnᵒ Corwine
mᣵ bartholew

Agreed with henery keny to make a fuffetient Cart way ouer ye bridge at bever Dam & alfo to make ye way fuffetient at both ends of ye bridg for wch worke being pformd he is to be payd by ye towne twenty fiue fhillings

Jos horn Is Choffen to Joyne with henery Skery In ye office as a feayler of Leather & both fworn before major hathorn

Agreed with peter prefkett to keepe ye Towne heard for this yeere—to begin keeping ye 10ᵗʰ of Aperill & to Continew keeping of ym till ye 14ᵗʰ october and If any Catle be loft he is feafonably to look ym vp & to bring ym to there feuerall owners.

And This being pformd he Is to Resᶜ ffrom ye feuerall owners of ye Catle According to there ꝑportion ye fume of fixteen pounds In ye like pay yt formerly hath bene payd

Capt walter price & Jnᵒ Curwin are Apoynted & Impowred In behalfe of ye towne to Anfwer at Ipfwich Court

In an Action of Replevy between Nath¹ Putnam & Jn°
Peefe Coftable In Refufeing to pay Rats toward ye New
meetting howfe & also to Anfwer In an Action betwen Jn°
Putnam & Jn° peafe Coftable & In an Action between
Nekolas manning & ye felect men If occation

The felect men vewing a fton horse of ffranfis fkerys of
a bay Coller he is Allowd to be According to law

The felect men being meett to fetle ye Accompts with
Nickolas maning Conftable They haue taken a bill of him
for ye Cleering of his Accompts

[210] 28ᵗʰ : of march 1674
Att a meetting of ye felect men: being prefent

major hathorne
Capt Curwine
Capt. Price
mʳ bartholmew
mʳ Grafton
mʳ prince
Jn° Corwin

This bill byndeth me Nickolos
maning to pay or Caufe to be payd
vnto mʳ William Brown fenʳ or order
The fume of twenty three pounds &
eleuen pence wᶜʰ is dew to him ffor
m higginfons Rate (at or before ye
feirft of may Next—And to pay to The
felect men or there order ye fume of twenty eaight pounds
fiue fhillings eaight pence at or before ye 10ᵗʰ of Jun Next
ffor ye true pformance of ye promifes—I ye fayd Nickolas
manning doe bind myfelfe my Ares executr Admineftra-
tors & Aftignes In ye bond of eaighty pounds truly to be
payd as wittnes my hand this 28ᵗʰ march : 1674

Nicholas Maning*

mʳ Henery Bartholmew makeing Complaynt to ye felectmen They haue ordered as ffollewith

9-2ᵐᵒ 74

Thomas Rootts you may take Notice yᵗ mʳ Henery Bartholmew Is to Run his ffence as major hathorn hath fhowd
him, and It is ordered yt you fhale neather dyrecktly nor
Indyrektly medle or touch mʳ Bartholmews ffence upon
yoʳ perrill, & yt There fhall be Care taken In Convenient
time for a way to yʳ howfe ouer ye Banlk by mʳ bartholmews ffence by us how are ye felect men

Att a meetting of ye felect men ye 23ᵗʰ of 2ᵐᵒ 1674
being prefent

*Autograph.

major hathorn
Capt. Curwin
mr bartholmew
mr Graffton
Jno Curwin
mr Prince
Capt : Price

major hathorn hath ꝙuided one
bulle ffor ye towne heard for this
yeer ffor wᶜh he is to haue twenty
ſhillings

Alſo Capt Curwin hath ꝙuided a
Nother bull more for ye towne heerd
for wᶜh he is to haue twenty ſhillings

[211]   Agreed with William Lord to Continew In his
takeing Care off ye meetting houſe Riging ye bell & dig-
ging of Graues for one yeer more upon ye ſayme terms as
ye Laſt yeer: his time begining 26ᵗʰ 2ᵐᵒ 74

Dockter Knott hauing Returnd Thomas Robinſon ye
ſelectmen haue ordered Jnᵒ Corwin to pay to ye ſayd
Knott fiue pounds wᶜh is In pt towards Thomas Robinſons
Care wᶜh ffiue pounds Is In full payment ffor a pſell of
land Layd out to ye ſayd Jnᵒ Corwine In ye Common by
ye ſelectmen

Conſidering how yt William hollenworth by ſeuerell
loſſes by ſea Is brought low ye ſelectmen haue Granted
liberty to his wiffe to draw beer & ſyder & Ipſwch Court
Allowd of It whyle ye Court at ſalem

Thomas Robinſon being Returnd ffrom Dockter knott
ye ſelectmen haue Granted him a fortnights time to ſee to
ꝙuid for himſelfe & In Caſe he doth not Then ye ſelect
men will take Care to put him out to ſeruis

Agreed with ffrantis Skery ‖ to kepe & mayntayne
Sarah ‖ lambert & to ffree The Towne from all burden &
Chardge wt euer during her life   In Conſideration of
wᶜh ye ſayd ffranſis Skery Is to haue ten Akers of land If
It be ffound Common on this ſid Ipſwich high way—but If
on ye other ſyd off ye way Then twenty Aker and Alſo to
be exempted from his ſingle towne Rate during his life ;
ffor The true pformance of ye aboue ſayd premeſes ye
ſayd ffrantis Skery doth bynd him ſelfe his Ares executors
Admeniſtrators & Aſſigns during ye Life of ye ſaid Sarah
lambert

Wittˢ his hand The 23 2ᵐᵒ 74 ffrancis Skery
Wittnes Hen : Bartholmew Joseph Grafton

[212]   Granted to Georg Keafer liberty to ffell Therty trees for bark upon bakers Iland

William hollensworths wiffe hath liberty Granted her till feptember Next before fhe pays her meetting howfe Rate In ye mayntime ye towne to fatif fy Jn° ffif ke

Sarah lambertts Chyld was taken from Thomas Green-flyts wiffe & put to Thomas Greens wife ye 27ᵗʰ of march foe yt Thomas Greenflyts wife kepe ye Chyld Juft one yeer wont tow days

Agreed That there fhall be a ffreemens meeting on ye 2ᵗʰ day of may being faterday at ten of ye Cloke In ye morning for ye election of Govʳ: mageftrats & other Generall offecers and alfo to Choofe deputys for ye Geneˡˡ Court

The Wayghts & meffurs are deleuered Into Conftable Laks hands 6 May 74

18ᵗʰ : 3ᵐᵒ : 74

Major hathorn
Capt Corwin
mʳ bartholmew
decon prince
Jnᵒ Curwin

The felect being meett & were prefent Thomas Lemeer a Jarfyman being Receued Into this Jurifdiction Is alfo Admitted an Inhabetant Into ye towne for one yeer upon tryall

Edmund ffeberarys wife Jn° fanders wife Jn° Normans wife Robertt hodges wife and Jn° fiblys wife haue liberty to build a fmale pew In one halfe of ye hindermoft feats of ye woemens feats below quided they fett there pew at one end of yt feat & for ye bredth not to exeed ye fformer feat

Capt Curwin Is Ordered to widen ye ffeirft of ye mens feats below abought one ffoott & to ffinifh It up & Is to be done well—and he is to be payd for ye Coft out of ye hundred & twenty pounds dew from Jon ffifke to ye towne

[213]   Att a meetting of ye felectmen ye 23ᵗʰ of May 1674   It is Agreed yt mr Jofeph Gardner Richard Leech ffranfis Nurce how are Choffen by ye Towne to lay out land They or any tow of yᵐ are to meifr ouer Nathanell Putnam Nathˡ ffelton & Antony Nedoms land & to bring Returu to ye

major hathorn
Capt Curwin
mʳ bartholmew
decon Prince
Jnᵒ Curwin

Towne what Common land they ffind There & m͏ʳ Bartholmew Is Joynd with ym

Att a freemans metting ye 1ᵗʰ of Jun
Chof fen for Deputys for ye Gen͏ᵘ Court Capt Curwin &
m͏ʳ henery Bartholmew and declared by ye Conftable yt
they were Choffen for ye whole yeer

Att a towne meetting ye 13ᵗʰ : 4ᵐᵒ 74
Choffen for a Jury of tryalls for ye Next Court
m͏ʳ keafer

Jnᵒ Putnam	Jnᵒ Norman
Nicholas maning	manaffeh marfton
Nath͏ˡ Beadle	Jnᵒ Williams

The towne being meett to Confider of mr higinfons
mayntenance They ffinding It Recorded formerly That
they are Ingaged to pay mony haue left It to ye felectmen
to make a Rate Accordingly

Vpon a motion by Robert ffollett for about 15 Akers of
land It is left to m͏ʳ Bartholmew Gedny & ffranfis Nurce
to Vew ye land and bring Return to ye towne.

Vpon a motion mayd by Jonathan Curwin to bye a
fmale pfell of land Neer to m͏ʳ Gardners brooke It is alfo
left to mr Gedny & ffrantis Nurce to Vew It & bring Return to ye towne

[214] ffranfis fkery vpon his Requeft to ye towne Is
Clered from a former bargayne mayd with him about
farah lambertt, only he hath Ingaged to keep her whyle
Micchelmas Next In Confideration of w͏ᶜh he is to haue
his town Rate Allowd him

Att a meeting of ye felectmen 22ᵗʰ
Jun 1674: being prefent

major hathorn	
Capt Curwine	mr Phelip Cromwell hath taken
m͏ʳ bartholmew	Thomas Robinfon for one yeer as his
mr Grafton	feruent
mr Prince	
Jnᵒ Curwine	

Att a meetting of ye towne ye 15ᵗʰ of 6ᵐᵒ 74
Thomas Putnam Is Choofen for an eaights man to Joyne
with ye felect men for making of ye Contry Rate

Granted to Robett ffollett a fmale pfell of land of ten
Akers Nere william thaws & for wt there is more then ten

Akers If he hath It to pay to ye towne fiue fhilling an
Aker In tow yeer after It Is layd out

Granted to Thomas Green for ye keeping & mayntay-
ning farah lambertts Chyld whyle ihe Is eaighteen yeres of
Age all yt pfell of land Neer fam¹¹ Cutlers & wt It ffalls
fhortt of forty Akers—It Is to be mayd up out of land by
Jn° Pudnys & ye whole land is fecurety to ye towne for
ye keeping of ye Chyld during ye time this to be layd out
by ye layers out

Voted yt Jonathan Curwin fhall haue that fmale pfell
of land Neer mr Gardners brooke contayning about 220
Rod & tow men to be Apoynted to lay It out & Agree
with him for ye price

[215] 18ᵗʰ 6ᵐᵒ 74
Att a meetting of ye felectmen being prefent

major hathorn
Capt Curwin
mʳ Bartholmew
mʳ Grafton
mʳ Prince
Jn° Curwin

Thomas Clark Is Admitted an Inhabetant Into this towne
Edward berry Junʳ Is Admitted an
Inhabetant Into ye towne
Leftenant Putnam to fee yt ye
bridge ouer Ipfwech Riuer mayd
fuffetient & also ye bridge at bever Dam be Alfo mended
by ye end of September : Next.

fardgent leach & Ifrell Porter are Choffen & Impowred
to make ye way ffrom Leeches hill to ye horce bridge to
be mayd fuffetient by ye laft of September Next.

Jn° Pickering Is joynd with mʳ Ruke to fee yt all ye
highways be mended between Thos || Cromwels || Corner
To ye towne bridge & alfo yt ye way In ye fouth feld be
mended all to be done by ye laft of feptember Next.

Att a meeting of ye felect men 22ᵗʰ : 7 ᵐᵒ 74

Major hathorn
Capt Corwine
mr bartholmew
mr Grafton
mr prince
Jn° Corwine

Ther was warrents Given forth to Jn°
Ruk Jn° Pickering Edward fflint Richard Leech & Isrell Porter to make fuffetient all those Contry higeways yt ye
felectmen were prefented for laft
Salem Court

Capt Curwine & mʳ Bartholmew are deíired to Inqʳ wt
veffells are bound for VerGenia & to Agree with any

mafter for ye Carring away of farah Lambertt for wch they
have whole power

The felectmen having perufed Capt Curwines Accompt
of difburfments aboute ye fort have determened at ye next
metting to make a Rate for

[216]   The felectmen finding Nik manning Creftopher
babedge & Jn° marfton foe bakward In Clering there Rates
Comitted to ym doe Refolue & determen yt If there
Accompts are Not Clered by falem Court Next to Areft ym
& m^r Bartholmew Is Choffen to pfecnt ye fayme

	li	s	d
Conftable Lake ye menefters Rate In mony Committed to his hands for ye yeer 74, Is 52 - 12 - 84.	52	12	08

out of wch fum he Is to pay forty eaight
pounds to m^r higginfon ye Remaynder to
ye felectmen.

to ye Contry Rate	30	10	03
to ye towne Rate	72	14	05

Mr Richard

Constable Jn° Cleford menefters Rate mony forty eight pound to mr higgenfon ye reft ye town	52	16	09
Deptt to ye Contry Rate	24	16	06
to ye towne Rate	56	10	07
& twenty one 1hillings more In feverall m left out	00	18	00
	114	01	10

Conftable Thomas fflint his menefters Rate	26	03	09
Deptt to ye Contry Rate	20	01	08
To ye towne Rate	51	18	07

C^r p his Towne Rate by diuers bills payd	22	05	06
by ye menefter Rate 40 cords wood and mony 2^li 18^s	18	00	00
to ye Contry	19	00	00

[217]   Att a Generall Towne meetting held ye 28
1 ᵐᵒ 74 Voted that euery man that Is warned by ye ouerfeers of ye high way to worke upon ye ways If he deth
not Apere himfelfe or fend a man fhall forffitt for euery fuch
Neglect toe fhillings & euery man that hath a team being
warned as aboue yt doth not Come fhall forffitt for euery
fuch Neglect fiue fhillings & alfo It Is further Agreed yt
ye ouerfeers of ye high way have ffull power to Agree with
all fuch as fhall worke upon ye high ways wt they fhall
haue p day

Choffen for ye Grand Jury: Choffen for ye Jury of tryalls

famuell Gardner fenʳ	mʳ Ely hathorn
Bartholmew Gidny	Jnᵒ Price
Nathˡ Putnam	Jnᵒ hathorn
Thomas Rootts	Jnᵒ higinfon
William Trafke	ferdgent ffelton
Josⁿ Raye	Ifrell Porter
Joseph Hutchefon	ffranfis Nurce

Voted by a full Vote of ye towne that there Is as
much land Granted upon ye Common or pen at ye uper
end of mʳ Bartholmews or Thomas Rootts land for to build
a New meeting houfe for ye wrfhip of God—And It Is
left to ye felectmen to lay out ye fayd land

It Is Agreed by a ffull and fre Vote of ye Towne for
mʳ Nikoletts Continuence amongft vs during his life

The layers out of land are Apoynted to lay out Rob
ffolletts land & mʳ Batter Is alfo Joyned with ym or any
tow of yᵐ with mʳ Batter.

[218]   Att a meetting of ye felectmen ye 10ᵗʰ 9 ᵐᵉ 74
being prefent

major hathorn
Capt. Curwin
mʳ Grafton
mʳ Bartholmew
mr Prince
Jnᵒ Curwin

Agreed yt ye Conftables are to
fetle there Accompts Next tuefday
& 'any man that doth Not Clere his
Accompts then to be Arefted ye Next
Coort

Agreed that the towne houfe fhall be fett up by the
priffon & William douton to Rayfe Itt with what fpeed he
Can

ffranſis Nurce being In debt to ye towne ſix pownds 8
ſ s: he doth Ingadge to pay ye ſayd ſome In a fortnight In
ſhingles for the Towne howſe at ffifften ſhillings ꝑ thou-
ſand, or as tow Indifferent men ſhall prize yᵐ being
equaly Choſſen

Att a towne meetting 2ᵗʰ 10 ᵐᵒ 74
Voted that there ſhall be ffiffty pound Rayſed more by
ye ſelect men Then was formerly Allowd to Capt. Curwine

Voted that Mʳ Norrice ſhall have ten pounds Allowd
him out of ye towne Rate for this preſent yeer   It is In
Conſideration of keeping ſcoole In his own howſe.

[219]   A liſt of ſuch as have diſburſt for ye Towne &
are to be payd out of This towne Rate mayd ye 24ᵗʰ of
ye 10 ᵐᵒ 74 ye ſome being 181ˡⁱ : 03 : 07

by Capt Curwine for diſburtſments one ye

	li	s	d
fort formerly	82	01	04
more to Capt Curwin for diſburſtments & his deputyſhip	17	03	00
mʳ Norrice a bill : of ten pounds	10	00	00
major Hawthorne ſix pounds	06	00	00
famuell Verry for killing a wolfe	01	10	00
Jnᵒ Lvke his bill	01	13	00
Jnᵒ Pickering	02	15	00
Thomas Putnam	03	00	00
mʳ Batter	08	19	06
Jnᵒ Gidny fenʳ	04	00	07
Capt Curwin for Will : lord	03	05	00
mʳ Norrice	00	00	00
Edward fflint for mending ways	03	05	06
Jnᵒ Putnam for mending ye wooden bridge	00	17	00
by ſerdgent Leach & Isrell Porter for mend-ing ye highway between froſt fiſh brooke & ye horse bridg	03	14	00
by Joſeph Gardner	02	16	10
by mr Grafton & decon prince for mending ye highways	03	14	00

by m^r Bartholmew for his deputyſhip ye
yeer 73 : 12^{ll} : ſs : d : more for deputyſhip this yeer : 7^{ll} : more paid Jno Green
22ſs 8^d 20 : 02 : 08
Jno Giles killing a wolfe   01 : 10 : 00
Thomas ffuller & henery Wilkins for killing
   tow woolfs laſt march   03 : 00 : 00
ye widdow Pope for killing of tow wolffs   03 : 00 : 00
to Robertt hibard for worke at ye fort   00 : 06 : 00
to m^r Gedny   01 : 09 : 06
to a bill to ffranſis ſkery for keeping of
   Sarah lambert   01 : 00 : 00
Zakery Marſh Good Greenſlet   00 : 05 : 00
to ſemvll Peckman half towne Rt   00 : 04 : 06

[220] p Contra a liſt of bills given out

                                            li   s.   d.

To major hathorn a bill Tho flint 5 : ‖ &
   will lake : 1 - 0 - 0 ‖   06 : 00 : 00
to Capt Curwine to Will^e Lake   40 : 00 : 00
to Capt Curwin to Jno Clifford   30 : 00 : 00
to Capt Curwin to Thos fflint   32 : 09 : 04
to m^r bartholmew : to J : C : 8^{ll} : 0 : 0 : &
   lake : 12 :   20 : 02 : 08
to m^r Grafton & deoon Prince   03 : 10 : 00
to Jno Putnam : Thos flint   00 : 17 : 00
Jno Giles for a wolfe : Thos Flint   01 : 10 : 00
Samuell Verry to Tho : flint   01 : 10 : 00
Joſepth Gardner J. Cliford   02 : 16 : 10
to Thomas ffuller hen : willkins ⎱
to Thomas fflint Conſtable   ⎰   03 : 00 : 00
to Good : pope - Tho fflint   03 : 00 : 00
to Jno Ruke - to will : lake   01 : 13 : 00
to m^r Gidny to will : lake   04 : 00 : 07
to m^r Norrice to will : lake   05 : 00 : 00
to m^r Norrice to Jno Peaſe   05 : 00 : 00
to m^r Gidny Thomas flint   01 : 09 : 06
to Edward fflint : will : lake   03 : 05 : 06
ffranſis ſkery - to Clefford   01 : 00 : 00
to Zak : marſh - to Thos fflint   00 : 05 : 00
to Samuell Pickman to will : lake   00 : 04 : 06

to Serdgent Leech & Is Portr Tho. flint   03 : 14 : 00
to ffranſis Skery - Creſtʳ babedge   02 : 10 : 00
to Mʳ Batter a bill to will lake   04 : 10 : 00
Josᵉ Miles Is abayted his towne rate : J :
  C : 00 will lord to Jnᵒ Cliford   07 : 06 : 00
To William Lord a bill of fiue pownds
  toward his looking after ye meetting
  howſe for ye : yeer : 75   To Thomas
  flint wᶜʰ he Refuſed to pay   05 : 00 : 00
to mʳ Batter a bill to Creſtopher babedge   04 : 09 : 06

[221]   Att a meetting of yᵉ Selectmen : ye 9ᵗʰ 12 ᵐᵒ
1674

It Is Voted yt Capt : Curwin mʳ Bartholmew & Jnᵒ
Curwin are Apoynted to lay out a high way Throw ye
land yt vas formrly old Good hucheſons - ſoe as may ‖be‖
moſt Convenient for ye Inhabetants ye farmers to Come
to ye meetting howſe.

Thomas ffuller ſenʳ Is Resd & Allowed of as an Inhabitant with his whole ffarm belonging to Salem. This Is
done by his on Conſent

                       *Thomas ffuller

Thomas ffuller ſenʳ Is Ingaged to make a ſuffetient Cart
way ouer beachy brooke - ye wᶜʰ being done he Is to be
Allowed his whole meetting howſe Rate that he was formerly Rated

major hathorn
Capt Curwin
mʳ Bartholmew
mʳ Grafton
dekon prince
Jnₒ Curwin

Att a meetting of ye ſelectmen yᵉ
26ᵗʰ 12 ᵐᵒ 74 being preſent Capt
Curwine & mʳ Bartholmew being
Choſſen to lay outa higway for ye
Conveniency of ye farmers to Come to
ye meetting howſe haue done as ffoll from there meetting
howſe a Rod & halfe wide by ye ſid of Joſeph hutcheſons
ffence puided It Goos Clere of ye ſwamp & from thence
upon a ſtraght lyne to Thomas Putnams orchard & from
thence a Rod & holfe wide Through Thomas Putnams
Ground downe to ye New bridg ouer Ipſwch Riuer & a
Nother way from Nathˡ Ingorſons to ye Corner of Joſeph

*Autograph.

huchefons fence* & foe by ye meetting howfe foore Rod wid & from ye Corner of Joseph hutchefons vp to hadloks to meett with ye Contry high way tow pole wide

[222]   7 1ᵐᵒ 7 4/5
The felectmen of falem being Apoynted by ye Genˡˡ Court to deuid ye ffoott Company of falem haue done as ffolloweth

The lower Company There bounds to begin at Jnᵒ Prices that fyd of ye lane being there weftermoft bounds & foe from Ruben Gupys to Jnᵒ Gupys & foe downward to mordekays Neke Joseph Gardner being Apoynted by ye Genˡˡ Court there Cheefe Comandʳ

The other Company to begine there eaftermoft bounds from there weftermoft & foe to take all ye Inhabetants upward of Glaff houfe North ffields & all others without ye feld farms Ryall fyd & all within ye bounds of falem and Jofeph Getchell Is Apoynted as a Conftant drum to ye vper Company ferdgent leach & fardgent ffelton are Apoynted to be of ye Vper Comp ferdgent Pickering & ferg fwenerton haue liberty wᶜʰ Comp to take alfo mʳ Gidnys Is Apoynted for a howfe of entertaynment for ye uper Company

It Is Agreed that there Is a Generall towne meetting to be warnd one fryday being ye 12ᵗʰ of march 74 : for ye Choyce of felectmen & Conftabls & ye faterday ffollowing for ye fremen to meett for ye Nomenation of mageftrats & Choyce of debutys for ye Generall Court & a Commffʳ for ye Carring of ye Votes to ye fhire towne & to make Choyce of a County Treffr

Layd out In ye pen or Comon at ye uperend of Thomas Roots his fence for ye fetting of a New meetting howfe about 100 ffoot each way leauing a way of one pole wid between ye meetting howfe & Thomas Roots his ditch

Att a Generall Towne meetting held ye 12ᵗʰ : march 1674 Choffen for Conftables for this yeer

Jnᵒ Turner
Manaffah Marfton
Jnᵒ Prokter

The towne haue Accepted of Jnᵒ Clifford . In ye Roome of Jnᵒ Turner he hauing mayd an Agreement with ye fayd Cliford

*In the margin, " next mr Baylys."

[223] Att a Generall Towne meetting 7 4/5: 12th: 1mo:

Choffen for felectmen for this yeer

Major hathorn   dockter wells
Capt: Corwine   Nik manning
Jn° Curwin   Ed fflint
Philip Cromwell

Voted yt ffraniis Skery Is to be Allowed fiue pounds from ye towne for wch he doth Ingagd to keep farah lambertt for one yeer from this day & alfo he Is Allowd ffiffty ihillings more for keeping farah lambertt from mickollmas laft till this day

Voted yt ye mony iix pownds feueenteen fhillings & 3^d ye ouer plofe of m^r higenfons debt Is Committed Into ye hands of ye felectmen to difpofe of to William Douton toward ye building of ye town howfe & deleuered Into major hathorns hands

Voted that the ten Aker lott fformerly Granted to Jn° born & fold to old weeks It Is left to ye felectmen to order the fayd lot to be layd out In Cafe ther be foe much Vacant land there

There being a petetion prefented by feuerall of ye Inhabetants Conferning Rams It Is Voted af ffolloweth

That w^t euer Rams are taken upon the Towne Commons from the laft of July to ye laft of october ye owners of ye fayd Rams are to forffitt for euery fuch defect ten fhillings to ye town

m^r famuell Gardner m^r Bartholmew Gedny & ffranfis Nurce being Apoynted to fell a pfell of land for ye paying of m^r higenfons debtts haue done Accordingly & ye towne haue excepted of there Accompt

[224] Att a ffreemens meeting ye 13th: 1mo: 74/5 Choffen for a Commifr to Carry ye Vots to m^r Gidnys & meett ye reft of ye Commifr m^r Jonathan Curwin

m^r Batter & William Brown Junr are Choffen deputys for ye Gen^{ll} Court for this prefent yeer

(*To be continued.*)

NEWSPAPER ITEMS RELATING TO ESSEX COUNTY.

(*Continued from Vol. XLIII, page 96.*)

Since our last, we have the following Account of Damage done by the late Storm, *viz.* Capt. *Barns,* in a Snow from *Cadiz,* cast away and lost in *Ipswich* Bay, and one Seaman, and a Passenger drowned. *Moody* of *York,* from *Minas, Nash* from the Eastward, and a Sloop with Boards, all ashore near *Plymouth.* The following Vessels were cast away to the Northward of the Gurnet, *viz.* Capt. *Bell* from *Maryland* with Corn and Pork, the Vessel lost, but some of the Pork saved. Capt. *Wing* from *Lisbon,* Vessel and Cargo lost, and the Master and Mate, with 3 Men more drowned. A Sloop from the West Indies laden with Molasses, bilg'd, and a Schooner from *Beverly,* supposed to be lost.

Boston Evening Post, April 26, 1756.

Since our last, we received an Account of the following Vessels being lost in the Storm therein mentioned, viz. A Schooner in Barnstable Bay; another, Moody, from Minas to Newbury; another, Nash, from Scituate to the Eastward; A Sloop, Malcomb, from Boston to the Eastward; A Sloop, Wing, from Lisbon to Boston five drowned; A Schooner belonging and bound to Rhode Island, from the West-Indies; A Fishing Schooner belonging to Beverly; A Coasting Scooner sunk in Cape-Ann Harbour; and a Schooner, Bell, from Maryland bound hither, cast ashore.

Boston Gazette, April 26, 1756.

ON THURSDAY NEXT, at *Eleven o'Clock A. M. will be exposed for Sale by publick Vendue, at the Royal Exchange Tavern in Boston, by Virtue of a Decree of the said Court, the Hull of the Snow* Endeavour, *Thomas* Barns *late Master, as she now lays stranded on* Ipswich *Beech, together with her standing and running Rigging, Sails, Cables, Anchors; and other Appurtenances, now at*

(273)

Mr. James Perkin's *Store, where they may be viewed before the Sale. At the same Time and Plac? will be also sold the Hull of the Sloop* Free Mason, *as she now lays on* Marshfield Beech, *together with her Cables, Anchors, standing and running Rigging, all to be seen at Mr.* John Rowe's *Store.*

per Curiam,

John Payne, *Dep. Regr.*

Boston Evening Post, May 10, 1756.

RUN-*away from his Master* Robert Macintire, *of* Salem, *on Monday the 3d Instant, an Apprentice Lad, named* Benjamin Orne, jun. *(who was lately impress'd into* Colonel Plaisted's *Regiment) about 18 Years & 1-2 old, about 5 Foot high, a well sett, sturdy fellow: Had on, either a blue Searge Suit, lin'd with black, or a gray Jacket with a spotted flannel one under it, wears a Cap, and had Pewter Buckles in his Shoes. Whoever shall take up said Apprentice, and convey him to his abovesaid master in* Salem, *shall have* ONE DOLLAR *Reward, and all necessary Charges paid by*

ROBERT MACINTIRE.

Salem, May 6, 1756.

Boston Gazette, May 17, 1756.

Ran away from the Subscriber at Newbury, *about the 15th of April last A Negro Fellow named* Daniel, *about 20 Years old of a middle size. He had on when he ran away, a brown Kersey Jacket, check'd woollen Shirt, a pair of red broad Cloth Breeches, and a mill'd Cap. He formerly belong'd to Capt.* Edward Sheaf *of* Charlestown. *Whoever will secure said Runaway, so that his Master may have him again, shall have* TWO DOLLARS *Reward, and all necessary Charges paid. All Masters of Vessels, &c., are caution'd against concealing or carrying off said Negro, as they would avoid the Penalty of the Law.* Joseph Cottle.

Newbury May 10th 1756.

Boston Evening Post, May 24, 1756.

All Persons having Demands on the Estate of the Rev. Mr. Ames Cheever *late of* Manchester, *deceas'd, are desired to bring in their Accounts to* Isaac Mansfield, *jun. Adminstrator of said Estate, at* Marblehead:, *and all Persons indebted to said Estate, are desired speedily to pay the same, as they would avoid further Trouble.* TO BE SOLD by the said *Isaac Mansfield,* A likely, strong and healthy NEGRO WOMAN, fit for Town or Country.

Boston Gazette, June 7, 1756.

On the 29th of last month, *Moses Richards* and *Abijah Johnson,* of *Rowley,* going down the River in a small Canoe, it overset, and they were both drowned.

Boston Evening Post, June 7, 1756.

Salem, 26 June, 1756.

All Sellers of Tea, Coffee and China Ware, in the County of Essex *are hereby Notified to pay the Excise due to the Subscriber, on the Fourteenth Day of* July *next, at his Dwelling-House, in* Salem *aforesaid, where Attendance will be given for that purpose,* by

Peter Frye, *Farmer.*

N. B. *No accounts will be received, unless they are according to Law.*

Boston Evening Post, June 7, 1756.

Ran away the 22d Day of this Instant May, two Negro Men Servants from Newbury, *the one belonging to Mr.* Joseph Swasey *of* Newbury, *of a light-pale Complection, and of midling Stature: Had on when he went away, a homespun Coat, Swanskin Jacket, and a white Jacket and Trowsers, named* Cebrew *The other from* Timothy Greenleaf *of* Newbury, *of midling Stature and black as most Negroes are, a fat plump lusty Fellow; he has a sly Look with his Eyes, wears the Button of his Hat before, a white Jacket with black Spots in it, and one striped Jacket and a pair of Cloth Breeches, named* Newport.

Whoever shall take up the said Negroes or either of them and convey them to either of said Masters, shall have TWO DOLLARS *Reward for each, and and all necessary Charges paid.*

Joseph Swasey.
Timothy Greenleaf.

All Masters of Vessels and others are forbid carrying off said Negroes or concealing them, on Penalty of the Law provided.

Boston Evening Post, June 14, 1756.

We hear from *Marblehead,* that several of their Fishermen are come in from the Grand Bank with their second Fairs, but neither saw or heard of any *English* or *French* Ships of War.

Boston Evening Post, June 21, 1756.

The Thursday Evening before last, as Mr. John Lyndes of Leicester, was coming from Salem to Lyn, another Man came up with him, upon which they ran their Horses, when Mr. Lyndes run foul of a Horse he had turn'd loose before, by which he was jerk'd off his horse, had his shoulder drove into his Breast, and died in about two Hours after.

Boston Gazette, July 19, 1756.

Ipswich, August 17th, 1756.

On the 10th Instant died here, after a short Confinement, the Honourable *Thomas Berry,* Esq; in the 62d Year of his Age; and on the 12th Instant he was very decently intered. He was esteemed a skilful Physician, and as such has been greatly serviceable. Providence early employed him in publick Stations. He was several Years a Representative for this Town, and afterwards many Years one of his Majesty's Council; he was Judge of the Probate of Wills for the County of *Essex,* first Justice of the Inferiour Court of Common Pleas, a Justice of the Peace, and Colonel of the third Regiment of Militia in the County of *Essex;* the four last of these Offices he sustained at the Time of his Death. He had many valuable and agreable Accomplishments, and has been extensively useful, vigorously improving the Talents committed to Him. We doubt not but that he is now partaking of the glorious Rewards of the Real Christian, and faithful Servant of God and his Generations. His Death is Lamented among us as a publick Loss.

Boston Gazette, Aug. 30, 1756.

To be sold at the House of Joseph Newhall, *Innholder, in* Newbury *on Tuesday the 14th Day of* September *next, at Two of the Clock in the Afternoon, by the Subscriber, Administrator of the Estate of* Moses Coker, *deceas'd, having Licence therefor from his Majesty's Superiour Court of Judicature, at publick Vendue to the highest Bidder, the Homestead of the said late* Moses Coker, *consisting of a good Dwelling-House, Barn, and four Acres and a half of Land adjoining, with a good Well on the Premises, pleasantly and advantageously situated for Trade and Business, in the most popular Part of the Town of* Newbury.

Newbury, Aug. 24, 1756.   RICHARD LONG.

Boston Gazette, Aug. 30, 1756.

On Saturday the 21st of last Month, at Night, the House of Mr. John Wardell at Andover was burnt to the Ground, with Household Furniture, wearing Apparel, and all that was therein consumed, excepting the Family, who with great Difficulty escaped with their Lives.

Boston Gazette, Sept. 6, 1756.

Whereas Solomon Smith *and* John Upton *alias* Upcut, *both of* Salem, *were impress'd to serve in the present Expedition against* Crown-Point, *on the 31st of August last, but have deserted that Service: Whoever shall deliver either of said Deserters to a proper Officer of* Salem, *shall be paid* FIVE DOLLARS *Reward: The above Deserters are both pretty short well-sett Men:* Smith *wore when he went away a handsome light colour'd Cloth Jacket, blue ribb'd Stockings;* Upton *had on a red course Waistcoat, is something pock-fretten, speaks broken English.*

Salem, 18 Sept. 1756.   BENJ. PICKMAN, Col.

N. B. *They were seen a few Days since on the Road going to* Boston.

Put on board a new Vessel at *Newbury,* (supposed thro'
Mistake) and brought to *Boston,* an Anchor of between
2 & 300 Weight; the Owner by describing the Marks
and paying the Charges may have the above Anchor
again; inquire of the Printers hereof.

Boston Gazette, Oct. 11, 1756.

*To be sold by publick Vendue, on Wednesday the 20th
Day of* October *Instant, at the House of Mr.* Dan Clark,
Inholder in Topsfield, *a fine comodious Farm lying in said*
Topsfield, *with a good Dwelling House, Barn and
Orchard, containing about Ninety eight Acres; also one
half Right of Land in* Gilmantown, *call'd Lot no.* 42, *in
the second Range; also a Right of Land in* Townsend
between Groton *and* Lunenburg; *and also a Right of Land
in* Falmouth *in* Casco-Bay: *All which Parcels of Land
were lately the Estate of Mr.* William Rogers *of* Topsfield.
October 11th 1756.

Boston Evening Post, Oct. 18, 1756.

TO BE SOLD

By Samuel Gardner *of* Salem, *a strong and healthy
Negro Woman who can do all Household Work well.*
The same Day, (Tuesday) a Man belonging to *Chebacco,* was killed by a flash of Lightning in his Barn,
into which he went to secure himself from the Violence of
the Storm. The same Flash instantly set the Barn on
Fire, which in a little Time was entirely consumed.

Boston Evening Post, Oct. 25, 1756.

Haverhill Oct. 23. On Wednesday last died after a
long and languishing sickness, the Honourable *Richard
Saltonstall,* Esq; aged about 54 Years, and was this Day
interr'd; who was for some Time one of His Majesty's
Council, and for many years one of the Justices of the
Superiour Court; all which, with his other Offices in the
Militia, he discharg'd with undoubted integrity.

Boston Gazette, Oct. 25, 1756.

Tuesday Afternoon last, we had a sudden and very violent Squall of Wind and Rain, attended with but two or three Claps of Thunder, which did little or no Damage; but we hear from Chebacco, in Ipswich, that a Barn was struck by the Lightning, and consum'd, with all its Contents, which were considerable. A young Man being out at Work in the Field, and observed the Squall a-coming, ran to the Barn for Shelter, and had scarcely got in before it was set on Fire; 'tis imagined he was instantly struck dead by the Lightning, being burnt to a great Degree before he could be got out.

Boston Gazette, Oct. 25, 1756.

These are to notify the Proprietors of *Ipswich Canada* (so called) in the County of *Worcester,* that have not paid their Taxes of *two Pounds thirteen Shillings and four Pence,* granted at their Meeting, *January* 25th 1753. And also another Tax of *Sixteen Shillings,* granted at their Meeting *Octob.* 25, 1753, ditto 31st *October,* 1754, a Tax of *Nineteen Shillings and four Pence;* ditto 2d June 1756, on Adjournment a Tax of twelve Shillings & five Pence, which Times of Payments are elapsed; and whereas many of the Proprietors have hitherto neglected to pay hte Taxes aforesaid.

These are to notify the Proprietors of *Ipswich Canada* (so called) in the County of *Worcester,* that have not paid their Taxes of *two Pounds thirteen shillings and four Pence,* granted at their Meeting *January* 25th, 1753 and also another Tax of 16 *Shillings* granted at their Meeting *October* 25, 1753, ditto 31st *October* 1754, A Tax of *19 Shillings and four Pence;* ditto 2d June 1756, on Adjournment a Tax of twelve Shillings & five Pence which Times of Payments are elapsed; and whereas many of the Proprietors have hitherto neglected to pay the Taxes aforesaid: These are to notify said Proprietors, that if they do not pay the aforesaid Taxes forthwith unto Mr. *Francis Goodhue* their Treasurer, that his Rights will be sold at publick Vendue to the highest Bidder, on the first Wednesday in

January next, at the House of Capt. *James Reed,* Innholder in *Lunenburg,* at One O'clock Afternoon.
Ipswich, Nov. 24, 1756.

> Benj. *Goodridge,*
> *Abijah Smith*
> *Francis Goodhue*
> Committee.

Boston Evening Gazette, Nov. 29, 1756.

Thursday Night last began a very heavy Storm of Snow at N. W. which continued all the next Day; in the midst of it, Capt. Smith who left London the 8th of October, arrived off Marblehead, where he was obliged to anchor; and the Storm still increasing he was forc'd to cut away his Main and Mizen-masts, in order to save the Vessel. Capt. Smith with great Difficulty rode it out, having one Man froze to Death, and the rest almost spent: He came tow'd up yesterday by three fishing Vessels, having nothing but his bare Foremast standing.

Boston Gazette, Dec. 20, 1756.

We hear from Marblehead, that on Friday last the Town mustered with Drums beating and Shovels flying, and in a few Hours clear'd the Road from thence to Salem (being 5 miles) notwithstanding the Snow in general was between 3 and 4 Feet deep.

Boston Gazette, Dec. 27, 1756.

We hear from Almsbury, that last Tuesday Morning, a young Man of that Town was found in a Swamp froze to Death.

Boston Evening Post, Jan. 24, 1757.

To be sold on reasonable Terms, the Mansion House in Haverhill, *that did belong to the Honourable* Richard Saltonstall, *Esq: and about Forty three Acres of the best Land adjoining, with an Outhouse, and other Buildings which is a beautiful and well finish'd Seat, pleasantly situated, having a fair Prospect of the Town and Ferry, by a Navigable River's Side; and in every Respect well accomodated for a gentleman of Fortune. For the Particulars of which you may enquire of* Hugh Hall, *Esq: or Messi's* Samuel Winthrop *and* John Leverett, *all of* Boston, *or of me the Subscriber at Haverhill.*

N. B.   *I have about 140 Acres of other Land also for Sale, which is good Mowing, Tillage, and Pasture Land, convenient for said seat.*

ENOCH BARTLET.

Boston Evening Gazette, Jan. 31, 1757.

Capt. Symonton in A Schooner from this Place for Casco-Bay, was last Wednesday cast away on Plumb Island near Newbury; The Vessel lost but Lives sav'd.

Boston Evening Gazette, Feb. 7, 1757.

A few Days since arrived here Capt. *John Sandford,* late Master of a Brigantine belonging to this Town, from whom we have the following Account, *viz.* That on his Voyage to *Europe* in *October* last, he was taken by A *French* Privateer from *Louisbourg,* of 8 Carriage and 10 Swivel Guns, and that he found on board the Privateer, Mr. *Solomon Lane,* and Company, of *Cape Ann,* who had just before been taken on Bank Quero.

Boston Evening Post, Feb. 21, 1757.

Capt. Orne who sail'd from Salem on the 1st of December last, for the Leeward Islands, was taken off Bermuda by a French Xebeck, from Martineco for Marseilles, and in their Passage for Europe, met with a large Ship which they took for an English Man of War, and accordingly stood for Madeira: While Capt. Orne was at Madeira, there came in a Privateer from England, which sail'd from thence the 28th of December last, the Captain of which reported. That on the 1st of January towards Dusk, he saw a Fleet of Ships steering W. by N. that he kept to Windward of them all Night, in order to make what they were in the Morning, and to his dissapointment found them to be French Men of War full of Men; and notwithstanding he was chas'd by one of them for several Hours, he got clear: That afterwards they stood their former Course W. by N. by which he imagin'd they were bound for Louisbourg. Capt. Orne who gives this Account, arrived at Salem, last Friday Evening, and also says, that the above Captain inform'd him that Admiral Byng had been three Days on his Tryal when he sail'd, and twas tho't it would take three more in examining the Witnesses, &c.

Boston Evening Gazette, Feb. 28, 1757.

All Licenc'd Persons, and those that have Permits to sell spiritous Liquors, &c in the Towns hereafter mentioned, in the County of *Essex,* are hereby notified to attend and pay their Excise in Manner following, *viz.* Those of the Town of *Lynn,* at Mr. *Norwood's,* Innholder in said Town, on Monday the 28th Instant; those of *Marblehead,* the 29th and 30th Instant, at Mr. *Samuel Roger's* Innholder; those of *Salem, Beverly, Boxford, Danvers, Topsfield, Middleton and Wenham,* on the 1st and 2d of *April* next at Mrs. *Pratt's,* Innholder in *Salem;* those of *Manchester,* on the 5th of *April* at Mr. *Allen's;* those at *Cape-Ann,* at Mr. *Broom's* on the 6th and 7th of said Month.

N. B. It is desired that proper Care may be taken by those licenc'd Persons, that their Accounts be made up according to Law, for no other will be accepted.

Boston Evening Gazette, Mar. 14, 1757.

To be Sold the North-westerly Part of the Mansion House of Capt. John Stacy, *late of* Marblehead, *deceas'd, formerly called the Bunch of Grapes Tavern, in said* Marblehead, *with a piece of Garden Ground near the same; any Person minded to purchase the same, may apply to* Mr. John Brown *in* Boston, Ichabod Plaisted *Esq; in* Salem, *or* Nathan Bowen *in* Marblehead.

Marblehead, March 17.
Boston Evening Gazette, March 28, 1757.

By a Vessell arrived at *Cape-Ann* in a short Passage from *Barbadoes,* we have advice, that Capt. *Eleazer Johnson* and Capt. *David Ouchterlony* in two ships from this

Port, Capt. *Warner* in a Ship from *Salem,* Capt. *Taylor* in a Sloop from *New York,* and the Capts. *Pine and Millar* in Sloops from *Philadelphia,* were taken by the *French* Privateers, the first carried to *Martineco,* the others into *Guadaloupe.*

Boston Evening Post, April 4, 1757.

Having seen Proposals for Printing Observations on the Doctrines, that I have Published in my late Discourses upon I Tim. I. 15. *by a Friend to Truth, and Lover of* Mankind, *(as he is pleas'd to call himself) I desire the Author to give the Publick his* Name *with his Observations: For it is look'd upon mean and cowardly, like* the Indians *sculking in the Bushes, for any Man to publish the* Name *of an Author and oppose his writings, without letting the Publick know also the* Name *of the Antagonist. And if the Author of those Observations should refuse this reasonable request, now he has timeous Notice, I shall think he is afraid of an Attack; and I believe the Publick will generally think him unworthy of Notice.*

Newbury, April 15, 1757. J. Parsons.

Observations on the Doctrines, and Uncharitableness, &c. of the Rev. Mr. JONATHAN PARSONS of *Newbury;* are in THE Press, and in great Forwardness; such as are inclined to become Subscribers (agreable to the Proposals in our last Monday's Gazette) are desired to be *speedy, otherwise they will loose the Benefit of being* Subscribers.

Boston Gazette, April 18, 1757.

Sundry Writings of considerable Consequence, were left in the Hands of Nathaniel Martin of Andover, *by* John Eastman *late Resident of said* Andover, *belonging to* Samuel Daly, *of* Providence, *in the County of* Providence, *Said* Martin *desires the Owner may have the same, by making out his Claim, and paying the Charges.*

Boston Gazette, April 18, 1757.

All Persons having Demands on the Estate of the Rev. Ames Chever, *late of* Manchester, *deceas'd, and have not*

*yet brought in their Claims; are desired to bring them in
to* Isaac Mansfield, *Jun. Administrator on said Estate at*
Marblehead. *And all Persons indebted to said Estate,
are again desired to make speedy Payment to said Administrator; as he is determined to settle said Estate as soon
as may be. To be* SOLD *a Negro Woman belonging to
said Estate—enquire of said Administrator.*
Marbelhead April 19, 1757.

Boston Gazette, April 25, 1757.

JUST PUBLISHED.

(And sold by the Printers hereof:)
A DISCOURSE on PSALM cxviii. 18, 19. Deliver'd
November 25, 1756. Being a Day appointed by Authority,
for a publick THANKSGIVING thro' this Province, By
JOHN TUCKER A. M. Pastor of the first Church in
Newbury.

Boston Gazette, April 25, 1757.

*This Day Published, (Price 1 s.) and to be sold by the
Printers hereof;*
OBSERVATIONS *on the Doctrines, and Uncharitableness &c. of the Rev. Mr.* JONATHAN PARSONS *of*
Newbury; *as exhibited more especially in his late* DIS-
COURSES *upon* I Tim. I. 15. *This is a faithful Saying,
and worthy of all Acceptation, that Christ Jesus came
into the World to save Sinners; of whom I am chief. By
a Friend to Truth, and Lover of Mankind.*

Boston Gazette, May 30, 1757.

We hear a Fishing-Schooner is arrived at Marblehead
which belong'd there, and had been taken on the Grand
Bank by a Letter of Marque Snow from France, bound
to Louisbourg, mounting four Guns, with 25 Men: The
Master of the Schooner ransom'd her for 150 l. Sterl.
and went himself with the Snow to Louisbourg as Hostage 'till the Ransom be paid. It is said a Number of
Blanks were on board the Snow ready for filling up, to
ransom Vessels, the Frenchman expecting to make a
good Fare of Ransomers among our Fishing Vessels.

Boston Gazette, June 13, 1757.

(To be continued.)

EXTRACTS FROM THE DIARY OF SAMUEL HORTON OF NEWBURYPORT.

COPIED FROM THE ORIGINAL NOW IN POSSESSION OF
EBEN BRADBURY OF NEWBURYPORT
BY HON. J. J. CURRIER.

March 17, 1772 Esquire Lee's schooner launched in my brothers yard

March 18, 1772 Robert Hoopers brig launched at half past ten P. M.

April 6, 1772 Robert Jenkins ship raised

July 16, 1772 ditto   launched

May 7, 1773 Capt Dunlaps ship launched

May 27, 1774 Capt Smiths ship launched

May 30, 1774 Mr. Roch's ship raised

Oct. 24 1774 ditto   brig   "

Aug. 24, 1774 Mr. Gray's ship launched built by Col. Toppan

April 1, 1775 George Jenkins launched his sloop

July 4, 1776 Frigate (26 guns) launched at Mr. Greenleafs yard—ashore but hauled off July 14, 1776

Jan. 15, 1777 Frigate raised in my brothers yard

June 2, 1777 Capt Tracy's (20 gun) ship launched

June 26, 1777 a sixteen gun ship launched at Mr. Stephen Cross' yard

July 23, 1777 James Tracy sails with his frigate for Cape Ann—gets ashore on the bar but is hauled off during the night

Aug. 21, 1777 Capt William Friend in a sixteen gun ship built in Mr. Stephen Cross' yard sailed (See Coffin's History, page 254.)

Oct. 18, 1777 Capt Nathaniel Tracy's brig (16 guns) launched

Feb. 6, 1778 Brig built on Capt Henry Titcombs wharf by my brother for Mr. John Tracy launched

Mch 15, 1778 Sailed Nathaniel Tracy's brig, 16 guns, built by my brother, for Cape Ann in command Capt Fletcher

May 15, 1778 John Tracy's privateer sailed for Portsmouth Capt James Johnson

July 23, 1778 Mr. Corbits ship, launched to carry 16 nine pounders—ditto Sailed Sept. 2, 1778 for Beverly in command Capt Hugh Hill

Feb. 1, 1779 launched Mr. George Corbits brig Experiment

May 11, 1779 Frigate launched from Mr. Cross' yard

May 15, 1779 launched from my brothers yard a fine sharp schooner built for Mr. Nathaniel Tracy

July 3, 1779 ye Pallace, Sky Rocket and Capt Gideons in a brig sailed for Boston to join ye fleet for Penobscot.   Two more ships are going I suppose to-morrow

Aug. 13, 1779 Mr. John Tracy's brig launched from my brothers yard

Sept 16, 1779 Ship for Mr. Geo Corbitt raised

Oct. 12, 1779 Brig built by my brother owned by John Tracy in command Capt Lee over set for lack of sufficient ballast

Nov. 23, 1779 Ships built by Mr. Greenleaf and Mr. Cross sailed for Boston

Jan. 22, 1780 Capt Collier sailed in Mr. Hoopers ship about 20 guns

April 18, 1780 Mr. Cobbitts ship 18 guns launched

May 8, 1780 ditto sailed Capt Cathcart commander

Nov. 4, 1780 Mr Corbitts ship raised in my brothers yard

Jan. 11, 1781 Capt Coats sailed in a new ship owned by Mr. Tracy, letter of Marque

CAPT. RICHARD MORE'S PETITION FOR A LICENCE TO KEEP A PUBLIC HOUSE IN SALEM, 1686.*

To the hone^{r}d County Court Sitting in Salem December 2^{end} 1786.

The humble petition of Richard Moore Serne^r Humbly Sheweth

That yor petitioner hath bine An Inhabitant in New England aboue Sixty years being one of the first comers into this land, In which time through Gods Blefing vpon my Endeauo^{rs} my owne & ffamilies nefsesities haue bine Suplyed without being An object of Charitie, & prouidence hath Inabled mee to bare my Share of Publique Charge my days through Gods good prouidence haue bine lengthened out to Old Age being about Seauenty Seauen years old by reason of Infirmities Attend[ing] old Aige my hands are not Soe Capable of Ministring to my Nefsesities as formerly. I in all humble maner pray this hone^{r}d court to grant mee a licence to keepe A publique houfe of Enter-[t]ainment to Sell Beere Sider Wine &c I haueing Conuencences of Houfing for entertainment of houfe & Man & other Conueniences equrably Sutable for such an Imploy in which If yor Hono^{r}r pleafe to Grant mee ye faue^r of A licence I fhall Carefully intend the keeping of Such good ord^r as the Law requires & giueing Such entertainement as may bee to Satiffaction of all pfens And Shall bee yor hono^{r}s obliged humble Serut.   Richard More Sen. Granted.

Essex County Court Files, Vol. XLVI, leaf 114.

*Capt. Richard More came in the Mayflower in 1620. His gravestone now in the Charter Street Burying Ground, Salem, is the only contemporaneous stone now remaining over the grave of a Mayflower passenger. For extended account, see Mayflower Descendant, Vol. III, pp. 193-201.

MILITARY ORDER IN RELATION TO A NEW FLAG, 1684.

Haverhill May 31: 1684.

To Lieu^t: John Gold

In obedience to a let^r I recied last night from o^r Maj^r: Gen^{ll}: with a comand from him in this vacancie of a setled Serg^t: Maj^r: for ye North Regim^t: in Essex to issue our warrant to ye Comission^d officers for a speedy survey of ye state & condition of ye soldiers under their comand wth respect to their armes & amnunition & other furniture as ye Law requirs each man to haue.

These are in his Maj^{ts} Name & and for his service to will and require you to make diligent search & survey how & in w^t manner all your Soldiers are fitted & furnished wth armes amunition & other furniture in all respects required by Law and in pticul^r y^t you wth ye rest of ye Committee of Militia of your Towne survey to giue acco^t of yor Towne stock of armes & amunition & to see y^t it be complet & full and you in y^r place as Comand of of ye foot & as Comittee man are required to take speedy effectuell carre y^t all defects be repaired & supplyed, of all, w^c you are to giue me a pticul^r acco^t und^r yor hands y^t according to his Mag^t Gen^{ll} comand, I may certifie him and my hand by or upon ye last of June next in w^t state & posture yor Company is in: & therefore I pray faile not to send me yor acco^t by ye 20 of June next y^t I may haue time to performe to is required of me.

In y^r Maj^t Gen^{ll} Letter I haue order also to require you w^c I hereby do wth all convenient speed to provide a new flight or suit of Colours for yor foot company ye grand feild or flight whereof is to be Green wth a red crofs in a white feild in the angle according to antient customs of o^r owne English nation & ye English plantations in America & our owne practice in o^r ships & other vessels. The bullets to be put into yor Colours for distinction & dignitie not being yet determined you may leave out at present wth out damage in making them or hindrance to or after determination, s^r faile not.

yor friend & servant

H. Saltonstall.

Massachusetts Archives.

(288)

SAMUEL CURWEN OF SALEM, LOYALIST.
1715-1802.

From the pastel made by Blyth in 1772, and now in the possession of the
Essex Institute.

HISTORICAL COLLECTIONS

OF THE

ESSEX INSTITUTE

| Vol. XLIII. | October, 1907 | No. 4 |

ESSEX COUNTY LOYALISTS.

In July, 1783, the British Parliament appointed a Commission to make a diligent and impartial inquiry into the losses and services of the king's faithful subjects who had suffered during "the last unhappy dissension in America." The volumes containing the notes of the proceedings and evidence were retained by one of the Commissioners and in time were presented to the Smithsonian Institution at Washington. They are now preserved in the Library of Congress. The following abstracts include all information relating to Loyalists who came from Essex County, Mass.

Evidence on the Claim of HENRY ATKINS, late of Newbury Port, Massachusetts Bay.

HENRY ATKINS, Son to Claimant, sworn: Says that he is informed by Capt. Murphy of the Ship Lion which sailed from London in June last that his Father died at Waltham Stowe about the 5th of June 1786. Capt. Murphy brought a message from Capt. Holmes to that effect. Witness is the only son of the Late Henry Atkins. He has seven sisters all in the States. His father was a native of Boston & in 1772 he was appointed Weigher & Gauger at Newbury Port & did the duty of that office until 1775 when he was prevented by the Americans. Says his father declared his sentiments openly in favour of Gt. Britain & was confined a close Prisnr for Two months

when he gave Bail & was confined to his House & Garden.
In 1778 he came to Halifax leaving his family, all but the
Witness & went to England in 1780, and in 1782 received
£40 pr an. from the Treasury. Witness has remained
here ever since 1778 & is emploied in the pay Mr. Genrs
office. When Witness left Newbury Port he left Books
& Cloathes worth £20 Str. Says they were taken by the
Rebels from the House of Col. Jones. Believes that all
the expenses charged in the acct were incurred, but he cannot posatively swear that he did not receive his sallary to
1782, when his allowance commenced. The Place of
Weigher & Gauger was worth £80 pr. an., but he cannot
say what part was Sallary & what fees.

———

Case of WILLM. BROWN, Esq., late of Salem. Claimt.
sworn saith: He is a native of Massachusetts, representative of two respectable families by his Father & Mother's
Side, the one Brown, the other Dudley. Remarkable for
their attachment to the Brit. Government, & two of the
most respectable families in Massts.

Was bred to the Study of Law, but turned his attention
to Improvement of his Estate. Was elected Representative for Salem in 1762. Continued in the Assembly 7 yrs.
in 1768. There was an alarm about the Stamp Act which
occasioned a Confederacy among the Colonies for Corres-
pondence. The Assembly of Massts. voted for Corres-
pondence. Lord Hilsboro required the vote to be re-
scinded. Claimt. voted for rescinding which lost him his
Popularity. This lost him his seat at the next election.

In 1774 resided on his own Property at Salem. Col. of
Militia of Essex Co. & Judge of the Superior Court of
Massts. Was one of the persons who addrest Govr.
Hutchinson. Never joined any rebel Committee or any
Association. Was appointed Judge of Superior Court by
Strong recommendations of Govr. Hutchinson. Was one
of the Mandamus Council.

In Aug., 1774, heard of the Danger in which Mandamus
Council were, & continued at Boston till the Evacuation in
March, 1776. Went home to England in the Packet from
thence. Bore Sr. Wm. How's Despatches to Govert. Re-

mained in England till Feby., '81, when he was appointed Govr of Bermuda. Recd. his Salary as one of the Judges, £200 per ann. & gratuities, till he was appointed Gover. Salary was paid from Date Commencing June, 1774.

Recd. in Aug., '75, by Genl. Gage's order £100 Ster. In March, 1776, recd. £200, in England of the Lords of the Treasury, in Common with the Mandamus Council. On appointment to Bermuda, applied to Treasury & recd. £100, and £200 on the expiry. of Judges Commission. When his appointment as Gover. took place. His present Salary £750 Ster. per ann. in England. He went to Bermuda in Decr., 1781, & has staid there ever since. His name was in the act against notorious Conspirators.

Produces his appointment as Col. of Militia by Govr. Hutchinson in 1771.

Produces his appointment of Judge of Superior Court of Massachusetts Bay by Genl. Gage June, 1774.

Produces Massachusetts Gazette, 15 Sep., 1774, containing Resoln. of a Committee that he should be requested to resign his office as Mandamus Councillor, and his ansr. that he would not from pursuasions or Threats do any thing derogatory to the character of a Councillor of his Majesty's Province.

Claimt. was possessed No. 1 of 9,663 acres in Lyme, Colchester, & New London in Co. of New London, Connecticut. 4,000 acres purchased by his Grandfr. of J. Harris 1718. Produces Deed from James Harris to Col. Saml. Brown of 4,000 acres in Lyme Township in Considn. of £1,600 Cury., New Eng. £666 Ster., dated 1718. Produces survey of sd. 4,000.

Produces Deed from James Harris to Saml. Brown of 2,865 acres in Town of Lyme in Considn. of £2,250 New Eng. Cury., dated 1723, £803 Ster.

Produces old memr. of a Deed from W. Gardner to S. Brown, being in the hands of Saml. Huntingdon, an Attorney at Norwich.

Produces Copy of said Deed, which appears a Deed from Wm. Gardiner to Col. Saml. Brown of 635 acres in Township of Colchester in Considn. 1,400 Connect. Cury., £500 Ster., dated 1724.

Produces Copy of Deed from Aaron Stark to Saml. Brown of 45 acres in Colchester in Considn. £50 Cury., dated 1725. £50 Cur. equal to 15.

Produces Copy of Deed from James Harris to Col. S. Brown of 37 acres in Colchester in Considn. £50., dated 1726.

Produces Deed from Danl. Davis to Col. Brown of 80 acres in Colchester in Considn. £160 Cur., dated 1727. £160 equal to 51 Ster.

Produces Deed from S. Peck to Col. S. Brown of 300 acres in Lyme in Considn. £700, dated 1728. £700 equal to 225 Ster.

Produces deed from James Harris to Col. Brown of 176 acres in Colchester in Considn. of £316, dated 1728. £316 equal to £102 Ster.

Produces Deed from Jas. Harris to Col. Brown of 172 in Colchester & New London in Considn. £345, dated 1728. £345 equal to £111 Ster.

Produces Deed from Danl. Galusin to Col. Brown of 145 acres in Lyme in Considn. £350, dated 1729. £350 equal to 113 Ster.

Produces Deed from S. Tubbs to Col. Brown of 21 acres in Colchr. in Considn. £42, dated 1729. £42 equal to 13 Ster.

Produces Deed from R. Staples to Col. Brown of 48 acres in Colchester in Considn. £110, dated 1729. £110 equal to £35 Ster.

Produces Deed from A. Gillet to Col. Brown of 165 acres in Colchr. in Considn. £120, dated 1729. £120 equal 38 Ster.

Produces Deed from James Harris to Col. Brown of 200 acres in Lyme in Considn. £140, dated 1729. £140 equal to 45 Ster.

Produces Deed from James Harris to Col. Brown of 626 acres in Lyme in Considn. £3,450, dated 1729. £3,450 equal to £1,114 Ster.

Produces Copy of Deed from Jas. Harris to Col. Brown of 26 acres in Colchester in Considn. £50, dated 1729. £50 equal 16 Ster.

Produces Copy of Deed from A. Gillet to Col. Brown of

128 acres in Colchester in Considn. £105, dated 1729. £150 equal to 17 Ster.

The whole contains 9,663 acres. Considn. amts. to £3,883. 13 8. Ster.

Claimts. Grandfr. continued in Possession dur. his Life; died in 1731; then went to Claimt.'s Father by Will of his Grandfather.

Produces Copy of Grandfather's Will, whereby he devises all his Lands &c. in Lime, Colchester, & New London to his eldest Son Samuel Brown in Tail Male. Remr. in Tail male to Wm. Like Remr. in T. Male to Benjn. Remr. in Fee to his right Heirs.

Willm. & Benjamin are dead without Heirs Male. Claimt. is the eldest son of Samuel Brown but says the ultimate Remr. under his Grandfr.'s Will would go to the children of all his sons.

Claimt.'s Father was in Possession. Died in 1742 without a Will. Claimant is entitled as Heir in Tail Male. Claimt. has been in Possession ever since, till the Troubles. There was no Recovery suffered. This Estate has been Confiscated.

Produces Copy of Conviction Feby., 1779, New London Co., and of forfeiture of the Claimt.'s real & personal Estate.

Produces Copy of Sale under Hand of Benjamin Huntingdon who was appointed adm. by the Court with acct. of Sale of 5,216 for the sum of 10,711 lawful M., and that there remained unsold 3,600 acres.

Debts found due abt. £700 Continental Cury.

Claimt. admits a Debt of £900 Ster. with 4 yrs. Int. due in 1774, & £480 lawful with about a yrs. Int.

All this was under Lease. Tenants were to pay Money; were also to make fences & other Improvements. Rent about £300 lawful per. ann., with other covenants on part of Tenants. Claimt. produces Leases to as above. Vals. the Estate at 40 sh. per acre.

The Estate laid all together between Connecticut & Thames River & its situation made it very valuable. 10 miles from New London, 10 miles from Norwich Market Towns & Seaports, one pt. was only 5 miles from Connecticut River.

Says he has laid out himself £7,000 Str. in buildings, in Repairs, in clearing & Wells. Was laid out in different Farms. Some of the best part was worth £3.12 Ster. per acre. 1,000 acres of this were thus good.

Claimt. says the best has been sold. The administrator values what remains unsold at 1 Gu. per acre. Claimt. says he has generally known farms in that neighbourhood sell at more than 40 sh.

Was possessed of an house at Salem. This was his Grandfather's bought at several times. The whole about 2 acres. Produces several Deeds of purchase of small pieces by his Grandfr. 1 by his Father, 1 by himself. Considn. abt. £240 Ster.

His Grandfr. built an house upon it, & Wharf. Left it by Will to Claimt.'s Father in fee. His Father was in Possession & it came on his Death to Claimt. & his Sisters. They were the only children. Produces Deed from his Sister & her Husb., Joseph Blaney, Conveying to Claimt. her share in the Prems. & other Lands in Considn. £800. Dated 1762.

This Estate was afterwards divided and consisted in 1774 of:

House in which Claimt. lived, which he values at £2,000 Str. 52 feet by 37. A very handsome House in the centre of the town. Vals. this house, Garden, orchard & offices at £2,000 Ster.

There was also another house on the Prems. where Claimt.'s Mother lived. Claimt. built this in 1763. Cost £350 Ster.

A house & wharf in the above mentd. Grounds. This house was divided into 2 Tenements & let at £12 lawf. per ann., other 1-2 at Do. Wharf let at £14 Ster. per ann. Vals. this at £1,000 Ster.

Land & Warehouse let to S. Flagg. Claimt. built this store. Cost £350 Ster. Let at £20 Ster. per ann. Vals. at £550 Ster. It included a small piece of Land at £3 Ster. per ann.

Was also possessed of 4-9 of a house in Salem in another part of the Town. Claimt. took this on a settlement of accts. with the Executor of his Uncle & laid out about

£145 Ster. in repairing it & let it. This had become divisible amongst the Family in these shares. The whole house let at £20 Ster. Vals. his share at £400. Produces Deed shewing his Title to these 4-9. Was entitled to 1-2 a cellar under the Town house, built by his Grandfr. and a Mr. Turner. Claimt. entitled to 1-2. American Committee estimate it at £110 Ster. Claimt. vals. it at the same.

Was also possessed of 37 acres at Stage Point in Salem, consisting of 8 parcels purchased at Different Times by Claimt.'s great Grandfr., his Grandfather, his Father & himself. Considn. £323 Ster.

Produces the several purchase Deeds, except 1 or 2, which had decayed. The Land lies opposite to Town of Salem. Was in a state of great Improvemt., divided into 12 Lots. 11 Lots let 53.15.6 per ann. Ster., exclusive of 9 acres. Worth 13.10 Ster.

Vals. this Est. at £50 Ster. per acre. Settled on Claimt. by his Grandfather, in the same way as the Lands in Lyme, &c.

Was possessed of a Farm about 4 miles from Salem called forest River farm, consisting of about 157 acres with 10 Rights, or rights for 10 Cows. 4 acres to a right. Purchased at different times by his Grandfr., his Father & Claimt. himself. Considn. £23.5.0—£397.4.0. 420.9 Ster. Has not these Deeds.

This Estate is left in Tail Male to Benjamin Brown, then to Claimt.'s Father in Tail, under his Grandfather's Will. Claimt. now is entitled to it as Heir in Tail. This was let to one Venning at £35 Ster. per ann.

Besides Rents Tenant was to supply ye Family with Butter cheaper than the market price, 6d. instead of 8d. per pound. Vals. this at £1,500 Ster.

Was possessed of 2-3 of 4,000 acres in Charlton. Produces Deed from W. Cowper to S. Brown of 2,000 acres in Oxford in Considn. £500, dated 1718. £500 equal 208 Ster. Produces Deed of other 2,000 acres to his Grandfr. in Considn. 400, dated 1717. 400 equal to 166 Ster.

Claimant's Grandfather gives these Lands to S. Brown, father to Claimt., in fee. 2-3 come to Claimt. on his

Father's Death.   Vals. these at 155 per acre.   Forest lands
no Improvements, brought in no Rent. These Lands are
within 15 miles of Worcester, the Shire Town, which
makes them valuable.

Claimt. also was possessed of 2-3 of 165 acres in Fitchburg in Midx. Co., purchased by S. Brown, Claimt.'s
Grandfr., before the year 1731.   Produces survey taken
in 1769, whereby it apprs. that 165 acres in Fitchburg are
surveyed as the Property of W. Brown.

Claimt.'s Grandfather leaves these lands to his Son Ben-
jamin in fee.   On Benjamin's death, came to Claimt.'s
Father & to his Uncle Willm.   His Uncle Willm.'s share
was disposed of & went to a Col. Willard.   The share of
Claimt.'s Father came by Descent to Claimt. & his Sister.
Part is sold.

Claimts. present share is 2-3 of 165 acres, forest, unimproved Lands.   It appears by a mem. that Claimt. asked
£150 lawful for these 165 acres in 1774, £112 Ster.

Claimt. was entitled to 2-3 of 110 acres in Ashley, purchased by Claimt.'s Grandfr. before the yr. 1731; left by
him to Benjamin on his death, descended to Claimt.'s
Father, & Uncle Willm.   His Uncle Willm.'s share went
to Col. Willard.   Father's share came between Claimt. &
his Sister.   Produces Survey in 1769, whereby there
apprs. a Lot of 110 acres belonging to W. Brown.   This
survey was made for purpose of dividing the Estate from
Claimt.   Produces Rect. of Tax for Lands in Ashley Aug.
1773.

Produces mem. of an Agreement made by Col. Willard
who had authority to sell from Claimt., that one Laurance
was to have these Lands at 18 sh. per acre, forest unimproved Lands.   Was also entitled to 2-3, 285 acres in
Fitchburg.   The whole was purchased by Claimt.'s
Grandfr., by him on his death left to Benjamin.   Came to
Claimt.'s Father & Uncle Willm.   Claimt.'s Father's
share came on his Death to Claimt. & his Sister.   Produces Survey in 1768, whereby 285 acres are stated as belonging to Claimt.   Claimt. entitled to 2-3 of this.

Produces Quit Claim from persons who had purchased
from the Representative of his Uncle Willm. his share.
Shd. have expected 3 Dollars per acre.

Says that the expenses attending these Lands from paymt. of Taxes makes them of high value. After the Taxes due for a course of years upon them are discharged.

Claimt. was entitled to a share of Lands in a large Grant in the Province of Main. This was originally a Grant of 600,000 acres to Lacon Clarke. He did not perform Conds. but his representatives—granted—reserving 100,000 acres to ——— to 10 associates on Considn. they performed —. They granted to 20 associates, receiv. 100,000 acres. These 20 associates grant 300,000 acres to Col. Waldo on Considn. of his getting a renewal of the Patent & performing the Conds. Waldo got the Patent 40 yrs. ago, & performed the Conds. Claimt. thinks his Grandfather had 1 of the 20 Association shares, amounting to 5,000 acres. Half this came to Claimt.'s father. Claimt. now claims 2-3 of 2,500.

Produces Rect. for 30 sh. of Wm. Brown in full for Taxes on one half a share in lands belonging to the Property called the 20 Associates of Lincolnshire Co. Signed W. Appleton, 1768, Proprietors Treas. Produces Do. 17 shils. in 1768.

These Taxes were not annual but from time to time called for as the expenses were incurred in general about the Lands.

These Lands left to Claimt.'s Father & Uncle Willm. Claimt.'s Father's share came 2-3 of it to Claimt. Vals. the 2,500 acres at £150 Ster.

Was entitled to several Lots in the town of Hadley. Produces acct. of the sd. Lots Copied from proprietor's Books, whereby appear 32 Lots in Claimt.'s name, containing different Quantities of Land. They are 2 miles in length, but some of them very narrow, quite strips. Knows not how to value them. Claimt.'s share is 2-3 of Moiety, 1,060 acres.

These lands were left by Claimt.'s Grandfr. to Benjamin. Came on his Death to Claimt.' Uncle & Father. Claimt. is entitled to 2-3 of his Father's share.

Claimt. was entitled to a moiety of a proprietor's right in Yarmouth, No. 95. Produces Letter from Proprietor's Clerk. Vals. it at 33.15. Claims 2-3.

Produces Evidence respecting his Lands in Springfield
These Lands are sold & Claimt. withdraws his Claim for
them.

Claimt. is in the notorious Conspirators Act. Under
this act the Estates of the persons therein mentioned are
forfeited. Claimt. says this extends to forfeiture of Estates Tail.

Claimt. was possessed of several Negroes on his Estate
at Connecticut in No. 11. When Claimt. thought of improving his farm in Connecticut he purchased 3 Negroes
& 1 Woman, whom he left on this Estate. Afterwards
purchased 3 or 4 which were sent to the farm on Claimt.'s
Estate which his agent's Son was in Possession.

These Negroes were on the Estate. The admr. of the
Estate would not sell them, having Doubts about the Le-
gality of such sale, but let them go away as they liked.
They are all lost to Claimt.

The admr. in his acct. of sale of Claimt.'s Estate mentions 11 Negroes living on the Estate when Govr. Brown
left it. Vals. at £45 each.

Furniture at his Dwelling house in Salem, propertioned
to the goodness of the house. Saved his Plate & Linen.

This Loss appears to have been accidental. The furniture was left in the house, & was removed on acct. of fires.
By removal & pillaging most of it was lost or spoilt. The
Library was under the same Circumstances. Vals. furniture £500, Library £150. £500 for furniture includes
2 slaves who have got their liberty, owing to the Confusion
of the States Debts.

Produces Certificate of Sale of real & personal Estate of
Claimant in the Province of Massachusetts, of a sum equal,
so far as had been sold, to 11 sh., 6d. Ster., £3,024.

Claims allowed by Commrs. on the Estate in Massachusetts, £934 Lawful, Intst. 401. Claimt. supposes about
700 lawful fairly due.

Claimt. says he was also in possession of some other real
Estate in Salem. 2 rights, or right of 2 Cows in great
Pasture of Salem. Purchased by his Grandfr. Vals. them
at £9 Sterl. each. Had made use of one right himself, &
let his Mother make use of the other. Pew in first meet-

ing house, belonged to his Grandfr. Vals. it at £33.15. Pew in St. Peters Church. Vals. £9 Ster.

Produces Deed from Wm. Eppes to Claimt. of a Pew in St. Peters Church in Considn. £12 Lawful.

Pew in a Meeting house. Produces Deed from Committee of proprietors of North Meeting house to Claimt. of half a Pew No. 16 in Considn. £15.5, lawful 1772. Vals. at £12.

Produces Deed of another Pew, No. 18. Considn. £28.10, lawful 1772. £21 Ster.

Do. No. 19 in 1773. Considn. £24.10 Lawful.

DR. JOHN PRINCE: Remembers Govr. Brown living at Salem. His mansion house, built by his Grandfather was a large house, 3 stories, 17 Rooms, large handsome Rooms, Garden, offices, Stables, Compleat. Thought the best house & the best situation in the Place.

It has been bought since the Confiscation by a relative of Witness at about £2,250 Ster. Thinks this a large Price. Thinks it would have fetched nearly the same sum before the Troubles. Knew the House when Claimt.'s Mother lived. Remembers Claimt.'s building it. Is a handsome house with 3 Rooms on a floor. This has been sold since the Confiscation to Nathan Goodall, who gave £750 Ster. Vals. it in 1774 at near that sum.

Remembers the house & the wharf. There were several persons who held different parts of the wharf. The wharf run 200 feet at least on the river. Should think this together must have been worth £1,000.

House where Flagg lived. Remembers Claimt. building store. Has been purchased by a relative of Wits. for £900 lawful. Vals. it above £500 Ster.

Knew the House where Gardiner lived. This belonged to the Family as Wits. thinks, undivided between Claimt. & his Cousin. This house has been purchased since Confiscation at £900 Ster. Thinks the whole house worth that money.

On being asked how it could be worth so much as rent was so little, says purchasers used to think themselves well off if they got 3 or 2 1-2 per cent. for their money.

Knew his lands at Stage Point. Remembers Claimt. in

Possession, opposite to the centre of the Town, on the other side River, divided into different Lots. Thinks it consisted of about 40 acres. One spot was particularly valuable. It was a place where ships hauled down to repair. Claimt. has been told by a Tenant since the Confiscation that a small spot of 1-2 acre brought in £45 Ster. in one year from the Profits of Ship hauling on it. That near the river was useful for drying fish, the other Land was chiefly grass, very convenient to the Town. A very valuable Tract. Thinks this would fairly have been worth from 50 to 60 Ster. per acre. That next the water was richly, worth £60 Ster. per acre.

Remembers him in Possession of Mening's Farm. Was valuable. It was good land, well situated. Vals. the farm at £10 Ster. per acre, but speaks doubtfully.

As to Charlton Lands. Wits. had himself Lands in a Town near Charlton which he sold at 30 Ster. per acre. They had small Improvements upon them. Such Lands were obliged to pay Taxes, tho. unimproved, but it was not usual to Escheat them. Used to be sold for non payment of Taxes.

His house at Salem was well furnished.

Remembers he had Rights in the great Pasture of Salem. Thinks them worth £9 Sterl. each.

Has heard he had large Property in Connecticut. It was reckoned very valuable. Thought valuable from being so near London & Norwich. Speaks highly in favour of his Character.

Further Evidence in Case of GOVR. BROWN. As to property in Massachusetts. Produces Copy of Deed from Jos. Bowditch to Claimt. of a piece of Land in Southfield in cons. £75 Lawful, 1764.

Produces Copy of Deed from Saml. Sarasy to Col. Saml. Brown of parcel of Salt Marsh in Salem County, 1 acre & ½ in considn £20 passable Money, 1728.

Produces Deed from Ebenezer Bowditch to Claimt. of a Lot in Salem containing 4 acres & ½ in considn £200 Lawful, 1760.

Produces Copy Conveyance from Luckin Thorndike, Israel Hutchinson, Dummer Jewett, the Commrs. of forfeited Estates, of a Parcel of Land in Salem on part of which the Mansion House formerly of Claimant stands, to Elias Haskel Derby in considn £6,050, in Massts. Govert. Securities. They sell the same in fee & warrant the same in the name of the Commonwealth, to the Purchaser in fee.

Produces Copy of Deed from Wm. Hynd to Col. Brown of 12 acres in Marblehead in a Place called the Plain farms in Consid. £50 Curt. Passable Money New England, 1728.

Produces Copy of Deed from John Marston to Col. Saml. Brown of a Parcel of Land in Stage Point in Salem, Contains about 3 acres in considn £54 Cury, dated 1718.

Produces Deed from Wm. Saunders to Col. Saml. Brown of 100 acres within Township of Salem in consr £400 Cury., dated 1711.

Produces Copy of Deed from James Derby to Col. Saml. Brown of a house & Land in Salem in considn £60 Cury., dated 1716.

Produces Copy of Deed from Jos. Flint, to Col. Sam. Brown, of 3 or 4 acres in Salem in Considn of £50 Cury., dated 1722.

Produces Certificates to Claimts being possessed of a Pew in Meeting house at Salem & vals. at £20 Str. Signed Jas. Jeffrey Clerk of the Proprietors of Meeting house, April, 1786.

Produces Certificate that Claimt. was entitled to 2-3 of 18 & ½ Common Rights in Great Pasture of Salem which have been sold by Commrs. of Confiscated Estates, signed Jos. Clough, Clerk of Proprietors, April, 1786.

Produces Certificate that Col. Saml. Brown was one of original 20 Associate Grantees of Land in Penobscot. 5,000 acres to each share. Silvanus Burn, Proprs. Clerk, May, 1786. Certificate that Claimt. was owner of one half the aforesaid share in 1774.

Produces Certificate signed John Downing, Peter Boyer, Committee for settling with Comrs. of Sale, that Comrs. of Sale sold in Co. of Worcester Lands the Property of Claimt. to amount of £2,450 Lawful, equal to £1,860 Str.

N. B.—Claimt's Agent Joseph Blaney says in a Letter, he is informed the Commrs. sold 1,700 acres for the sum mentd. in the above Certificate.

As to Property in Connecticut, Produces affidavit of Ebenezer Backus that he knew Claimant's Estate in Colchester, Lime & New London, tho' not exact No. of acres, very valuable from its situation, good farms & builds., well timbered, as valuable as any Land in Province. Divided into farms, vals. it at 15 Dollars per acre.

Evidence on the Claim of GEORGE DEBLOIS, the Elder, late of Salem, now of Halifax, Mercht.

Claimt. Geo. Deblois being sworn says that he is a native of England, came to America in 1761 & settled at Salem as a mercht., continued there till Apl., 1775, always sided with Government of Great Britain on Commencement of troubles. Took a part in the Disturbance on Stamp Act, made himself obnoxious by signing an address to Govr. Hutcheson on his going home to Engd. in 1774. Also signed an address with ye Loyalists to Genl. Gage in Sumr. 1774, on his first coming to Salem. By these Acts had become so obnoxious that he was obliged to fly from Salem, meant to go to Boston but found it impossible, obliged to embark himself & family for Halifax, April 1775.

Made no submission at any time prior to this to the Rebels. Was called upon to take arms at the affair of Lexington with the Americans but refused. Ever since has remd. under Protection of Brit. Govment.

Property.

Real Property Claims 1 Acre & 1-2 but withdraws.

States Loss of Merchandise left at Salem when he fled to amount £438.11.5 Massts. Lawful Money. Produces extracts from his Books to prove Merchandise left behind at Salem, which extract is in manner following:

Amount left at Salem　　.　　.　　£299. 0. 6 1-2
　　　　　　　　　　　　　　　　　£438.11. 5 1-2

　　　　　　　　　　　　　　　　　£438.11.5 1-2

By advance Claimt. explains Freight, Insur., Commission. Cannot state what part has been seized by the Committee of Sequestr. thereof. Cannot say how much of this has been lost, some part has been sold by my Agent.

States Value of furniture left at Salem of which he admits he has recvd. a great Deal.

Value 170. 5. 9. Masst. C.

Recvd. 103. 19. 6.

_____

66.16. 3.

Has no Acct. of the manner in which the rest of the furniture was lost. Has no account of China broke to pieces, £60. Ship Martha. The Co-partnership of Gilbt. Lewis, Stephen, George, Snr., & George, Jnr., Deblois, Merchts. at N. York Shipt on Board the Martha from London in Feby. 27, '78, a cargo of English goods to the value of £6,731.12.10 Sterling, which ship & Cargo was taken by the Shannon Sc., Geo. Collin, & carried into Halifax & there condemned under ye Prohibitory Act. Cargo was insured in London. Insurers returned prem. to the amount of £1,300 Str., which he bels. is the whole yet recovered. A Claim for the whole has been lodged in England by one of the Partners—Gilbert.

Debts.—States amnt. of Book Debts & notes still due from persons in the United States, £1,138.9.10 1-2 Mss'ts. M. This Acct. contains some Debts due before the Co-partnership.

Sloop Hawke, having a cargo on board belonging to the afsd. Partners was cast away on Point Charles on Delaware & plundered by Americans. Estimates his share at £260 Str.

Witness, PETER FRY, ESQ., formerly of Salem:

Knew Claimt. Lived 3 or 4 doors from me. Always appeared by acns. & words a good subject. Knew of his signing address to Govr. Hutchinson & Gen. Gage. Knew that he had made himself obnoxious from his attachmnt. to Brit. Govnt. Was driven from Salem by the Difficulties of the times to avoid insults & being obliged to serve in American Army. Never recollects any Instance of his submission to Americans.

Thinks Claimt. left his Stores in the care of Mr. Pincheon at Salem. Mr. Pincheon showed me a cask of hard ware of Claimt.'s & sd. the Rebel Comt. had taken part of Claimt.'s furniture left behind, but knows not but that it was saved to him.

Claimt. kept a large Store at Salem, had large Dealings, probably large Debts due to him.

Claimt. was a man of an excptl. character, being a Church of Eng. man, more expected to be a Tory.

DR. JOHN PRINCE, formerly of Salem :

Knew Claimt. His conduct that of a subject attached to G. Britain. On Gen. Gage's arrival signed the address with the Loyalists. He had become obnoxious to the other party. Left Salem on acct. of his Principles. Brought away great part of his property, but left store & goods in charge of a friend, Mr. Pincheon. Left great part of his furniture behind. Claimt. of a fine Char. in every respect.

Evidence on Case of GEORGE DEBLOIS, Jnr., late of Newbury Port, Masst.

Claimt. being Sworn, says:

He is a native of Bost. Resided in America till 1775. At beginning of Troubles was settled in Newbury in Masst. Conduct uniformly as a Loyalist. Several times called upon to take up arms after Battle of Lexington by the Americans, but refused. At no time took any part with them, or made submission.

In April 1775 embarked with his family for River St. Johns. His motive was attachmt. to Brit. Government and has remd. constantly under protection of Brit. Govt. ever since.

Claimt. son of Lewis Deblois of Boston. Examined formerly at the Board in England. Produces Certificates of Govr. Tryon, dated Jany. 24, 1777, of his having taken an Oath of Allegiance to the King, and Certificate dated 20th Octr., 1777, signed by Wm. Coffin, Clerk of the Volunteer Co., to show he was a Volunteer of Massachusetts Co. of Vols.

Property.—Possessed a store at Newbury built on Land taken by Lease, which lease expired 1779, but he was to have Leave to remove store. Store was worth £100 Mass money.

Ship Martha. Claimt. one of the 3 Partners concerned in the Ship Martha. £1,300 that & upwards has been recd.

Furniture on board the Hawke which he was removing to Settle at Philadelphia, to the amt. of £200 Sterling. Sloop was carried away & plundered by Americans. Merchd. on board sd. Sloop 1-5 Share, about £260, States no part was saved.

Debts.—State Debts due to Amt. £905.17.4 1-2 Mss. money, of which he has recvd. upwards of 300 Mss. M.

DR. JOHN PRINCE:

Knew Claimt. Always considered him to be a Loyalist. Thinks he left Newbury to avoid Troubles. He was markd. at Newbury as a Loyalist. There were few Loyalists there. Knew he had a store at Newbury.

PETER FRY ESQ.:

Knew Claimt. Have heard him mentioned as one attached to Brit. Govrnmt. & that he had left Newbury on acct. of the Troubles of the Times.

Case JOSEPH HOOPER, Marblehead. As soon as the restraining act passed he Signed a Protest & induced others to sign it, contrary to the Resolutions of the Town of Marblehead, where he resided. He followed the business of a Rope maker & was a Mercht. His house was called Tory Hall from his known adherance to Govt. He was obliged to go armed for some time before he left America. The troops left Marblehead a short time before the battle of Lexington. He continually lived with the officers of the British Army.

After the battle of Lexington, Capt. Bishop in the Lively Ship of War, blocked up the Port & he was chosen by the Town as a friend to Govert. to mediate for them.

After this he was constantly attacked & insulted and frequently put in danger of his life. Then attempts were made to burn his house in the night. He killed one man in the attempt.

On the 1st of May 1775 a Town meeting was held at Marblehead & all adherent to the British cause, were ordered to renounce their alligance, he was the only person in the Town who refused to make a temporary submission.

They immediately drew up a form of recantation, which a friend of his who was of the committee, brought to him

& told him he must sign before the Friday following or his life would be the forfeit. He then thought it prudent to get off, which he did in a Ship of his fathers to Bilboa in Spain & lay 42 nights on some dried Fish. He came from Spain to England, since which time he has never been to America.

Certificates from Gen. Gage & Judge Brown to Loyalty to Property from others, but they cannot be received.

SIR WM. PEPPERELL. Believes Mr. Hooper to be a Loyalist & has understood that he has suffered considerably by his Loyalty. He supposed him to be a person of Property, when he was in America & still thinks he was. His Father was a very steady Loyalist.

The Claimant called again to speak to Property says he built a House, bought the land in 1772 of Benj. Matson Esq., says he thinks the Land cost him before he began to build, twixt £3 & 400 Stg. The building of the House cost him £2500 Stg. The out Buildings, fence, &c., cost him £500. It was just finished before the troubles. He values the whole at £3500 & is concious it must have cost him more. Plate, Furniture, Wine, liquors, Linnen, in his opinion were worth at least £500.

A large Rope walk he swears was his own property. He values this with tools & implements at £2500, it cost him that & he could had £2000 from a person to take him into Partnership. The Rope Walk he hears is not destroied. He thinks it would let for £70 or £80 pr. annum. His father is not in Possession. He says all his Property at Marblehead is confiscated as will appear by an affidavit of his Fathers which was produced & read. His Father was active last August. It appears by the same that the Property was the sons. He had a right in two other Rope Walks. He left all his Papers at Salem. He values this Interest at £300.

A House & Land at Newbury Port, his title to this is in right of his Wife, it belonged to her. It belonged to her Father & Mother, it has been valued at £1875, there is a mortgage on it for £600. He values his loss to him at £1000. Does not know that it is Confiscated his Wife is in Possession.

150 acres Lands at Marblehead, these he would only have at his Father's death. He has a Deed of Gift for them. He values them at £500.

For Hemp Cordage English & West Indian goods. He swears he had those in his Rope Walk to the value of £400. Furniture, Plate, &c., &c., in his Father in Law's house £189.

He had two Negroes which are liberated by the Congress. Succeeded to two by his Father in Law, one lives with his Wife & one is dead.

He had 5 Horses, two he drove in his Phaeton, one he rode. These cost him £20 each & 2 cart horses. He values them at £50.

He had two carriages which he values at £80.

Upon a ballance there was £400 due him in America.

He claims Loss of business in his Rope Walk for 9 years at £700 pr. an. Says he made that by his business. He realized about £400 pr. an., by his trade in the Fisheries, &c.

The Interest of his estate for 9 years at £300 pr. an. He formerly had £100 pr. an. from the Treasury from 1777. He is reduced by Mr. Wilmot & Coke to £80.

SAM'L CURWEN, Esq. Has Known Mr. Hooper since his infancy. Mr. Curwen lived at Salem only 4 miles from Marblehead, says the Hooper family were always esteemed Loyal. He does not himself know any acts of their Loyalty. He knows he carried on the Rope business & always considered him as the owner of the Rope Walk. He cannot put any value on his Rope Walk or on his House. He knows the woman he married. Believes her Father is a Loyalist he does not know what fortune she had, believes her father had failed some years before. Mr. C— came away before Mr. Hooper. He has heard nothing of Mr. Hoopers conduct by which he displeased the Rebels. Says Mr. Coombs could give the Board some information, but he is at present out of town. Says he knows nothing more of Mr. Hoopers case & Mr. Monro is desired to inform Mr. Hooper that the Board will require further evidence to Coroborate Mr. Hoopers testemony.

PETER FRYE, Esq. He lived at Salem. Hooper lived at
Marblehead. He was a rope maker. He believes the Rope
Walk was his own. It was made at a very considerable
expense. He thinks it might have let for £100 pr. an.
He thinks he could have bought & built the whole for
£2000 Lawful. He always considered both Father & Son
as very Loyal subjects. Knows his House, it was one of
the best houses in Town. It would have cost him £2500
S. with the out buildings. He was at great expense in
clearing the ground for the foundation. If he had been
to buy the house he would have thought £2000 a high
price for it. At auction he thinks it would have sold for
£1500, it was well furnished. He thinks that the furniture, plate, &c., might be worth £350. He has heard
that Mr. Hooper had a concern in another Rope Walk.
He has rode around the House at Newbury Port. Mr.
Hooper got it by his Wife. He thinks it might be worth
£7 or 800. He Knows Mr. H. had Negroes, but does not
know the number. He had two or three Carriages. Being
asked as to the price of Carriage Horses, he says £10 is a
high price. He says that he might make £500 pr. an. of
his Rope Walk, sometimes more. He does not know if
Mr. Hoopers Property is confiscated & doubts if the proscription Laws prevents persons who are attainted from
inheriting property. Says he never knew of Property coming by a man's wife being confiscated when she remained in
this Country. This goes to the Estate at Newbury Port &
the principle which he lays down as to Inheritence applies
to the estate in reversion to him at his fathers death.

Decision.

That Mr. Hooper is a Zealous & Steady Loyalist.

They value his House at... ... ...£1450
Plate, Furniture, Liquors, Linnen, &c. &c... 300
His Rope Walk at 1450
Part concern in two others... 150
Tar, Hemp, Cordage & Merchandise... 200
Two Negroes 80

Carriages... 40
Balance Debts 400
Allowance from the Treasury... ... ... 80 pr. an.

Case of BENJN. MARSTEN, late of Marblehead, Massachusetts.

Claimant sworn saith:

He is a native of America. Resided at Marblehead when Troubles began. From the first declared his sentiments freely & publicly in favour of Brit. Govert. Was one of the select men of the Town, & always ready to Execute the Laws in support of Brit. establish'd Government.

In Novr., 1775, went from Marblehead to Boston to join the Brit. Went as soon as he could in an open Boat which was accompanied with considerable Hazard. Continued with the Brit. at Boston & came with Gen. How to this Province. Was once employed to Convey a spy who was going into the Enemy's Country.

On coming into the Province had intended to go into the Military Line, but was disappointed on which he went to sea in a Mercht. vessel as super Cargo. Was taken Prisoner on his first voyage in 1776. Was carried into Plymouth, & kept prisoner 6 months, & treated with uncommon severity owing to the Principles which he was known to have entertained & profest.

Claimant was in Possession of an Estate at Marblehead, an house with buildings, Garden, orchard &c., containing about one acre.

Claimant lived upon it. Produces Deed of Conveyance from Rachel Majery to Claimt. of a Messuage in Marblehead Containing 2 acres of Land in Considn. £450, dated 1760. Laid out as much more as the Purchase money in Repairs and additional Builds. Sold one acre for about £225 Sterl.

Vals. the above estate at £600 Ster.

On Claimant's leaving Marblehead, it was taken Possession of by Committee. It has been since leased to one Marston Watson, Nephew to Claimt. There was no Mortgage or Incumbrance on this Estate.

A Store divided into two Tenements in King street, Marblehead. Produces Deed from Richd. Reed to Claimt. of a Tract of Land in King Street, Marblehead, with part of a Warehouse in Considn. £100, dated 1764. Produces Release from Robt. Hooper to Claimant of all his right in the aforesaid Premises in Considn. £5, dated 1764. Richd. Hooper had an old mortgage.

Claimt. built a new store after the Purchase at £150 lawful, divided into 2 Tenements, at £6 Ster. per ann. Kept the other himself. Vals. the whole at £13.10 Ster. per ann.

Vals. it at £180 Ster.

Produces a private Letter from his Nephew, Marston Watson, at Marblehead, May, 1782, by which it appears that Claimant's personal Estate had been sold. The real Estate was then unsold, but 3 Commrs. had been appointed to take an acct. of Charges upon all Claimant's Estate. Letter says there would be probably little surplus. Claimant says he owed about £550 Ster., of £70 of which was due in London.

1-5 of a Farm commonly called Bootman's Farm. The whole farm consisted of 60 acres with 1-5 of the Stock. The farm had belonged to his wife. Claimt. & his Wife Conveyed this to Isaac Mansfield Jany., 1773, in order that he might reconvey the Premises to Claimant. This was the way by which married Women made Conveyances answering the purpose of a Fine.

Produces Deed from Claimant & Wife to Isaac Mansfield, dated Jany. 9, 1773. Isaac Mansfield Conveyed the Premises to Claimant immediately after the former Deed was recorded but Claimt. has not this Deed at present.

Claimant & his Wife's Brors. & Sisters used to let this & the whole produce was a clear £120 lawful Mon. amongst the five. It came to his Wife as her Share on the Death of an Elder Brother.

Produces Copy of Will of his Wife's Father, Joseph Sweet, dated 1744, devising to his Son, Joseph, a farm consisting 65 acres, with buildings, stock, utensils, &c. Joseph Sweet, the Son, was in possession & died intestate without, Children. 1-5 came to Claimt.'s Wife.

Vals. them at £220 Ster.

Claimt. has not heard anything of the sale of this. Thinks a Brother & Sister of Claimt.'s Wife now living at Marblehead who are entitled to equal shares in it with Claimt.'s Wife.

1-5 of house in Marblehead, his Wife. Conveyed by Claimt. & Wife to Isaac Mansfield, in order to be Conveyed to Claimt. Produces Deed from Claimt. & Wife to Isaac Mansfield in 1772. Has not the Deed whereby Isaac Mansfield reconveyed. Had belonged to Joseph Sweet. Left to him by his Father's Will, and was Mrs. Marston's share on her Bror.'s death. The whole of this house let at £16 per ann. Vals. his share at £45 lawful. Knows nothing of the sale.

9 acres of pasture near Marblehead, Wife's Est. Produces Copy of Will of Joseph Sweet, dated 1744, giving to his Daugr. Sarah Sweet—afterwards Claimt.'s Wife—3 Cows, Commonages in Marblehead in Tail. This Consisted of about 9 acres.

Produces Exemplification of Recovery in 1763, in order to cut off the entail, and Deed to land, the leases of Recovery by which the said Premises are declared to be Conveyed for use of Claimant & his Heirs.

Claimt. was in Possession of this. Has not heard of the sale. These Commonages were worth £15 Ster. each. It was the Common Price.

Lost furniture & merchandise according to Inventory. Part left in Claimt.'s house at Marblehead. Part sent to different friends at different times in order to be secured. They were soon found out & have been seized & sold.

He had 3 Negroes. 2, a Woman & Child, were left at Mr. Bassets. Thinks they have been liberated by the State, but thinks they now live' at Mr. Bassets. Worth £55, the two.

Had a young man left him with a friend. He thinks he has been liberated. He went from the person with whom Claimt. left him. He afterwards went to sea & was lost. Worth £25 lawful.

Was in Possession of all the different articles in Inventory & has lost them all, amounting with Negroes to £451.18.8 lawful.

Adds in his Claim now £25.10 Sterling for various articles of personal property. The several articles were found out by Commrs. & Sold.

Claims for rents from the fall of 1775.

Claimant now resides at City of St. Johns, New Brunswick.

PETER FRY, Wits:

Knew Claimant. Certainly a Loyalist, uniformly so. Knew he had a house at Marblehead. Remembers his building it. In 1777 there was an Execution on a Judgement against Claimant and an order to appraise this house, & set off part in satisfaction of this Debt. It was then appraised & Witness was one of the Commrs. who appraised it, but cannot perfectly recollect what it was appraised at. According to his present Judgement would vote it at £500 Ster.

Claimt. had rendered himself obnoxious & Wits. does not think it probable that he should gain any benefit, from the Lease granted by Commrs. to his nephew.

Knew Claimt.'s Wife. Remembers her Brother Joseph. Died without Children. There were Cow Commonages in the Lands near Marblehead. Thinks them worth about £12 Ster. each.

Knew that he had Negroes. Wits. thinks that those Negroes only were liberated who would take up arms. Does not remember any general act for liberating.

His furniture was tolerably good. Cannot form any exact Judgement. Thinks it likely he might have had to the amount in his Inventory.

REVD. MR. WEEKS:

Knew Claimt. He was certainly a Loyalist. Knew his house at Marblehead. Remembers him in Possession of it. Remembers he had a Store. Remembers Claimant's Wife, Sarah Sweet.

Knew No. 3 Bartman's Farm. It belonged to several relations, of which Mrs. Marston was one. The family used to have a Dinner there every year. It was well stocked. Remembers he had Negroes. Remembers the Boy. His house was handsomely furnished. He had a pretty Library. He was a man of some education.

Case OWEN RICHARDS. He was born in Wales & went to America in 1774. He was a Custom house officer, Settled at Boston as a Tidesman. Produces the appointmt dated 8th April, 1768. His Sallary was £25 pr. an. & 1sh. 6d. when emploied. He was sent to Marblehead when the Port of Boston was shut. He was unable to do any duty after the Battle of Bunker Hill. He always did his duty like a Loyal subject & therefore he was treated more severely. He staid at Marblehead near a year & left Boston at the Evacuation.

He came to England in April, 1777 & applied to the Treasury who gave him £30 pr. an., which was Confirmed by Messrs. Wilmot & Coke & he still receives it. He has never received any sallary since he left America.

Certificates to the proper discharge of his duty from Mr. Hallowell, &c. & from Gover. Hutchinson & Chief Justice Oliver, they speak fully to Loyalty. Mr. Hallowell says in his Certificate that he had a house in Boston.

Case of THOS. ROBIE, late of Massachusetts Bay. Claimt. Sworn Saith. He is a native of America, lived at Marblehead when Troubles broke out, did not take an active part, but shew'd himself inimical to the measures of the Rebels. Left Marblehead about the 6th May, 1775 & came to this Province, thought himself hardly safe in person as he had been threatened. He was reckoned a Tory & they were told the Tories would be put in the front of the Battle. Hostilities commenced on the 19th April. Claimant left New England in May following, brought away some of his effects, there was then no Impediment to bringing away his effects if he had Convenience of Trunks—Vessels. Says his name was in the list Act of Prescription. Left his house chiefly in the care of his Wife's Grandmother.

In 1776 his house was entered upon by a Committee. Part of the effects were sold by his Wife's Grandmother, part of the effects were stole. The house was his own, built it himself. Purchased the Land about 1772 in considn £140 Str. Built the house at about ₣750 Str. There were two Mortgages upon it, one for £400 & the other for £800. No Interest having been paid, as Claimt. had no advantage of the house, the sum is now laige, admits the Mortgages are to the full value of the Estate now. The Mortgagee took Possession in 1783, but have since brought an action here for the Debt and got Judgement. Claims Debts £1,410.

Produces an Acct. of Goods in his store in Decr., 1777, then seized by a Committee & sold. Produces Affidt. of Richard Harris that in Dec., 1777, several articles were then in Possession of the Committee as the Property of Claimant & sold, & the money, amounting to £427.19.11 Lawful Mon. of sd. State paid by the Committee of whom Harris was one to Henry Gardner, Treasurer.

Produces Rect. by Henry Gardner, Treasury Office, 18 Jany. 1780, recd. of Committee of Marblehead 427.19.11 of the Estate of Thos. Robie. Claimt. cannot fix the sterling amount of this sum.

Produces further Acct. from Fras. Felton that Claimt's Estate real & personal was taken Possession of & that several articles of personal Estate was sold.

The Act produced mentions only Sundry articles in the Hardware Business. Fras. Felton was one of the Marblehead Committee.

Produces affidt. from Richd. Harris that Committee took Possession of Claimant's house & Land at Marblehead & leased & improved the same for the Benefit of the State. Vals. them at £40 per ann. Rent.

In Octr., 1783, one of the Mortgagees got Possession. Produces Certificate from Genl. Thos. Gage dated London, 5 Ap., 1776, that Claimt. did before 19th Apr., 1776, deliver in writing a Declaration purporting his hearty Disapprobation of the Measures adopted by the Americans against Supremacy of Brit. Parlt.

It appears that the sum paid into the Treasury is in Sterling very little £20 or 30. According to several Letters from Claimant's friends in Marblehead, but Claimant says many of his effects were stollen out of his store, after they took Possession of it.

Produces an acct. of several articles sold by his Wife's Grandmother to amount of £209, laid out in Government Notes.

FOSTER HUTCHINSON, Esq., Wits. Knew Claimt. understood him a friend to Brit. Govermt. and an enemy of the Measures pursued by the Americans. Is satisfied he is amongst the persons proscribed. He was amongst the persons who addrest Govr. Hutchinson. He never recanted, some of them did.

REVD. MR. WEEKS. Knew Claimt. Considered him as a friend to Brit. Govr. always. Knew he had a brick house at Marblehead. Kept a store, chiefly in the Hardware Business. Left the Country early, came away before Trials & Proscriptions in general, but all the persons who addressed Govr. Hutchinson & did not recant were he thinks proscribed.

THOS. BROWN, Wits. Claimt. signed the address to Govr. Hutchinson. Remembers seeing his name in the Newspapers, proscribed as an Enemy to his Country & people, forbid to have any Dealings with him. This was owing to his signing the address to Govr. Hutchinson. He had declared against New Importation agreement.

Some of the persons who addresst Govr. Hutchinson recanted. Claimant never recanted.

Had a large Store & good Business. He suffered greatly in Trade in Consequence of his Declaration of his Principles, and of signing the address. His Business was almost ruined by it.

Case of NATHANIEL TAYLOR, Esq., late of Massts. Claimant sworn saith : He is a native of America. Lived at Boston. He was Deputy Naval officer there. Had been in that office from the year 1755. Benjamin Pemberton was the Principal. Claimt. acted as his Deputy for many years. Afterwards acted as Deputy to the sons of Sir Francis Bernard. Produces the last appointment from John Bernard in 1772.

He was discharging the Duties of this office when the Troubles broke out. When Boston Port was shut up, he went first to Plymouth, then to Salem & executed the office there. During this time he was stationed at Salem, from Aug., 1774, till after the Battle of Lexington, he was desired by Genl. Gage & the Quarter Master General to send Provisions for the King's Service to Boston which he did & sent in many vessels while he was in the Custom house at Salem in the year 1775. He understood there was a Design to seize his person & hold him as an Hostage in case Genl. Gage should seize any person at Boston, on which he made his escape & got on Board a man of war & got to Boston. Continued at Boston till Evacuation, having left a person to execute his office at Salem. Came to Halifax on the Evacuation & from thence to this Province. His name is in the first Act of Proscription.

FRENCH WAR PRISONERS, 1747.

Yeiterday arrived here a Flagg of Truce Ship in 21 Days from Quebec, which has brought from thence about 170 Perfons Who have been taken and carried thither Captive since the War commenc'd with France.

A List of Prifoners that came in the Flag of Truce from Quebec taken by L'Castor, at Sea, June 21, 1746, Francis Cox, James Felt, and Samuel Buffington of Salem; & Lewis Reading of Marblehead. Taken by Monfieur Rumsey Jan. 30, 1746/7, Anthony Woodbury, Lieut Joseph Stockman and Wm Stockman of Newbury.

Bofton Post Boy, August 17, 1747.

ENGLISH NOTES ABOUT EARLY SETTLERS IN NEW ENGLAND.

Communicated by Lothrop Withington, 30 Little Russell Street, W. C., London (including "Gleanings" by Henry Fitz Gilbert Waters, not before printed).

(*Continued from Vol. XLI, page* 292.)

SHEAFE.

RICHARD SHEFF, of the parish of Cranebroke, in the county of Kent, clothier, 21 June, 1557, proved 24 September, 1557. To be buried in the parish church of Cranebroke, in St. Thomas chancell, beside the body of my father there. To the High Altar of the said Parish, for my tithes negligently forgotten or withholden, six shillings eight pence. I will that there be bestowed upon an altar cloth for the altar dedicate to God in the said chancell, and for other necessaries there, by the discretion of my executors and overseers, five pounds. I give towards the reparations of the said church and for my burying place, forty shillings. I will that there be given and distributed among prests, clerks, and poor people on the day of my burial, by the discretion of my executors, four pounds. I will that there be distributed among prests, clerks, and poor people at my month's mind, by the discretion of my executors, forty shillings. I will that there be yearly kept in the parish church of Cranebroke, by the space of four years next after my decease, one obett, and that at the same there be distributed (as before) to pray for my soul and all Christen souls yearly, forty shillings, by the discretion of my executors.

I give and bequeath to Elizabeth my wife two hundred pounds of currant money of England, to be paid to the said Elizabeth, her executors and assigns, in manner and form following, that is to say, within one quarter of a year next after my death twenty pounds, and so every quarter one next following one other twenty pounds till the said sum of two hundred pounds be wholly and entirely paid. To every of my daughters now being unmarried, that is to say, Margaret Sheff, which at the making of this my will is of the age of sixteen years and a half, Alys Sheff, of the age of fifteen years and a half, Margery Sheff, of the age of eighteen* years and

---

*I would suggest that this number, which was in Roman characters, should be thirteen. The age of Anne I cannot explain, unless XI was put by mistake for IX.—H. F. W.

a half, Mary Sheff of the age of eleven years and three quarters, and Anne Sheff, of the age of eleven years, at Easter next before the date of this my present Testament and last Will, fifty pounds to be paid to every of them at and in the day of their several marriages, and if it fortune any of my foresaid daughters not to be married before they attain and come unto the age of twenty-five years then I will to every of my said daughters so not married before the said age of twenty five years the said sum of fifty pounds.

I will that Thomas my son stand and be charged with the bringing up of all my said daughters, &c. I will and give to Thomas Sheff my son one of my goblets of silver. I give and bequeath to Johanne Knachebull my daughter one other of my goblets of silver and I will and give to Elizabeth my wife my best goblet of silver with the cover of silver to the same appertaining, also my salt of silver and gilt, and all my silver spoons. To Katheryn Love my daughter one silver pot with a cover to the same and a scripture thereupon parcell gilt. I will and give to Anne Knachebull, daughter of Richard Knachebull and Johanne my daughter, three pounds six shillings eight pence, to be paid to her in the day of marriage. Certain other bequests to wife Elizabeth. I will that Thomas Sheff my son shall yearly keep for Elizabeth my wife two kine summer and winter upon my lands in Cranebroke. I will that Thomas Sheff my son shall keep and bring up my two "wanyars" till such time as either of them have a calf, then I will both the heifers and the calves to Mary and Annie Sheff my daughters. I will that Thomas my son shall yearly during the term of sixteen years next after my decease deliver or cause to be delivered to Elizabeth my wife or to her assigns, at the messuage which I now dwell in or at my messuage where Robert Clachynden now dwelleth, situate in the parish of Cranebroke aforesaid &c., twenty loads of good wood ready made without anything to be paid for the same by the said Elizabeth my wife (if she) so long remain sole and unmarried. I will give and bequeath to William Sheff my son four hundred pounds, &c., which four hundred pounds I will that land be bought with the same within two years next after my decease, to the use of the said William my son, by my overseers and executors. I will and give to Walter Hendley, my cousin, my best gown, my best coat, welted with velvet, my best doublet of "satten." To John Sheff my brother five pounds in two years, &c. To Matthew Cryr my gown faced with grograin and one of my russet coats. To Sir John Baker, Knight, five pounds. To Mr Richard Baker Esq. five pounds.

The residue to my son Thomas Sheff, which Thomas I do ordain and make of this my present Testament my sole executor. (Son William spoken of as under twenty-two years of age.) Then follows the last will, being a disposition of the lands and tenements. To wife a life estate in sundry lands, &c. Son Thomas to have the messuage, lands, and tenements, &c., in Cranebrook, with remuinder to son William, then to the next heirs of son Thomas. To son William my marsh lands in the parish of Ibe* church, in the county of Kent aforesaid, with remainder to Thomas, then to the heirs of William.

Witnesses : George Atkynson, vicar, Richard Courtop, William Cortopp, Henry Allard, Water Henley.

Wrasteley, 34.

RICHARD COURTHOPP of Cosins Bleane in Kent gen^t, 21 October 30, Eliz: proved 12 February, 1588. The poor of Cranebrooke and of Cosinns Bleane, To my mother one hundred pounds. To my brother William Sheafe one hundred pounds, and to my sister the wife of the said William Sheafe one hundred pounds. To my cousin Peter Courthoppe of Canbrooke the elder and to Alexander Courthoppe of Godderds Green in the said parish, to each of them fifty pounds. Fifty pounds each to cousins Richard Courthopp of Buckinghamshire and Richard Courthopp of Dover. My cousin Thomas Lynche the elder, of Staple in Kent gen^t. Certain servants named. The residue to my father in law Mr. Doctor Lawse and to my well beloved cousin Thomas Lynche the elder of Staple whom I constitute and appoint executors.

Commission issued at above date to Henry Lawse of Cosine in the Blean &c. to administer &c. for the reason that Thomas Lawse Doctor of Laws and Thomas Lynche senior, the executors named in the will, expressly renounced.

Leicester, 25.

JOHN ROBERTES (written often in the will Roberdes) of Brenchly in the Diocese of Rochester 16 September 1592, with a Codicil without date annexed, proved 4 March 1593. To the churchwardens of that parish towards the breaking of the ground where my body shall be buried and towards the reparations of the church there forty shillings. To be bestowed at my burial towards the relief of the poor forty shillings. To an honest and godly preacher to preach at my burial ten shillings. To the poor of Brenchly every year for

*This must be Ivychurch, a parish a few miles N. W. of Romney or New Romney, one of the Cinqueports.   H. F. W.

five years after my decease twenty shillings. My godchildren. To my daughter Elizabeth sixscore pounds at age of twenty or day of marriage. My other daughters. To wife Margaret my silver cup which was my father's (and other property). The house where my son George now dwelleth. Sixteen cords of wood to be delivered for my wife every year during her widowhood at the house where my son George now dwelleth. Sundry servants named. To Joane Shefe and Thomas Shefe, my daughter's children, three pounds six shillings eight pence each at their respective ages of eighteen, and to Katharine Sheefe my said daughter's child five pounds at eighteen. To Elizabeth and Agnes Shefe, two more of my daughter's children, forty shillings each at eighteen. My daughter Grynnete's children Sara and Samuel, at eighteen, Daughter Sara wife of John Maundie. The child she goeth withal. Son George to be sole executor and Thomas Shefe of Cranbrooke and his son Richard Shefe to be overseers. Margaret the daughter of my son George. Lands and tenements in Brenchly and Horsmonden. Reference to will of John Downar of Brenchly, deceased. Andrew Davies a witness.

Rochester Wills, Vol. 18 (1591-1605), *L.* 306.

WILLIAM HYDER. An inventory &c. entitled A Note of Lynnen and Woollen apparell with other necessaries and certain Commodities packed up in my Trunks C 1. March 1603. Among the items I have noted Twelve tobacco pipes with a white box—viii^d, Four Burning glasses at xii^d apiece. One leaden pot to put tobacco in i^s, Twenty two Fishing hooks vi^d, One pound of leaf tobacco v^s, One Case of bottles with nine glasses xvii^s, Five pints aqua vitae at xii^d the pint v^s, Five pints of Huscabaugh at xvi^d—vi^{s}viii^d. If it please God that I die in this my intended voyage for the East Indias &c, I would have gold rings of fifteen shillings apiece to be caused to be made for my father and mother in law, my brother Richard Hider and his wife, my sister Sheaf, my brother and sister Hovenden, my cousin William Moodey, John Skynner, Thomas Baker, Richard Roystall, Lambert Beckwith, George Clough, Isaac Allin and my brother John Hider with my cousin Edward and his wife.

Then follows a more formal will wherein he styles himself of London merchant. He refers to Captain Colthurst and makes bequests to surgeon, surgeon's mate, and sailors &c. Signed 19 January 1604.

Commission issued 16 June 1606 to Richard Hider his natural brother to administer &c.   *Stafford, 41.*

(*To be continued.*)

EDMUND LEWIS OF LYNN AND SOME OF HIS DESCENDANTS.

BY GEORGE HARLAN LEWIS OF LOS ANGELES, CAL.

(*Continued from Vol. XLIII, page 256.*)

Children of Jonathan and Lucy:

481. STILLMAN, b. Dec. 20, 1796; m. Nancy Chapin of Waterford, Vt.
482. TRUMAN, b. Jan. 1, 1799; never married.
483. ISAAC, b. June 5, 1801; m. Betsey Chase of Concord, Vt.
484. LUCY, b. Mar. 24, 1803; m. Seth Burroughs of Kirby, Vt.
485. POLLY, b. Jan. 31, 1806; unm.
486. RHODA, b. Feb. 21, 1808; m. Benjamin Nutter of Kirby, Vt.

218 Isaac Lewis, born Feb. 4, 1766, and was brought up in the family of Benjamin Lewis (205), at Milford, N. H. He removed from Roxbury, Vt., to Williamstown, Vt., where he died July 27, 1824. He married, Oct. 14, 1789, Elizabeth Cram, born at Lyndeboro, N. H. Jan. 2, 1764, daughter of David and Mary (Badger) Cram, who died Feb. 26, 1845.

Children of Isaac and Elizabeth, born at Roxbury, Vt.:

487. BETSEY, b. Sept. 27, 1791; d. Dec. 3, 1838; m. James Hatch, b. Apr. 27, 1787; s. of Asa and Roxanna (Delano) Hatch.
488. JONATHAN, b. July 2, 1793; d. June 14, 1870, at Williamstown, Vt.
489. CYNTHIA, b. Apr. 15, 1795; m. Elam Clark.
490. MOSES, b. May 19, 1797.
491. SOPHIA, b. Aug. 10, 1799; m. Sanford Hatch.
492. DAVID CROSBY, b. Aug. 4, 1808.

222 James Lewis, born in Billerica, Mass., Jan. 26, 1761, was a major in the militia. He removed to Groton, May 24, 1796, and was a deputy sheriff from 1809 to 1813. He was a justice of the peace from Feb. 25, 1811, until his death; postmaster at Groton from Sept. 9, 1815, until July 1, 1826, and also appointed postmaster for Pepperell in 1818. He was appointed coroner for life on July 4, 1803. He was a democrat. He bequeathed to

his sons James, Aaron, Levi, Andrew, Frederick A. and
William C., one dollar each ; to his son Merric all the rest
and remainder of both real and personal estate, he to support and maintain his (James) beloved wife Lucy in his
present mansion house.   He was married at Billerica by
Rev. Henry Cummings on Dec. 19, 1782, to Lucy Crosby,
born Nov. 10, 1765, daughter of Hezekiah and Lucy
(Kittredge) Crosby of Billerica.   He died in Groton, Dec.
24, 1828, and his wife followed him six days later.

Children of James and Lucy, six born in Billerica, and
the last two in Groton :

493. JAMES, b. Feb. 1, 1785.
494. AARON, b. Dec. 11, 1786.
495. LEVI, b. Nov. 28, 1788.
496. ANDREW, b. Oct. 19, 1790.
497. LUCY, b. June 15, 1792; d. Dec. 31, 1794.
498. MERRIC, b. July 25, 1795.
499. FREDERICK AUGUSTUS, b. Sept. 10, 1798.
500. WILLIAM CROSBY, b. Sept. 15, 1800, m. 3 times and had son,
      Winslow R., who lives in New Haven, Conn.

226 Seth Lewis, born in Billerica, Mass., Sept. 22,
1766, family record (May 6, 1766, town record). He lived
in Townsend, Mass., and late in life moved to Lunenburg,
where he died June 23, 1833.   He married, Sally Marshall,
who died in Lunenburg, Nov. 17, 1834, aged 67 years.

Children of Seth and Sally Lewis :

501. MARSHALL, b. Oct. 16, 1794.
502. ERI, b. July 29, 1796.
503. SALLY, b. June 24, 1798 ; d. July 11, 1802.
504. ITHRA, b. Jan. 14, 1801.
505. NANCY, b. Feb. 8, 1803; d. Sept. 11, 1825, unm., in Lunenburg.
506. HAMOR, b. Aug. 20, 1805.

243 Asa Shedd Lewis, born in Groton Mass., June
25, 1790.   He was a farmer in Groton until about 1830,
when he removed his family to Weston, Vt., and after
living there several years, moved back to the same place
in Groton where he first lived, and where Asa, Abi and
Reuben died. His will, dated Dec. 4, 1862, was filed Jan.
6, 1863.   He married, first, Elizabeth Marble, born in

Somerset, Mass., April 1, 1794, who died in Groton Aug. 16, 1818. He married, second, Jan. 19, 1820, Mindwell H. Shattuck, b. Feb. 27, 1800, who died in Groton Dec. 31, 1854. She was the daughter of Moses and Abigail (Wood) Shattuck of Pepperell, Mass. He married, third, Harriet P., who survived him.

Children of Asa Shedd and Elizabeth, born in Groton:

507. REUBEN, b. Sept. 13, 1816.
508. ELIZA ANN, b. July 13, 1818; d. in Nashua, N. H., Dec. 29, 1866; m. John Gardner Wright, b. in Dighton, Mass., July 11, 1815, a farmer at Somerset, Swansea and Groton, Mass., and Concord, N. H., where he died. They had 11 children.

244a Samuel Lewis, born Aug. 24, 1779; married Hannah M. Bradley, born June 20, 1782. He lived at Claremont, N. H., Cabot, Vt., and later at Northfield, Vt., where he died Oct. 28, 1846. His widow died at Moretown, Vt., Nov. 21, 1854.

Children of Samuel and Hannah:

509. SILAS, b. April 4, 1810, at Claremont, N. H.
510. CYNTHIA, b. July 31, 1811; m. David Perigo; lived at St. Johnsbury, Vt.
511. ALVIRA, b. Nov. 8, 1812; d. Sept. 29, 1841.
512. FANNY, b. Nov. 6, 1814; m. Ephraim French Bailey; d. April 28, 1856, at Moretown, Vt.
513. SUSAN, b. April 24, 1817; m. Alvin Smith; d. Jan. 25, 1854, at Roxbury, Vt.
514. HANNAH M., b. Aug. 11, 1819; m. Andrew Bailey; d. Jan. 18, 1893, at Cornish, N. H.
515. GEORGE R.   ⎫ All b. June 20, 1821, and d. within four weeks
516. WILLIAM H.   ⎬ after.
517. EMILY B.   ⎭

244b John Lewis, born in Washington, N. H., in 1781. He married, July 27, 1806, Rhoda Baldwin, born in Billerica, Mass., in 1785, and died in Townsend, Mass., Nov. 3, 1860. He lived in Townsend, Mass., and died there on or about Feb. 7, 1866.

Children of John and Rhoda:

518. ANN MARIA, b. Nov. 13, or 15, 1806 (two records); d. Nov. 29, 1806, in Billerica.
519. CHARLES HENRY, b. April 10, 1808.

520. BENJAMIN FRANKLIN, b. Feb. 12, 1810; d. Nov. 7, 1814, in Townsend.

521. ANN MARIA, b. Jan. 23, 1812; d. Nov. 6, 1887, in Shirley, Mass.; m., first, Nov. 29, 1832, Silas Shattuck, b. in Townsend; d. in Shirley, June 1, 1846, son of Silas and Sally (Bailey) Shattuck of Shirley. He lived in Mason, N. H., and Shirley, Mass. She m., 2d, Feb. 27, 1849, Joel Adams. Lived in Shirley. Five children.

522. HARRIET ELIZABETH, b. Feb. 26, 1814; d. Feb. 4, 1894; m. Feb. 6, 1838, Walter Fessenden of Townsend, Mass., b. in Groton, Mass.; d. Jan. 28, 1884; son of Benjamin and Lavinia (Stevens) Fessenden of Townsend. Lived in Townsend. Three children.

523. BENJAMIN FRANKLIN, b. July 26, 1816.

524. SARAH JANE, b. Oct. 18, 1818; m. Nov. 12, 1845, Elijah Tracy, b. in Cornish, N. H., who d. Oct. 31, 1873. They both were deaf mutes. No issue.

525. MARY, b. July 27, 1821; d. July 10, 1825.

526. ALBERT, b. May 11, 1824.

527. MARY AUGUSTA, b. Mar. 23, 1826; d. Feb. 20, 1832.

528. NANCY CATHARINE, b. Oct. 6, 1828; m. Apr. 29, 1849, George Robinson of Townsend, Mass., who d. Dec. 21, 1893. One child.

244c   Isaac Lewis, married Mary, or Polly, Holt, born in Townsend, Mass., Sept. 14, 1786 ; died Sept. 8, 1851. He left his wife and family, and nothing is known of him.

Children of Isaac and Mary:

529. WALTER, was in trade in the West Village of Townsend, Mass.; d. unm.

530. ALEXANDER.

531. JULIA.

247   Asa Lewis, born July 19, 1778, in Groton, Mass., and lived there during his life. He was a wheelwright by occupation, and died June 10, 1846. He married, first, Lucy Fletcher, born April 28, 1777, who died in Groton Sept. 29, 1835, daughter of Lieut. Ezekiel and Bridget (Parker) Fletcher. He married, second, Martha, sister of his first wife, who died Feb. 4, 1856, æ. 70 years.

Children of Asa and Lucy, born in Groton:

532. LUCY, b. Feb. 4, 1803; d. Feb., 1849; m. Levi Burgess of Concord, Mass. Three children.
533. WILLIAM, b. June 18, 1804; m. Jane Bond Wadleigh.
534. HARRIET, b. Apr. 13, 1806; m. Josephus Morton (2d wife).
535. MARY, b. Mar. 25, 1808; m. Josiah Cushman of Kingston, Mass.
536. SARAH, b. June 15, 1810; m. Josephus Morton.
537. ASA, b. Nov. 5, 1812; d. 1863; m. Maria Pollard of Boston; was a book publisher in Boston.
538. LUTHER, b. June 26, 1815; m. Achsah Cole of Belfast, Me.
539. LOUISA, b. Sept. 6, 1818; m. J. Perkins Tyler, or Taylor, of Woburn, Mass.
540. BENJAMIN, b. Mar. 16, 1820; m. Lucy Horton in 1846; lived at Worcester, Mass.

251 Henry Lewis, born in Groton, Mass., July 5, 1788, and died June 18, 1832. He was a truckman, and lived in Boston. He married, June 16, 1811, Hannah S. Allen, born March 20, 1793, and died Oct. 3, 1835, daughter of Samuel and Martha (Trask) Allen.

Children of Henry and Hannah S., born in Boston:

541. GEORGE HENRY, b. Dec. 16, 1811; died in U. S. naval service during the civil war.
542. EDWARD, b. July 14, 1813; was in the U. S. naval service during the civil war, and never heard from.
543. MARTHA ANN, b. Aug. 5, 1815; d. Feb. 8, 1897; m. William Hall; lived in Boston. Five children.
544. LORENZO TURNER, b. Feb. 7, 1817.
545. BERNARD (M.), b. March 12, 1819.
546. LOTHROP, b. Aug. 19, 1822; d. June 7, 1841, unm., in New York.
547. JOHN WILLIAM, b. Mar., 1825; d. 1852, at sea.
548. MARY ANN, b. June 9, 1828; m. in Boston, Aug. 31, 1851, John Briard Brimblecom, b. in Marblehead Aug. 16, 1828, son of Nathaniel and Elizabeth (Briard) Brimblecom. Four children.
549. WILLIAM HENRY, b. Aug. 5, 1830.

252 Ebenezer Lewis, born in Groton, July 25, 1790, was a blacksmith, and lived in Boston until 1819, when he removed to Windham, N. H., and was employed in the blacksmith shop at the mills. In 1828 he built a house in the centre of the town, in which he lived until

his death, Nov. 12, 1869. He formed a partnership with
Silas Dinsmore, and carried on blacksmithing in a shop
which stood where the Presbyterian church now is. He
married, Oct. 13, 1812, Mary, daughter of Jonathan Hamblett of Dracut, Mass. She was born Feb. 3, 1791, and
died Feb. 10, 1875.

Children of Ebenezer and Mary, three born in Boston,
Mass., five born in Windham, N. H.:

550. JULIA ANN, b. Mar. 7, 1813 (Bible record); d. Oct. 31, 1897; m.
Stephen Brown; lived at Barnstead, N. H. Two children.
551. EBEN AUGUSTUS, b. April 3, 1815.
552. ANDREW, b. June 1, 1817.
553. MARY E., b. Oct. 9, 1819; d. May 3, 1855; m. John Hartwell
Tower of Saxonville, Mass. Three children.
554. JOHN B., b. Mar. 2, 1821; m. Catherine ——; lives at South
Bangor, Franklin Co., N. Y.
555. CHARLES, b. Sept. 2, 1828; m. 1st, Ellen E. Taylor; m. 2d,
Oct. 19, 1881, Mary A. (Estes) Gloyd, dau. of D. and Maria
Estes of Lynn.
556. CORNELIUS COOLIDGE, b. Mar. 2, 1831; m. Sept. 14, 1859, Cor-
delia M. Studley. No issue.
557. LUCINDA F., b. Sept. 29, 1833; m. John G. Bradford, b. in Pel-
ham, N. H., Jan. 8, 1830. They reside in the old homestead
of her father, in Windham, N. H.

254 Luther Lewis, born in Groton, Mass., Nov. 12,
1795; lived in Groton, Charlestown and Boston, where he
died Oct. 27, 1842. He married in Boston, May 20, 1824,
Susanna Wallis Curtis, born in Charlestown, Aug. 7, 1807,
and died there June 9, 1844, daughter of Lebbeus and
Susanna Wallis (Frothingham) Curtis.

Children of Luther and Susanna W. born in Boston:

558. SUSAN, b. Dec. 21, 1825; d. Mar. 21, 1901, in Chelsea, m. at
Ashburnham, Mass., April 1850, Walter Searle of Chelsea,
4 children.
559. CHARLES BENJAMIN, b. Aug. 13, 1827.
560. HENRY FROTHINGHAM, b. Oct. 21, 1829.
561. LUTHER, b. Nov. 2, 1832.
562. Frederick Thomas, b. Nov. 2, 1839.
563. William Henry Huggaford, d. young.

258 Robert Lewis, born in Lynn, April 8, 1774 or 1775 (recorded in both years), and died Dec. 28, 1854 æ: 79 y. 8 m. 24 d. His will made Dec. 27, 1854 gives to wife Hannah all estate of every description wherever, after her decease; to go to his children, Sally Rich: Mary Stone: Robert: Abigail Fowler: Asa: Benjamin H: Otis: Warren: Jacob M. and to his wife's daughter Hannah, wife of Nathaniel Boynton.

He married, first, Aug. 13, 1797, Abigail Phillips, probably the daughter of William and Sarah (Bartlett) Phillips of Marblehead, who died Aug. 23, 1810. He married, second, Mar. 31, 1812 Hannah, widow of Benjamin Humphreys who was lost at sea in 1802. She was born in Marblehead, Mar. 16, 1778, and was the daughter of Benjamin and Jemima (Gale) Humphreys of Marblehead. She died Feb. 12, 1855. All the sons worked at shoemaking in winter and went fishing in the summer.

Children of Robert and Abigail, born in Lynn:

564. SALLY, b. Mar. 29, 1797; d. Dec. 4, 1872; m. in Lynn Aug. 4, 1816, Stephen Rich, b. in Berlin, Mass., Jan. 4, 1792; d. in Lynn, Mar. 23, 1870, son of James and Hannah (Baker) Rich of Nantucket. He was a shoemaker and grocer in Lynn, and had born in Lynn: (1) Abigail Phillips, b. Nov. 30, 1816; m. Oct. 5, 1836, Edwin Breed. (2) Mary Etta, b. Apr. 6, 1819, d. young. (3) William Allen, b. Oct. 26, 1821; m. Caroline G. Stone. (4) Sally Maria, b. Sept. 15, 1823; m. 1st Dunshuttle; m. 2d George Arrington. (5) Martha Ellen, b. Sept. 15, 1823; m. John Hamilton Brown. (6) Stephen Sumner, b. July 7, 1826. (7) Elbridge Everett, b. May 25, 1832. (8) Eliza Jane, b. Jan. 13, 1834; m. Henry M. Batchelder. (9) Otis, b. Oct. 24, 1838; d. June 30, 1856.

565. MARY, b. 1801; d. in infancy.

566. MARY HODGES, b. Dec. 3, 1804; d. June 4, 1878, m. in Lynn, Oct. 1, 1820, Williams Stone, b. Apr. 26, 1796, d. in Lynn, Feb. 28, 1865, son of Caleb and Anna (Williams) Stone of Lynn. He was a wholesale fish dealer. His father Caleb Stone was a Frenchman who came ashore at Nahant on a bunch of sea weed from a whaling vessel that was wrecked off Nahant. Children born in Lynn: (1) Emeline, b. Apr. 4, 1821. (2) William, b. Apr. 10, 1823. (3) Mary Abigail, b. July 26, 1826. (4) Anna Williams, b. Feb. 5, 1829. (5) Harriet Ellen, b. 1836. (6) Lucinda Priscilla.

567. WILLIAM, b. Mar. 25, 1806; removed to Cape Cod, and when about to be married he went to Boston to buy furniture. He reached there and nothing was ever heard of him after. A case of mysterious disappearance.

568. ROBERT, b. June 16, 1808.

569. ABIGAIL, b. Aug. 6, 1810 (Nabby in Lynn Record), d. Oct. 13, 1873, m. in Lynn, Dec. 10, 1826, Samuel Fowler Jr. b. in Lynn Apr. 19, 1803, d. there Dec. 28, 1887, son of Samuel and Elizabeth (?) Fowler of Lynn. He was a shoemaker and lived in what is now Swampscott. Children born in Lynn: (1) William, b. June 2, 1827. (2) Elizabeth, d. in Salem. (3) Ann Boynton, b. Aug. 21, 1836; d. July 1878; m. I. A. Trask (gs). (4) Rebecca Newhall, b. May 21, 1840; d. Feb. 17, 1883 (gs); m. James P. M. S. Pitman. (5) Robert Lewis, b. Jan. 17, 1843.

Children of Robert and Hannah, born in Lynn:

570. ASA, b. May 28, 1814.

571. BENJAMIN HUMPHREYS, b. Sept. 18, 1816.

572. OTIS, b. Oct. 2, 1818.

573. WARREN, b. Dec. 8, 1820.

574. JACOB MEEK, b. Oct. 13, 1823; d. Jan. 4, 1905; m. Oct. 13, 1845, Roxanna Wilkins Stone, b. in Lynn Jan. 12, 1826, and d. Aug. 14, 1905, daughter of Joshua and Sally Stone. No issue. They celebrated their golden wedding in 1895. He was engaged in shoemaking, fishing, a grocer, a shoe manufacturer for 25 years, and his last years in the real estate and insurance business. He was elected to public office more times than any other man in Lynn. He was a member of the Water Board for eight years; Common Council in 1852-3, Alderman for 9 terms in succession from 1859 to 1871, and Mayor of Lynn from 1873 to 1887. He was of great influence in conducting negotiations in the settlement of the great strike in 1860, and he was founder and organizer of the Lynn Mutual Aid Association. He was one of the oldest and most respected citizens at the time of his death. He was greatly interested in the genealogy of his family and while Mayor he examined all the records of the city. From what he gathered and knew personally and his brother Warren, now living, has confirmed, I have obtained much that is given in this publication. He was a genial, whole-souled gentlemen of quiet thoughtful habits, his tendencies always being apart from a love of display.

260 John Lewis, called 3rd, born in Lynn Feb. 13-15, 1779 : married June 13, 1799, in Lynn, Martha Porter, b. Oct. 15, 1779 at Salem and died in Lynn Sept. 30, 1814, daughter of Thomas and Martha Porter of Salem. He died in 1805 and his widow married again.

Children of John and Martha, born in Lynn :

575.   HENRY, b. Oct. 10, 1799.
576.   JOHN, b. Oct. 9, 1802.
577.   ROBERT, b. Mar. 15, 1805: d. ae. 5 or 6 years.

261 Blaney Lewis, born in Lynn Oct. 7, 1780, was a cordwainer, and lived in Lynn. He married in Lynn Nov. 13, 1800 Elizabeth Humphrey of Marblehead, and died July 8, 1821. His widow died Jan. 7, 1828.

Children of Blaney and Elizabeth, born in Lynn :

578.   MARY, b. Jan. 14, 1801; d. 1868; m. in Lynn John Gibson, b. May 1800, and d. Oct. 5, 1862 (gs). Children: (1) James, b. July 27, 1820, moved to Reading. (2) Joseph, b. Nov. 26, 1822, d. Oct. 1826. (3) Martha Lavinia, b. Apr. 5, 1825. (4) Mary Elizabeth, b. Nov. 21, 1827. (5) Caroline Augusta, b. Jan. 19, 1830, m. Dow. (6) John. (7) Sarah, m. S. Heatley.
579.   MARTHA, b. Oct. 14, 1802; m. in Lynn Apr. 3, 1823, Hiram Williams, a carpenter. Children born in Lynn. (1) Mary Jane, b. Dec. 20, 1823. (2) Sarah Ann, b. Jan. 22, 1826. (3) Sidney Ingalls, b. Nov. 27, 1827, d. Aug. 12, 1848. (4) Rebecca Maria, b. Sept. 3, 1834. (5) Blaney. (6)Adaline (twin). (7) Blaney (twin).
580.   BLANEY, b. Aug. 15, 1804; m. and removed to Cape Cod.
581.   LEVINA, b. Mar. 7, 1807; m. Oct. 12, 1823 in Lynn, Joseph Batcheller.
582.   BETSEY, b. June 30, 1809; d. Apr. 18, 1810.
583.   RUTH, b. July 2, 1811; d. Dec. 20, 1812.
584.   ELIZABETH, b. Dec. 8, 1813; d. Dec. 30, 1846; m. Aug. 19, 1832; Henry Washington Alley. Children born in Lynn. (1) John H. (2) William. (3) Mary Adelaide, b. Mar. 28, 1841, d. Aug. 13, 1842. (4) Blaney Otis, b. June 11, 1844; d. Sept. 18, 1844. (gs)
585.   REBECCA MATILDA, b. Dec. 10, 1816; m. Mar. 5, 1834, in Lynn, John J. Foster, d. June 2, 1852 (ae. 38 years gs), from Salem. Children born in Lynn: (1) Lydia Ellen, b. Apr. 28, 1836. (2) John Henry, b. Apr. 30, 1839. (3) Joseph Franklin, b. Aug. 31, 1841. (4) James Marsh, b. Sept. 19, 1843. (5) Phebe Ann Elizabeth, b. Oct. 23, 1847.

586. ALFRED, b. abt. 1820; d. Apr. 7, 1892 (ae. 72 y. Lynn Rec.); m.
in Lynn, June 6, 1850 Lydia Maria, daughter of Allen Smith
Rich of Lynn, and had a daughter Dora B.

263   Nathaniel Lewis, called Nathan, born in Lynn
Jan. 22, 1783, was a cordwainer and lived in Lynn
where he died in 1832. His widow was appointed administratrix of his estate July 3, 1833, and on Aug. 20, was
allowed $150 for care of two small children. He married
first, in Lynn Nabby Floyd, born in Lynn Feb. 10, 1789
and died Oct. 9, 1828, daughter of Hugh and Abigail
Floyd of Lynn. He married, second, in Lynn (published
Nov. 15, 1829) Elizabeth Curtin.

Children of Nathaniel and Nabby, born in Lynn:

587. ELBRIDGE GERRY, b. Aug. 10, 1807.
588. LEONARD, b. Dec. 7, 1810.
589. BICKFORD, b. June 10, 1813.
590. ADLINE, b. Nov. 28, 1815; d. June 1, 1886; m. Nov. 13, 1834,
Amos E. Mower, b. Aug. 30, 1810, d. Apr. 4, 1880, son of
John jr. and Sarah Mower of Lynn. Children born in Lynn;
(1) Maria, m. —— Mellen. (2) James E. B. (3) Charles F.
b. July 10, 1845. (4) Earl A. b. Oct. 11, 1846, m. Emmeline
Page.
591. AARON LUMMUS, b. July 16, 1818.
592. MARIA, b. Sept. 20, 1820, m. in Lynn, June 13, 1841, James
Chase, b. in Weare, N. H., Mar. 17, 1819, and d. in Lynn
Oct. 14, 1889, son of John Chase of Weare, N. H. Children
born in Lynn. (1) Charles E. b. Oct. 20, 1842. (2) Addie, b.
Nov. 25, 1847.

264   Henry Lewis, born in Lynn, Jan. 20, 1785 ;
was a shoemaker and lived in Lynn. He married, first,
in Lynn, Nov. 15, 1807, Huldah Ingalls, born in Lynn,
July 25, 1788, who died there Sept. 19, 1813, daughter
of Edmund and Huldah (Batcheler) Ingalls of Lynn. He
married, second, in Lynn, June 29, 1817, Eunice Foster,
born in Groveland, Jan. 2, 1791, who died May 17, 1884,
at the great age of 93 y., 4 m., 15 dys., daughter of Reynolds and Elizabeth Foster.

Children of Henry and Huldah, born in Lynn:

593. HARRIET, b. Jan. 28, 1808; m. in Lynn, June 6, 1844, Blaney
Graves, b. Jan. 27, 1811; son of Mark and —— Graves;
no issue.

594. HENRY, b. Sept. 26, 1809. Went to California in 1849; remained until a short time before his death, when he returned to Lynn and died unm. on July 30, 1875.

Children of Henry and Eunice, born in Lynn:

595. GEORGE WASHINGTON, b. Apr. 12, 1818.

596. HULDAH, b. Oct. 15, 1819; m. in Lynn, June 1, 1843, Benjamin Lovett of Beverly. Children: (1) Ellen; (2) Lewis; (3) William H.; (4) Frank E.; (5) Israel; (6) Martha F.

597. EUNICE ELLEN, b. Oct. 3, 1821; m. in Lynn, June 18, 1851, C. Warren Johnson, b. June 2, 1323, son of Caleb Johnson of Lynn.

598. ELIZABETH CONANT, b. Jan. 1, 1823; m. in Lynn, Nov. 5, 1850, Charles H. Gamage, b. in Bristol, Me., in 1822; son of Joseph Gamage.

599. IVERS FOSTER, b. May 3, 1826.

600. AROLINE AUGUSTA, b. Nov. 28, 1828; d. Nov. 25, 1885.

601. ABBY JANE, b. July 31, 1831; d. —— 1890; m. in Lynn, Feb. 18, 1857, Augustus A. Oliver, b. in Malden, in 1832; son of Henry Oliver. Children: (1) Anna; (2) Grace; (3) Fred.

268 Amos Lewis, born in Lynn Oct. 17, 1794; was a shoemaker in Lynn, where he died May 20, 1869. He married in Marblehead, Nov. 22, 1819, Ruth Brown, born in Danvers and died in Lynn May 4, 1867, aged 75 y., 21 days, daughter of Ebenezer (of Reading) and Ruth (of Marblehead) Brown.

Children of Amos and Ruth, born in Lynn :

602. AMOS NELSON, b. Dec. 23, 1820; d. in Lynn, Oct. 25, 1868; m. Apr. 22, 1842, Ruth M. Barker of Marblehead; no issue.

603. BETSEY PREBLE, b. Mar. 28, 1823; m. in Lynn, May 31, 1842, Enos Hoyt Gordon, b. in Henniker, N. H. Children b. in Lynn: (1) Adrian Frank, b. April 10, 1845; (2) Charles Edwin Lewis; (3) Mary Eliza; (4) William Hoyt; (5) Abby Isabel.

604. ABIGAIL FIELDING, b. July 30, 1824 ; m. in Lynn, Sept. 27, 1846, Joseph H. Valpey. Lived in Detroit, Mich. Children: (1) Eliza Ellen, b. in Lynn, Aug. 9, 1847; (2) Abba Frances, b. Sept. 13, 1849; (3) Lewis Nelson, b. July 6, 1854; (4) Celia Louise, b. Dec. 7, 1858.

605. CHARLES EDWIN.

606. SARAH PREBLE, b. 1842; d. Oct. 13, 1848.

269 George Lewis, born in Lynn, May 31, 1800, was a stone mason and lived in Lynn, where he died intestate, May 12, 1880. He married in Lynn, Jan. 19, 1826, Mary Felton of Marblehead, born May 20, 1801, and died in Lynn Nov. 25, 1885, daughter of Joseph and Mary Felton of Marblehead.

Child of George and Mary, born in Lynn:

607. MARY JANE, b. July 14, 1826; pub. in Lynn, Nov. 26, 1848, with John H. Bradshaw, b. Oct. 12, 1823, and d. Nov. 9, 1859. Children: (1) Edward Cook; (2) George Lewis; (3) Margaret S.; (4) Caroline.

275 Benjamin Lewis, born in Lynn, Nov. 3, 1796, and died there Oct. 18, 1868. He married in Lynn, Oct. 7, 1819, Betsey Farrow, born in Bristol, Me., Sept. 15, 1799 (gs), and died May 5, 1877, daughter of John and Betsey Farrow.

Children of Benjamin and Betsey, born in Lynn:

608. LYDIA, b. Feb. 7, 1822; m. in Lynn, July 8, 1841, John Richards Parrott, b. in Lynn, Dec. 25, 1818; son of Nathaniel and Catherine Parrott of Lynn. (Mrs. Catherine Parrott became the third wife of Joseph Lewis, No. 281.)
609. BENJAMIN WILSON, b. April 12, 1824; d. May 12, 1824.
610. MARTHA, b. Jan. 29, 1826; d. in infancy.
611. FRANCES ELLEN, b. 1828; m. Apr. 19, 1853, Lemuel Lord, b. Apr. 29, 1826; son of Brackett Lord of Lynn.
612. MARTHA ELIZABETH, b. Aug. 16, 1830; d. Dec. 30, 1849.
613. NATHAN, b. Aug. 16, 1830; d. Sept. 25, 1832.
614. JAMES WARREN, b. Oct. 15, 1833; m. 1st, in Lynn, July 25, 1858, Lydia O. Salter, b. in Sullivan, Me., dau. of William and Hannah Salter. He m. 2d, in Lynn, Nov. 14, 1865, Annie Mackintosh, b. in New Brunswick.
615. RUTH ANN, b. 1836; m. in Lynn, Jan. 1, 1857, Algernon S. Fisher, son of Moses S. Fisher.
616. BENJAMIN ADDISON, b. 1838; m. in Lynn, April 21, 1861, Susan M. Kendrick, b. at South Orleans, daughter of Zebedee and Augusta (Small) Kendrick.
617. CATHERINE AUGUSTA, b. Mar. 22, 1840; m. in Lynn, Aug. 1, 1867. Richard J. Nichols, b. June 15, 1839, son of Nathan and Harriet H. Nichols of Lynn.

279 John Richards Lewis, born in Lynn, June 20, 1804, and died there Feby. 17, 1843. He lived in Lynn and was a teamster. He married in Lynn, May 22, 1825, Martha G. Knapp, born in Marblehead, May 14, 1804, and died in Lynn, Feb. 17, 1889, daughter of Samuel and Grace Knapp of Marblehead.

Children of John Richards and Martha G., born in Lynn:

618. SAMUEL AUGUSTUS, b. Nov. 15, 1825.
619. CLARISSA ANN, b. Jan. 5, 1829; d. Feb. 12, 1843.
620. JOHN WESLEY, b. May 20, 1830.
621. RICHARD EVERETT, b. Sept., 1835; d. June 18, 1852.
622. HANNAH R., b. July 21, 1838; d. Aug. 20, 1864.
623. MARGARETT ANN, b. Feb. 17, 1843; the same day her father died. She m. Mar. 9, 1872, Edward Henry Knight, b. in Salem, son of William and Lydia Knight.

281 Joseph Lewis, born in Lynn, Oct. 6, 1790, was brought up by his uncle Benjamin (144), whom his mother married, and was often called his son. He married, first, in Lynn, Oct. 10, 1813, Rebecca Lummus. He married, second, in Lynn, Dec. 23, 1819, Fanny Ashbee. He married, third, in Lynn, Dec. 25, 1831, Mrs. Catherine Parrott, widow of Nathaniel Parrott (see No. 608).

Children of Joseph and Rebecca, born in Lynn:

624. ELIZA ANN, b. Jan. 9, 1814; m. Feb. 26, 1835, George W. Watts, b. Apr. 12, 1809, son of Daniel and Betsey Watts of Lynn.
625. SALLY JANE, b. Sept. 15, 1817.

Children of Joseph and Fanny, born in Lynn:

626. CAROLINE AUGUSTA, b. Aug. 16, 1825.
627. JOSEPH WARREN, b. Nov. 22, 1827.
628. JOSEPH WARREN, b. June 23, 1828; d. Apr. 19, 1829.

283 Benjamin Richard Lewis, born in Lynn, May 26, 1793; removed to Northampton, Mass., and later to Westfield, Mass., where he died Mar. 31, 1868. He married in Lynn, Oct. 29, 1815, Hannah, daughter of Samuel and Grace (Guiller) Knapp of Marblehead. Grace Guiller was a friend and playmate of General Lafayette, who, on his last visit to this country in 1824, went to Marblehead to call upon her. At this interview Hannah and her son were present. She died at Westfield, Mar. 14, 1869.

Children of Benjamin R. and Hannah, first 3 born in Lynn, rest in Northampton :

629. HANNAH KNAPP, b. Aug. 26, 1816; m. at Northampton, Jan. 23, 1839, Addison Bryant, son of Ashael and Eunice Bryant of Chesterfield, Mass. Lives in Janesville, Wis. Children: (1) Helen, b. Dec. 18, 1839, in Montague, Mass.; m. Nov. 24, 1863, Lewis B. Lathrop of Lockport, N. Y., in Chicago, Ill.; (2) Frances, b. Dec. 8, 1841, in Westfield; (3) Addison Lewis, b. Aug. 5, 1848, in Westfield; (4) Willis C., b. June 5, 1852, in Great Bend, Pa.; d. in Westfield.

630. BENJAMIN FRANKLIN, b. Oct. 22, 1820.

631. ALBION WESLEY, b. Aug. 4, 1823; d. Oct. 12, 1826, in Lynn.

632. ALBION WESLEY, b. May 8, 1828.

633. MARTHA ELLEN, b. May 8, 1828; d. in infancy.

634. MARTHA ELLEN, b. Nov. 28, 1830; d. Apr. 1, 1835, at Northampton.

635. MARY GRACE, b. June 8, 1834; m. Charles Henry Stebbins, son of Edy and Rebecca (Wetherbee) Stebbins of Westfield, Mass. She died at Northampton, Mar. 30, 1907.

636. EDWARD TALBOTT, b. July 25, 1837; unm.; lives in Milwaukee, Wis.

287 Thomas Lewis, born in Lynn, Jan. 7, 1801, was a cordwainer and lived in Lynn, where he died Jan. 25, 1839. He married, first, in Lynn, July 6, 1819, Mary Harris of Marblehead, born in 1800 and died in Lynn, Jan. 20, 1829. He married, second, Oct. 18, 1829, Nancy Briant.

Children of Thomas and Mary, born in Lynn :

637. ELIZABETH ANN, b. Nov. 17, 1819; m. in Lynn, Jan. 28, 1841, John B. Twisden, b. Nov. 3, 1816; d. Apr. 13, 1886; son of Samuel Twisden. Children: (1) Mary Elizabeth, b. Feb. 14, 1842; d. Nov. 24, 1844; (2) Sarah Jane, b. Aug. 24, 1845; (3) Nancy Ellen, b. Mar. 20, 1848; (4) John Henry, b. May 27, 1854; d. May 29, 1894.

638. BURRILL TURNER, b. Sept. 19, 1825.

639. THOMAS HARRIS, b. Jan. 6, 1829.

Children of Thomas and Nancy, born in Lynn:

640. CHARLES WARREN, b. Nov. 28, 1832.

641. MARY ELLEN, b. May 10, 1835; m. 1st, Nov. 19, 1856, Charles A. Johnson, b. in Lynn, Dec. 17, 1833; d. Jan. 10, 1884; son of Jacob I. and Mary Johnson. She m. 2d, Dec. 15, 1886, Eben H. Downing, b. in Lynn, Aug. 14, 1839, son of Eben P. and Sarah Downing of Lynn.

288 Richard Lewis, born in Lynn, Nov. 6, 1802, was a shoemaker and lived on Summer St., Malden, Mass., during his married life and died there Jan. 18, 1878. He married, Nov. 16, 1825, Hannah Farnham, born in Andover, Mass., Sept. 30, 1804, who died at Malden, May 25, 1886, daughter of Timothy and Sarah (Berry) Farnham of Andover, Mass. In 1832 they adopted a daughter of her brother, Lydia Ann Farnham, born Aug. 28, 1830, and died Nov. 30, 1855, who married July 20, 1850, William Coffin Peabody and had two children: (1) Elizabeth Frances; (2) George. All are now dead.

Child of Richard and Hannah, born in Malden:

642. HENRIETTA FARNHAM, b. Sept. 8, 1840; m. May 3, 1871, James Scales, b. Aug. 8, 1830, in Rotherhithe, London, Eng.; son of James Boughton and Caroline Maria (Bisley) Scales. Child: (1) Josie Gertrude, b. Sept. 5, 1872; m. Nov. 12, 1894, Henry Austin Dunshee. Live on the homestead of Richard in Malden, Mass.

294 Stephen Lewis, born in Lynn, Jan. 4, 1794, was a silk dyer and finisher, employed at the Malden Dye House for many years, and later moved to Lynn, where he died Mar. 10, 1855. He married at Malden, April 8, 1821, Dolly Wood, born in Bradford, Mass., Apr. 28, 1793, who died April 26, 1861, daughter of Lieut. Thomas and Dolly (Carleton) Wood of Bradford.

Children of Stephen and Dolly, first 3 born in Malden, last in Lynn:

643. GEORGE, b. Apr. 7, 1823; d. Sept. 9, 1848; unm.
644. JANE, b. Oct. 2, 1825; m. at Woburn, Mass., Nov. 16, 1848, Henry Symonds, b. Jan. 17, 1819; d. Jan. 27, 1873; son of Zebadee and Amittia (Webber) Symonds, of Lincoln, Mass. Children: (1) Clara Josephine, b. Nov. 2, 1849; m. May 8, 1872, Dwight M. Clapp, b. June 5, 1846, son of Moses and Almira (Russell) Clapp of Southampton, Mass.; (2) Emma Frances, b. July 30, 1852; m. Charles B. Dennis, son of Willard and Hannah Dennis of Fitchburg, Mass.
645. ALMIRA, b. Oct. 1, 1829; m. —— Heath.
646. CHARLES WINSLOW, b. Jan. 7, 1832. His birth record and his father's will call him Winslow. In the record of his marriage he is Charles Winslow and in the record of his death he is Charles W., a soldier.

302 Nathaniel Lewis, born in Lynn, Feb. 28, 1799, is called junior in the birth records of his children, his father being then alive.

No. 147. Nathaniel, born in 1768, married Rebecca (Richards) and died Jan. 24, 1824, and had a son Nathaniel (286), born (May 29), 1799, who d. Dec. 30, 1822.

No. 150. Nathaniel, also born in 1768, was called junior, also married a Rebecca (Clark) and had a son Nathaniel (302), also born in 1799. (Feb. 28.) This continued similarity in names and births has led to confusion and the descent has been carefully investigated. This explanation is made to correct an error made by Alonzo Lewis in Lynn Records—where he copied them, and it is verified by Ex-Mayor Jacob M. Lewis, who knew the families.

He was a shoemaker and lived in Lynn. He married, first, Nov. 11, 1824, Abigail A. Perkins, who died Nov. 28, 1829. He married, second, Sept. 16, 1830, his first wife's sister, Louise Perkins. They were daughters of Jonathan and Margaret Perkins. He died Nov. 2, 1867.

Children of Nathaniel and Abigail, born in Lynn:

647. ALLEN WEBSTER, b. June 17, 1825.
648. JOHN CONWAY, b. Nov. 28, 1827.

Children of Nathaniel and Louisa, born in Lynn:

649. MARY ABIGAIL, b. Oct. 9, 1831; d. young.
650. WILLIAM PRESCOTT, b. Aug. 17, 1833; d. May 9, 1860.
651. EMELINE AUGUSTA, b. Oct. 24, 1835; m. Aug. 27, 1856, in Lynn, Francis Henry Broad.
652. ADELAIDE V., b. ——; m. Joseph Parsons at Northwood; d. in Lynn.
653. LAURA E., b. ——, 1843; m. in Lynn, Jan. 13, 1863, Henry Merrill, son of Samuel B. and Lucretia Merrill.
654. CHESTER PERCIVAL, b. Nov. 18, 1844; was in Co. M, First Heavy Artillery and taken a prisoner and died at Florence, S. C.
655. CLARA JANE, b. Jan. 28, 1847; m. in Salem.
656. HORACE PECK, b. Feb. 28, 1850; m. 2d, July 29, 1889, Annie B. Swainamer, in Lynn.
657. OLIVER PERRY, b. April 9, 1852; m. and d. in Northboro, N. H.

307 Joseph Lewis, born in Lynn, Mar. 21, 1796, was a teamster and fish dealer. He lived in Lynn and was called "junior," No. 281 being "senior." He died in Lynn, Sept. 14, 1873. He married, first, Dec. 11, 1823, Lydia R. Lewis (276), born April 9, 1798, who died Nov. 29, 1828. He married, second, Sept. 30, 1830, Lydia Goldsmith, born Feb. 12, 1798, who died May 1, 1848, daughter of Joseph and Lydia (Ireson) Goldsmith of Lynn. He married, third, in Lynn, Jan. 1, 1857, widow Irene Hastings, aged 50 years, born in Uniontown, Me., daughter of Thomas Jones, who survived him.

Children of Joseph and Lydia R., born in Lynn:

658. JOSEPH WARREN, b. Feb. 28, 1824; d. young.
659. EVERETT EUSTIS, b. Dec. 23, 1824; d. Oct. 28, 1853; m. July 28, 1847, Jane B. Hammond, dau. of John and Hannah Hammond.
660. LYDIA MARIA, b. May 18, 1826.
661. ELIZABETH ANN, b. Nov. 4, 1828; m. in Lynn, Nov. 15, 1849, Benjamin Spear, son of William Henry Spear of Boston.

Children of Joseph and Lydia, born in Lynn:

662. HARRIET, b. Feb. 19, 1832; m. July 3, 1851, Robinson L. Weeks, son of Ninphus Weeks.
663. JOSEPH WARREN, b. Oct. 3, 1834; d. Aug. 10, 1852.

311 Jonathan Blaney Lewis, born in Lynn, Nov. 22, 1799, recorded as Blaney and recorded as Jonathan Blaney in deed of his father's heirs (Essex Co. Deeds, v. 261, f. 212), Oct. 8, 1831. He married, Nov. 13, 1823, Abigail A. Marshall, born in Salem in 1805; died in Lynn, Oct. 29, 1882. He died Oct. 17, 1876.

Children of Jonathan Blaney and Abigail A.:

664. EDWARD, b. Feb. 2, 1825; d. Oct. 26, 1856.
665. CHANDLER, b. July 26, 1827; moved to Rockport, Me.
666. ANGELINA, b. Feb. 11, 1834; d. Oct. 19, 1850.
667. WARREN A., b. ——, 1838; d. Sept. 6, 1882, of a fractured spine, æ. 44 yrs.

313 Joseph Felt Lewis, born in Lynn, Sept. 2, 1804, was a fish dealer and was found drowned on the Chelsea marshes on Dec. 10, 1872. He married in Lynn,

Oct. 27, 1834, Almira Davis, who died March 23, 1857, æ. 52 years.

Children of Joseph Felt and Almira :

668. JOHN EDWIN, b. Oct. 14, 1835; d. Oct. 9, 1836.
669. JOSEPH EDWIN, b. Feb. 11, 1838.
670. MARY EMILY, b. Aug. 22, 1840; d. July 27, 1842.
671. EMILY ADELAIDE, b. Jan. 2, 1846; m. in Lynn, May 22, 1864, Gustavus Hall of Lynn.

318   James Lewis, born in Lynn, Feb. 11, 1802, was a shoemaker and lived in Lynn where he died Oct. 25, 1877. He married, first, in Lynn Oct. 13, 1825, Malinda Short, born in West Newbury, May 3, 1804, who died Dec. 7, 1842. He married, second, Martha Stone of Marblehead, who was born Jan. 2, 1816 and died Mar. 26, 1897, daughter of Benjamin and Hannah Stone.

Children of James and Malinda, born in Lynn :

672. THEODORE AUGUSTUS, b. Feb. 9, 1827.
673. JAMES HERMON, b. Feb. 13, 1831; d. May 17, 1896: m. 1st, Jane Burrill, b. in Lynn; m. 2d, May 19, 1881, Fanny Brown at Hamilton; m. 3d, widow Mary (Raymond) Ellis, b. in Danvers, dau. of Robbins and Elizabeth Raymond. No issue.
674. WILLIAM, b. Jan. 25, 1835; d. July 28, 1856; unm.

Children of James and Martha, born in Lynn :

675. BENJAMIN FULLER, b. Oct. 12, 1845; m. 1st, at Plymouth, Mass., Apr. 24, 1871, Sarah Elizabeth Pierce, b. in Plymouth, Dec. 27, 1849, and d. Sept. 14, 1893, dau. of Benj. and Lydia Pierce. Children: (1) Frank Burton, b. in Lynn, May 30, 1875, d. June 26, 1898. He m. 2d, Apr. 19, 1897, widow Mary (Hodge) Healey, b. Sept. 12, 1858, dau. of Freeman O. and Olive Hodge.

326   Thomas Vickary Lewis, born in Lynn, Sept. 3, 1820, and died Mar. 25, 1899. He married in Lynn, Oct. 2, 1842, Lydia Maria Ireson, born in Lynn, Feb. 20, 1823, daughter of Benjamin and Martha (Putnam) Ireson of Lynn. His widow survives him.

Children of Thomas Vickary and Lydia Maria, born in Lynn :

676. MARTHA ELLEN, b. Oct. 31, 1846; d. Apr. 13, 1849.
677. ANNIE MARIA, b. Sept. 10, 1854.
678. THOMAS HERBERT, b. Apr. 12, 1861; d. Apr. 5, 1887.

341 Thomas Lewis,* born in Boston, May 24, 1808, removed from Boston, Sept. 21, 1829 and located himself as a merchant and general storekeeper at Shelbyville, Ill., where he died April 28, 1838. He married in 1833, near Vincennes, Ind., Jane Armstrong, born in Kentucky, Nov. 7, 1812, daughter of William and Mary Armstrong. After his death she married, second, Dr. William Keller of Shelbyville. They moved to Sullivan, Ill., in 1844, where she died July 18, 1855, of cholera as did her husband three days after.

Children of Thomas and Jane:

679. THOMAS, b. and d. in infancy.
680. THOMAS, b. and d. in infancy.
681. THOMAS, b. Feb. 20, 1837 in Shelbyville, Ill.

344 Abiel Smith Lewis, born in Boston, July 15, 1814. He and his brother William Gustavus, were shipping and commission merchants in the West India and African trade with a store on Long wharf, Boston, for many years trading under the name of A. S. & W. G. Lewis. He removed to Framingham, Mass., in 1851 where he died Mar. 2, 1895. He was a state senator in 1856. He married, first, in Roxbury, Apr. 17, 1842, Elsie E. Davis, born in Roxbury, Aug. 12, 1822, and died in Framingham, Mar. 25, 1853, daughter of Charles and Harriet (Fellows) Davis of Roxbury. He married, second, in Framingham, Nov. 16, 1854, Eliza D. Upham, born in Boston, Sept. 30, 1830, who died in Framingham, Dec. 8, 1861, daughter of Charles and Elizabeth (Curtis) Upham of Boston. He married, third, Dec. 6, 1865, Harriet Phipps Richardson, born in Medway, June 9, 1841, who died on Long Island, Boston Harbor, July 16, 1871, daughter of George and Harriet N. (Phipps) Richardson of Framingham. He married, fourth, Dec. 30, 1874, Mary Blake Humphreys, born in Dorchester, Feb. 28, 1841, daughter of Henry and Sarah Blake (Clapp) Humphreys of Dorchester.

Child :

682. ELSIE SUSAN (adopted), b. in New Orleans, La., Jan. 20, 1849; m. April 21, 1870, Paymaster George E. Hendee U. S. Navy.

*Thomas Lewis had a brother Joseph who m. and lived in St. Louis, Mo., and had (1) William F. ; (2) Herbert; (3) Sarah L., m. —— Bradley; (4) Josephine.

Children of Abiel Smith and Eliza D. born in Framingham:

683. MARION, b. Dec. 11, 1855.
684. EVA, b. June 27-28, 1857; m. June 21, 1888, Frederick H. Ellis.

Child of Abiel Smith and Harriet P. born in Framingham :

685. GEORGINA, b. July 4, 1868; m. Dec. 28, 1891, J. P. Carl Weis of Providence, R. I.

345 William Gustavus Lewis, born in Boston, Aug. 21, 1816, was in business with his brother Abiel S. (344). He removed to Framingham in 1856, where he bought the Capt. R. Fiske farm at Salem End, and later acquired several estates in the vicinity, and entered quite extensively into agriculture. In 1881-2 he was president of the Middlesex South Agricultural Society. A selectman in 1890. He died in Framingham, Feb. 25, 1901 (gs). He married, in Roxbury, Oct. 13, 1841, Mary Ann Davis Dudley, born in Boston, Aug. 9, 1821, daughter of David and Hannah (Davis) Dudley of Roxbury, Mass. Children of William G. and Mary Ann :

686. MARY AUGUSTA, b. in Boston, Aug. 22, 1842; m. Dec. 2, 1868, Frederick Waterston Clapp, b. Feb. 25, 1843; d. Nov., 1879 (Thanksgiving day), son of Nathaniel B. and Mary B. (Clapp) Clapp. Children: (1) Fanny Lewis, b. Sept. 25, 1869; (2) Frank Nathaniel, b. Oct. 2, 1870; (3) Gustavus, b. Oct. 28, 1871; (4) John Wilson, b. Mar. 10, 1873; (5) Amy Dudley.
687. CHARLES DUDLEY, b. Sept. 26, 1844, in Roxbury.
688. WILLIAM GUSTAVUS, b. Nov. 24, 1846; d. Aug. 26, 1847, in Roxbury.
689. FRANCES WILSON, b. Mar. 7, 1851 in Roxbury; m. June 15, 1875, James Henry Humphreys, b. Mar. 6, 1850, son of Henry and Sarah Blake (Clapp) Humphreys. Lives in Dorchester. Child: (1) Bertha.
690. ELSIE ELIZABETH, b. Dec. 21, 1852, in Framingham; d. July 25, 1858.
691. HELEN GERTRUDE, b. Sept. 28, 1857, in Framingham; m. June 6, 1883, George Evans Whitney, lives in Cambridge.

351 John Lewis, born in Boston, Jan. 21, 1819, died in Malden, June 27, 1892. He married in Malden, Sept. 24, 1843, Eliza Tufts, born in Malden, Jan. 17, 1824, daughter of Joseph Warren and Eliza Tufts of Malden. Children of John and Eliza, born in Malden:

692. JULIA ELIZA, now living in Malden.

693. GEORGIANA ATWOOD, b. Feb. 11, 1848; d. Nov. 19, 1849.

694. GEORGIANA ATWOOD, m. —— Foljambe.

357 Nathaniel Lewis, born in Malden, Sept. 21, 1827, was a farmer removed to Minnesota in 1857, thence to Indiana in 1859, and in 1870 to Otisfield, Me. He died in Everett, Mass., July 10, 1899. He married in Boston, in 1857, Lydia Farnham b. in Pittsfield, Me., Nov. 3, 1836, daughter of Joseph and Kessia Farnham of St. Albans, Me.

Children of Nathaniel and Lydia:

695. AUGUSTA H., b. in Louisville, Ky., in 1859; m. Ernest B. Eldredge. Lives in Leicester, Mass.

696. EMMA BELLE, b. in Otisfield, Me., in 1860; m. William Taylor. Lives in Westboro, Mass.

697. GEORGE ATWOOD, b. in Otisfield, Me., in 1869; unm. in 1901; a hotel clerk in Boston.

358 Thomas Lewis, born in Boston, July 21, 1829; married, Oct. 17, 1850, in Boston, Elizabeth Ann Scadding, born in Boston, April 1, 1830, who died in Medford, Jan. 7, 1897, daughter of John and Phebe (Pierce) Scadding of Woburn, Mass. Lives in Medford, Mass.

Children of Thomas and Elizabeth Ann:

698. HANNAH PIERCE, b. in Boston, Oct. 14, 1852; m. in Everett, Mass., Jan. 15, 1872, Augustus Baldwin, b. in Malden, June 24, 1845, son of Charles and Sarah (Ward) Baldwin of Malden. He was a mill overseer, and lived in South Walpole, Mass., Lebanon, and now in Manchester, N. H. Children: (1) Mary Elizabeth, b. Nov. 14, 1874, in Everett, Mass.; m. W. E. Blakeley, Sept. 11, 1897. (2) Thomas Lewis, b. Mar. 23, 1876; d. in Everett, April 5, 1876. (3) William Augustus, b. Feb. 14, 1878, in Everett. (4) Grace Marion, b. Dec. 22, 1881, in Everett. (5) Irene Beatrice, b. May 25, 1892, in Lebanon, N. H.

699. SARAH LIZZIE, b. in Malden, June 22, 1855. Lives in Medford, Mass.
700. MARY FRANCES, b. in Malden, May 12, 1864. Lives in Medford, Mass.

362 Franklin Henshaw Lewis, born in Boston, July 20, 1825 ; merchant in Boston, where he died, Aug. 28, 1871. His widow lives in Brookline, Mass. He married, in Fall River, Dec. 27, 1848, Sarah Borden Durfee, born in Fall River, Dec. 14, 1829, daughter of Matthew Challenor and Fidelia (Borden) Durfee of Fall River.

Children of Franklin H. and Sarah B.:

701. FRANKLIN HENSHAW, b. Nov. 27, 1849; d. unm., Apr. 25, 1891.
702. SARAH BORDEN DURFEE, b. Nov. 28, 1851; unm.; lives in Boston.
703. LUCY SHAW, b. Jan. 7, 1854; m. June 20, 1881, Louis Robeson, b. Aug. 24, 1844, son of Thomas and Sibyl (Washburn) Robeson. Child: Sibyl, b. May 11, 1892. Lives in Brookline.
704. WALTER SHANNON, b. July 5, 1856; d. Apr. 15, 1859.
705. JOSEPHINE, b. Jan. 28, 1859; unm.; lives in Boston.
706. JAMES DANFORTH, b. Aug. 3, 1861; m. in Newburyport, Sept. 14, 1894, Mrs. Anna Cora Hale. Child: Ann Cora, b. Feb. 24, 1897, in Newburyport. Lives in Los Angeles, Cal.

379 Thomas Lewis, born in Lynn, Sept. 29, 1776 ; was a sea captain, and was lost at sea Jan. 2, 1804. He married, in Lynn, April 30, 1797, Polly Alley.

Children of Thomas and Polly, born in Lynn :

707. THOMAS, b. Oct. 29, 1797; died Nov. 27, 1800.
708. SALLY, b. Jan. 10, 1800; d. Oct. 11, 1800.
709. SALLY, b. Jan. 10, 1802; m. April 1, 1822, James Gaven.
710. MARY (twin), b. June 23, 1804; d. Sept. 7, 1805.
711. SUSANNAH (twin), b. June 23, 1804.

381 Isaac Lewis, born in Lynn, April 12, 1785, and died there Feb. 7, 1814. He married in Lynn, Nov. 15, 1807, Jane Tufts, born Aug. 19, 1789, daughter of David and Jane Tufts of Lynn. After his death she married, second, July 3, 1817, Richard Mansfield of Saugus, and after his death she married, third, John Putnam of Saugus.

Children of Isaac and Jane, born in Lynn :

712. MARY JANE, b. Feb. 15, 1808; d. Sept. 18, 1823.
713. SUSAN, b. Apr. 6, 1810; d. Mar. 2, 1811.
714. SUSAN, b. Feb. 12, 1812.

384 Jesse L. Lewis, born in Lynn, April 16, 1792 ; married, first· in Lynn, Jan. 1, 1819, Nancy Barry, born Mar. 4, 1799, daughter of James and Sally Barry, who died April 2, 1837. He married, second, in Lynn, Nov. 30, 1843, Elizabeth Townsend, widow of Daniel Townsend. She died Feb. 28, 1860. He died in Lynn, Sept. 19, 1874.

Children of Jesse L. and Nancy :

715. NANCY JANE, b. Jan. 21, 1819; d. July 18, 1849.
716. SUSAN HENRY, b. Nov. 10, 1821, in Portsmouth, N. H.
717. ISAAC HENRY, b. Mar. 23, 1824, in Portsmouth, N. H.
718. MARY ELIZA, b. Mar. 15, 1826; d. Dec. 26, 1834, in Lynn.
719. SAMUEL BARRY, b. Mar. 7, 1828; d. unm., June 7, 1849.
720. SARAH BRIMBLECOM, b. Jan. 26, 1830; m. June 13, 1850, Benjamin A. Homan, b. May 7, 1829.
721. JOHN T., d. Mar. 1, 1855, æ. 23 y.
722. HENRY G., d. Oct. 16, 1857, æ. 23 y.
723. MARY ELIZA, b. Mar. 31, 1837.

395 John Lewis, born in 1780 ; married Ann Jencks Voce.

Children of John and Ann Jencks :

724. SAMUEL.
725. JESSE.
726. ALFRED ; m. Martha Coit.
727. JOHN N., m. Jan. 20, 1839, Betsey Oxx.
728. SARAH ANN, m. Washington Ling.
729. CAROLINE, m. Jonathan D. Waldron.
730. MARY MASON, b. 1814; m. James Nichols Palmer.
731. ELEANOR, d. in infancy.
732. ELEANOR, m. Alexander Manchester.

399 Benjamin Lewis, born in Dighton, Mass., Feb. 14, 1785 ; died in Providence, R. I., June 11, 1848. He

married, first, Mary Sprague, who died Oct. 25, 1823, æ. 38
years. He married, second, in Providence, Aug. 15, 1824,
Mary Hopkins Mann, born Dec. 2, 1805, and died Dec.
5, 1874, daughter of David E. and Amy (Hopkins) Mann.
He was a mason by occupation, and lived in Providence,
R. I.

Children of Benjamin and Mary :

733. LYDIA GARDNER, b. July, 1815; d. June 17, 1885; m. George
W. Briggs, b. Feb. 25, 1811; d. April 1, 1839. Children: (1)
George D., b. in Swansey, Aug. 20, 1836; m. Celestinia L.
Jencks. (2) Mary E., b. June 1, 1838; m., Aug. 11, 1868,
Charles H. Bliss, b. Aug. 22, 1837, who was drowned off
Watch Hill from the steamer Metis, which was burnt Aug.
30, 1872. After jumping overboard, he was struck by a
trunk on the head, which so stunned him he was unable to
swim, otherwise he might have been saved. (3) Albert L.,
b. Feb. 13, 1845; m. Mary Cobb of Dighton, Mass. (4) Clara,
b. Sept. 24, 1855; d. April 10, 1856. (5) Walter B., b. Oct.
15, 1858; unm.

734. MARY S., b. Dec. 2, 1817; d. Dec. 24, 1817.

735. DEXTER BOSWORTH, b. Sept. 20, 1820.

Children of Benjamin and Amy :

736. SARAH HOLBROOK, b. Aug. 1, 1825; d. May 23, 1826.

737. HENRY HOPKINS, b. Mar. 10, 1827.

738. MARTHA LANKSFORD, b. Feb. 7, 1829; d. April 13, 1845.

400 James Lewis, born in Dighton, Sept. 10, 1787;
died in Providence, R. I., Feb. 7, 1872 ; married, first, May
26, 1816, Celia Chace, born Nov. 17, 1795, and died Oct.
6, 1836, daughter of Caleb and Rosamond (Bullock)
Chase. He married, second, May 18, 1837, Nancy Whit-
taker, born May 13, 1812, and died July 21, 1858. He
married, third, Nov. 7, 1859, widow Mary A. Talbot, who
died Feb. 10, 1888, æ. 81 years. He was for many years
a mason, and built some of the most substantial buildings
in Providence, including the Arcade. He amassed considerable wealth, and was highly esteemed by his fellow-
citizens.

(To be continued.)

SALEM WARNINGS, 1791.

Essex ss.   To either of the Constables of the Town of
Salem in s^d County GREETING.   You are in the Name of
the Commonwealth of Massachusetts directed to warn and
give Notice unto

Samuel Stone of Danvis county of Essex
Eunice Marshall of Danvis in the county of Essex
John Curley Butcher of Rhodeisland
Wid Moley Felt of Beverly in the County of Essex
Charles Heridon of Watertown Currier
Samuel Haselton dyer from Old ingland
Mary Wetmore of Ipswich in the County of Essex
Mary Tucker of Danvis wever county of Essex
Theadeus Willington Butcher of Waltham
James Goldthwrit of Danvis Shoemaker county of Essex
Phebe Farrer of Mansfield in Conneticut
Genney Cowins of Jersey
Benj^a Watkins New Castle New hampshier
Dorethy Coffin New Castle New hampshier
Caleb Maning of Charlstown Chaise maker
Joseph Wheeler of Marblhead mariner County of Essex
Thomas Maning of Charlestown Chaise maker
Ephraim Smith of Concord Carpenter
Elijah Johnson of Scituate Leather dresser
Ezekiel Wellman of Lynfield County of Essex Leather
    dresser
Ezekill Moriall of New Hampshire Butcher
John pope Baker of Danvis County of Essex
Abraham Forster Butcher of New Rowley County of
    Essex
Andrew Hibbard Methuing Shoemaker
Janney Flint of Cancer Widow

Nehemiah Adams of Ipshwich County of Essex Cabbinet
    Maker
Robert Upton Labourer of Amherst New Hampshire
Rich⁴ Mason painter of Lynn in County of essex
John Weyburt of Boston Blacksmith
Willᵐ Chandler of Rowley Taylor
Caleb Smith of Milton Shoemaker
Thomas Barnes of Boston Chair maker
William Mathews mariner of Old Ingland
John Burns Bos'n on the seas in urope
Ester Thurston of New Rowley
Jacob Reed of Danvis Labourer County of Essex
Gorge Heuslar of Germany
Gorge Bruce of Uburn Butcher
Rachel Mogerage of Stoneham
Sarah dove of Beverly in County of Essex
Joseph Rider of plymouth fisherman
Elizabeth William of Charlstown
Thomas goss of Spain mariner
Edwin Dolton of Ireland
Bartholo Brown of Danvis county of Essex carpenter
John plant Labourer of Halifax
Samuel Galaway of Ipshwich Baker
David Osborn Baker of Roxbury
Nathaniel Trumbull whealrite of Charlestown
Elizabeth pickwoth Marblehead
Peter Clough Mariner of Amesbury County of Essex
John Dunkin of Scotland Mariner
Wᵐ Fitch Moriss of Ireland Mariner
Abraham Mulbot fisherman of Marblehead county of
    Essex
Abegil Wendal of Boston
James Fisher of Virginia
Noah Higby wever of Meddletown Connecticut
Walter Richards Labourer of Lynn
Willᵐ paterson of Marblehead County of essex
Rich⁴ Carter of Old Ingland
Jacob Poland of Beverly wever county of essex
Willᵐ Bradshaw of Scotland Mariner
James Wood of Old Ingland Mariner

John Erwin wever of Scotland
Butler forgety of Ireland Schoolmaster
Mathew Leech of Italy fisherman
Abegil Safford of Ipswich
Rich Mullin fisherman of Ireland
William Burden Mariner of Old Ingland
Samuel Homan of Old Ingland
Samuel Marshall Taner Danvis Baker
Jon^a Pierce Lancester County Worster, Blacksmith
Nathan Marray of Newport Blacksmith
Alexander Anderson of Scotland
Ezekil goldthewit Smithfield Rhode island
Charles Hamilton old Ingland Mariner
Genney Glassford Marblehead
Emmons Smith of Ipswich Labourer
Richd Hall of Ireland fisherman
Humphrey Fears of Cape Ann Labourer County Essex
Elizabeth Moss Marblehead County of Essex
John Kent of Sheepscutt River Mariner
John Glover of Dorchester Baker
Jon^a Tant of Milton Carpenter
John Scallgon of Ireland Labourer
Samuel Gail of Marblehead fisherman
Amos Clough of Byfield County of Essex Mariner
Sophia Brown of Germany
Willm Owr of Derry New Hampshire
Mary Cally of Marblehead County of Essex
Lemuel Horton of Milton
John Wood of Lynn Labourer
Willm Adkins of London Ship Carpenter
Henery Brown of Halifax Mariner
Susanah Candesh of Marblehead
Joseph Dewing of Neadham neare Boston
Francis Ryan of Ireland
Joseph Hart of Readin house Carpenter
Nath^el Gould Topsfield
Willm Holmes of Old Ingland Labourer
Woodard Abreham of Charlestown
James Canada of Sheepscutt Fisherman
Ebenezer Phelps Readin precint Labourer

Thomas Haneford Casco Bay portland Mariner
Jonᵃ D. Bosson of Roxbury
Joseph Mansfield of Lynn hatter
Jeptha Lathe of Uburn Taylor
Jonᵃ Ingils of Andover Shoemaker county of Essex
Sam¹ Stocker of Cambridge hatter
Wᵐ Jinkins of Malding Cabinet Maker
Israel Moneys of Topsfield Labourer County of Essex
James Wright of Scotland Baker
Edward Burns Ireland Mariner
Joseph Felt Marblehead Mariner County of Essex
Joseph Ayres of Old England Mariner
Robert LFavar Topsfield County of essex, Taylor
John Crane of Isle of Man
Daniel Chadwick falmouth
Joseph Thomson of Beverly Mariner County of Essex
John Rikey of Scotland Mariner
Lake Killey of Newfoundland Mariner
Lucy Woodman Widow
Anna Jackson Widow
Mary Heigh of Marblehead
Edward Shaullere of Germany
John Francis of Spain Mariner
Sam¹ Dale of Danvis Whealright
Banjᵃ Trask of Beverly Blacksmith
Francis Sheldon of Lynnfield Labourer
Dunkin McPherson Scotland Labourer
John Williams Ship Carpenter of old Ingland
Amos Rice of Boston Joyner
Robert Cowen Scotland painter
John Bodg Mariner Old Ingland
James Ward of New York Mariner
Joseph Saul Mariner of Jersey
Genney Mc Cunib of Ireland
Volentine Runnels Mariner West of Ireland
Edmond Patch of Ipshwich County of Essex
Obediah Gross of Hingham house Carpenter
Micah Wilds of Braintree
John Sanders of Marblehead
William Coles of Marblehead Mariner

Moses Hood of Topsfield Labourer, County Essex
James Harinton Virginia Mariner
William Daniels of Hingham Botbilder
Alexander More of Scotland Mariner
James Green of Malden Baker
John Moraity of Ireland Clerk
Joseph Rider Janes Mariner Plymouth
William Paterson of Old Ingland Mariner
William Owin Mariner of Boston
Thomas Farely Mariner of Old Ingland
Elijah pirkins of Topsfield County of Essex Chair maker
Joseph Chandler of Andover Labourer
James Elmer of Old Ingland Mariner
Ruben Black of Casco Bay Labourer
John Kelly of Ireland Tobaconist
Thomas Patfield of old Ingland Labourer
Jonᵃ Peabody of Middletown fisherman
Jacob Caldwell of Ipswich county of Essex fisherman
David Kief of Ireland Labourer
Patrick Peland of Ireland Mariner
John Arther of Ireland Labourer
Joseph Cook of Cambridge Butcher
Stephen Hood of Chelsea Labourer
Absalome Gatrage of Maryland Labourer
Samˡˡ Ball Old Ingland Mariner
patrick Conner of Ireland Labourer
Thomas Peston of Old York Mariner
Richᵈ Collins of Ireland Labourer
James Hamscom of portsmouth New Hamshire Labourer
Wᵐ Joyes of Boston Rope-maker
George pirkins of Exeter N. Hampshier Sailmaker
Thomas Tiplady of Old England Labourer
Hubartis Mattoon of New Market Blacksmith
John Bugess of Ireland Mariner maried Gavet
Ebed Lewis of Hingham Ship Carpenter
Samuel Biship of Marblehead Labourer
John Deal of Danvis Labourer
John Harvey of Old Ingland Tallow-chandler
Eleazer Bisby of Marshfield Labourer
Abigil porter of Beverly County of Essex widow

John Deverex of Old Ingland Labourer
John Battor Old Canary Blacksmith
John McVay of Ireland Mariner
Obediah Willcookes of Rhode Island Mariner
Andrew Truelove of Ireland Mariner
Henery parker of Urope Mariner
Gorge Lassall of Rhode Island Mariner
John Honey of Old Ingland Mariner
William Sage of Connetticutt Carpenter
William pirkins Damascottey Mariner
Thomas Squires Mariner of Old Ingland
Benj[a] Chamberlain of Chemsford Mariner
Timothy Pentergrass of Ireland mariner
pierce evooy Old Ireland mariner
Ebenezer Nuting of Cambridge mariner
Ebed Stodard of hingham Shoemaker
Abraham Knowlton of Ipswhich Cabinet maker
David Malcolm of town of Warrin eastward Mariner
Nathaniel Hichins of Lynn Carpenter
John Bishop of Marblehead Labourer
Amos Lfavour of Topsfield Taylor County of Essex
James Creely of Urope mariner
Widow Lydia King of Eastham Cape Cod
Jon[a] Brown of Lynn Carpenter County of Essex
John pirkins of Topsfield Husbandman
Jeremiah Longway of Quebeck mariner
Anna Longway of Dongester South Boston
Elisabeth Kelly of Ireland Widow
Rich[d] Nicholls of Rhode Island fisherman
Edward Euling of Jersey Mariner
John Elleson Old Ingland Labourer
Joseph Crookshank of Old Ingland mariner
James Clarage of Portsmouth Ship Carpenter
Polley Larrance Widow
John Gunnerson of portsmouth Boat builder New Hamshier
Thomas Keene of Halifax fisherman
John Dawson of guensey Labourer
Abijah Hichins of Lynn Carpenter
John Williams of Ireland mariner

John Batter of Ireland Blacksmith
John Ustur of Ireland mariner
Isaac Pirkins of Topsfield yoman
John Mcpherson of Ireland Mariner
Jon^a Gould Labourer
Francis Loveing Rope maker Old France
John Walker of Scotland mariner
Frederick Chappell of Rhode Island mariner
Robert Bartlett of Marblehead Labourer
Joseph Franks of Ireland Labourer
James Robinson Ireland fisherman
Ester Bean of Old Ingland Widow
Benj^a Billstone Old Ingland Rope maker
Jacob page of Charlston Mariner
Nathan Pirkins of Kitery Mariner
Seth King of Portsmouth goldsmith
Hannah Willard of Boston Widow
Solomon Webber of Old York Laborer
Ralf Crane of Stoken husbandman
Jon^a Brown of Readin husbandman
Richd Phillips of Lynn
William Flood of Malldin Labourer
Thomas Galley of Marblehead Labourer
Mary Galley of Marblehead Widow
George Shavell of Old Ingland Labourer
Margerate Andriss of Boston
John Jenkins of Scituate County plymouth Tayler
Timothy Brant of Readin Mariner
Sarah Coneway of Marblehead Widow
Susanah Tucker of Marblehead Widow
Lydia Kelly of Lynn Widow
Benj^a Shaw of Danvis Baker
Sarah Williamson of Marblehead Widow
Robert Summers of Old Ingland Labourer
Morris Caben of France Mariner
Peter Flood of Maldon Labourer
Robert Pirkins of Duglas Laborer
John Willis of Old Ingland Mariner
John Shaw of Danvis Mariner

who is lately come into this Town for the purpose of abiding therein not having obtained the Towns Consent therefor, that they depart the limits thereof with thier Children & others under their Care within fifteen days. And of this precept with your Doings thereon you are to make return into the Office of the Clerk of the Town of Salem within Twenty days Next coming that such further proceedings may be had in the premises as the Law directs. Given under our hands & Seals at Salem aforesaid this Thirtieth day of May A. D. 1791.

Edwd Norris
John Hathorne
Joseph Sprague   Selectmen
Jonathan Waldo   of
Nathl Richardson   Salem

Essex ss. Salem eighteenth of June 1791. In obedience to the within I have Warned and given Notice to the Within named persons with there Children and Others under their Care to Depart the Limits of this Town as I am within Commanded by Reading the within precept and by Leaveing a Copey of the Same at their Last usall place of Abode.

Samuel Jones Constable.

Essex Institute Manuscript Collections, Salem MSS.

INDEX.

(353)